P9-DGV-308

ESSAYS IN ACCOUNTING THEORY IN HONOUR OF JOEL S. DEMSKI

Joel S. Demski

[Photo Courtesy of Accounting Hall of Fame at the Ohio State University]

ESSAYS IN ACCOUNTING THEORY IN HONOUR OF JOEL S. DEMSKI

Edited by

Rick Antle[1], Frøystein Gjesdal[2] and Pierre Jinghong Liang[3]
[1]Yale School of Management, [2]Norwegian School of Economics and Business Administration
[3]Carnegie Mellon University

 Springer

Library of Congress Control Number: 2006934309

ISBN-13: 978-0387-30397-0   ISBN-13: 978-0387-30399-4 (e-book)
ISBN:10: 0-387-30397-9   ISBN:10: 0-387-30399-5 (e-book)

Printed on acid-free paper.

Printed in the United States of America.

9 8 7 6 5 4 3 2 1

springer.com

Dedication

This book is dedicated

to

Joel S. Demski

Contents

About the Editors

Rick Antle (PhD Stanford) has been a faculty member of the University of Chicago (1980-1985) and the Yale School of Management (1985 -), where he was promoted to full professor in 1989. He served as the Senior Associate Dean at Yale from 2000 to 2005.

Frøystein Gjesdal (PhD Stanford) has been a Professor of Managerial Economics at the Norwegian School of Economics and Business Administration (NHH) since 1979 (full professor since 1986). He is currently Head of the Department of Accounting, Auditing and Law. He has also been an academic visitor at Stanford University, Yale University, London School of Economics as well as University of Florida.

Pierre Jinghong Liang (PhD University of Florida) has been a faculty member (associate professor since 2004) of the Tepper School of Business, formerly known as the Graduate School of Industrial Administration, at the Carnegie Mellon University located in Pittsburgh, Pennsylvania.

Contributing Authors

Rick Antle
Yale School of Management

Anil Arya
Ohio State University

Peter Bogetoft
Royal Agriculture University of Denmark

John Christensen
University of Southern Denmark – Odense

Ronald A. Dye
Northwestern University

John C. Fellingham
Ohio State University

Gerald A. Feltham
University of British Columbia

Mark Finn
Northwestern University

Hans Frimor
University of Southern Denmark - Odense

Joseph J. Gerakos
University of Pennsylvania

Frøystein Gjesdal
Norwegian School of Economics and Business Administration

Jonathan C. Glover
Carnegie Mellon University

Thomas Hemmer
University of Houston

Steven Huddart
Pennsylvania State University

John S. Hughes
University of California at Los Angeles

Christopher D. Ittner
University of Pennsylvania

David F. Larcker
Stanford University

Carolyn B. Levine
Carnegie Mellon University

Pierre Jinghong Liang
Carnegie Mellon University

Brian G. Mittendorf
Yale School of Management

Suresh Radhakrishnan
University of Texas at Dallas

William P. Rogerson
Northwestern University

Douglas A. Schroeder
Ohio State University

Andrew W. Stark
Manchester Business School

Gary L. Sundem
University of Washington

Shyam Sunder
Yale School of Management

Preface

Since the 1960s, Joel Demski has been a potent force in the accounting scholarship and education. Always the rebel, Joel sees any set of received doctrines as more of a target (in the military sense) than as being set in stone. Early in his career, Joel was part of a group of pioneers that broke from tradition and began the amazing expansion of accounting thought into the era of information economics. A prolific writer, he has made path-breaking contributions both in accounting and in economics. His work is always consistent in invoking modern economic rationale and unapologetic in building sound reasoning based on first principles. The result has been scholarship that is both innovative and fundamental.

The "Impossibility" debate is a quintessential example of Joel's fundamental insights and his unflinching belief in scientific spirit. In a provocative and influential article published in The Accounting Review, he showed the inconsistency between an information view of accounting and the formulation of any set of universal, normative accounting standards. This "impossibility theorem" raised a deep and fundamental question about the long-standing academic efforts to contribute to the codification and conceptualization of accounting principles. A lively debate ensued, with a special thread pinning him with Professor Raymond Chambers, another influential accounting scholar. In the debate, Joel held steadfastly to information economics reasoning, and their exchanges produced a great deal of insight from both sides. The benefit to accounting scholarship, and to the efforts of those charged with setting accounting standards in practice, was enormous. This is but one example; see Chapter 1 of this volume for a comprehensive review of Joel's contribution to the literature.

As an educator, he has profoundly influenced the lives of his many students. He has been an inspiration to his doctoral students at Stanford, Yale, and Florida, giving generously of his time and his energy. He had a similar effect on those who have had the opportunity to attend his PhD courses in other universities: Carnegie-Mellon, Emory, Michigan, Odense (now Southern Denmark) and Ohio State, among others. It is important to note that Joel's teaching efforts have not been confined to doctoral students. He has shown a consistent and steadfast commitment to classroom teaching at all levels: doctoral, MBA, undergraduate and even high school, much to the good fortune of some lucky algebra students in New Haven, Connecticut.

Although perhaps required for clarity, it invites misunderstanding to write of Joel's contributions to scholarship and education in separate paragraphs for, above all, he believes in a unity of purpose in teaching and research. He has been consistent in bringing latest research into classrooms, and firm in his belief that research is not worth doing if it can only be taught at the doctoral level. He calls this the "Ralph" test, named after a fictional student in his textbooks (who in turn was named for his undergraduate roommate at the University of Michigan). His two more recent major textbooks, Managerial Use of Accounting Information (1994) and Accounting Theory: an Information Content Perspective (2002 and co-authored with John Christensen), are testaments to his educational efforts.

As a member of the broader academic community, he has been tireless in building scholarly environments and in caring for his resident institutions and the profession at large. Every university at which he was employed, Columbia, Stanford, Yale, and now Florida, was made better by his consistent advocacy of scholarship, tough standards, and complete commitment by all its participants. Outside the universities, he served as the president of the American Accounting Association and represented the academic community in the Financial Accounting Standards Advisory Council.

Joel Demski is a special individual. His uncompromising scholarly standards, stubbornness in his approach to every academic endeavor, and his willingness to give of himself have not changed in his entire career spanning five decades. These are some of the reasons he is one of the most respected scholars today.

Joel has received many awards and accolades. He received the AAA Seminal Contribution to Accounting Literature Award in 1994 and was inducted into Accounting Hall of Fame in 2000. He is an Honorary Doctorate of Odense University (now University of Southern Denmark). He is a recipient of the Elm-Ivy Award (for outstanding contributions to the relationship between Yale and the city of New Haven), the AICPA Award for Outstanding Contributions to the Accounting Literature and the AAA Outstanding Educator Award.

This volume in Joel's honour, along with a companion conference (to be held on October 15, 2005 in Gainesville Florida), is one way for all of us, some of the beneficiaries of his life-long academic endeavors, to express our gratitude and admiration for all he has done for the members of the profession, for the field of accounting, for the institutions he has helped build, and, more personally, for us.

We are grateful for the support from Joel's colleagues and friends, many of whom are contributors to this book. We thank Min Cao and Edwige Cheynel for able research assistance. We also thank staff members of Springer (the publisher) and in particular, Jack Rogers, Judy Pforr, and Deborah Doherty for their constant support in bringing the idea of the book into fruition. Finally, we wish to thank Amy Hendrickson from Texnology, Inc. and Rosemarie Lang of the Tepper School of Business at Carnegie Mellon for their excellent editorial support, which was indispensable in putting together the volume.

Rick Antle, Yale School of Management

Frøystein Gjesdal, NHH

Pierre Jinghong Liang, Carnegie Mellon University

September 2005

Chapter 1

JOEL S. DEMSKI: A LEADER IN ACCOUNTING SCHOLARSHIP

Gerald A. Feltham
Sauder School of Business, University of British Columbia, Vancouver, British Columbia, CANADA V6T1Z2

Abstract: Joel Demski has made significant contributions to accounting research and education for nearly forty years. This paper reviews and highlights many of his scholarly contributions. He has been innovative and thought provoking – always at the leading edge of our discipline

Key words: Accounting Theory

1.   INTRODUCTION

I have been asked by the organizers of this conference to write and present a paper that describes and comments on Joel Demski's contributions to accounting scholarship. I am very pleased to accept this invitation and to participate in this wonderful event. We have been good friends for thirty-seven years.

Joel obtained his Ph.D. from the University of Chicago and joined the faculty of Columbia University in 1966. I obtained my Ph.D. at the University of California, Berkeley, and joined the faculty at Stanford in 1967. Chuck Horngren had been Joel's supervisor at the University of Chicago and had come to Stanford in 1966. He was very impressed by Joel and in 1968 he encouraged the Stanford faculty to invite Joel out on a recruiting trip.[1]

---

[1]   At that time, the Stanford accounting faculty consisted of five full professors (Chuck, Bob Jaedicke, Bob Sprouse, Ozzie Nielson, and Jerry Wentworth) and one assistant

Joel and I met for the first time when he came to Stanford on his recruiting trip. He had been an engineering undergraduate, while I had majored in accounting. Nonetheless, we had both studied accounting and management science in our Ph.D. programs, and we were both interested in management accounting, particularly as it related to management decisions. Furthermore, we both received appointments to Stanford's Decision Analysis group as well as to the Accounting group.

Our dissertations were quite different, but Joel had read both my dissertation and that of my fellow student John Butterworth. He immediately became interested in the information economic analyses John and I used to explore the relationship between information and the payoffs from management decisions. Hence, Joel and I quickly formed a close bond.

2. THE SIXTIES – A TIME OF CHANGE

To appreciate Joel's early contributions to accounting scholarship, one must have some understanding of the nature of accounting thought at the time Joel entered the Ph.D. program in the early sixties. The following is a brief sketch of some salient aspects of that setting. The changes that took place in the sixties profoundly affected subsequent accounting thought and research. Joel was at the forefront of that change, along with a small band of other Ph.D. students at Chicago, most notably, Bill Beaver, Ray Ball, Phil Brown, and Ross Watts. However, right from the start, Joel's work differed dramatically from their empirical research on financial reporting. He soon joined in applying information economics to accounting, which was initiated at Berkeley by John Butterworth, Ted Mock, and myself.

2.1 Accounting thought prior to the mid sixties

Up through the fifties, and into the sixties, classical accounting thought viewed accounting as a *measurement activity* that provides "truthful" descriptions of events -- statements of "fact" that can be used by a variety of decision makers. There was little or no explicit exploration of the impact of accounting reports on the resulting decisions and consequences.

---

professor (me). Bob Swieringa, now Dean at Cornell, joined us in January 1969, and Bill Beaver came as an Associate Professor in September 1969.

2.1.1   From cost to value based accounting principles

Much of the accounting thought prior to 1950 had focussed on developing a coherent approach to matching costs and revenues within a going concern. This is epitomized by the classic work by Paton and Littleton (1940). However, in the fifties and sixties, accountants were becoming increasingly concerned about the implications of price changes, both general and specific. Many thought that we can and should produce more useful balance sheets and accounting measures of income.

Two economists, Edwards and Bell were among the authors who made specific proposals for "improving" accounting reports. Their underlying perspective is revealed by the following quote from their 1961 book:

We have suggested that there are two central objectives toward which accountants should point ... The principal purpose to be achieved by the collection of accounting data ... to provide useful information for the evaluation of past business decisions and of the method used in reaching those decisions. ... Evaluation by both insiders and interested outsiders provides the key to the successful functioning of a private, free enterprise economy. If the task is performed effectively, resources will be allocated efficiently. If accountants do not provide the data necessary for measuring performance, resources are misallocated and both business firms and the community at large suffer as a consequence.

Edwards and Bell devote more attention to the use of accounting information than do most accounting authors of that era. Nonetheless, they do not provide much analysis of the links between their proposed reports, the resulting decisions, and economic consequences. They proposed reporting more than one profit measure, leaving it to the decision maker to choose the most relevant measure for the decision at hand.

2.1.2   Exhortations to explicitly consider the user

With the movement away from "cost-based" to "value-based" accounting measures, several accounting authors began to call for more explicit analysis of the users of accounting reports. Perhaps the most influential exhortation came from *A Statement of Basic Accounting Theory* that was published in 1966 by a committee of the American Accounting Association. The following quote highlights the committee's call for a user perspective in accounting research.

The greatest accounting need both at present and in the future is the determination of the nature of information needs of users of accounting communications. No one really knows what individuals or any organization wants, or what they should want, and there is a need for some fundamental research on this question. ... Research here should ... involve investigating the interrelations of the decision models of the users with the nature and form of the information required and of the accounting model itself.

2.1.3   Cost accounting

Cost accounting began to develop at the beginning of the twentieth century. During the nineteenth century, most "cost" information was gathered by engineers outside the accounting process. However, identification of the cost of goods sold and inventories in manufacturing organizations resulted in the incorporation of cost accounting within the accountant's double-entry bookkeeping system.

In 1923, Clark, an economist, clearly articulated and analyzed the view "that there are different kinds of problems for which we need information about costs, and ... the particular information we need differs from one problem to another." And in 1937, Coase, another noted economist, emphasized the nature of opportunity costs. Such costs are not recorded in the accounting system, but they are an important ingredient in rational analysis of whether to take a particular action.

Cost analysis for decision making began to become an important part of the accounting literature in the 1940s, as reflected in a National Association of Cost Accountants' 1945 statement on the uses and classifications of costs:

Cost accounting is a means to an end, and not an end in itself. Accordingly, any study of the field of cost accounting should start with a study of the ends to be served--the uses to be made of cost data. Only by clearly describing and relating the various purposes for which costs are to be used is it possible to determine the types of cost data needed for each purpose and the principles and techniques which should govern their development.

Interestingly, while much was written about cost analysis for decision making, this discussion had only limited impact on the recording and reporting activities of the accounting system.

2.2   Decision-facilitating information in organizations

The call for a user perspective in accounting was in part a reflection of the developments in several disciplines outside of accounting. These changes had a significant effect on research in business schools in general, and had a particularly transforming effect on accounting research. The 1960s became a pivotal era of change in accounting research. In particular, the developments in this era contributed to a heavy emphasis on the examination of the decision-facilitating role of accounting information.

2.2.1   Statistical decision theory

Information only plays a role in decision making if there is uncertainty regarding the consequences of the decision maker's actions. Hence, the development of a clear, consistent approach to the examination of decision making under uncertainty was a key ingredient to the implementation of a formal economic analysis of the user perspective in accounting research.

Two economists, von Neumann and Morgenstern, developed an axiomatic structure for constructing utility functions that represent individual preferences under uncertainty. von Neumann had done preliminary work in this area in 1928, but the key work was completed and published in 1944.

To consider information, one needs a mechanism for specifying how information affects the decision maker's beliefs. Statistical decision theory employs probability theory, and in particular Bayes' theorem, to determine posterior beliefs given prior beliefs about observed and unobserved (e.g., future) events. There was considerable work in the 1940s and 1950s that considered various forms of stochastic relations among events and the inferences to be drawn from the observable events with respect to the unobservable events (e.g., future events).

2.2.2   Information economics

Statistical decision theory developed representations of decision-maker preferences, identified the relation between information and posterior beliefs, and identified optimal decision rules based on those posterior beliefs. From this developed an area of research referred to as information economics. This area of study treats the acquisition of information as an object of choice and seeks to provide insights into the optimal acquisition and use of information. In 1961, Stigler wrote:

One should hardly have to tell academicians that information is a valuable resource: knowledge *is* power. And yet it occupies a slum dwelling in the town of economics. Mostly it is ignored: ... There are a great many problems in economics for which this neglect ... is no doubt permissible or even desirable. But there are some for which this is not true, and I hope to show that some important aspects of economic organization take on new meaning when they are considered from the viewpoint of the search for information.

While the "information search" literature had little direct influence on accounting, it was important in developing a heightened interest in information in economics.

Another stream of information economics research was initiated by Marschak, who focused on information in organizations. He published his first paper dealing with information in organizations in 1955 and ultimately linked up with Radner to write the *Economic Theory of Teams* in the early 1960s (although it was not published until 1972). This work analyzed the optimal use of information by multiple decision makers within an organization, assuming that the decision makers differed in the information they received but had the same prior beliefs and preferences. The identical preference assumption was ultimately viewed as unacceptable, but this work did much to stimulate economic analysis of the use of information in organizations.

Marschak (with Miyasawa 1968) also contributed to the comparative analysis of alternative decision-facilitating information for a single decision maker. Blackwell (1951, 1953), a statistician, provided the foundational work in this area in his analysis of the comparison of experiments in settings in which the information provided by the experiments are used to make decisions (inferences). Marschak interpreted information structures as experiments.

2.2.3   Operations research

During the second world war, the allies called on scientists to assist them in developing strategies that would assist in the war effort, particularly with respect to a variety of operational activities. This brought scientists into contact with management decision problems. After the war, groups of scientists became involved in what become known as operations research (or management science). They carefully examined management decisions and sought to identify the optimal decisions to make in a given setting.

By the end of the 1950s, there was a significant body of management science literature. For example, in 1957 a text book by Churchman, Ackoff, and Arnoff describe inventory models, linear programming models, waiting-time models, replacement models, and bidding models. In the *Journal of Accountancy* (1955), Churchman and Ackoff point out that

The accounting approach to providing information for executives has been based on two fundamental themes: (1) provision of information that is "open-ended," *i.e.,* might be useful for a number of different purposes and rarely is sufficient by itself to define a policy for the executive; and (2) provision of data that can be checked by well defined operations on the accounts and records of the company.

They called for the development of "operational accounting" that provides "research information," which is "not open-ended, and suitable for any conceivable use, but is specifically geared to making predictions." They also called for reports of opportunity costs and other useful information that may not be readily verifiable.

Accountants became interested in operations research, and in the fifties we begin to see simple mathematical models in the accounting literature. Trueblood, a well known accountant, wrote a paper in *Journal of Accountancy* (1960) commenting on the implications of operations research for accounting. He saw the increased demand for decision relevant information and felt that firms should have comprehensive integrated information systems (controlled by accountants) that provided the desired information. He also felt that operations research might be useful in addressing the following issue:

> ... there are today no generally accepted criteria for the design of an integrated information system for a firm -- for deciding what information is needed, how frequently the information is required, how accurate it needs to be, and how information is to be originated and transmitted.

3. THE LATE SIXTIES AND EARLY SEVENTIES

Now that the stage has been set, we begin to explore Joel's contributions to accounting research over the last forty years. These contributions are truly impressive, and cover a broad range of innovative analytical accounting theory. Furthermore, in addition to Joel's direct contributions to accounting research, he mentored a number of Ph.D. students who produced significant contributions in their dissertations and subsequent research. Many are in attendance at this conference.

Joel has published approximately eighty papers in major refereed journals in accounting and economics. I will explicit reference to more than half of his papers, plus key papers produced by his Ph.D. students from their dissertations. However, I do not mention all of Joel's papers, and one should not infer that I think an omitted paper is less important than those I have included. I have tried to develop a useful taxonomy for classifying many of his papers. Some papers may be omitted because they do not fit into my taxonomy, or I may not have had time to remind myself of the content of some papers.

3.1 Integrating planning models and variance analysis

Operations research models played an important role in Joel's research from the very beginning. Initially his research focused on the use of historical information, and variance analysis in particular, in providing feedback for control. He argued that it was important to recognize that results could differ from plans due to at least three factors: errors in the form of the planning model used to predict the consequences of actions; errors in estimating the planning model parameters; and inefficiencies in implementing the plans. These errors and inefficiencies interacted and it is not a trivial process to assess the economic impact of these errors. However, Joel provides an approach that identifies the aggregate economic consequences of the three factors.

Joel's research in this area is reported in the following sequence of papers.

- An extension of standard cost variance analysis, *Accounting Review* (1967), with Dopuch and Birnberg.
- An accounting system structured on a linear programming model, *Accounting Review* (1967).
- Predictive ability of alternative performance measurement models, *Journal of Accounting Research* (1969a).
- Decision-performance control, *Accounting Review* (1969b).
- The decision implementation interface: effects of alternative performance measurement models, *Accounting Review* (1970).
- Implementation effects of alternative performance measurement models in a multivariable context, *Accounting Review* (1971).

This is an impressive set of papers, especially when you consider that they were all published within five year's of Joel's graduation from the University of Chicago. Of particular note is the fact that Joel's single-authored 1967 paper received the 1967 AICPA Award for Outstanding Contributions to the Accounting Literature, and his 1970 paper won the AAA's 1969 manuscript contest. The first of these two awards was selected by a joint AICPA/AAA committee that considered all papers published in the preceding five years, whereas the AAA manuscript contest is open to any accounting researcher who had received his Ph.D. in the preceding five years.

In my cost analysis course at UBC, I continued, until I retired, to use some of the techniques proposed by Joel in the papers listed above. The traditional variance analysis that is found in virtually all cost and management accounting texts provides only a superficial description of the differences between plans and results. I want my students to be able to think about the economic consequences of avoidable differences and of the failure to anticipate unavoidable differences. Developing that kind of analytical skill is at the heart of Joel's early work. It emphasizes insightful analysis rather than computational rules. In fact, this is a hallmark of all of Joel's contributions to accounting scholarship.

3.2 The decision-facilitating role of information

We now shift our focus to the beginnings of information economic research in accounting. The roots are found at Berkeley[2] in the mid-sixties, but the blossoming takes place at Stanford in the late sixties and early seventies.

3.2.1 Initial applications of information economics to accounting

In the mid-sixties, Hector Anton challenged his Berkeley Ph.D. students to think deeply about the nature of accounting and its role in society. In addition, in an organization theory course we were exposed to Marschak and Radner's work on information economics, including draft chapters to their book, *Economic Theory of Teams,* which was published in 1972. As a result, John Butterworth, Ted Mock, and I wrote dissertations applying information economics concepts to accounting.[3]

I developed a general multi-period decision model in which there were explicit representation of the link between past and future events and the information available about past events. In addition, I used a dynamic inventory model to illustrate several key concepts: decision model simplification, relevance (reporting more detailed information about past events), timeliness (reporting information earlier or more frequently), and accuracy (reporting more precise information about prior events).

---

[2] Roy Radner was at Berkeley and Jacob Marshak was at UCLA. Their joint work influenced Ph.D. students at both institutions, but it was the Berkeley students (notably, John Butterworth, Ted Mock, and myself) who had a sustained impact on the accounting literature.

[3] John's dissertation *Accounting systems and management decision: an analysis of the role of information in the management decision process,* was a runner up for the 1967 McKinsey Foundation Post-Doctoral Dissertation Award, and was the basis for Butterworth (1972).

My dissertation, *A theoretical framework for evaluating changes in accounting information for managerial decisions*, won the 1967 McKinsey Foundation Post-Doctoral Dissertation Award, it served as the basis for Feltham (1968) – which was a winner of the 1968 AAA Manuscript Competition, and Feltham (1972) is a revised version that was published as AAA Research Monograph #5.

Ted's dissertation, *The evaluation of alternative information structures*, served as the basis for Mock (1969, 1971).

I assumed there is an *information evaluator* who applies a cost/benefit approach to selecting an accounting information system, and the information evaluator need not be the decision maker.   Hence, I considered the possibility that the decision maker might make suboptimal use of the information he receives.   Furthermore, if the information evaluator is also the decision maker, then a cost/benefit approach can be applied to both decision rules and the information system.

3.2.2   The "Felski" Partnership

After his arrival at Stanford, Joel and I began discussing information economics and its implications for accounting.   We soon came up with the ideas for two papers and we began to work on them simultaneously.   Both were published in the *Accounting Review*.
- The use of models in information evaluation, *Accounting Review* (1970);
- Forecast evaluation, *Accounting Review* (1972).

The first was more memorable than the second, and this is reflected in the fact that the first was awarded the 1970 AICPA Notable Contribution to Accounting Literature Award.   Hence, Joel received this prestigious award twice while he was still an Assistant Professor.

We identified the key components of the information evaluation model and the issues involved in its implementation.   Most noteworthy was our summary and classification of a variety of contemporary research with respect to how it contributed to our understanding of elements of the information evaluation model, or constituted a very simplified approach to information evaluation.   One can view this discussion as describing how positive research on the use and consequences of information can be related to normative research on the choice of an accounting system.

Later, Tom Dyckman of Cornell University would refer to us as "Felski" since he said: "you can't tell them apart."   Of course, that is not true, since I have always had more hair than Joel – at least on the top of my head!

3.2.3   Information evaluation: complexity and simplicity

Joel and I regularly worked as a team while we were at Stanford, but we each had our own single-authored research.   Joel was particularly interested in implementation issues and this led to the following two papers;
- Some decomposition results for information evaluation, *Journal of Accounting Research* (1970).
- Information improvement bounds, *Journal of Accounting Research* (1972).

While decomposition of the evaluation problem would ideally simplify the analysis, Joel's analysis in the first paper is quite complex. I shall never forget the comment made by a Ph.D. student when Joel presented the paper at a Stanford accounting research workshop. The student, who did behavioral experimental research in his dissertation, described Joel's analysis as "an appendix looking for a paper"!!!

3.2.4   Cost determination

In 1969 the AICPA asked the Stanford accounting faculty to examine the area of cost determination. Chuck Horngren and Bob Jaedicke were well known for their textbooks and papers dealing with cost accounting. The AICPA had previously focused on financial reporting and had neither engaged in nor supported research in cost accounting. However, the government was threatening to establish cost accounting standards, particularly with respect to cost-plus contracting, and the AICPA were anxious to establish cost accounting standards as part of their domain.

Our proposal followed the cost analysis approach that had begun to develop in the forties (and had been exposited by Clark).

- Research proposal for cost measurement criteria, *Journal of Accountancy* (1960), coauthored by Joel, Chuck Horngren, Bob Jaedicke, and myself.

In this user decision model approach, we planned to examine decision contexts to identify the relevant costs. The objective was to identify the nature of the "true" cost for a given decision context and then seek to measure or predict that cost as accurately as possible. However, as we worked on the project, Joel and I became dissatisfied with our approach. We began to argue with Chuck and Bob regarding what we could say using this "conditional truth" approach, and began pushing an information economics approach. (Remember, Chuck and Bob were well established full professors, while Joel and I were green assistant professors.)

The information economics approach recognized that decision makers frequently used simplified decision models and simplified procedures for determining costs. The issue is not one of attempting to develop decision models and cost accounting procedures that are faithful to the truth. Instead, the objective is to develop decision models and cost accounting procedures that efficiently trade off the economic consequences of the actions taken, the cost of the information used in making decisions, and the cost of the decision analysis.

The resulting product was too abstract for AICPA tastes and they chose not to publish our report. However, Bob and Chuck had been farsighted enough to specify in our contract that if the AICPA chose not to publish the report, then the publication rights reverted to us. It was ultimately published as

- Cost Determination: A Conceptual Approach (1976), Iowa State University Press.

Joel and I were listed as the authors even though we had tried to convince Chuck and Bob to be listed as well. (Chuck said he did not want to have to explain what we had done).

I found working with Joel on this project to be stimulating and enlightening. We had many significant discussions about how to approach each of the issues we faced. This profoundly affected my teaching of cost analysis to undergraduates and MBA students, first at Stanford and then for my thirty-three years at UBC.

3.2.5   Multi-decision maker information evaluation issues

The following three papers illustrate Joel's ability to understand and communicate the implications for accounting of developments in other fields (particularly economics).

- General impossibility of normative standards, *Accounting Review* (1973).
- Rational choice of accounting method for a class of partnerships, *Journal of Accounting Research* (1973).
- Choice among financial reporting alternatives, *Accounting Review* (1974).

Our initial information economic analyses focused on single-decision-maker settings, whereas these papers consider settings in which there are multiple decision makers. Furthermore, unlike the Marschak and Radner "team", Joel considers settings in which the decision makers have diverse personal preferences.

The first is an application of the Arrow impossibility theorem with respect to the aggregation of diverse preferences in settings in which there are no exchanges between decision makers. The second is an extension of Wilson's (1968) examination of decision and risk-sharing preferences within a partnership (which Wilson calls a syndicate), given optimal partnership contracts. In Joel's model, the partners must choose an information system in addition to the partners' actions. Conditions are identified in which the partnership contract creates a "team", i.e., the decision makers agree on the choice of information system and the actions taken given the signals from that system.

The third paper considers the impact of public information in a general equilibrium model, with consideration of the impact of private investor information. This analysis was later developed more fully by others, but

Joel provided leadership by identifying a fruitful area for future research. As stated before, he is consistently at the leading edge of the field.

4. SHIFT IN FOCUS: EXPLORING THE DECISION-INFLUENCING ROLE OF ACCOUNTING

In 1971 I left Stanford to return to Canada. Each year I returned to Stanford to attend summer camp and to work with Joel on the *Cost Determination* book. In 1975-76 I returned to Stanford on a sabbatical leave. We completed the book and began a new era of accounting research.

In the introduction to the *Cost Determination* book, Joel and I recognize that cost information can be useful for both facilitating and influencing decisions. The book, and most of our prior research, focused on decision-facilitating information and analysis. However, as we completed the book during my sabbatical year, we began to explore the decision-influencing role of information and analysis.

This latter research considers the link between performance measures and incentives. This was the point at which I began to think seriously about incentives. However, when I went back over Joel's research I found that he had given this some serious thought much earlier. The following briefly describes two papers that reflect his thoughts. This is followed by a description of our early joint work in agency theory.

4.1 Joel's early research on incentives

Joel's early research had focused on the use of accounting information as a feedback for making better decisions -- identifying "errors" in planning models and their implementation. As time progressed, Joel began to consider the manager as distinct from the firm's owner, and the use of accounting numbers as performance measures used to motivate the manager's decisions.

Two papers are significant here.

- Optimal performance measurement, *Journal of Accounting Research* (1972).
- Uncertainty and evaluation based on controllable performance, *Journal of Accounting Research* (1976).

The first paper is noteworthy because it explicitly considered: two individuals with personal preferences (an owner and a manager); the manager selects a productive act; the manager's compensation is a function of a performance measure (statistic); there is a reservation utility level; and there is   uncertainty that may influence the monetary outcome, the performance statistic, and the compensation. Extensions to the basic model include: selection of a personal information system by the manager, multiple periods, and multiple managers.

The manager does not have any direct preference (e.g., cost or disutility) with respect to his action. Hence, it is not a classic agency theory model, and we could dismiss some of the results by noting that the first-best result can be obtained by paying fixed wage if the principal is risk neutral, or offering an efficient risk-sharing contract if the principal is risk averse (and outcome is contractible). However, I think it is noteworthy because this paper points us in the direction of considering the role of performance measures in an incentive contracting setting. It illustrates Joel's insightfulness and innovativeness – he is again at the leading edge.

The second paper considers a multiple manager setting from a syndicate (i.e., efficient risk sharing) perspective. The key feature was an examination of the "controllability" criterion -- which holds that a manager should only be held responsible for outcomes to the extent he influences that outcome. Joel demonstrates that implementation of this criterion can lead to inferior results due to inefficient risk sharing.

4.2   Information asymmetries in economic analysis

The initial work in information economics had focused on a single decision maker or multiple decision makers who either had the same information (e.g., the theory of risk sharing) or acted cooperatively if they had different information (e.g., the economic theory of teams). In the early seventies, economists began to analyze exchanges between individuals who had different information.

In 1975-76 I was on sabbatical leave at Stanford, I sat in on a Ph.D. seminar Joel was teaching and we both sat in on a sequence of courses taught by Joe Stiglitz and Sandy Grossman. This sequence examined a variety of recent papers on information economics, with a significant section on the papers dealing with information asymmetries.

Joel and I were particularly influenced by a paper on sharecropping by Stiglitz. It explored the economic reasons for the use of three alternative types of contracts between a farmer and a land owner: pure wage, land rental, and sharecropping. Key features of this analysis were that the farmer and the land owner maximized their own utility and the farmer had preferences with respect to both the effort he expended and his financial return. Risk sharing issues may arise, but if the land owner is very wealthy, then he is essentially risk neutral and would bear all the risk in a first-best contract. In that setting, any risk born by the farmer must be due to either an inefficiency or an incentive to motivate more than a minimal level of farmer effort. We felt that the economic arguments used in this paper could be extended to a re-examination of the management control function of accounting.

4.3   Agency theory and accounting: The beginnings

In the Ph.D. course that Joel was teaching, we read a 1975 monograph on measurement in accounting by Yuji Ijiri. Ijiri exhorted accountants to reconsider the stewardship role of accounting. He believed it was a foundational role for accountants and that it had been largely ignored during the preceding thirty years as we focussed almost exclusively on the decision-facilitating role of accounting information.

Joel and I agreed with Ijiri's call for a reconsideration of the stewardship role of accounting, but we did not agree with his measurement approach. He emphasized truth and approximation to truth. The cost/benefit tradeoffs in the choice of accounting procedures and the use of accounting numbers were largely ignored. The sharecropping paper by Stiglitz gave us a means of introducing cost/benefit analysis of accounting information that is used to influence management decisions. A major appeal of this area of research for accountants was that reporting what had occurred was directly valuable in an agency relation.

Joel and I proceeded to write a paper in which we considered two types of information asymmetries: pre-contract differences in knowledge about the skill of the manager and post-contract differences in the observability of the manager's actions. The former results in the "adverse selection" problem, while the second results in the "moral hazard" problem.

We established conditions under which the first-best results could be achieved (i.e., the information asymmetries did not result in inefficiencies) and explored the role of payoff-contingent contracts in mitigating the problems created by these information asymmetries.

In the moral hazard setting, we explicitly considered the potential benefits of contracts that provided distinctly different compensation levels depending on whether the payoffs exceeded some "standard".

The resulting paper was
- Economic incentives in budgetary control systems, *Accounting Review* (1978).

It did not receive any awards at the time, but in 1994 it was awarded the American Accounting Association's Seminal Contribution to Accounting Literature.

5.   EXTENSIONS OF AGENCY THEORY

Our 1978 paper was the first of a long sequence of papers that explore various aspects of the use of performance measures, such as accounting reports, in influencing managers' (agents') action choices. Joel has been directly involved in numerous significant papers in this area, and has also contributed to many other significant papers through his mentoring of Ph.D. students. The following categorizes a number of these papers.

5.1   Optimal contracts and the value of additional performance measures.

Our analysis in the 1978 paper was restricted to linear contracts based on the firm's payoff. We did not know how to derive optimal contracts, but Bengt Holmstrom was a Ph.D. student in Joel's class in 1976 and he produced a pathbreaking dissertation that characterized optimal incentive contracts. In addition, Bengt identified key conditions under which additional performance measures reduce agency costs. The following are two of Bengt's many noteworthy papers in this area.
- Moral hazard and observability, *Bell Journal of Economics* (1979).
- Moral hazard and teams, *Bell Journal of Economics* (1982).

Frøystein Gjesdal was also a Ph.D. student in Joel's 1976 seminar. He further explored the impact of performance measure characteristics on the principal's expected payoff.
- Accounting for stewardship, *Journal of Accounting Research* (1981).
- Information and incentives: The agency information problem, *Review of Economic Studies* (1982).

Joel's early work on variance analysis naturally led him to explore the acquisition of additional performance information conditional on the information provided by a primary performance measure. In the following two papers, Joel worked with Stan Baiman who had been his Ph.D. student in the early seventies, (i.e., in the pre-agency theory era).
- Economically optimal performance evaluation and control systems, *Journal of Accounting Research* (1980).
- Variance analysis procedures as motivational devices, *Management Science* (1980).

Rick Lambert, another of Joel's Ph.D. students also produced an insightful variance analysis paper.
- Variance Investigation in agency settings, *Journal of Accounting Research* (1985).

The additional information acquired at the end of the period can be valuable either because it is influenced by the agent's action or because it is informative about uncontrollable events that influence the primary performance measure. In a very simple paper, Joel and his former Ph.D. student, Rick Antle, highlighted an interesting implication of the two types of relevant performance measures.

- Controllability principle in responsibility accounting, *The Accounting Review* (1988).

They pointed out that management accounting texts generally emphasize the "controllability principle," i.e., in evaluating an agent, exclude measures that are not influenced by the agent's action. Rick and Joel then proceeded to illustrate that this was an inappropriate perspective. In particular, while an agent's actions may influence production costs and not revenues, an optimal incentive contract will use both revenues and costs in evaluating the agent if the revenues are informative about uncontrollable events that affect costs. This paper is noteworthy because it took what we had learned from our agency theory analyses and used it to provide a more insightful perspective in teaching management accounting. While it was published as a note in the "education" section of *The Accounting Review*, it has been widely cited by accounting researchers.

5.2   Private pre-decision information

The early information economics research had focussed on decision-facilitating information, which is received by the decision maker prior to selecting his actions. The agency models referenced above focus on verified decision-influencing information that is reported after the agent has taken his actions. Joel again provided leadership through his involvement in research that considered both types of information in a single model. Of particular note is the introduction into the agency model of private pre-decision information, i.e., information observed by the agent, but not the principal, prior to the agent taking his action.

As noted above, Joel has produced a number of papers that provide an information economics perspective on variance analysis. Variances represent differences between actual results and standards or budgets that may be based on unverified reports made by the managers being evaluated. This led John Christensen, another of Joel's Ph.D. students, to consider pre-decision information that is observed by the agent, but not the principal. He establishes that communication of the agent's private information to the principal can be valuable in contracting even though the agent's message is unverified.

- Communication in agencies, *Bell Journal of Economics* (1981).
- The determination of performance standards and participation, *Journal of Accounting Research* (1982).

In addition to working with some of his former Ph.D. students, Joel began in the eighties to work with David Sappington, an economist. They coauthored at least fourteen papers, some published in accounting journals, and others published in economics journals. One of the most noteworthy of these papers examines a setting in which the agent's effort is exerted to acquire pre-decision information about the consequences of an investment choice that the principal delegates to the agent.

- Delegated expertise, Journal of Accounting Research (1987).

The investment choice requires no effort on the part of the agent, but the investment is both costly and beneficial to the principal. If the agent makes his investment choice based solely on his prior beliefs, then the first-best result can be attained by paying him a fixed wage and instructing him to make the investment choice that maximizes the principal's expected net payoff. In that setting there is no moral hazard problem associated with the investment choice. However, the acquisition of pre-decision information is costly to the agent, and potentially benefits the principal by facilitating the agent's investment choice. Incentives are provided to induce the agent to exert costly effort to acquire the decision-facilitating information. A particularly interesting aspect of the model is that the moral hazard problem associated with the information acquisition effort induces a moral hazard problem with respect to the agent's investment choice. The identification of the induced moral hazard problem was a significant contribution to the literature.

Prior to the "delegated expertise" paper, Joel wrote a paper with Stanford colleagues Jim Patell and Mark Wolfson in which the agent chooses both a productive act and a performance measurement system.

- Decentralized choice of monitoring systems, *The Accounting Review* (1984)

The agent receives private information about the production technology after he has taken his productive action, but possibly before he chooses the performance measurement system. The paper demonstrates that it can be optimal for the principal to allow the agent to choose the performance measurement system that will be used in calculating his compensation.

Later Joel wrote a paper with Ron Dye in which the agent receives private information about the output characteristics for the set of projects available to him.

- Risk, return, and moral hazard, *Journal of Accounting Research* (1999).

Each project is characterized by the mean and the variance of a sample of cash flows that will be generated if the agent exerts zero effort. The agent can choose to exert positive effort, which will increase the mean of the cash flows generated by the chosen project. After observing the set of available projects, the agent makes an unverified announcement of the mean and variance for his choice of project and effort.

The paper does not try to identify an optimal contract, but, instead, the principal selects from the class of contracts that are linear functions of the sample mean and the sample variance, augmented by quadratic penalties based on deviations between the sample mean and sample variance and the mean and variance announced by the manager. The principal is risk neutral, so that the variance of the cash flows has no direct significance to him. However, the variance will affect the riskiness of the agent's compensation if the compensation varies with the reported cash flows. Hence, the principal is concerned about both the mean and the variance of the agent's project choice, since the latter will affect the risk premium that must be paid to the agent. A simple linear contract of the cash flows would be a very blunt instrument in this setting. By considering a more complex, yet constrained, class of contracts, the authors are able to generate examples that provide interesting insights into the issues that arise when the agent controls both the mean and the variance of the reported cash flows.

5.3   Multiple agents

Early agency theory models typically assumed the principal had only one agent, or he could optimally contract with each agent separately. Joel was again at the forefront in examining the nature of optimal contracts in multi agent settings. There are two broad classes of multi-agent models in the literature. One basic type consists of models in which there are multiple productive agents, and the other type consists of multi-agent models in which one is a monitor of the productive agent(s).

5.3.1   Relative Performance Measures

As noted above, in our single-period models we have at times considered what I call insurance informative measures. These measures are not influenced by the agent's actions, but are informative about the uncontrollable events that influence the primary performance measure that is influenced by his actions. The performance measures for other firms or agents whose outcomes are influenced by correlated uncontrollable events are often given as examples of insurance informative measures.

The analysis is straightforward if the agents act independently, and that may be a reasonable assumption in settings in which the agents are managers in different firms. However, Joel and David Sappington realized that managers in the same organization may be induced to coordinate their actions if the performance measures for the two agents are correlated and the performance measure for one agent is used as an insurance informative measure for the other.

- Multi-agent control in perfectly correlated environments, *Economic Letters* (1983).
- Optimal incentive contracts with multiple agents, *Journal of Economic Theory* (1984).

The second paper is widely cited. It illustrates how a relative-performance contract can induce the two agents to both exert low effort, so that they both have low outcomes and can claim their poor results are due to "bad" uncontrollable operating events. The authors then demonstrate that coordinated shirking can be avoided, and still obtain some of the benefits of insurance informative measures. For example, the first agent's contract can be based on his own action informative performance measures, and then the second agent's contract can be a relative performance contract based on the action informative performance measurers for both agents.

5.3.2 Decentralized contracting

The preceding papers with David Sappington assume that while the agents can coordinate their actions, they cannot change the compensation received by the agents given the performance measures reported. However, in the following paper, Joel and David consider a setting in which the principal contracts with the first agent who in turn contracts with the second agent.

- Line-item reporting, factor acquisition, and subcontracting, *Journal of Accounting Research* (1986).

This paper assumes there are two factors of production. Initially, there is a single agent who provides one factor, and the other is provided by the principal. Settings are considered in which the two suppliers choose how much they will each supply, versus one in which the agent chooses both quantities. The analysis is then extended to settings in which the two factors are supplied by different agents. Under centralized contracting, the principal contracts with both agents, whereas with decentralized contracting, there is subcontracting between the two agents. Subcontracting can be beneficial to the principal if the first agent has information about the second agent's action that is not available to the principal.

This paper is simple, yet rich in insights. Given my own current work on multi-agent models with Christian Hofmann, I am glad I rediscovered this paper. This allows us to properly acknowledge that some of our insights are essentially the same as some provided by Joel nearly twenty years ago.

5.3.3 Transfer pricing

Inter-divisional transfers of goods and services are common in multi-divisional firms, and every management accounting text includes some discussion of the use of transfer prices in developing divisional performance measures. Therefore, it is not surprising that various authors, including Joel, have developed multi-agent models to explore the incentive issues that arise due to inter-divisional issues. One of Joel's contributions to this area is a paper with John Christensen.

- Profit allocation under ancillary trade, *Journal of Accounting Research* (1998).

As the title suggests, a key feature of this two-agent model is that the inter-divisional transfers are a small part of each division's activities. The incentive mechanisms for each agent are based on divisional profit measures, which are primarily affected by the agent's primary activities. The profits on inter-divisional transfers create performance measure noise with respect to the primary incentive problems. As in many of Joel's papers, the model here is simple, but reflects some key characteristics of the phenomena being examined, and therefore yields interesting insights.

5.3.4 Monitors and productive agents

In most agency models the performance measures are assumed to be verified by some unspecified monitor who reports truthfully. However, if the monitor's verification and reporting activities are personally costly and noncontractible, then both the productive agent (e.g., manager or worker) and the monitor (e.g., auditor or supervisor) are agents with whom the principal contracts.

Rick Antle (one of Joel's Ph.D. students) introduced the auditor as an agent.

- The Auditor as an economic agent, *Journal of Accounting Research* (1982).
- Auditor independence, *Journal of Accounting Research* (1984).

Joel later worked with David Sappington to explore the implications of collusion between a productive agent and a monitor.

- Hierarchical structure and responsibility accounting, *Journal of Accounting Research* (1989).

This insightful paper demonstrates how a "whistle blowing" mechanism can be used to efficiently induce both the productive agent and the monitor to report truthfully to the principal.

5.4   Double moral hazard with limited contractible information

In two of their most intriguing papers, David Sappington and Joel consider settings in which incentive issues arise with respect to both the principal and the agent, and there is limited contractible information.

- Resolving double moral hazard problems with buy-out agreements, *The Rand Journal of Economics* (1991).
- Sourcing with unverifiable performance information, *Journal of Accounting Research* (1993).

In the first paper, the principal and the agent both provide productive effort that influence the firm's terminal value. The agent takes his action first, and it is observed by the principal before taking his own action. There is *no contractible information*. However, firm ownership is transferrable and the final owner will know its terminal value when realized. The principal initially owns the firm, and he can offer the agent a contract which specifies two options from which the principal will choose after observing the agent's action. The first option is to pay the agent a pre-specified wage and retain ownership of the firm. The second option requires the agent to buy the firm at a pre-specified buyout price. Interestingly, in this simple setting with no contractible information, the agent can obtain the first-best result.

In the second paper, the final outcome is contractible and is influenced by the agent's action. The principal does not take an action and does not observe the agent's action. However, the principal does privately observe a signal that is influenced by the agent's action and influences beliefs about the outcome. The contract can be a function of the outcome plus a report by the principal with respect to the signal he observed. The principal's contract choice problem has two types of incentive constraints: one with respect to the agent's action choice, and the other with respect to the principal's reporting choice. It may be optimal to ignore the principal's report in the contract, but the paper provides settings in which the contract with the agent is less costly to the principal if it is carefully constructed to also induce truthful reporting by the principal.

I find the two papers to be intriguing because they demonstrate how creative contracting can overcome limitations in the available contractible information.

5.5   Multiple periods

Virtually all the agency models mentioned above consider only a single period. However, multi-period issues are of central importance in accounting, and multi-period models have become common place in recent years. Not surprisingly, Joel and his Ph.D. students were among the first to explore multi-period agency models.

5.5.1   Consumption smoothing

Rick Lambert, one of Joel's Ph.D. students, extended the basic single period agency model to consider the implications of contracting with a single agent for two periods.
- Long-term contracts and moral hazard, *Bell Journal of Economics* (1983).

The agent is assumed to have time-additive preferences with respect to consumption, so that he prefers "smooth consumption" across periods. If the agent does not have access to borrowing and lending, then the principal will offer contracts with "smooth compensation." However, this is unnecessary if the agent can borrow and lend. The agent's utility for consumption and disutility for effort are assumed to be additively separable, and this implies that the agent's wealth at the start of each period affects his effort choice. Anyone analyzing multi-period agency models must be very mindful of the effect of the agent's consumption and action preferences.

5.5.2   Accounting choice

The effectiveness of accounting measures, such as accounting income, as performance measures depends in part on the rules used to calculate those measures and the agent's ability to influence the calculations. Many papers in the agency theory literature consider relatively abstract performance measures and do not attempt to capture the unique characteristics of accounting measures. However, Joel has been a leader in providing relatively simple models in which the performance measure reflects key characteristics of accounting income.

The initial paper by Rick Lambert assumed the agent's preferences are time-additive and, thereby, created a direct preference for borrowing and lending in order to smooth consumption. In virtually all of Joel's multi-period papers, he assumes the agent's preferences are represented by an exponential utility function defined over his aggregate consumption minus his aggregate effort costs. Hence, the agent is only concerned about his net consumption, not its timing. This simplifies the analysis by avoiding a direct demand for borrowing and lending to smooth consumption, and by avoiding wealth effects on the agent's action choices. This allows Joel to focus the use of accounting measures in the efficient inducement of the agent's effort across periods, with emphasis on the settings in which the agent can influence the accounting measure.

5.5.2.1   Revenue recognition.

Joel' paper with Rick Antle on the impact of alternative revenue recognition rules is an example of this type of analysis.

- Revenue recognition, Contemporary Accounting Research (1989).

This paper is notable both because it examines how an important accounting rule affects the information content of accounting income, and because it considers more than one use of the information provided by accounting income.   In particular, the paper considers the use of reported accounting income by investors in making consumption choices over time, and its use as a performance measure for providing management incentives over time.

5.5.2.2   Endogenous measurement choice.

The Antle and Demski "revenue recognition" choice paper assumes the accounting measurement rule is chosen exogenously.   However, Joel has other papers in which the measurement rules, or even the amount reported, are chosen endogenously by the agent.   We saw that in some of the previously mentioned single-period papers, and the following two-period model paper has that characteristic.

- Performance measure manipulation, *Contemporary Accounting Research* (1998).

In this paper, the agent directly chooses the reported first-period output after privately observing the actual first-period output plus partial information about the second-period output.   The aggregate output for the two periods is audited, but the agent can over- or under-state the first-period output.   The agent's communication channel is limited, so that the Revelation Principle does not apply.   Hence, the optimal contract may induce lying.   Of particular note is the fact that the model provides a simple setting in which income smoothing, i.e., understating (overstating) the first-period output when it high (low), can be optimal.   Interestingly, this result is obtained even though the agent's preferences are such that the agent is concerned only with his total net consumption, not its timing.

In the preceding paper, the agent's report is constrained, but within the constraints the agent can say whatever he prefers.   In a subsequent paper with Hans Frimor and David Sappington, Joel considers a two-period, multi-task model in which the agent exerts both productive and manipulative effort in each period.

- Efficient manipulation in a repeated setting, *Journal of Accounting Research* (2004).

The productive effort influences the probability of a good outcome for the principal, which in turn increases the probability of a favorable performance report. The manipulative effort (which Feltham and Xie 1994 call "window dressing"), on the other hand, does not affect the probability of a good outcome but increases the probability of a favorable performance report when there is a bad outcome. Incentives to induce productive effort, also create incentives for manipulative effort. A key feature of this multi-period model is that manipulative effort in the first period can have a carry-over effect to the second period. The principal is assumed to have some control with respect to the extent of the carryover. The paper identifies settings in which the principal prefers to limit the carryover, and other settings in which he prefers to facilitate the carryover. As with many of Joel's papers, the model is relatively simple, but provides a rich set of insights.

5.5.3   Renegotiation

The initial agency theory research generally assumed that principal/agent contracts are written in terms of verified performance measures and that the principal and agent can reliably commit to implementing the terms of the initial contract. However, in recent years researchers have introduced unverified performance measures and limited commitment. Of particular note recently is exploration of two-period settings in which the principal and agent cannot commit to not renegotiate the initial contract at the end of the first period.

The following are two of Joel's contributions to this literature.

- Performance measure garbling under renegotiation in multi-period agencies, *Journal of Accounting Research* (1999), with Hans Frimor.
- Accounting policies in agencies with moral hazard and renegotiation, *Journal of Accounting Research* (2002), with Peter Christensen and Hans Frimor.

A distinctive feature of the models in these two papers is that the agent privately observes the first-period outcome before contract renegotiation occurs. We know from other papers in the literature that renegotiation results in less effective contracts when the performance measures are publicly reported. The paper with Hans Frimor demonstrates that renegotiation results in another form of distortion when the first-period outcome is privately observed. In particular, in this setting the optimal contract induces the agent to "garble" (manipulate) his report of the first-period outcome. That is, the agent's report does not fully reveal what he observed. This is an interesting illustration of the well-known fact that the

Revelation Principle does not necessarily apply if there is limited commitment.

In the paper with Peter Christensen and Hans Frimor, renegotiation takes place after the agent has taken his first action (which may be randomly chosen) and before he takes his second-period action and observes the first-period outcome. At the renegotiation stage the principal offers the agent a menu of contracts from which he chooses by reporting his first-period action. After the agent has observed the first-period outcome, he reports it to the principal and receives the first-period compensation specified by the renegotiated contract. The second-period compensation is paid after the agent observes and reports the second-period outcome. The agent's outcome reports are constrained by the firm's auditor who ensures the reports are consistent with the firm's accounting policies. Five reporting policies are considered. All ensure that the aggregate reports cannot exceed the aggregate realized outcome, but they differ with respect to the feasible manipulations within that constraint.

6. COST ANALYSIS

Joel's research in the sixties explored cost analysis issues, and cost determination was the focus of the book we published in 1976. Approximately twenty years later Joel returned to the analysis of costing issues, teaming up with his former Ph.D. student, John Christensen.

- The classical foundations of "modern costing," *Management Accounting Research* (1995).
- Product costing in the presence of endogenous subcost functions," *Review of Accounting Studies* (1997).
- Factor choice distortion under cost-based reimbursement, *Journal of Management Accounting Research* (2003).

This work reflects Joel's constant desire to provide insights into accounting using fundamental concepts and analysis. Activity-based costing had developed during the eighties and into the nineties as a popular topic in cost accounting texts. In their 1995 and 1997 papers, John and Joel examine activity based costing using neoclassical economic analysis of a firm's production technology and costs. Classification and aggregation are major themes, with emphasis on understanding their relationship to characteristics of a firm's production technology.

The 2003 paper examines the impact of costing procedures on the results that occur if a cost-reimbursement system is used in contracting between a buyer and a supplier. The production technology in the 2003 paper is the same as in the 1997 paper, and some of the results from the 1997 paper are used in the 2003 paper. However, the 2003 paper is more explicit in specifying a setting in which costing plays an important role. Alternative costing systems essentially represent alternative simplifications, and which simplification is preferred depends critically on the characteristics of the production technology.

7. APPLICATION OF THEORETICAL ANALYSIS IN ACCOUNTING

While some of Joel's research paper are very complex, the vast majority use relatively simple models to make important conceptual points about the interaction between accounting and economic activity. Furthermore, he has developed the ability to explain information economic analysis in simple terms that can be grasped by undergraduate students, graduate students, and faculty who are not analytical researchers. Joel believes "theory is practical." That is, if you learn how to think carefully and insightfully about a field such as accounting, you will make more effective decisions. Hence, he believes that our theoretical research should impact our teaching and empirical research.

7.1 The use of theory in accounting instruction

I do not know what Joel had done in his teaching at Columbia, but as soon as he arrived at Stanford in 1968, Joel and I began to integrate theoretical quantitative analysis into the introductory management accounting course in the MBA Core. We were relatively new assistant professors, but with the support of the senior faculty (Chuch Horngren, Bob Jaedicke, and Bob Sprouse), we took a bold step in our teaching. I continued that type of approach when I moved to UBC, and I know Joel has consistently adopted this type of approach throughout his career.

When we started in 1969, we used a new managerial accounting text by Nick Dopuch and Jake Birnberg. Joel joined them as a co-author in the second and third editions, bringing to bear the insights he had gained from his teaching at Stanford, plus what we had learned from our information economic research on cost determination.

- Cost Accounting: Accounting Data for Management Decisions, Harcourt (second edition 1974, third edition 1980).

At approximately the same time, Joel wrote a short paperback explaining, in relatively simple terms, the key elements of information economic analysis.

• *Information Analysis.* Addison-Wesley (1972, second edition 1980).

This book was designed to help both students and researchers to develop their ability to insightfully examine information/decision issues.

The development of information economic theory relevant to accounting has grown significantly since those early days. These theoretical developments are important ingredients in the two textbooks Joel has published in the last dozen years.

• Managerial Uses of Accounting Information. Kluwer (1994).
• Accounting Theory: An Information Content Perspective. McGraw /Hill-Irwin (2002), with John Christensen.

These two books are rich in illustrations of the application of information economic theory (including agency theory) to accounting issues. As noted earlier, Joel is a master of developing simple models to illustrate major theoretical insights. While these texts are written for undergraduate and masters students, Ph.D. students and accounting researchers can learn much from them.

7.2 The Use of Theory in Empirical Research

Joel has not participated in any empirical research, but empirical researchers would be well served to understand Joel's contributions to accounting theory. As a starting point, I recommend they read the two textbooks mentioned above. In addition, I recommend they read the following paper coauthored with David Sappington.

• Summarization with errors: A perspective on empirical investigation of agency relationships, *Management Accounting Research* (1999).

7.3 Perspectives on accounting research and education

As a leading accounting scholar for four decades, it is not surprising that Joel has frequently written and presented papers that provide his perspective on accounting research and education. In many cases these papers were written at the request of a conference organizer or editor, who knew that Joel could be relied upon to provide interesting, unique insights. It would be too large a task for me to try to comment on each paper or to even give a succinct summary of this set of papers. However, I provide a list of the papers that are published in refereed journals, so that we gain some sense of how extensive they are.

• The use of models in information evaluation, *The Accounting Review* (1970), with Jerry Feltham.
• The nature of financial objectives: A summary and synthesis, *Journal of Accounting Research* (1974), with Bill Beaver.

- Models in managerial accounting, *Journal of Accounting Research Supplement* (1982), with David Kreps.
- Accounting research: 1985, *Contemporary Accounting Research* (1985).
- Positive accounting theory: A review, *Accounting, Organizations and Society* (1988).
- The changing landscape of academic accounting, *Revision & Regnskabsvaesen* (1995).
- Corporate Conflicts of Interest, *Journal of Economic Perspectives* (2003).
- Endogenous expectations, *The Accounting Review* (2005), AAA Presidential Lecture.
- Accounting and Economics, *The New Palgrave Dictionary of Economics*, 2nd edition (2005).
- Analytical Modeling in Management Accounting Research, *The Handbook of Management Accounting Research* (2005).

8. MAJOR AWARDS

I conclude this tribute to Joel, with a reminder that, in addition to the awards he received for specific papers, he has received two major broad-based awards from the academic accounting profession.

8.1 AAA Outstanding Educator Award

In 1986, at the mid-point of his academic career, Joel received the American Accounting Association's Outstanding Educator Award. He had participated in revising the cost accounting text with Nick Dopuch and Jake Birnberg and had significantly and creatively affected the teaching of management accounting to Stanford MBAs. Also, as noted above, he had written (1972) and revised (1980) his book on information analysis. However, there is no doubt that a major reason he received the outstanding educator award was his insightful instruction and guidance of many Ph.D. students (including those here today) who have gone on to produce outstanding research.

It is now twenty years later. I believe that a strong case can be made for awarding him a second outstanding educator award – based solely on his contributions since the first award.

8.2   Accounting Hall of Fame

Joel was inducted into The Accounting Hall of Fame (located at Ohio State University) in 2000. Bill Beaver is the only one from our generation who preceded Joel in receiving this prestigious honour. It reflects the breadth, and particularly the depth of Joel's sustained contribution to accounting scholarship. I conclude my tribute to Joel with excerpts from the citation which Chuck Horngren read at Joel's induction into the Accounting Hall of Fame.

Known for the originality and rigor of his research, this distinguished and consummate scholar has played a leading role in accounting research for over three decades. ...

His path breaking work on applications of information economics and agency theory to accounting is presented in 60 published journal articles, 5 books, and over 25 other published papers. His work and that of the countless students he inspired has created a new domain for accounting theory. He is one of the most widely cited authors in the accounting literature and many of his papers have been awarded national prizes for their importance and influence. One of his first papers, "An Accounting System Structured on a Linear Programming Model," won the 1967 AICPA Award for Outstanding Contributions to the Accounting Literature and 3 years later, another paper, "The Use of Models in Information Evaluation" (written with his former colleague Gerald Feltham), captured the same award. Another early paper, "Decision Implementation Interface ..." won the 1969 American Accounting Association Competitive Manuscript Award. His articles have been required reading for doctoral students for over three decades, and his doctoral seminars, which he has delivered to many universities, are nationally know for their insights and their capacity to inspire and prepare students for research. His most recent book, Managerial Uses of Accounting Information, brings this important work and his insightful thinking about fundamental accounting problems to interested students at all levels.

For many years, he has played an active role in the American Accounting Association. He has served on many of its committees and editorial boards. Next year he will serve as its president-elect. He has also been a member of the editorial boards of the Journal of Accounting Research and many other journals. He is known as a true scholar for his probing mind and uncompromising pursuit of excellence. He is also well-known as a mentor and as a superb example for others because of his willingness to invest himself in the work of his colleagues and students.

His many honours include an honorary doctorate from Odense University in Denmark, the American Accounting Association's Outstanding Educator Award (1986), multiple awards of the AICPA-AAA Outstanding

Contribution to Accounting Literature Award (1967 and 1970), and the University of Florida Foundation Research Professorship.

... He is the 64th member of the Accounting Hall of Fame, ...

REFERENCES

American Accounting Association, 1966, *A Statement of Basic Accounting Theory*. American Accounting Association, Chicago.

Blackwell, D., 1951, Comparison of experiments, *Proceedings of the Second Berkeley Symposium on Mathematical Statistics and Probability*, University of California Press, Berkeley, 93-102.

Blackwell, D., 1953, Equivalent comparison of experiments, *Annals of Mathematical Statistics* 24: 267-272,

Butterworth, J. E., 1972, The accounting system as an information function, *Journal of Accounting Research* 10:1-25.

Churchman, C. W., and R. L. Ackoff, 1955, Operational accounting and operations research, *Journal of Accountancy* XCLX, 33-39.

Churchman, C. W., R. L. Ackoff, and E. L. Arnoff, 1957, *Introduction to Operations Research*. Wiley, New York.

Cyert, R. M., and J. G. March., 1963, *A Behavioral Theory of the Firm.* Prentice-Hall: Englewood Cliffs, New Jersey.

Clark, J. M., 1923, *The Economics of Overhead Costs*. University of Chicago Press: Chicago.

Coase, R. H. The nature of costs, *Economica* 4:386-405.

Edwards, E, I., and P.W. Bell, 1961, *The Theory and Measurement of Business Income*, University of California Press, Berkeley.

Feltham, G. A., 1968, The value of information, *The Accounting Review* 43, 684-696.

Feltham, G. A., 1972, *Information Evaluation: Studies in Accounting Research #5*, American Accounting Association, Sarasota, Florida.

Feltham, G. A., and J. Xie, 1994, Performance measure congruity and diversity in multi-task principal/agent relations, *The Accounting Review* 69:429-453.

Ijiri, Y., 1975, *Theory of Accounting Measurement: Studies in Accounting Research #10*, American Accounting Association, Sarasota, Florida.

March, J. G., and H. Simon, 1958, *Organizations*. John Wiley and Sons, New York.

Marschak, J., 1955, Elements of a theory of teams, *Management Science* 1:127-137.

Marschak, J., and K. Miyasawa, 1968, Economic comparability of information structures, *International Economic Review* 9: 137-174.

Marschak, J., and R. Radner, 1972, *Economic Theory of Teams*, Yale University Press, New Haven.

Mock, T. J., 1969, Comparative values of information structures, *Journal of Accounting Research: Selected Studies*, 124-159.

Mock, T. J., 1971 Concepts of information value and accounting," *The Accounting Review* 46, 765-778.

National Association of Cost Accountants, 1945, *The Uses and Classifications of Costs*, N.A.C.A. Research Series Bulletin Number 7.

Paton, W. A., and A. C. Littleton, 1940, *An Introduction to Corporate Accounting Standards*. American Accounting Association.

von Neumann, J., and O. Morgenstern, 1947, *Theory of Games and Economic Behavior.* Princeton University Press, Princeton.

Stigler, G., 1961, The economics of information, *Journal of Polictical Economy* 69: 213-285.

Stiglitz, J. E., 1974 Risk-sharing and incentives in sharecropping," *Review of Economic Studies*, 269-288.

Trueblood (1960), R. M., 1960, Operations research -- a challenge to accounting, *Journal of Accountancy* CIX: 47-51.

Wilson, R., 1968, On the theory of syndicates, *Econometrica* 36:110-132.

PART I

GENERAL THEORY

Chapter 2

FAIR VALUE, ACCOUNTING AGGREGATION AND MULTIPLE SOURCES OF INFORMATION

John Christensen and Hans Frimor
University of Southern Denmark

Abstract: Accounting information is formed by an aggregation of the information available to the accounting system. Introduction of fair value accounting represents a new solution to the accounting aggregation problem as market information is merged into the accounting system. Multiple sources of information are available to market participants and accounting information is but one of these sources. Fair value information is available to the accounting system, to the public, and to individual market participants, hence, the aggregate information available in the economy – aggregate informativeness – depends on the confluence of accounting information and other sources of information. Particularly, the price process might well be informative but is influenced by the accounting policy chosen and, hence, it is not obvious the introduction of fair value accounting leads to an improvement in aggregate informativeness. Fair value accounting may destroy the aggregation mechanism of the market.

Key words: Fair value, Accounting Aggregation, Information

1.   INTRODUCTION

FASB and IASB have been promoting fair value accounting in response to the demand for accounting information that is more in line with market valuation of the firm. This idea has been picked up in many of the studies on quality of earnings, and indeed one of the measures of quality of earnings that has been suggested is exactly the extent to which the accounting value mimics the market value. The argument behind this is straightforward provided accounting is the only source of information. If the purpose of the accounting information is valuation of the firm, introduction of fair values will certainly improve the valuation. The accounting value of the firm will be better aligned with the market value of the firm.

In the presence of multiple sources of information the picture changes. Often some information is provided by the financial reports while other sources of information directly feed the market participants. The accounting system can only process the information it has access to and the resulting financial report will reflect that. Furthermore, the accounting system aggregates information. In the presence of multiple sources of information it becomes important how the private information of the investors and the accounting information interact under various regimes. Mixing information sources is complicated and adding fair values to the accounting system might have a negative effect due to the interaction. The investors might not be able to "undo" the accounting aggregation.

Our task is to analyze the interaction among accounting reports, investors' private information and market valuation. The accounting system has access to accounting information and market information with noise and must provide an aggregated report. The market participants also have access to market information. The market determines price based upon the accounting report and the investors' private information, taking into account that the market participants learn from the price. Consequently, a rational expectations equilibrium is employed. In this setting the information processing is not invertible and the choice of accounting policy becomes more involved. Fair value accounting does not uniformly dominate transaction based accounting. The choice of accounting policy must reflect the influence of accounting on information aggregation in the market. Transaction based accounting can be preferred even when it seems the accounting system has comparative advantage in assessing fair values.

2.   THE MODEL

We consider a two period pure exchange economy with a single firm, an associated auditor, a riskless asset, and a set of atomistic investors. Trade takes place in the first period while consumption takes place in the second. Prior to the opening of the market each investor costlessly observes two pieces of information pertaining to the payoff from the firm's assets, $\tilde{x}$. Firstly, an auditor assists in the release of a public signal, $\tilde{V}_t$, concerning the future value of the risky asset and secondly, each agent observes a private signal, $\tilde{y}_i$, pertaining to the same.

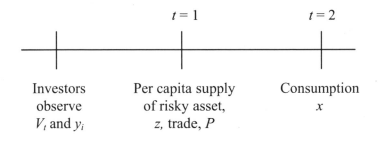

Figure 1. Timeline

We will assume the payoff of the risky asset consists of two elements:

$$\tilde{x} = \tilde{\varepsilon}_A + \tilde{\varepsilon}_E.$$

The accountant/auditor has comparative advantages in predicting parts of future payoffs. We will let $\tilde{\varepsilon}_A$ denote the fact the accountant/auditor is uniquely qualified in assessing this part of the payoff, while the comparative advantage is less pronounced when it comes to assessing the remaining component, $\tilde{\varepsilon}_E$. Specifically, we will assume the accountant/auditor observes two signals, $\tilde{y}_A$, and $\tilde{y}_E$. For simplicity, we will assume

$$\tilde{y}_A = \tilde{\varepsilon}_A$$

and

$$\tilde{y}_E = \tilde{\varepsilon}_E + \tilde{\varepsilon}_{AU}.$$

That is, the accountant/auditor can(not) assess $\tilde{\varepsilon}_A$ ($\tilde{\varepsilon}_E$) perfectly. This corresponds to a situation in which the auditor observes information contained in the books of a company, $\tilde{y}_A$, but also observes additional information, $\tilde{y}_E$, not on the company's records. The question we want to address is whether all available information should be reflected in the released financial statement, $(\tilde{y}_A, \tilde{y}_E)$, or whether only information reflecting transactions and the largely mechanical accounting treatment thereof should be reported, $\tilde{y}_A$. The accounting report, V_t, is designed to be the expected payoff given the information which is released in the accounting system.[4] Consequently, it depends on the particular accounting policy chosen or invoked through regulation. In the artificial world of the model the solution is of course simple, both pieces of information should be released – separately.   Though the problem exists in our simple setting, the problem is of particular concern, when many pieces of information are aggregated. In practice, for example, line items are reported with a single number. That is, the underlying transactions and the effects of accounting treatment – including effects of valuation – are aggregated and not reported separately. In our particular model, we will say the accounting policy/regime is transaction based if $V_t = V_T$, where

$$\tilde{V}_T = E[\tilde{x} \mid \tilde{y}_A],$$

and accounting is said to be market based if $V_t = V_M$, where

$$\tilde{V}_M = E[\tilde{x} \mid \tilde{y}_A, \tilde{y}_E].$$

Assuming all stochastic variables are normally distributed,

$$\begin{pmatrix} \tilde{\varepsilon}_A \\ \tilde{\varepsilon}_E \\ \tilde{\varepsilon}_{AU} \end{pmatrix} \sim N(\underline{0}, \Sigma_\varepsilon),$$

where

$$\Sigma_\varepsilon = \begin{bmatrix} \sigma_A^2 & 0 & 0 \\ 0 & \sigma_E^2 & 0 \\ 0 & 0 & \sigma_{AU}^2 \end{bmatrix},$$

it follows

$$\tilde{V}_T = \tilde{y}_A,$$

---

[4]   Note that this choice of accounting value sidesteps the problems attached to scaling issues. It is the information content of the accounting variables, $(\tilde{y}_A, \tilde{y}_E)$, that are important, not the scaling. The scaling is the expected value of the firm.

whereas

$$\tilde{V}_M = \tilde{y}_A + \frac{\sigma_E^2}{\sigma_E^2 + \sigma_{AU}^2} \tilde{y}_E.$$

Similarly, the agent's private information,

$$\tilde{y}_i = \tilde{\varepsilon}_E + \tilde{\varepsilon}_i,$$

where $\tilde{\varepsilon}_i \sim N(0, s^2)$, is independent of any other stochastic variable.

3.   ACCOUNTING POLICIES

The above model corresponds to the situation where an auditor not only observes transactions but also information pertaining to the value of the firm's assets and liabilities. Given there are multiple sources of information the question arises of how these should be aggregated into summary statistics, i.e., accounting numbers. The primary guidance in making decisions is found in the accounting standards.

When deciding whether accounting should be transaction or market based, a criterion for choosing is needed. Following Schipper and Vincent (2003) we focus on "the extent to which the reported earnings faithfully represent Hicksian income, where representational faithfulness means 'correspondence or agreement between a measure or description and the phenomenon that it purports to represent.'" Empirically the time series properties of earnings are used for evaluating the quality of earnings. Persistence captures the ability of accounting earnings to represent the long term sustainable level of earnings. It is assumed that persistence is of importance to investors as they have a long term perspective. In the same vein the predictive ability of earnings has been advocated as a measure of quality, cf. Lipe (1990). The relation to decision usefulness is obvious as long term earnings and long term returns are aligned. Also the variance of earnings has been suggested as a measure of quality simply because smoothing is associated with high quality earnings.

In another stream of empirical research earnings quality has been linked to the discretionary accruals in the financial statements. The rank order here is that more discretionary accruals lead to lower quality earnings. The argument is that the discretionary accruals are closely related to management reporting and management incentives might lead to biased reporting. Along these lines Leuz et al. (2003) argue that the resulting smoothed earnings are less informative as a result of management discretion. One common problem embedded in all these measures is that they might not measure the phenomenon they try to measure as noted by Schipper and Vincent (2003). The assumptions of the persistence, predictive ability, and variance measures are that the time series of economic income is nice and smooth in itself. For example, if the income series is inherently volatile, a low variance earnings series might not faithfully represent the income series but at the same time this earnings series will exhibit high quality earnings. Also the discretionary accruals might at the same time be managed and informative. Consequently, the view on earnings of Leuz et al. (2003) might not be the only explanation. On this Demski (1998) finds that smoothed earnings might be even more informative than the non smoothed earnings provided it is possible to control the incentives and furthermore smoothing might carry information on its own. For an accountant this finding is rather comforting as most of the accountant's skills are used in converting a cash flow series into an earnings series and accruals are central for this transformation.

When seen through the Feltham-Ohlson[5] framework, one interpretation is that the ease of assessing market value is a unifying criterion in defining earnings quality. Regarding the subset of financial reporting users, which the investors constitute, this idea corresponds well to the information content point of view in ASOBAT. In our setting, a similar operationalization of an earnings quality measure is the expected squared valuation error. For example, a possible criterion for choosing between accounting principles could be to choose the accounting principle that minimizes the accounting valuation error

$$E[(x - V_t)^2 \mid Inf_t],$$

where the information used in forming the conditional expectation is the same information entering into the formation of V_t, i.e., $Inf_A = \tilde{y}_A$ and $Inf_M = (\tilde{y}_A, \tilde{y}_E)$. The ranking of transactions versus market based accounting is clear using this criterion, as market based accounting clearly dominates transaction based accounting:

$$E[(x - V_M)^2 \mid Inf_M] = Var[x \mid Inf_M]$$
$$< Var[x \mid Inf_T] = E[(x - V_T)^2 \mid Inf_T].$$

[5] Feltham and Ohlson (1995).

Many proponents of market based accounting seem to be employing a similar criterion in forming their opinion, and, ignoring manipulation concerns, this seems quite reasonable. Market based accounting does in fact provide more information to the market than does transaction based accounting. The problem is a criterion based on accounting valuation error implies a narrow focus on accounting information, disregarding other sources of information available in the economy. As Christensen and Demski (2003) write, "It is simply naive to treat accounting as the sole or primary source of information. This admonition comes in two forms. One is the fact that when the accounting system does not recognize some event, it does not follow outside observers are unaware of that event.... Second is the fact that multiple sources of information do not simply 'add together.' They combine in a far from straightforward fashion."

The astute reader will – of course – have noticed that in the above we have defined valuation error as the difference between realized payoff and expected payoff. In a multiperiod world a natural generalization is to define accounting valuation error as the difference between book value of equity and (future) market value of equity. From Beaver and Demski (1979) we know market values are hard to assess – especially when markets are incomplete – but also that market value equals expected future payoff less a risk premium. Furthermore, taking information dissemination effects into account, it could well be the case the difference between book value of equity and market value of equity is minimized by revealing nothing![6] As we wish to avoid problems in assessing risk premia and as we dislike a measure which in some respects is too sensible to the price formation process, we will use posterior variance of the future payoff conditional on all information available to investors as our criterion when ranking different accounting policies.

4.   PRICING

Each agent invests in the two assets so as to maximize his expected utility of consumption. Provided agents are rational (Bayesian) the expectation, $E_i[\cdot]$, is affected by public as well as private information available to the agent and, hence, each agent's demand depends on his private information. If individual demand is affected by private information, then in general market clearing price(s) is a function of the information

---

[6]   Demski and Feltham (1994) model the effects of information dissemination.

available to all the agents in the economy. Sophisticated investors realize this and thus price may provide investors with information in addition to their private information. At the individual level the information available in the economy is the private information, y_i, the accounting information, V_t, and the market price of the risky asset, P. Rational investors form a conjecture regarding the price formation, $f(\cdot)$. This conjecture influences individual demand through their expectation, and thus the market clearing price is a function of the conjecture, $T(f(\cdot))$. If the market clearing price is formed according the conjecture – if $f(\cdot)$ is a fixed point in the mapping T – then the conjecured price functional is a self fulfilling rational expectations equilibrium.

In order to evaluate the consequences of alternative accounting policies we analyze how the price is formed in rational expectations equilibria corresponding to the alternative accounting policies. This will enable us to assess the posterior variance under alternative accounting policies. The choice of accounting policy is endogenized, cf. Demski (2004). A partial analysis of the accounting choice is misleading as the reaction of investors to all information is disregarded.

In modeling the price formation we will use a version of the Hellwig (1980) model in which the number of investors/agents in the economy is infinite. As noted, agents trade and consume over two periods, i.e., trade takes place in the first period and the proceeds from first-period trade are consumed in the second. Let the agents in the economy be indexed by $i \in [0, 1]$. Each agent allocates his individual initial wealth, W_{0i}, between the riskless and the risky asset. At $t = 2$ the risky asset pays $\tilde{x}$ units of the single consumption good, while the riskless asset pays off 1. Taking the riskless asset as a numeraire and letting P be the price of the risky asset, the agent's terminal wealth, $\tilde{w}_{1i}$, is

$$\tilde{w}_{1i} = w_{0i} + z_i(\tilde{x} - P)$$

where z_i is the agent's holdings of the risky asset. Agents maximize their expected utility of consumption, $E_i[u_i(\tilde{w}_{1i})|Inf_i]$, where u_i is the agent's utility function and Inf_i is the agent's information. We will assume agents have negative exponential utility with risk aversion, r. Thus, $u_i(w_{1i}) = -\exp\{-r\ w_{1i}\}$, which implies individual demand for the risky asset is independent of the agent's initial wealth. That is, each agent solves

$$\max_{z_i} \int_{-\infty}^{\infty} -\exp\{-r(w_{0i} + z_i(x - P))\}g(x \,|\, Inf_i)dx$$

$$= \exp\{-rw_{0i}\} \max_{z_i} \int_{-\infty}^{\infty} -\exp\{-rz_i(x - P)\}g(x \,|\, Inf_i)dx$$

where $g(x \mid Inf_i)$ is the conditional probability density function. We also assume per capita supply of the risky asset, $\tilde{z}$, is random. More specifically we assume $\tilde{z} \sim N(0, \sigma_z^2)$ and independent of any other stochastic variable.

To derive a rational expectations equilibrium we assume investors conjecture the equilibrium price is an affine function of aggregate economic information and the random per capita supply of the risky asset[7]

$$\tilde{P}_t = \pi_0' + \pi_1' \tilde{V}_t + \pi_2' \tilde{\varepsilon}_E - \gamma' \tilde{z}. \tag{1}$$

Note the parameters π_i' and γ' depend on the accounting policy governing the reporting. Investors directly observe the statistic

$$\hat{y}_i = y_i - \frac{\text{cov}(\tilde{y}_i, \tilde{V}_t)}{Var(\tilde{V}_t)} V_t$$

as well as V_t, whereas investors neither observe $\tilde{\varepsilon}_E$ nor $\tilde{z}$, but are able to infer the following statistic:

$$\hat{P}_t = \pi_2' \tilde{\varepsilon}_E - \gamma' z - \frac{\text{cov}(\pi_2' \tilde{\varepsilon}_E - \gamma' \tilde{z}, \tilde{V}_t)}{Var(\tilde{V}_t)} V_t.$$

As $(V_t, \hat{y}_i, \hat{P}_t)$ is a simple transformation of (V_t, y_i, P_t), each set has the same information content, but the former is easier to work with.

Immediately it seems we need to derive two rational expectations equilibria, one under a transaction based policy and one under the market based policy. However, as

$$\lim_{\sigma_{AU}^2 \to \infty} V_M = V_T$$

it follows the rational expectations equilibrium under the transaction based policy is but a special case of the equilibrium under a market based policy.

---

[7] Admati (1985) considers a continuum agent economy, and argues that in such an economy a unique linear rational expectations equilibrium exists.

Consider a market based policy; then given the conjecture, (1), V_M, $\hat{y}_i$, and $\hat{P}_M$ are jointly normally distributed:

$$\left(V_M, \hat{y}_i, \hat{P}_M\right)' \sim N\left(\underline{0}, \Sigma_M\right).$$

$$\Sigma_M = \begin{pmatrix} \sigma_A^2 + \dfrac{\sigma_E^4}{\sigma_E^2 + \sigma_{AU}^2} & 0 & 0 \\ 0 & k + s^2 & \pi_2 k \\ 0 & \pi_2 k & \pi_2^2 k + \gamma^2 \sigma_z^2 \end{pmatrix}$$

where

$$k = \sigma_E^2 - \frac{\left(\dfrac{\sigma_E^4}{\sigma_E^2 + \sigma_{AU}^2}\right)^2}{\sigma_A^2 + \dfrac{\sigma_E^4}{\sigma_E^2 + \sigma_{AU}^2}}$$

Now,

$$(x, V_M, \hat{y}_i, \hat{P}_M)' \sim N\left(\underline{0}, \begin{array}{cc} \sigma_x^2 & \Sigma_{xM} \\ \Sigma_{Mx} & \Sigma_M \end{array}\right)$$

and

$$\Sigma_{Mx} = \begin{pmatrix} \sigma_A^2 + \dfrac{\sigma_E^4}{\sigma_E^2 + \sigma_{AU}^2} \\ \sigma_E^2 - \dfrac{\sigma_E^4}{\sigma_E^2 + \sigma_{AU}^2} \\ \pi_2\left(\sigma_E^2 - \dfrac{\sigma_E^4}{\sigma_E^2 + \sigma_{AU}^2}\right) \end{pmatrix}.$$

Letting

$$(B_1 \ B_2 \ B_3) = \Sigma_{xM} \Sigma_M^{-1} \tag{2}$$

it follows

$$E\left[\tilde{x}|V_t,\hat{y}_i,\hat{P}_M\right]=V_M+B_2\hat{y}_i+B_3\hat{P}_M \;; \text{i.e., } B_1=1$$

and

$$Var\left[\tilde{x}|V_t,\hat{y}_i,\hat{P}_M\right]=\sigma_E^2+\sigma_A^2-\Sigma_{xM}\Sigma_M^{-1}\Sigma_{Mx}$$

independent of the realization of $(V_t,\ \hat{y}_i,\ \hat{P}_M)$, and the investors have the usual demand function,

$$z_i=\frac{E\left[\tilde{x}|V_t,\hat{y}_i,\hat{P}_M\right]-P_M}{rVar\left[\tilde{x}|V_t,\hat{y}_i,\hat{P}_M\right]}.$$

The market clearing condition is

$$\int_0^1\frac{1}{rVar\left[\tilde{x}|V_t,\ \hat{y}_i,\ \hat{P}_M\right]}\left(V_M+B_2\hat{y}_i+B_3\hat{P}_M-P_M\right)\ di=z, \qquad (3)$$

which reduces to

$$z=\{V_M+B_2(\varepsilon_E-\frac{\text{cov}(\varepsilon_E,\ V_M)}{Var[V_M]}V_M)+B_3(\pi_2\varepsilon_E-\gamma z-\pi_2\frac{\text{cov}(\varepsilon_E,\ V_M)}{Var[V_M]}V_M)$$
$$-\pi_0-\pi_1 V_M-\pi_2\varepsilon_E+\gamma z\}/rVar\left[\tilde{x}|V_t,\ \hat{y}_i,\ \hat{P}_M\right].$$

$$(4)$$

Isolating P_M in this equation yields

$$P_M=(1-B_3)^{-1}\left\{V_M+B_2(\varepsilon_E-\frac{\text{cov}(\varepsilon_E,\ V_M)}{Var[V_M]}V_M)\right.$$
$$\left.-B_3(\pi_0+(\pi_1+\pi_2\frac{\text{cov}(\varepsilon_E,\ V_M)}{Var[V_M]})V_M-rVar\left[\tilde{x}|V_t,\ \hat{y}_i,\ \hat{P}_M\right]z\right\},$$

$$(5)$$

which is linear in the information variables. That is, given investors believe price is linear in information and supply, according to the conjecture (1), the resulting price-information-supply relation is indeed linear. Thus, if the coefficients in (1) are the same as the coefficients in (5), then (1) is a self fulfilling rational expectations equilibrium. That is, (1) is a rational expectations equilibrium if and only if the following equations hold (equate coefficients in (4)):

$$1 - B_2 \frac{\text{cov}(\varepsilon_E, V_M)}{Var[V_M]} - B_3 \pi_2 \frac{\text{cov}(\varepsilon_E, V_M)}{Var[V_M]} - \pi_1 = 0 \tag{6}$$

$$B_2 + B_3 \pi_2 - \pi_2 = 0 \tag{7}$$

$$-B_3 \gamma + \gamma = rVar\left[\tilde{x} \mid V_t, \; \hat{y}_i, \; \hat{P}_M\right] \tag{8}$$

$$\pi_0 = 0. \tag{9}$$

PROPOSITION 1   *A unique solution,* $(\pi_1, \; \pi_2, \; \gamma)$, *exists to the set of equations (6), (7), and (8).*
PROOF.   Manipulating (6), (7), and (8) yields that π_2 is the solution to the following cubic equation:

$$\left[\hat{k} - \pi_2 k\right]^3 - \sigma_z^2 \left[r\hat{k}s(1 - \pi_2)\right]^2 \left[\pi_2(k + s^2) - \hat{k}\right] = 0$$

where $\hat{k} = \sigma_E^2 - \sigma_E^4 /(\sigma_E^2 + \sigma_{AU}^2)$. Standard procedures yield that the equation has one real and two complex roots.   ∎

COROLLARY 1 *When* $\sigma_{AU}^2 \to \infty$

$$\pi_2 = \frac{\sigma_E^2(1 + r^2 s^2 \sigma_z^2)}{\sigma_E^2(1 + r^2 s^2 \sigma_z^2) + r^2 s^4 \sigma_z^2}$$

$$\gamma = \frac{rs^2 \sigma_E^2(1 + r^2 s^2 \sigma_z^2)}{\sigma_E^2(1 + r^2 s^2 \sigma_z^2) + r^2 s^4 \sigma_z^2}$$

and

$$\gamma / \pi_2 = rs^2. \tag{10}$$

Thus, when the auditor's talent in assessing the economic component of future dividends is severely limited, the expressions for π_2 and γ are relatively simple. As noted each investor observes V_M and y_i directly and $\varepsilon_E - (\gamma / \pi_2) z$ indirectly through the equilibrium price. Hence, the informativeness of the price system is injective in γ / π_2. Since $\varepsilon_E - (\gamma / \pi_2) z$ is 'economic value' plus noise, it follows the informativeness of price is decreasing in $\gamma / \pi_2 = rs^2$ (and σ_z^2), that is, the more risk averse the agents are or the noisier each agent's private information is, the less the aggregate information is reflected in price.

In the general case it is also possible to write up the expressions for π_2 and γ in terms of the parameters of the economy; however, in that case we have not been able to reduce these expressions into something easily interpretable.

5.   AGGREGATE INFORMATIVENESS

Our goal is to assess how different accounting policies affect the informativeness of the total set of informative variables available in the economy. In doing so, it appears from (10) that risk aversion and noise on the agent's private information plays a role in the sense that if the product of these parameters is relatively large, then we should expect the amount of information revealed by price to be modest. Also, if exogenous noise, σ_z^2, is large we expect price to reveal little, and if the auditor is very talented in the sense σ_{AU}^2 is small, then we expect little remains to be learned from price.

We will illustrate some insights with a couple of examples. In the first example the parameters are: $r = 0.1$, $\sigma_A^2 = \sigma_E^2 = 1$, $s^2 = 4$, and $\sigma_z^2 = 9$. Letting σ_{AU}^2 be on the horizontal axis and depicting the posterior variance, $Var\left[\tilde{x} \mid V_t, \hat{y}_i, \hat{P}_M\right]$, as a function of σ_{AU}^2 yields Figure 2 below.

The horizontal line is the posterior variance under a transaction based policy. The posterior variances intersect for $\sigma_{AU}^2 = 4.15$, hence in this example the auditor does not need much expertise relative to investors in estimating economic value before the market based system dominates the transaction based system, at least if we use the informativeness of the total of the informative variables in the economy. This example seems to confirm the folklore that market based accounting dominates transaction based accounting. As indicated, this may not always be the case.

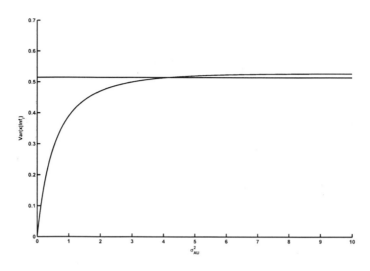

Figure 2

Changing parameters to: $r = 0.1$, $\sigma_A^2 = \sigma_E^2 = 1$, $s^2 = 1$, and $\sigma_z^2 = 2$, we get Figure 3 below.

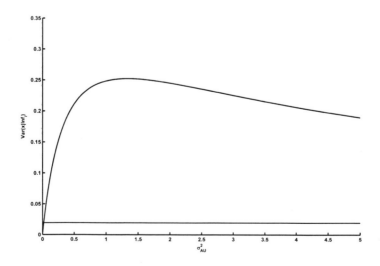

Figure 3

In this example the curves intersects at $\sigma^2_{AU} = 0.02$, hence for this set of parameters the auditor needs a precision which is more than 50 times higher than the precision with which the individual investor is able to assess economic value before the auditor's assistance is warranted.[8] In this example there is relatively little demand uncertainty and the investors are well informed of the market conditions as their private information has low variance. In that case the market mechanism is very powerful in aggregating the information from the investors. This leaves little room for the accounting system to supply market information. In fact, given the market is this well informed, going to market based accounting is inferior to transaction based accounting. Aggregating the market information into the accounting report makes the accounting report less useful to investors because this makes the market participants less able to infer the underlying state of nature.

Hitherto, we have assumed the auditor is knowledgeable with respect to his own shortcomings. That is, when σ^2_{AU} large, the auditor does not let his information influence the report to any great extent. The auditor is acting Bayesian in this respect.[9] Accounting on the other hand is in some sense less modest. Often accounting rules mandate how things must enter the financial statement. For example, it is possible to use either Historical Cost, Current Cost, Realizable Value, or Present Value as measurement basis according to IASB standards. In our setting the Present Value Base would be an accounting rule mandating that

$$\hat{V}_M = y_A + y_E = \varepsilon_A + \varepsilon_E + \varepsilon_{AU}.$$

Using this valuation base the fair value accounting incorporates the full effect of the auditor's perception of fair value as opposed to the interpretation of fair value we have used in our analysis. When the auditor is Bayesian, more noise is not necessarily bad, but when he is not, more noise and market based accounting can be a really sour combination.

---

[8] Considering the propensity amongst accounting students to take asset pricing classes, this might be too much to hope for.

[9] Given the amount of statistics in accounting programs this might be too much to hope for, too.

6.   CONCLUSION

Demski (2004) warns against a partial equilibrium view of the world. Using a partial equilibrium model, we have demonstrated the warning is not unfounded. A partial view on informativeness leaves the impression mark to market accounting dominates transaction based accounting in the sense accounting reports based on the former are more informative than accounting reports based on the latter principle. A less partial more inclusive view reveals this is not always the case. Once other sources of information are considered, the aggregate informativeness may be 'higher' in a transaction based regime than in a market based regime. In our setting with a single accounting item, only two policies exist and the choice between them is clearcut. Real life is of course less simple: for each component of each line item the proper accounting treatment needs to be determined. Should it be marked to market or should it be carried at historic cost? The preceding analysis indicates items which are easily valued should be marked to market, whereas items whose value is hard to assess should be carried at historic cost. We believe total informativeness considerations both in the sense of this paper and in the sense of manipulation concerns should inform the decision on accounting principle, line item by line item.

REFERENCES

Admati, A. R. (1985). "A Noisy rational Expectations Equilibrium for Multi-Asset Securities Markets," *Econometrica* 53, 629-657.

Arya, A., J. C. Glover, and S. Sunder (2003). "Are Unmanaged Earnings Always Better for Shareholders?" *Accounting Horizons* 17, 111-116.

Beaver, W. H. and J. S. Demski (1979). "The Nature of Income Measurement," *The Accounting Review* 54, 38-46.

Christensen, J. A. and J. S Demski (2003). *Accounting Theory: An Information Content Perspective*, Irwin/McGraw-Hill.

Demski, J. S. (1998). "Performance Measure Manipulation." *Contemporary Accounting Research* 14, 261-285.

Demski, J. S. (2004). "Endogenous Expectations," *The Accounting Review* 79, 519-539.

Demski, J. S. and G. A. Feltham (1994) "Market Response to Financial Reports," *Journal of Accounting and Economics* 17, 3-40.

FASB (2005). *The FASB Report*, February.

Feltham, G. A. and J. A Ohlson (1995). "Valuation and Clean Surplus Accounting for Operating and Financial Activities," *Contemporary Accounting Research* 11, 689-731.

Hellwig, M. (1980). "On the Aggregation of Information in Competitive Markets," *Journal of Economic Theory* 22, 477-498.

Leuz, C., D. J. Nanda, and P. Wysocki (2003). "Earnings Management and investor protection: An international comparison," *Journal of Financial Economics*

Lipe, R. (1990). "The Relation Between Stock Returns and Accounting Earnings given alternative Information," *The Accounting Review* 65, 49-71.
Schipper, K. and L. Vincent (2003). "Earnings Quality," *Accounting Horizons* 17, 97-110.

Chapter 3

EQUILIBRIUM VOLUNTARY DISCLOSURES WHEN FIRMS POSSESS RANDOM MULTI-DIMENSIONAL PRIVATE INFORMATION

Ronald A. Dye[1] and Mark Finn[1]
[1]Kellogg School of Management, Northwestern University

Abstract: This paper presents an equilibrium model of voluntary disclosures for the seller of an asset who receives a random sample of information of random size about the asset's value. Even though (a) antifraud rules prevent the seller from making false statements about the value of the items in his random sample, (b) all potential purchasers of the asset know that the seller's random sample always contains at least one sample element, (c) all potential purchasers of the asset interpret the seller's disclosure or nondisclosure in the same way, and (d) disclosure of any or all of the seller's sample information generates no proprietary costs, we show that in equilibrium there is a positive probability that the seller will make no disclosure at all, and that, when the seller makes no disclosure, the nondisclosed information is not the worst possible sample information the seller could have had about the asset's value. These results are contrasted with the "unravelling" result of Grossman [1980], Grossman and Hart [1980], and Milgrom [1981]. We show that, were potential purchasers of the asset to know the size of the seller's random sample, "unravelling" (i.e., full disclosure) would occur. We conclude that the randomness of the seller's sample size is key to determining the seller's equilibrium voluntary disclosure strategy.

Keywords: credible, voluntary, nonproprietary, equilibrium, disclosure policies

1. Introduction

As Feltham's survey in this volume demonstrates, Joel Demski has contributed enormously to the study of a large cross section of accounting research problems. Financial accounting theory is one of the areas to which he has made fundamental contributions. Demski [1973], Demski [1974], and Beaver and Demski [1979] are among the classics in financial accounting theory, and whenever we teach PhD classes in financial accounting and disclosure these articles constitute assigned readings for the first day of class. They collectively demonstrate many of the difficulties that a scientifically-based formulation of accounting standards faces: Demski [1973] notes that selecting among accounting standards is a quintessential example of a collective choice problem, and so Arrow's "impossibility theorem" [1951] suggests that there will be difficulties in selecting standards in a rational, nondictatorial way. Demski [1973] also observed that even if the concerns about the collective nature of the financial reporting choice problem could be ignored, any financial reporting system is fundamentally an information system, and so, according to Blackwell's theorem [1951], the only way one can be assured, in single person settings, that a decision maker will prefer one financial reporting system to another is if the partitions induced by the financial reporting system are ordered by "fineness," i.e., one financial reporting system provides strictly more information than does another financial reporting system. Since many proposed changes in financial reporting systems cannot be ranked by the fineness criterion (even those that are commonly reputed to be improvements in financial reporting – such as accounting for subsidiaries by consolidating them rather than accounting for them under the equity method), there is often no guarantee that a change in a financial reporting system will lead to an increase in a decision maker's welfare without knowing more about the specific problem the decision maker faces. Demski [1974] illustrated another problem with constructing financial reporting standards in multi-person settings: such changes almost invariably lead to wealth redistribution effects, and these wealth redistribution effects further exacerbate the political problem of choosing accounting standards. Finally, Beaver and Demski [1979] make the argument that universally agreed upon procedures for measuring income in perfect and complete markets is uncontroversial and straightforward, whereas constructing universal, agreed upon procedures for measuring income in imperfect and incomplete markets is difficult, if not impossible.

It is a testament to the importance of these articles by Demski that, even thirty years after some of them were written, they remain on PhD reading lists at premier research institutions. Moreover, the problems identified by these papers led to a shift in the direction of financial accounting research: instead of focusing on the construction of accounting standards, researchers began to study firms' voluntary disclosure policies.

But the literature on voluntary disclosure policies has run into stumbling blocks of its own. Simply put, the theory of voluntary disclosures (initially developed by Grossman [1981], Grossman and Hart [1980], and Milgrom [1981] ("GHM")) predicts that much more disclosure will occur than seemingly does occur. As conventionally articulated, that theory is asserted to predict that if (a) anti-fraud rules prevent a firm's manager from making false declarations about his private information, (b) investors know the manager has private information relevant to assessing the firm's value, (c) all investors interpret the manager's disclosures, or lack of disclosures, in the same way, and (d) there are no costs in making a disclosure (i.e., the manager's information is not proprietary), then a manager interested in maximizing his firm's market value will disclose his information so as to distinguish it from other, worse information about the firm's value he could have had. An important corollary to this result is that, when these four conditions are satisfied, the only circumstance under which, in equilibrium, a manager will not disclose private, value-relevant information that investors know he has is when his information is the worst possible.

The logic underlying GHM's result is very similar to the logic underlying Akerloff's [1970] original "lemon's" problem, even though the conclusions of GHM and Akerloff are nearly opposite to each other: Akerloff asserted that if sellers knew more about the quality/value of the products they are selling than do buyers of the products, information asymmetry will lead to the collapse of the market, that is, only the worst (among the observationally indistinguishable) quality products will be sold. In contrast, GHM's primary conclusion is that information asymmetry between buyer and seller poses no impediment to the operation of a market at all, provided sellers can make credible statements about the quality/value of the products they sell. To see the parallels in the logic underlying both results, just note that in Akerloff's setting the equilibrium "unravels"[1] because if multiple potential sellers with assets of varying quality are posited to offer their assets for sale at the same price, the "best" potential sellers (among those originally posited to sell the asset at this price) who possess assets with values that exceed this price will distinguish themselves by refusing to put their assets on the market. Similarly, in GHM's setting the equilibrium "unravels" because if multiple potential sellers with assets of varying quality are posited to make the same disclosure about the assets they possess, the "best" potential sellers (among those originally posited to make this common disclosure) will distinguish themselves by making a disclosure that reveals they possess higher valued assets.

Since the logic of GHM is so compelling, attempts to reconcile the theoretical predictions of the GHM theory with the actual disclosure practices have focused on altering one of the four assumptions (a)-(d). For example, Gigler [1994] and Newman and Sansing [1993] dropped assumption (a) and allowed managers to make disclosures the validity of which cannot be confirmed. Dye [1985], Jung and Kwon [1988], and Pae [1999] dropped assumption (b) by positing that investors may not be sure whether the manager has received information, Dye [1999] dropped assumptions (b) and (c) by positing that the manager's receipt of information is random, and that investors may be differentially informed about when the manager has undisclosed information, and

Jovanovic [1982], Verrecchia [1983], and Dye [1986] dropped assumption (d) by positing that the manager's information is proprietary.

The purpose of the present paper is to show that all four conditions (a)-(d) can be satisfied, and yet in equilibrium, with positive probability a firm's value-maximizing manager will not disclose information that investors know he has, and moreover this information need not be the worst possible information the manager could have had. The paper thus demonstrates that the usual articulation of the unravelling result - as described above - is incorrect without further qualification, and hence that no disclosure can constitute consistent value-maximizing behavior by firms even when the four conditions (a)-(d) hold.

We preview the model underlying this claim here, leaving the details of the model's formal articulation to subsequent sections. In the model we study, the number of *dimensions* of the manager's private information is random. Specifically, we assume that the manager receives a random sample of observations correlated with the firm's value, and that the size of the random sample is itself random, but always includes at least one sample element. We posit that antifraud statutes limit the manager's disclosures to those that can be confirmed by his sample evidence. More precisely, we consider a disclosure D to be credible if (and only if) D is a subset of the random sample S the manager receives. This requirement for a disclosure to be credible is natural, since the manager can confirm (what we call) a credible disclosure by displaying the relevant sample evidence. This notion of credibility prevents the manager from making believable statements such as "I [the manager] have disclosed all of my sample evidence," because while a disclosure D ensures $S \supseteq D$, it does not ensure $S = D$. From this, it also follows that a manager who received a sample of, say, size $n = 6$ can make credible statements regarding lower bounds on the size of the sample he received (e.g., for any $n' \leq 6$, he can claim that he received a sample of size at least n' by exhibiting n' elements from his sample), but he cannot make credible statements regarding the upper bound on the size of his sample.[2]

As we show formally below, this version of antifraud statutes does not affect whether the equilibrium unravels when the number of dimensions of the manager's private information is fixed and known to investors: in that case, equilibrium prices are (still) equivalent to the prices that would prevail were all of the manager's sample information public. But, when the dimensionality of the manager's private information is random, this specification of anti-fraud statutes allows for equilibria with less than full disclosure to emerge, even when conditions (a)-(d) hold.

In our model, knowledge of both the number of elements in the manager's sample and the maximum of the sample constitute a sufficient statistic for the sample with respect to the firm's value. The manager has an incentive to understate the realized number of elements in his sample, because a given value of the sample maximum leads to a more favorable inference about the firm's value, the smaller the size of the sample that generates the maximum. This is intuitive: the fact that a jewelry store has obtained a certificate asserting that a diamond is of investment grade clarity, cut, and color is more favorable evidence that the diamond is in fact "flawless" if only one jeweler were asked to certify the diamond than were one hundred jewelers asked. Likewise, learning from a toothpaste commercial that "four out of (a set of) five dentists highly recommended the toothpaste" is more favorable evidence of a toothpaste's quality the fewer the number of quintuples of dentists polled to achieve this 80% approval rating. Thus, if a seller/manager can make credible disclosures that the sample he received contained "at least X elements," but the seller/manager cannot make credible disclosures that his sample contained "at most X elements" (since, as noted above, statements of the latter sort cannot be confirmed by his sample evidence), then in equilibrium a value-maximizing manager will say nothing about the realized size of his sample because outsiders draw increasingly unfavorable inferences about the firm's value the larger the sample the outsiders believe the manager received (holding other details of his disclosure fixed).

Thus, following the manager's disclosure, investors must use a two-step process to make inferences about the unknown distribution generating the firm's value: first, they make inferences about the size of the sample the manager observed, and second, they use these size-related inferences in conjunction with the manager's disclosure to estimate the firm's value. We show that when the manager's sample is of random size, there is a nondegenerate interval I over which the (capital market's) assessment of the firm's expected value conditional on the sample maximum is not monotonically increasing in the sample maximum, even though when the manager's sample is of known, deterministic size, the (capital market's) assessment of the firm's expected value conditional on the sample maximum *is* globally increasing in the sample maximum. This happens because, over the interval I, an increase in the manager's reported sample maximum leads the capital market to infer that the number of elements in the manager's random sample has increased by so much they are led to revise downward their perceptions of the firm's value. This nonmonotonicity of the firm's conditional expected value over the interval I induces the manager to remain silent in equilibrium when the realized sample maximum falls inside I.

The formal model setup underlying our results is described in the next section, followed by a section that contains the statement of the main result. A brief conclusion precedes an appendix that contains all pertinent proofs.

2. Model setup

At the start of a period, everyone in an economy believes that the discounted expected value of a firm is ω, where ω is the realization of the unknown random variable $\tilde{\omega}$, the initial priors of which are given by the density $f(\omega)$.

The realization ω of $\tilde{\omega}$ is assumed unobservable to everyone, forever. However, during the period, the manager of the firm privately receives a random sample $\tilde{x}_1, ..., \tilde{x}_n$ of observations that are correlated with ω. Given $\tilde{\omega} = \omega$, we posit that each $\tilde{x}_i$ is independently and identically distributed (iid) according to the density $g(x_i|\omega)$.

The random dimensionality of the manager's private information, stated as the random sample size assumption below, is key to our main result.

Random Sample *Size* Assumption ("RSSA") The number n of elements in the random sample $\{x_i\}_{i=1}^n$ observed by the manager is the realization of some positive, integer-valued random variable $\tilde{n}$ with distribution $\Pr(\tilde{n} = n) \equiv h(n)$, $n \geq 0$, $h(0) = 0$, $h(n) < 1$ for all $n \geq 1$, with upper bound $\bar{n}$ (which may be finite or infinite).

That is, the manager always sees at least one observation x_i ($h(0) = 0$); he does not receive a predetermined number of observations ($h(n) < 1$ for all n). No other restrictions on the probability distribution $h(\bullet)$ are imposed other than those just stated in any of the results that follow.

In the following we restrict the manager's possible disclosures to those that can be "supported by the sample." By this, we mean:

Definition 1 *When the manager's random sample is* $\{\tilde{x}_i\}_{i=1}^{\tilde{n}} = \{x_i\}_{i=1}^n$, *a disclosure D is supported by the sample provided* $D \subset \{x_i\}_{i=1}^n$.

When a disclosure can be supported by the sample, the manager can exhibit one or more of the sample observations to confirm what was said in his disclosure. While a manager is certainly capable of fully disclosing his information when all disclosures must be supported by the sample, this restriction, with one exception, eliminates the manager's ability to communicate to investors that he has engaged in full disclosure when RSSA is in effect. For example, when $\bar{n} = 6$, were the manager's sample equal to $\{x_1, x_2, x_3\} = \{1, 7, 4\}$, then the full disclosure $D = \{1, 7, 4\}$ is indistinguishable from the partial disclosure $D = \{1, 7, 4\}$ when the manager's sample is $\{x_1, x_2, x_3, x_4, x_5\} = \{1, 2, 2, 4, 7\}$.

What can be credibly disclosed under this definition is a subset of the actual sample elements, and not the indices of those disclosed elements. That is, we are presuming that one cannot disclose, for example, that $x_1 = 5$ and $x_2 = 2$, but rather that "there were realized elements of the sample that included the observations 5 and 2." In our judgement, this presumed *inability* of the manager to disclose the index of a realized sample element, as opposed to the sample element itself, is a desirable feature of the "supported by the sample" definition, as it prevents the manager from indirectly signalling information about the size of his sample through his disclosure. If - contrary to what we presume - the manager had the ability to disclose the indices of his sample elements, then the manager could disclose that he received at least five sample elements, say $x_1 = 5$, $x_2 = 9$, $x_3 = 6$, $x_4 = 11$, $x_5 = 1$, through the simple disclosure $\{x_5 = 1\}$. In contrast, in our presentation, the disclosure $D = \{1\}$ provides no information about the size of the sample the manager received. As another example highlighting the distinction between the disclosure of sample elements and the disclosure of the indices of the sample elements, if indices could be disclosed, the disclosure $D = \{x_1, x_2, x_4\}$ would convey that the manager received at least four pieces of information, whereas – under our interpretation - the disclosure $\{5, 9, 11\}$ (note that $x_1 = 5$, $x_2 = 9$, $x_4 = 11$) would only reveal that the manager has received at least three pieces of information which had values $5, 9, 11$.

The one exception in which the manager can engage in full disclosure when his disclosure must be supported by the sample is when $\bar{n}$ is finite and the number of elements in his disclosure D is $\bar{n}$: in that special case, the manager can disclose to investors that he has no undisclosed information because investors know, when $\#D = \bar{n}$, there is in principle no other information the manager could have had. E.g., when $\bar{n} = 6$ and the manager discloses $D = \{1, 2, 2, 4, 7, 8\}$, then investors would know that the manager has engaged in full disclosure. This special case allowing the manager to communicate that he has engaged in complete disclosure can arise only because the upper bound $\bar{n}$ is both common knowledge and finite. Were $\bar{n} = \infty$, the manager cannot reveal that he has disclosed all of his information, even when he discloses a sample that contains an infinite number of elements.

We now introduce a formal definition of equilibrium for disclosures that can be supported by the sample. (In this definition and throughout the paper, risk-neutral pricing is presumed.)

Definition 2 *A disclosure equilibrium consists of a disclosure policy* $d^*(\bullet) = d^*(\{\tilde{x}_i\}_{i=1}^n)$ *and a pricing function* $P(\bullet) = P(D)$ *such that,*

(i) for each sample $\{x_i\}_{i=1}^n$, *the disclosure* $D^* = d^*(\{x_i\}_{i=1}^n)$ *maximizes* $P(D)$ *among all possible disclosures that can be supported by the sample:*

$$d^*(\{x_i\}_{i=1}^n) \in \arg \max_{D \subset \{x_i\}_{i=1}^n} P(D);$$

(ii) for any disclosure D expected under the disclosure policy $d^*(\bullet)$,

$$P(D) = E[\tilde{\omega}|\ d^*(\{\tilde{x}_i\}_{i=1}^{\tilde{n}}) = D];$$

(iii) for any disclosure D not expected under the disclosure policy $d^*(\bullet)$, *the value assigned to* $P(D)$ *must be belong to the closure of the set*

$$\{E[\tilde{\omega}|\{x_i\}_{i=1}^n]|\text{all samples } \{x_i\}_{i=1}^n \text{ that can support disclosure } D\}.$$

In words, an equilibrium consists of a pricing function and a disclosure policy such that, given a pricing function and a particular set of sample observations, the manager's disclosure policy maximizes the price of the firm among all possible disclosures supported by the sample, and given the disclosure policy, the pricing function correctly calculates the firm's expected value. The out-of-equilibrium specification described in (iii) requires that there be consistency between a manager's "unexpected" disclosure and the value investors assign to the firm were such an unexpected disclosure to occur. More precisely, for each unexpected disclosure D, there must be some sample $\{x_i\}_{i=1}^n$ that supports this disclosure for which the expected value of the firm given that sample equals the assigned price $P(D)$ for that disclosure.[3]

Restricting disclosures to those that can be supported by the sample in the GHM world where the manager receives a single datum q involving the firm/asset being sold leads to the same "full disclosure" conclusion as in GHM, using the same logic they employed.[4] We shall now show in the following Remark, by making specific assumptions regarding the prior distribution $f(\omega)$ of $\tilde{\omega}$ and the sampling distribution $g(x_i|\omega)$ of $\tilde{x}_i$ given $\tilde{\omega} = \omega$, that this full disclosure conclusion also extends to situations in which the manager receives a set of information consisting of a sample $\{x_i\}_{i=1}^n$ of *known* size n. The specific distributional assumptions we make are the following. We take $f(\omega) = \frac{\alpha w_0^\alpha}{\omega^{\alpha+1}}$, for $\omega > w_0 > 0$ (and is otherwise 0) and $\alpha > 1$, that is, $\tilde{\omega}$ is given by a Pareto distribution with parameters α and w. Also, given $\tilde{\omega} = \omega$, we assume the $\tilde{x}_i$ are iid with $g(x_i|\omega) = \frac{1}{\omega}$, $x_i \in [0, \omega]$ (and is otherwise 0), that is, $\tilde{x}_i$ is uniformly distributed on $[0, \omega]$.

(In the following remark, $\max D$ is the largest of $D's$ elements.)

Remark (*Grossman-Milgrom-Hart's "Full Disclosure" Result) When $\tilde{\omega}$ and $\tilde{x}_i$ adhere to the Pareto/Uniform distributional assumptions, $i = 1, 2, ..., n$, where the number n of sample observations the manager receives is common knowledge, then in any equilibrium, the price of the firm is exactly the same as it would be were the manager's information public:*

$$P(D) = \frac{(\alpha + n)\max\{w_0, \max D\}}{\alpha + n - 1}.$$

This conclusion follows because of three facts about the Pareto/Uniform conjugate distribution pair (see e.g., DeGroot [1970]). Fact 1: the maximum y of a sample $\{x_i\}_{i=1}^n$ of size n is a sufficient statistic for the sample with respect to the unknown parameter ω. Fact 2: given size n of the sample and the sample maximum y, the posteriors on $\tilde{\omega}$ are Pareto with parameters $\alpha + n$ and $\max\{w_0, y\}$. Fact 3: The expected value of a Pareto distribution with parameters α and w_0 is $E[\tilde{\omega}|\alpha, w_0] = \frac{\alpha w_0}{\alpha - 1}$; hence, the expected value of $\tilde{\omega}$, given the sample $\{x_i\}_{i=1}^n$ with maximum y is $\frac{(\alpha+n)\max\{w_0, y\}}{\alpha+n-1}$. The first fact documents that outsiders care about the sample $\{x_i\}_{i=1}^n$ in making inferences about ω only to the extent that they know the maximum of this sample. Thus, "fully" disclosing the sample (i.e., $d^*(\{x_i\}_{i=1}^n) = \{x_i\}_{i=1}^n$) is tantamount to disclosing the sufficient statistic $\max\{x_i\}_{i=1}^n$ of the sample. If the manager chooses to withhold some of his sample information, investors will merely assume that all of the undisclosed observations are smaller than the disclosed observations. The second and third facts, when combined with the first fact, imply that if $y = \max D$ is the highest reported sample observation, then investors will price the firm at $P(D) = \frac{(\alpha+n)\max\{w_0,y\}}{\alpha+n-1}$. Since this is increasing in y, the manager will respond by reporting the largest of his sample observations, thereby confirming investors' expectations.[5]

However, this result does not extend to the situation where RSSA is in effect. To see this, suppose the contrary, i.e., that full disclosure continues to be an equilibrium under RSSA. According to the Remark, when $D = \{x_i\}_{i=1}^n$, the firm will be priced at $P(D) = \frac{(\alpha+n)\max\{w_0,y\}}{\alpha+n-1}$, where $y \equiv \max D$. Notice that under RSSA, the price of the firm depends on the disclosure D in two respects. First, in determining the maximum of the sample; second, in determining the size of the sample. If the manager deviated to the singleton disclosure $D = \{y\}$, which is also supported by his sample, the firm would be priced at $P(\{y\}) = \frac{(\alpha+1)\max\{w_0,y\}}{\alpha}$. Since $\frac{(\alpha+n)\max\{w_0,y\}}{\alpha+n-1}$ is strictly decreases in n, it follows that, for any $n > 1$, the manager gets a higher selling price by deviating from a policy of full disclosure and understating the size of his sample. This is intuitive for reasons noted in the Introduction: a given report that the maximum of the sample is, say 5, is more favorable information about how big ω is, the smaller the sample maximum was drawn from.

The observation that full disclosure is not an equilibrium of this model is a variation on the results of Dye [1985] and Jung and Kwon [1988], who showed that full disclosure is generally not an equilibrium when the amount of information the manager has is random and unknown to investors. What the next section does is demonstrate the new result that equilibria exist in this model in which no disclosure ($D = \phi$) occurs with positive probability, notwithstanding that investors know that the manager always receives a sample of size one or more (recall $h(0) = 0$).

3.   Main Result

The main result of the paper is the following:

Theorem *When $\tilde{\omega}$ and $\tilde{x}_i$ adhere to the Pareto/Uniform distributional assumptions, $i = 1, 2, ..., \tilde{n}$ and $\tilde{n}$ satisfies RSSA, then the following is a disclo-*

sure equilibrium. When $\tilde{n} = n$, the realized sample is $\{x_i\}_{i=1}^n$, and $y \equiv \max\{x_i\}_{i=1}^n$,

> *(i) there exists a unique value $y^* > w_0$ such that,*
>
> > *(ia) if $y \geq y^*$, then $d^*(\{x_i\}_{i=1}^n) = \{y\}$;*
> > *(ib) if $y < y^*$, then $d^*(\{x_i\}_{i=1}^n) = \phi$.*

> *(iia) For $y \geq y^*$, $P(\{y\}) = y \times \sum_n \frac{\alpha+n}{\alpha+n-1} \times \frac{\frac{n}{n+\alpha}h(n)}{\sum_{\hat{n}} \frac{\hat{n}}{\hat{n}+\alpha}h(\hat{n})}$;*

> *(iib) $P(\phi) = P(\{y^*\})$.*

> *(iii) This equilibrium is supported by the off-equilibrium specifications: for any unexpected disclosure D with $\max D \equiv y'$:*
>
> > *(iiia) if $\#D < \bar{n}$, $P(D) = \frac{\alpha+\bar{n}}{\alpha+\bar{n}-1} \times \max\{w_0, y'\}$;*
> > *(iiib) if $\#D = \bar{n}$, then $P(D) = \frac{\alpha+\bar{n}}{\alpha+\bar{n}-1} \times y'$.*

> *(iv) With $\tilde{y} \equiv \max\{\tilde{x}_i\}_{i=1}^{\tilde{n}}$, $E[\tilde{n}|y]$ is weakly increasing in y everywhere, strictly so for $y < w_0$.*

Part (i) of the theorem contains the main result: for samples $\{\tilde{x}_i\}_{i=1}^{\tilde{n}}$ whose maximum y falls below some value $y^* > w_0$, the manager makes no disclosure, whereas for samples whose maximum exceeds y^*, the manager simply discloses the sample maximum with no supporting details - i.e., he does not disclose any other information about the sample.[6] While we leave the formal demonstration that this is a feature of an equilibrium to the appendix, we supplement the intuition sketched in the Introduction for this result here.

The logic of the unravelling result would seem to suggest, contrary to this result, that a manager with a sample whose sample maximum y is close to, but below, y^*, should receive a higher market price by disclosing y rather than saying nothing and being "pooled" with all those managers whose sample maximums are below y. As the proof shows, it is true that for y close to but below y^*, the expected value $E[\tilde{\omega}|\max\{\tilde{x}_i\}_{i=1}^{\tilde{n}} = y]$ is strictly increasing in y, which seems to support the idea that such managers would be better off separating themselves from other managers by making a disclosure and revealing y.

But this last observation is not enough to demonstrate that separating y from those realizations of $\tilde{y}$ falling in the set $[0, y)$ results in a higher selling price for the firm. The critical fact is that (as is shown in the appendix) $E[\tilde{\omega}|\{\tilde{x}_i\}_{i=1}^{\tilde{n}} = y]$ is strictly decreasing in y for all $y \leq w_0$. As a consequence, all managers with sample maximums $y \in (w_0, y^*)$ are better off pooling with managers who have sample maximums $y \leq w_0$ by making no disclosures of any kind.

It may seem odd that $E[\tilde{\omega}|\{\tilde{x}_i\}_{i=1}^{\tilde{n}} = y]$ strictly decreases in y for all $y \leq w_0$. Why does this occur? This is partially explained by part (iv) of the theorem: according to (iv), the inferred expected sample size giving rise to the realized sample maximum strictly increases over this interval. As a consequence, over this interval, an increase in the reported sample maximum leads investors to infer that the size of the manager's sample increased by so much that they reduce their estimate of $\tilde{\omega}$ conditional on the reported sample maximum. We can think of this as a form of "marketer's curse." In the context of product sales, for examples, it suggests that, sometimes, reporting better testimonials about a product can lead to lower assessments about the product's value, since the better testimonials lead potential purchasers to infer that more customers were screened to acquire the better testimonials.

This result is exclusively due to investors'/customers' uncertainty about the size $\tilde{n}$ of the sample: as was discussed above following the statement of the Remark, when n is deterministic, $E[\tilde{\omega}|\{\tilde{x}_i\}_{i=1}^n = y]$ is weakly increasing in y everywhere (strictly so for $y > w_0$).

One might argue that, since the latter is true, then the managers who should try to separate themselves from other managers are those managers with the very lowest sample maximums. But, they cannot. A manager with a low sample maximum cannot separate himself from a manager with a high sample maximum, because managers with high sample maximums typically will have other smaller sample realizations that they could have reported. Thus, managers with moderate to high sample maximums can mimic the disclosures of (that is, pool with) managers with very low sample maximums, but not conversely. There is nothing managers with very low sample maximums can do to prevent this mimicry/pooling.

It follows that, in this example, unlike the standard unravelling setting, outsiders who see no disclosure ($D = \phi$) do not infer that the manager had the worst possible sample information. Instead, upon observing no disclosure, outsiders only infer that, whatever the manager observed, its sample maximum was below y^*.

Part (ii) of the theorem describes the equilibrium pricing assignments associated with the equilibrium disclosures: for $y = \max D \geq y^*$, the price of the firm is linearly increasing in y. And, for the disclosure D with $\max D = y^*$, the price of the firm is the same as were the manager to make no disclosure.

Part (iii) of the theorem describes the market value assigned to the firm in the event of an off-equilibrium disclosure. If the manager makes an unexpected disclosure, then the price assigned to the firm is the one that results in the smallest possible expected value for $\tilde{\omega}$, consistent with the disclosure the manager makes. This entails having investors postulate that the manager's sample size is as large as possible, namely $\bar{n}$.[7]

4.   Conclusions

We have shown that when managers possess nonproprietary information of random dimension and managers cannot prove to investors whether they have engaged in full disclosure, then value-maximizing managers may well choose not to disclose their information even when their information is not the worst possible, their information is not proprietary, and investors know they possess the information. This result may help in explaining the actual disclosure practices of firms.

There remains a lot of work on disclosures to be done, of course. One of the points that Demski has emphasized throughout his research career is the endogeneity of virtually all facets of an economic environment. The preceding model takes as given all aspects of the information environment of the firm studied other than the private information received by the firm. We would expect that a firm's disclosure policy will depend on: what other sources of information about the firm are available to investors (e.g., by acquiring information on private account, through intermediaries, etc.), what kinds of disclosure policies its competitors adopt, the legal, regulatory, and competitive environment in which the firm's disclosures take place, etc. None of these factors is in fact exogenous, and a fuller, richer model of disclosures would endogenize all these factors. Another factor not considered in the present work is the robustness of an equilibrium disclosure policy to (minor) changes in what investors know about the distribution of the information the firm receives. Robustness has become a recent interest of Demski's as well (see, e.g., Arya, Demski, Glover, Liang [2005]). While most of the research on robustness has to date focused on the issue of the robustness of contracts, or allocation mechanisms, examining the robustness of disclosure policies may also help to resolve some of the anomalies in the disclosure literature. But the precise effects of robustness-related issues on firms' disclosure policies remain unknown presently. Given the breadth of Demski's research interests, we would not be surprised that, when another research conference toasting Demski's contributions to accounting on his 75th birthday takes place, we will have an opportunity to review Demski's new contributions to the analysis of such robustness issues, as well as many other foundational accounting questions.

Acknowledgments

We wish to thank Sri Sridhar for comments on an earlier draft of the manuscript, and the Accounting Research Center at Northwestern University for financial support.

Appendix: Proof of the main theorem

The key to proving the theorem is contained in the following lemma.

Lemma *With* $y \equiv \max\{\tilde{x}_i\}_{i=1}^{\tilde{n}}$,

(i) *over the interval* $y \leq w_0$:

(ia) $E[\tilde{\omega}|y] = w_0 \times \dfrac{\sum_n \frac{n}{\alpha+n-1} \frac{y^{n-1}}{w_0^n} h(n)}{\sum_{\hat{n}} \frac{\hat{n}}{\hat{n}+\alpha} \frac{y^{\hat{n}-1}}{w_0^{\hat{n}}} h(\hat{n})}$;

(ib) $E[\tilde{\omega}|y]$ *is strictly decreasing in* y;

(ii) *over the interval* $y \geq w_0$:

(iia) $E[\tilde{\omega}|y] = y \times \sum_n \dfrac{\alpha+n}{\alpha+n-1} \times \dfrac{\frac{n}{n+\alpha} h(n)}{\sum_{\hat{n}} \frac{\hat{n}}{\hat{n}+\alpha} h(\hat{n})}$;

(iib) $E[\tilde{\omega}|y]$ *is linearly increasing in* y;

(iii) $E[\tilde{n}|y]$ *is increasing in* y *everywhere, strictly so for* $y < w_0$.

Proof of the first part of the lemma

To proceed, we need to calculate the posterior of $\tilde{n}$, given that $y \equiv \max\{x_i\}_{i=1}^{\tilde{n}}$. Refer to this posterior as: $h(n|y) = \frac{h(y|n)h(n)}{\sum_{\hat{n}} h(y|\hat{n})h(\hat{n})}$. In the first part of the lemma, we restrict attention to $y \leq w_0$.

We start by calculating the cumulative distribution function $H(y|n) \equiv \Pr(\tilde{y} \leq y|n) = \int \Pr(\tilde{y} \leq y|n, \omega) f(\omega) d\omega$.

$$
\begin{aligned}
\int \Pr(\tilde{y} \leq y|n, \omega) f(\omega) d\omega &= \int_{w_0}^{\infty} \left(\frac{y}{\omega}\right)^n f(\omega) d\omega = \int_{w_0}^{\infty} \left(\frac{y}{\omega}\right)^n \frac{\alpha w_0^\alpha}{\omega^{\alpha+1}} d\omega \\
&= \frac{\alpha}{n+\alpha} \left(\frac{y}{w_0}\right)^n \int_{w_0}^{\infty} \frac{(n+\alpha) w_0^{n+\alpha}}{\omega^{n+\alpha+1}} d\omega = \frac{\alpha}{n+\alpha} \left(\frac{y}{w_0}\right)^n.
\end{aligned}
$$

So, the density $h(y|n)$ associated with $H(y|n)$ is given by

$$
h(y|n) = H_y(y|n) = \frac{n\alpha}{n+\alpha} \frac{y^{n-1}}{w_0^n}, \text{ for } 0 < y \leq w_0.
$$

Thus, the posterior for n, given $0 < y \leq w_0$, is:

$$
h(n|y) = \frac{h(y|n)h(n)}{\sum_{\hat{n}} h(y|\hat{n})h(\hat{n})} = \frac{\frac{n}{n+\alpha} \frac{y^{n-1}}{w_0^n} h(n)}{\sum_{\hat{n}} \frac{\hat{n}}{\hat{n}+\alpha} \frac{y^{\hat{n}-1}}{w_0^{\hat{n}}} h(\hat{n})}. \tag{3.A.1}
$$

Hence, since $E[\tilde{\omega}|y, \tilde{n}] = w_0 \frac{\alpha+n}{\alpha+n-1}$ for $y \leq w_0$, we conclude:

$$
\begin{aligned}
E[\tilde{\omega}|y] = E[E[\tilde{\omega}|y, \tilde{n}]|y] &= \sum_n \left[w_0 \frac{\alpha+n}{\alpha+n-1} \right] \times \frac{\frac{n}{n+\alpha} \frac{y^{n-1}}{w_0^n} h(n)}{\sum_{\hat{n}} \frac{\hat{n}}{\hat{n}+\alpha} \frac{y^{\hat{n}-1}}{w_0^{\hat{n}}} h(\hat{n})} \\
&= w_0 \times \frac{\sum_n \frac{n}{\alpha+n-1} \frac{y^{n-1}}{w_0^n} h(n)}{\sum_{\hat{n}} \frac{\hat{n}}{\hat{n}+\alpha} \frac{y^{\hat{n}-1}}{w_0^{\hat{n}}} h(\hat{n})}.
\end{aligned}
$$

The accompanying footnote shows that the ratio $\dfrac{\sum_n \frac{n}{\alpha+n-1} \frac{y^{n-1}}{w_0^n} h(n)}{\sum_{\hat{n}} \frac{\hat{n}}{\hat{n}+\alpha} \frac{y^{\hat{n}-1}}{w_0^{\hat{n}}} h(\hat{n})}$ is strictly decreasing over the interval $y \leq w_0$, as long as there is no single value of n for which $h(n) = 1$ holds.[8]

This proves the first part of the lemma.

Proof of the second part of the lemma

As in the case of the first part, we start by calculating the cdf $H(y|n) \equiv \Pr(\tilde{y} \leq y|n) = \int \Pr(\tilde{y} \leq y|n, \omega) f(\omega) d\omega$ for $y > w_0$. In this case, it is given by:

$$
\begin{aligned}
\int \Pr(\tilde{y} \leq y|n, \omega) f(\omega) d\omega &= \int_{w_0}^{y} 1 \bullet f(\omega) d\omega + \int_{y}^{\infty} \left(\frac{y}{\omega}\right)^n f(\omega) d\omega \\
&= \int_{w_0}^{y} \frac{\alpha w_0^\alpha}{\omega^{\alpha+1}} d\omega + \int_{y}^{\infty} \left(\frac{y}{\omega}\right)^n \frac{\alpha w_0^\alpha}{\omega^{\alpha+1}} d\omega - w_0^\alpha \omega^{-\alpha}|_{w_0}^{y} \\
&\quad + \alpha w_0^\alpha y^n \frac{1}{(n+\alpha)y^{n+\alpha}} \int_{y}^{\infty} \frac{(n+\alpha)y^{n+\alpha}}{\omega^{n+\alpha+1}} d\omega \\
&= 1 - \left(\frac{w_0}{y}\right)^\alpha + \alpha w_0^\alpha \frac{1}{(n+\alpha)y^\alpha} \\
&= 1 - w_0^\alpha y^{-\alpha} \frac{n}{n+\alpha},
\end{aligned}
$$

so:

$$
h(y|n) = \frac{\alpha n w_0^\alpha y^{-\alpha-1}}{n+\alpha}, y > w_0 \text{ and } n \geq 1.
$$

So, the posterior on $\tilde{n}$ is, for $y > w_0$:

$$
h(n|y) = \frac{h(y|n)h(n)}{\sum_{\hat{n}} h(y|\hat{n})h(\hat{n})} = \frac{\frac{n}{n+\alpha}h(n)}{\sum_{\hat{n}} \frac{\hat{n}}{\hat{n}+\alpha}h(\hat{n})}, n \geq 1. \tag{3.A.2}
$$

Observe that this conditional distribution for n does not vary with y over the interval $y > w_0$. Moreover,

$$
\begin{aligned}
E[\tilde{\omega}|y] = E[E[\tilde{\omega}|y, \tilde{n}]] &= \sum \left[y \times \frac{\alpha+n}{\alpha+n-1}\right] \times \frac{\frac{n}{n+\alpha}h(n)}{\sum_{\hat{n}} \frac{\hat{n}}{\hat{n}+\alpha}h(\hat{n})} \\
&= y \sum_{n} \frac{n}{\alpha+n-1} \frac{h(n)}{\sum_{\hat{n}} \frac{\hat{n}}{\hat{n}+\alpha}h(\hat{n})}. \tag{3.A.4}
\end{aligned}
$$

This proves the second part of the lemma.

Proof of the third part of the lemma

This follows immediately by calculating the conditional expectation $E[\tilde{n}|y]$ using the densities in (3.A.1) and (3.A.2) and then differentiating with respect to y. (Note that this is also part iv of the main theorem.)

Identification of the value of the equilibrium y^*

Taking the assignments of $P(D)$ in the statement of the theorem as given, define the set $\Delta \equiv \{y = \max\{\tilde{x}_i\}_{i=1}^{\tilde{n}} | \text{ the manager prefers to disclose his sample maximum rather than make no disclosure}\}$. That is, define Δ by:

$$
\Delta \equiv \{y|P(\phi) \leq P(\{y\})\}.
$$

We shall show in the subsection below entitled "Confirmation of equilibrium specifications," that Δ is characterized by a right-tailed interval, i.e., $\Delta = [y^*, \infty)$ for some y^*. Taking that characterization as given presently, we wish to identify the exact value of y^* in this subsection.

In order to be an equilibrium, all managers who possess sample maximums with $y \geq y^*$ must prefer disclosing their sample maximums to not disclosing them, and the manager whose sample maximum is y^* must be indifferent to disclosing it, i.e., $E[\tilde{\omega}|y^*] = E[\tilde{\omega}|\tilde{y} < y^*]$.

Define $\phi(y^*) \equiv E[\tilde{\omega}|y^*] - E[\tilde{\omega}|\tilde{y} < y^*]$. Notice $\phi(w_0) < 0$ (since, according to the first part of the above lemma above, $E[\tilde{\omega}|y]$ is declining in y for $y < w_0$). Thus, we confine our search for y^* to $y^* > w_0$.

Suppose $E[\tilde{\omega}|y] \leq E[\tilde{\omega}|\tilde{y} < y]$ for all y. Since $\lim_{y \to \infty} E[\tilde{\omega}|\tilde{y} < y] = E[\tilde{\omega}]$, this last inequality implies that for all sufficiently large y, $E[\tilde{\omega}|y] \leq E[\tilde{\omega}]$. But, since $E[\tilde{\omega}]$ is finite, and $E[\tilde{\omega}|y]$ is linearly increasing in y for $y > w_0$ (see the second part of the lemma above), this is impossible. Hence, for some $y > w_0$, $E[\tilde{\omega}|y] > E[\tilde{\omega}|\tilde{y} < y]$, i.e., $\phi(y) > 0$. So, by the continuity of $\phi(y)$, it follows that $\phi(y^*) = 0$ for some $y^* > w_0$.

Moreover, this y^* can be shown to be unique,[9] and $E[\tilde{\omega}|y^*] < E[\tilde{\omega}|y]$ for all $y \in (0, y_L)$ for some y_L sufficiently near zero.[10]

Confirmation of the equilibrium specifications

We first suppose that the manager's sample $\{x_i\}_{i=1}^n$ contains $n < \bar{n}$ elements. This then leads to three separate subcases.

First, $y \equiv \max\{x_i\}_{i=1}^n < w_0$. If the manager conforms to the hypothesized equilibrium behavior, the firm's price will be the "no disclosure" price $E[\tilde{\omega}|\max\{\tilde{x}_i\}_{i=1}^{\bar{n}} = y^*]$. In contrast, were the manager to deviate to any other disclosure (by disclosing any D' that can be supported by his sample), then according to the statement of the theorem, the firm will be priced at $P(D') = \frac{\alpha + \bar{n}}{\alpha + \bar{n} - 1} \times w_0$ We now show that the manager is better off conforming to equilibrium behavior. To see this, recall $y^* > w_0$, and so, by the lemma above, $E[\tilde{\omega}|\{\tilde{x}_i\}_{i=1}^{\bar{n}} = y]$ is strictly increasing in y for $y \geq w_0$. Thus, we have

$$E[\tilde{\omega}|\{\tilde{x}_i\}_{i=1}^{\bar{n}} = y^*] > E[\tilde{\omega}|\{\tilde{x}_i\}_{i=1}^{\bar{n}} = w_0].$$

But, notice:

$$E[\tilde{\omega}|\{\tilde{x}_i\}_{i=1}^{\bar{n}} = w_0] = w_0 \times \sum_n \frac{\alpha + n}{\alpha + n - 1} \times \frac{\frac{n}{n+\alpha} h(n)}{\sum_{\hat{n}} \frac{\hat{n}}{\hat{n}+\alpha} h(\hat{n})} \geq$$

$$w_0 \times \sum_n \frac{\alpha + \bar{n}}{\alpha + \bar{n} - 1} \times \frac{\frac{n}{n+\alpha} h(n)}{\sum_{\hat{n}} \frac{\hat{n}}{\hat{n}+\alpha} h(\hat{n})} = \frac{\alpha + \bar{n}}{\alpha + \bar{n} - 1} \times w_0.$$

So, any manager with a sample $\{x_i\}_{i=1}^n$ for which $y = \max\{x_i\}_{i=1}^n < w_0$ is better off conforming to the equilibrium behavior specified in the theorem than deviating to any other supportable disclosure.[11]

Second, $w_0 \leq y \equiv \max\{x_i\}_{i=1}^n < y^*$. If the manager conforms to the hypothesized equilibrium behavior, the firm's price also will be the "no disclosure" price $E[\tilde{\omega}|\max\{\tilde{x}_i\}_{i=1}^{\bar{n}} = y^*]$. Deviating to any disclosure D for which $\max D < w_0$ is undesirable for exactly the same reason it was undesirable in the first case above. We next show that deviating to any disclosure D' with $\max D' \equiv y' \in [w_0, y) \subset [w_0, y^*)$ is also undesirable. Indeed, according to the off-equilibrium specifications stated in the theorem, choosing any such deviation results in the firm being priced at $P(D) = \frac{\alpha + \bar{n}}{\alpha + \bar{n} - 1} \times y'$. This is less $E[\tilde{\omega}|\{\tilde{x}_i\}_{i=1}^{\bar{n}} = y^*]$, since

$$E[\tilde{\omega}|\{\tilde{x}_i\}_{i=1}^{\bar{n}} = y^*] \geq E[\tilde{\omega}|\{\tilde{x}_i\}_{i=1}^{\bar{n}} = y'] = y' \times \sum_{n=1}^{\bar{n}} \frac{\alpha + n}{\alpha + n - 1} \times \frac{\frac{n}{n+\alpha} h(n)}{\sum_{\hat{n}} \frac{\hat{n}}{\hat{n}+\alpha} h(\hat{n})}$$

$$\geq y' \times \sum_{n=1}^{\bar{n}} \frac{\alpha + \bar{n}}{\alpha + \bar{n} - 1} \times \frac{\frac{n}{n+\alpha} h(n)}{\sum_{\hat{n}} \frac{\hat{n}}{\hat{n}+\alpha} h(\hat{n})} = y' \times \frac{\alpha + \bar{n}}{\alpha + \bar{n} - 1}. \quad (3.A.4)$$

So, any manager with a sample $\{x_i\}_{i=1}^n$ for which $w_0 \leq y \equiv \max\{x_i\}_{i=1}^n < y^*$ is also better off conforming to the equilibrium behavior specified in the theorem than deviating to some other disclosure that can be supported by the sample.[12]

Third, $y = \max\{x_i\}_{i=1}^n \geq y^*$. If the manager conforms to equilibrium behavior, the firm is priced at $E[\tilde{w}|y] = y \times \sum_n \frac{\alpha+n}{\alpha+n-1} \times \frac{\frac{n}{n+\alpha}h(n)}{\sum_{\hat{n}} \frac{\hat{n}}{\hat{n}+\alpha}h(\hat{n})}$. Since $E[\tilde{\omega}|y] > E[\tilde{\omega}|y^*]$, it is clear that conforming to equilibrium behavior is clearly better than reporting any D with $\max D < y$.[13]

Having completed the confirmation that of the equilibrium specifications when the manager's sample $\{x_i\}_{i=1}^n$ contains $n < \bar{n}$ elements, we now turn to the special case where the manager's sample is of size $n = \bar{n}$. If the manager's disclosure D consists of $\#D < \bar{n}$ elements, then the preceding argument applies verbatim. If, however, the manager's disclosure D consists of $\#D = \bar{n}$, elements, that is, the manager discloses his entire sample, then a separate analysis must be conducted, because the off-equilibrium specifications are now restricted to $P(D) = \frac{\alpha+\bar{n}}{\alpha+\bar{n}-1} \times \max\{x_i\}_{i=1}^{\bar{n}}$. We have three additional subcases to consider.

First, suppose $w_0 \leq y \equiv \max\{x_i\}_{i=1}^{\bar{n}} < y^*$.[14] If the manager conforms to the hypothesized equilibrium behavior, the firm's price will be the "no disclosure" price $E[\tilde{\omega}| \max\{\tilde{x}_i\}_{i=1}^{\bar{n}} = y^*]$. In contrast, if the manager deviates to the full disclosure $D' = \max\{x_i\}_{i=1}^{\bar{n}}$, the firm will be priced at $P(D') = \frac{\alpha+\bar{n}}{\alpha+\bar{n}-1} \times \max\{x_i\}_{i=1}^{\bar{n}}$. Since, by the lemma above, $E[\tilde{\omega}|\{\tilde{x}_i\}_{i=1}^{\bar{n}} = y']$ is increasing in y' for all $y' \in [w_0, \infty)$, we have - in particular- for $y' = y$:

$$E[\tilde{\omega}|\{\tilde{x}_i\}_{i=1}^{\bar{n}} = y^*] \geq E[\tilde{\omega}|\{\tilde{x}_i\}_{i=1}^{\bar{n}} = y]. \tag{3.A.5}$$

Moreover,

$$E[\tilde{\omega}|\{\tilde{x}_i\}_{i=1}^{\bar{n}} = y] = y \times \sum_{n=1}^{\bar{n}} \frac{\alpha+n}{\alpha+n-1} \times \frac{\frac{n}{n+\alpha}h(n)}{\sum_{\hat{n}} \frac{\hat{n}}{\hat{n}+\alpha}h(\hat{n})}$$

$$\geq y \times \sum_{n=1}^{\bar{n}} \frac{\alpha+\bar{n}}{\alpha+\bar{n}-1} \times \frac{\frac{n}{n+\alpha}h(n)}{\sum_{\hat{n}} \frac{\hat{n}}{\hat{n}+\alpha}h(\hat{n})} = E[\tilde{\omega}|\{\tilde{x}_i\}_{i=1}^{\bar{n}} = y] \tag{3.A.6}$$

(notice that this last expression is $E[\tilde{\omega}|\{\tilde{x}_i\}_{i=1}^{\bar{n}} = y]$ and not $E[\tilde{\omega}|\{\tilde{x}_i\}_{i=1}^{\bar{n}} = y]$). Putting (3.A.5) and (3.A.6) together, we conclude that for all $\{x_i\}_{i=1}^{\bar{n}}$ with $w_0 \leq y \equiv \max\{x_i\}_{i=1}^{\bar{n}} < y^*$:

$$E[\tilde{\omega}|\{\tilde{x}_i\}_{i=1}^{\bar{n}} = y^*] \geq E[\tilde{\omega}|\{\tilde{x}_i\}_{i=1}^{\bar{n}} = y], \tag{3.A.7}$$

and so the manager will not deviate from the hypothesized equilibrium by fully disclosing his sample information.

Second, suppose $y'' \equiv \max\{x_i\}_{i=1}^{\bar{n}} < w_0$. Since $E[\tilde{\omega}|\{\tilde{x}_i\}_{i=1}^{\bar{n}} = y']$ is weakly increasing for all y' (and, in fact, is constant for $y' < w_0$), we conclude that for any $y > y''$,

$$E[\tilde{\omega}|\{\tilde{x}_i\}_{i=1}^{\bar{n}} = y] \geq E[\tilde{\omega}|\{\tilde{x}_i\}_{i=1}^{\bar{n}} = y'']$$

and so we can appeal to the inequality in (3.A.7) to conclude

$$E[\tilde{\omega}|\{\tilde{x}_i\}_{i=1}^{\bar{n}} = y^*] \geq E[\tilde{\omega}|\{\tilde{x}_i\}_{i=1}^{\bar{n}} = y'']. \tag{3.A.8}$$

Hence, a manager with sample $\{x_i\}_{i=1}^{\bar{n}}$ with $\max\{x_i\}_{i=1}^{\bar{n}} < w_0$ will not deviate from the hypothesized equilibrium by fully disclosing his sample information either.

Finally, consider $y'' \equiv \max\{x_i\}_{i=1}^{\bar{n}} > y^*$. In this case, fully disclosing his information is equilibrium behavior, and so there are no off-equilibrium concerns to consider.

This completes the analysis of all possible cases, and so completes the proof of the theorem.   ∎

Notes

1. Gertner [1998].
2. There is one exception to this last statement, discussed in the text below.
3. The requirement that the value assigned to $P(D)$ belong to the *closure* of the set

$$\{E[\tilde{\omega}|\{x_i\}_{i=1}^n]| \text{ among all samples } \{x_i\}_{i=1}^n \text{ that can support the disclosure } D\},$$

rather than the set itself is made to deal with the prospect, in case $\bar{n} = \infty$, that the number of elements in the manager's sample could be arbitrarily large.

4. To see this, let p_q be the price investors attach to the firm when $\tilde{q}$ is known to be q, and (as in GHM), assume $p_q \neq p_{q'}$ when $q' \neq q$. In the GHM setting when the manager's information set is $\{q\}$, the manager's only disclosures that can be supported by his sample are to disclose nothing ($D = \phi$) or else to disclose the exact value of the manager's sample information ($D = \{q\}$). If $S \subset Q$ consists of those realizations of $\tilde{q}$ for which no disclosure is postulated to occur, then $P(\phi) = E[p_{\tilde{q}}|\tilde{q} \in S]$. But, since $\sup\{p_q|q \in S\} > E[p_{\tilde{q}}|\tilde{q} \in S]$ unless S is a singleton, the managers with the "best" information q in S will separate themselves by disclosing $\{q\}$. So, S is at most a singleton, and every equilibrium entails full disclosure.

5. Of course, the manager is indifferent as to what gets reported when $y < w_0$.

6. The equilibrium conclusion that, when the manager discloses information, he discloses the most favorable sample observation among the sample observations he receives, is similar to Shin's [1994] demonstration that equilibrium disclosures can be described by what he refers to as "sanitization strategies." A fundamental difference between the present paper and Shin's work, however, is that, in Shin [1994], there is a positive probability of the manager receiving no information whatsoever. Consequently, in Shin's work, the manager may sometimes fail to make a disclosure of information that he receives for the same reason that managers in Dye [1985] sometimes do not make disclosures: investors cannot distinguish the manager's failure to disclose information because he is hiding information from the manager's failure to disclose information because the manager did not receive information. This contrasts to the model in the present paper where the manager always receives some private information, and investors know that the manager always receives some private information.

7. When $\bar{n}$ is finite, there must be separate off-equilibrium specifications for the cases where $\#D < \bar{n}$ and $\#D = \bar{n}$, since in the latter case investors know the manager has no undisclosed sample information. This eliminates any discretion in assigning off-equilibrium beliefs.

8. This ratio $\dfrac{\sum_n \frac{n}{\alpha+n-1} \frac{y^{n-1}}{w_0^n} h(n)}{\sum_{\hat{n}} \frac{n}{\hat{n}+\alpha} \frac{y^{\hat{n}-1}}{w_0^{\hat{n}}} h(\hat{n})}$ is of the form, with $g(n) \equiv \frac{n}{\alpha+n} \frac{1}{w_0^n} h(n)$:

$$\frac{\sum_n g(n)y^{n-1} \times \frac{n+\alpha}{n+\alpha-1}}{\sum_n g(n)y^{n-1}} = \frac{\sum_n g(n)y^{n-1} \times (1 + \frac{1}{n+\alpha-1})}{\sum_n g(n)y^{n-1}}$$

$$= 1 + \frac{\sum_n \frac{g(n)}{n+\alpha-1}y^{n-1}}{\sum_n g(n)y^{n-1}}$$

Differentiating the quotient $\dfrac{\sum_n \frac{g(n)}{n+\alpha-1}y^{n-1}}{\sum_n g(n)y^{n-1}}$ (and omitting reference to the denominator of the result), we see that $E[\tilde{w}|y]$ is strictly decreasing in y for $y < w_0$ if and only if the following inequality holds:

$$\sum_{n\geq 1} g(n)y^{n-1} \sum_{n\geq 2} \frac{(n-1)g(n)}{n+\alpha-1}y^{n-2} < \sum_{n\geq 1} \frac{g(n)}{n+\alpha-1}y^{n-1} \sum_{n\geq 2}(n-1)g(n)y^{n-2}.$$

Since all summands appearing in the sums $\sum_{n\geq 2}$ assume the value zero when $n = 1$, this can be replaced by:

$$\sum g(n)y^{n-1} \sum \frac{(n-1)g(n)}{n+\alpha-1}y^{n-2} < \sum \frac{g(n)}{n+\alpha-1}y^{n-1} \sum(n-1)g(n)y^{n-2}.$$

(In the preceding inequality, as well as in the inequalities that follow, a sum without an explicit index is presumed to range over $n = 1$ to $n = \infty$.) Equivalently,

$$y \sum g(n)y^{n-2} \sum \frac{(n-1)g(n)}{n+\alpha-1}y^{n-2} < y \sum \frac{g(n)}{n+\alpha-1}y^{n-2} \sum (n-1)g(n)y^{n-2}.$$

Since $y > 0$, with $k(n) \equiv g(n)y^{n-2}$, the last inequality is equivalent to:

$$\sum k(n) \sum \frac{(n-1)k(n)}{n+\alpha-1} < \sum \frac{k(n)}{n+\alpha-1} \sum (n-1)k(n)$$

or

$$\sum k(n) \left[\sum k(n) - \alpha \sum \frac{k(n)}{n+\alpha-1} \right] < \sum \frac{k(n)}{n+\alpha-1} \sum (n-1)k(n)$$

or

$$\left[\sum k(n) \right]^2 < \sum \frac{k(n)}{n+\alpha-1} \sum (n+\alpha-1)k(n).$$

With $a(n) \equiv \left[\frac{k(n)}{n+\alpha-1} \right]^{.5}$ and $b(n) \equiv [(n+\alpha-1) \times k(n)]^{.5}$, we can rewrite the preceding as:

$$\left[\sum a(n)b(n) \right]^2 < \sum a(n)^2 \sum b(n)^2.$$

This last inequality is the Cauchy-Schwarz inequality. Thus, if we only required the preceding inequality to hold weakly, we would be done by the Cauchy-Schwarz inequality. We must show, though, that the Cauchy-Schwarz inequality holds strictly for our assignments of the vectors $\mathbf{a} \equiv (a(1), a(2), a(3), ...)$ and $\mathbf{b} \equiv (b(1), b(2), b(3), ...)$.

The Cauchy-Schwarz theorem assets that the inequality is strict as long as $\mathbf{a}$ and $\mathbf{b}$ are not collinear. In view of how $a(n)$ and $b(n)$ are defined, for them to be collinear, we would require, at least, $(\frac{k(m_1)}{\alpha+m_1-1}, \frac{k(m_2)}{\alpha+m_2-1})$ and $((\alpha+m_1-1)k(m_1), (\alpha+m_2-1)k(m_2))$ to be collinear for some integers $m_2 > m_1 \geq 1$ (Note that there exists $m_2 > m_1$ such that $h(m_1) > 0$ and $h(m_2) > 0$ by the assumption that no single integer m exists at which $\tilde{n} = m$ with certainty.) Moreover, for any such m_1 and m_2, $k(m_1) \neq 0$ and $k(m_2) \neq 0$ by definition of $k(\bullet)$, so the aforementioned collinearity is equivalent to the collinearity of $(\frac{1}{\alpha+m_1-1}, \frac{1}{\alpha+m_2-1})$ and $(\alpha+m_1-1, \alpha+m_2-1)$. Now, collinearity of $\mathbf{a}$ and $\mathbf{b}$ would, at least, require the existence of some fixed constant c such that $\frac{c}{\alpha+m_1-1} = \alpha+m_1-1$ and $\frac{c}{\alpha+m_2-1} = \alpha+m_2-1$, i.e., $c = (\alpha+m_1-1)^2 = (\alpha+m_2-1)^2$, which is manifestly impossible (since $\alpha > 1$ and $m_2 > m_1 \geq 1$).

9. To see this, note that

$$\frac{d}{dy}\phi(y) = \frac{\partial}{\partial y}E[\tilde{\omega}|y] - \frac{k(y)}{\int_0^y k(y)dy} \times [E[\tilde{\omega}|y] - E[\tilde{\omega}|\tilde{y} < y]],$$

where $k(y)$ is the density of $y = \sup\{y_i\}_{i=1}^{\tilde{n}}$. For $y > w_0$, we know

$$\frac{\partial}{\partial y}E[\tilde{\omega}|y] = \sum_n \frac{n}{\alpha+n-1} \frac{h(n)}{\sum_{\hat{n}} \frac{\hat{n}}{\hat{n}+\alpha}h(\hat{n})} > 0.$$

Thus, at any $y^* > w_0$ for which $\phi(y^*) = 0$, i.e., for which $E[\tilde{\omega}|y^*] = E[\tilde{\omega}|\tilde{y} < y^*]$, we have $\phi'(y^*) > 0$. This proves uniqueness: given the continuity of $\phi(y)$, there cannot be two or more y^*s satisfying $\phi(y^*) = 0$, all of which approach zero "from below."

10. To see this, notice that if $E[\tilde{\omega}|y] \leq E[\tilde{\omega}|y^*]$ for all $y < w_0$, then we would have $E[\tilde{\omega}|y < y^*] < E[\tilde{\omega}|y^*]$, contrary to what the equilibrium specification of y^* demands. Hence, there exists an interval of $y's$, say $(0, y_L)$ for some $y_L < w_0$ such that $E[\tilde{\omega}|y] > E[\tilde{\omega}|y^*]$ for all $y's$ in this interval.

11. Moreover, it should be noted that the off-equilibrium assignment in this case is consistent with the requirements stated in the definition of the equilibrium. If $\max\{x_i\}_{i=1}^n < w_0$, then there are samples

$\{x_i'\}_{i=1}^{\hat{n}}$ of arbitrarily large sample size $\hat{n}$ for which (i) $\{x_i\}_{i=1}^{n} \subset \{x_i'\}_{i=1}^{\hat{n}}$ and (ii) $\max\{x_i'\}_{i=1}^{\hat{n}} = w_0$, yielding expected value $E[\tilde{\omega}| \max\{x_i'\}_{i=1}^{\hat{n}} = w_0] = w_0 \times \frac{\alpha + \hat{n}}{\alpha + \hat{n} - 1}$. For sufficiently large $\hat{n}$, it follows that the expected value $E[\tilde{\omega}| \max\{x_i'\}_{i=1}^{\hat{n}} = w_0]$ can be made arbitrarily close to w_0. Hence, (the closure of) such samples will support the off-equilibrium pricing specification $P(D) = a + bw_0$ made in the statement of the theorem.

12. As in the first case, it should be noted that the off-equilibrium assignment in this case is consistent with the requirements stated in the definition of the equilibrium. That is, when $\max\{x_i\}_{i=1}^{n} \in [w_0, y^*)$, then there are samples $\{x_i'\}_{i=1}^{\hat{n}}$ of arbitrarily large sample size $\hat{n}$ for which (i) $\{x_i\}_{i=1}^{n} \subset \{x_i'\}_{i=1}^{\hat{n}}$ and (ii) $\max\{x_i'\}_{i=1}^{n} = \max\{x_i\}_{i=1}^{n}$, yielding expected value $E[\tilde{\omega}| \max\{x_i'\}_{i=1}^{\hat{n}} =] = \max\{x_i\}_{i=1}^{n} \times \frac{\alpha + \hat{n}}{\alpha + \hat{n} - 1}$. For sufficiently large $\hat{n}$, this expectation can be made arbitrarily close to $\max\{x_i\}_{i=1}^{n}$. Hence, (the closure of) such samples will support the off-equilibrium pricing specification $P(D) = a + b \max\{x_i\}_{i=1}^{n}$ made in the statement of the theorem.

13. As in the previous cases, it is easy to exhibit samples that converge to the assigned off-equilibrium expected values and that support any off-equilibrium disclosures that may occur.

14. The reason for considering this case first will be apparent below.

References

Akerloff, G., "The Market for 'Lemons': Quality Uncertainty and the Market Mechanism," *Quarterly Journal of Economics* 1970.

Arrow, K., *Social Choice and Individual Values*, Yale University Press 1951.

Arya, A., Demski, J., Glover, J., and P. Liang, "Quasi-Robust Multi-agent Contracts," University of Florida working paper 2005.

Beaver, W. and J. Demski, "The Nature of Income Measurement," *The Accounting Review* 1979.

Blackwell, D., "Comparison of Experiments," *,Proceedings of the second Berkeley Symposium on Mathematical Statistics and Probability,* ed. by J. Neyman, University of California Press, Berkeley and Los Angeles 1951.

Demski, J., "The General Impossibility of Normative Accounting Standards," *The Accounting Review* 1973,

Demski, J., "Choice Among Financial Reporting Alternatives," *The Accounting Review* 1974.

DeGroot, M., *Optimal Statistical Decisions* (New York: McGraw Hill) 1970.

Dye, R., "Disclosure of Nonproprietary Information," *Journal of Accounting Research* 1985.

Dye, R., "Proprietary and Nonproprietary Disclosures," *Journal of Business* 1986.

Dye, R., "Investor Sophistication and Voluntary Disclosures," *Review of Accounting Studies* 1999.

Feltham, G. "Joel S. Demski: a Leader in Accounting Scholarship," in this volume.

Gertner, R., "Disclosure and Unravelling," in *The New Palgrave Dictionary of Economics and the Law* (New York: Stockton Press), 1998

Gigler, F., "Self-enforcing Voluntary Disclosures," *Journal of Accounting Research* 1994.

Grossman, S., "The Informational Role of Warranties and Private Disclosures about Product Quality," *Journal of Law and Economics* 1981.

Grossman, S. and O. Hart,."Disclosure Laws and Takeover Bids," *Journal of Finance* 1980.

Jovanovic, B., "Truthful Disclosure of Information," *Bell Journal of Economics* 1982.

Jung, W. and Y. Kwon, "Disclosure When the Market is Unsure about Information Endowment," *Journal of Accounting Research* 26, 1988.

Milgrom, P., "Good News and Bad News: Representation Theorems and Applications," *Bell Journal of Economics* 1981.

Newman, P. and R. Sansing, "Disclosure Policies with Multiple Users," *Journal of Accounting Research* 1993.

Pae, S., "Acquisition and Discretionary Disclosure of Private Information and its Implications for Firms' Productive Activities," *Journal of Accounting Research* 1999.

Shin, H., "News Management and the Value of Firms," *Rand Journal of Economics* 1994.

Verrecchia, R., "Discretionary Disclosure," *Journal of Accounting and Economics* 1983.

Chapter 4

SYNERGY, QUANTUM PROBABILITIES, AND COST OF CONTROL

John Fellingham and Doug Schroeder
Ohio State University

Abstract: A standard control problem is analyzed using quantum probabilities. There are some advantages of conducting the analysis using the axiomatic structure of quantum probabilities: (1) there is synergy associated with bundling activities together, and, hence, a demand for the firm; (2) information occupies a central place in the analysis; (3) accounting information questions can be related to other information sciences. The main result is that control costs decline when aggregate performance measures are used; aggregation arises naturally. An implication is that the common practice of acquiring individual measures may be misguided in an environment where synergy is a first order effect. Also, double entry accounting appears well suited for processing information in a synergistic context.

Key words: Aggregation, Agency, Quantum Probabilities, Synergy

1.   INTRODUCTION

Exploiting synergy is a fundamental objective of firms. Synergy exists if it is more efficient to bundle activities than to engage in each separately. In an uncertain environment a definition of synergy invokes expected values: the expected value of the bundled activities strictly exceeds the sum of the expected values if the activities are performed separately. Synergy supplies an explanation for the existence of firms, as, absent synergy, separate activities could be conducted as efficiently purely in a market setting.

In this paper we are interested in the general question of how to process information in a firm. As synergy is a fundamental precursor to firm formation, it seems sensible to address the question in a setting in which synergy is of first order importance. Typical sources of synergy are economies of scale and scope (frequently modeled without uncertainty).

Arya (2002) describes synergistic gains to information in an adverse selection setting where there exists no production synergy. That is, two independent but potentially value-enhancing activities undertaken simultaneously can yield more favorable trade-offs between production and rationing to control the agents' information rents than when the activities are undertaken individually. In this paper we consider an inherently uncertain (quantum) setting in which synergy arises from bundling productive activities. A primary information processing result is reductions in control costs arise from employing aggregate performance measures for agents who supply unobservable inputs.

This paper augments a recurring theme in accounting on the merits of aggregation. A commonly cited reason to aggregate information is bounded rationality: limits on information transmission, reception, and processing can make aggregated information desirable. Benefits to aggregation, even with fully rational participants, include cancellation of errors in product costing (Datar and Gupta 1994), conveying information via choice of aggregation rule (Sunder 1997), protecting proprietary information (Newman and Sansing 1993), and substituting for commitment (Arya, Glover, and Sunder 1998, and Demski and Frimor 2000). By exploiting information processing capacity created via superposition,[10] quantum information adds another avenue for aggregation to be beneficial. A natural accounting response follows: aggregate measurement of bundled activities is more efficient both in terms of synergy and control cost than individual measurement of each activity.

In this paper synergy is modeled using quantum probabilities, the probabilities used to describe Nature in the subatomic realm. One advantage of the approach is that synergy is a first order effect of the uncertain environment. That is, when uncertainty is described by quantum probabilities, synergy is a direct implication. A further advantage is that quantum probabilities follow an axiomatic development with its inherent advantages of abstraction and rigor of analysis.[11] An implication of the axioms is that productive and measurement activities are inextricably linked; it is not possible to talk about productive activities without explicit recognition of the measurement activity.

---

[10] Superposition, and other quantum physics terms, are defined in the axiomatic development of Appendix 1.

[11] As discussed in Appendix 1, quantum probabilities reflect the superposition principle and are fundamentally different from a mixture of classical probabilities used to describe non-quantum phenomena (Feller, 1950, Zuric, 1991, Tegmark and Wheeler, 2001, Nielsen, 2003, and Davidovich, 2005).

The axiomatic development of synergy allows posing specific questions. As more activities are bundled in the firm, more agents are employed to perform the activities. If the agents are subject to moral hazard, how can the agents' behavior be efficiently controlled? In particular, is it best to use aggregate (firm-wide) performance measures? Or, perhaps, is it better to acquire disaggregated individual (divisional) performance measures? In other words, is there a trade-off between the benefits of bundling activities (as if the activities were free of moral hazard) and the cost of controlling moral hazard? Furthermore, is collusion a pressing concern?

The results are stark. Proposition 1 supplies necessary and sufficient conditions for positive synergy, that is, when there is demand for bundling activities. Proposition 2 demonstrates that, under those conditions, aggregate performance measures reduce the cost of control relative to individual performance measures. In other words there is no trade off between synergy and moral hazard. Whenever it makes sense to employ aggregate measures of bundled activities, control costs decline.

When applied to an economic setting, the axioms imply the existence, and allow analysis, of a number of phenomena besides synergy, itself. For example, the axioms imply the choice of how to measure an activity subject to moral hazard, affects the choice of the activity. That is, different measurement methods yield different output probabilities, which, in turn, imply different equilibrium activity choices in the standard moral hazard problem.

Another intriguing implication is the appropriateness of double entry accounting as the information processor in a synergistic environment. In one sense, accounting numbers are well suited for documentation of the output of several non-separable activities. That is, the emphasis is on recording joint output, rather than the delicate exercise of assessing (perhaps by allocating responsibility to or via some other value assessment of) inherently non-separable sources.

There is a fundamental similarity between double entry accounting and the outcomes of quantum probabilities. Quantum probabilities describe subatomic units whose properties can be one of two possibilities: plus or minus charge, for example, or up or down spin. Hence, quantum probabilities are binary in the sense that they supply a probability for only two outcomes — a "success," say, and the complement is the probability for a "failure." Double entry accounting similarly makes judgments of a binary type. Is revenue to be recognized or not? Is an expenditure an asset or an expense?

The paper is organized as follows. In section two quantum probabilities are introduced (mathematical details are discussed in appendix 1). A numerical example illustrates how synergy can occur in the presence of quantum probabilities. There is no moral hazard problem in the example, nor is there moral hazard in Proposition 1 which supplies the general condition for when bundling is accompanied by strictly positive synergy. In section three a basic moral hazard problem is introduced as well as a benchmark control numerical example. Section four compares the cost of control for the same agents when aggregate or individual performance measures are employed. Proposition 2 supplies conditions for when the cost of control declines for aggregate performance measures; the conditions are similar to the conditions of Proposition 1. Whenever the conditions imply bundling is efficient absent moral hazard, aggregate measures produce a decline in the cost of control when confronted with moral hazard.

Section five contains a discussion of some of the implications. In the presence of synergy driven by quantum probabilities, there are two deleterious effects of individual, rather than aggregate, measurement. First, the cost of control increases. Second, behavior is altered so that the synergy is destroyed. Implications for different organizations are briefly considered. Further, the appropriateness of double entry accounting in a synergistic environment is entertained briefly. Concluding remarks are in section six.

2.   QUANTUM PROBABILITIES AND SYNERGY

Quantum probabilities describe the behavior of sub atomic units, which often behave as waves. Hence, representation of the probability measures relies on trigonometric functions, like sine and cosine, which represent the behavior of waves. Also, the activity generating the probability measure can be thought of as an angle measured in degrees (or radians). The quantum probability for a success (or failure) conditional on activity (angle) θ_1 is as follows. The probabilities are derived from the representation of quantum mechanical behavior in Appendix 1.

$$P\left(\text{success}|\theta_1\right) = \sin^2 \frac{\theta_1}{2}$$

$$P\left(\text{failure}|\theta_1\right) = 1 - \sin^2 \frac{\theta_1}{2} = \cos^2 \frac{\theta_1}{2}$$

Also derived in the appendix are the probabilities for success when the activities are bundled together.

$$P\left(\text{success}|\theta_1,\theta_2,\ldots\theta_n\right)=\sin^2\sum_{j=1}^{n}\frac{\theta_j}{2}$$

$$P\left(\text{failure}|\theta_1,\theta_2,\ldots\theta_n\right)=\cos^2\sum_{j=1}^{n}\frac{\theta_j}{2}$$

Notice that, for n = 1, bundled probabilities reduce to the individual expressions.

The probabilities stated above allow for a crisp representation of synergy and for the conditions when synergy is positive. The first step is to represent expected values. In order to do so, assign a value of one to a success and zero to a failure.[12]

$$EV\left(\theta_j\right)=\sin^2\frac{\theta_j}{2},$$

The expected value for bundled activities:

$$EV\left(\sum_{j=1}^{n}\theta_i\right)=\sin^2\sum_{j=1}^{n}\frac{\theta_j}{2}$$

Synergy is defined as the difference between the expected value of a set of bundled activities and the sum of the expected values if the activities are engaged in individually.

Definition. $\text{Synergy}=EV\left(\sum_{j=1}^{n}\theta_i\right)-\sum_{j=1}^{n}EV\left(\theta_j\right)$

---

[12] Expected value for quantum phenomena is more carefully defined in Appendix 1.

Some numerical examples are supplied.

	$\theta_1 = \theta_2 = 60°$	$\theta_1 = \theta_2 = 90°$	$\theta_1 = \theta_2 = 120°$
$EV(\theta_1)$	.25	.50	.75
$EV(\theta_2)$	.25	.50	.75
$EV\left(\sum_{i=1}^{2}\theta_i\right)$	.75	1.0	.75
Synergy	.25	0	-.75

From the numerical examples it is seen that synergy can be positive or negative (or zero). We wish to analyze situations where there is a demand for bundling activities together. Hence, we are particularly interested when synergy is strictly positive. As presented in Proposition 1, the condition is

$$0 < \sum_{i=1}^{n}\theta_i < 180°. \quad \text{(The proof is in Appendix 2.)}$$

PROPOSITION 1.

If $0 < \sum_{j=1}^{n}\theta_j < 180°$, then Synergy > 0.

If, and only if, $0 < \sum_{j=1}^{n}\theta_j < 180°$, then

$$EV\left(\sum_{j=1}^{n}\theta_j\right) > EV\left(\sum_{j=1}^{n-1}\theta_j\right) + EV(\theta_n)$$

Whenever the activity angles involved sum to less than 180°, the expected value from the activities increases when the activities are bundled together. Furthermore, from part (ii), adding to the bundle an additional activity, θ_n, increases synergy if, and only if, the sum of the resulting angles is less than 180°. That is, activity angles will be added to the bundle only until the sum reaches 180°.

It is an implication of the axioms — in particular, the measurement axiom — that measuring individual activities destroys synergy. The logic was used in the proof of Proposition 1, so it is presented as a corollary here.

Corollary
When activities are measured individually, Synergy = 0.

In quantum physics a measurement activity collapses the quantum uncertainty, interference disappears, and the quantum object behaves according to classical rules. How this happens is mysterious and the source of controversy. See, for example, chapter 29 in Penrose, 2004. In physics the idea that measurement choices affect the underlying reality of the thing measured was hard to accept. In an economic setting the intuition may be somewhat more palatable, especially in the context of a control problem. That is, it is not inconceivable that what is measured may affect the equilibrium choice of an agent compensated based on the measurement. Furthermore, in a moral hazard setting control costs are non-trivial and may affect the benefits available from synergy. The next section introduces a basic control problem in order to investigate the moral hazard problem in a synergistic environment.

3. BASIC CONTROL PROBLEM

A control problem arises when the action, θ, is not generally observable; all that is observable is the outcome of the action. Any attempt to control the act — discourage the agent from shirking — must be based on the observable outcomes only. The development here follows Christenson and Demski, 2003. The objective is to provide a parsimonious set-up in which information is a legitimate force, thereby allowing crisp discussion of the results.

In order to treat risk aversion as a first order effect and changes in risk aversion as second order, use a constant absolute risk aversion (CARA) preference representation for the agent: $U(x) = -e^{-rx}$, where r is the risk aversion parameter (as in Amershi, et al, 1985). Suppose, further, there is a cost, c, associated with a particular effort level, and the cost is in terms of dollars. The agent's utility function is domain additive in wealth and cost of effort (as in Fellingham, et al, 1985).

$$U(x,c) = -e^{-r(x-c)} = -U(x)U(c),$$

where r is the Arrow-Pratt risk aversion parameter.

Further assume the agent chooses between a high effort θ_H and a low effort θ_L, with associated costs c_H and c_L. Let p be the probability of success if the agent works hard, and q the probability otherwise, where q is less than p. Reward the agent with compensation I_S if a success is observed and I_F for a failure. Finally, let RW be the agent's reservation wage (value of alternative employment). The risk neutral principal's problem is to induce a high effort level subject to the standard individual rationality and incentive compatibility constraints.

Individual rationality constraint:

$$pU(I_s,c_H) + (1-p)U(I_F,c_H) \geq U(RW)$$

Incentive compatibility constraint:

$$pU(I_s,c_H) + (1-p)U(I_F,c_H) \geq qU(I_s,c_L) + (1-q)U(I_F,c_L)$$

The constraints can be treated as equalities, as any slack is a loss to the risk neutral principal. Utilizing the domain additive representation can further simplify the linear system:

$$pU(I_s) + (1-p)U(I_F) = U(RW + c_H)$$
$$qU(I_s) + (1-q)U(I_F) = U(RW + c_L)$$

Consider a numerical example with the following parameters.

$$\theta_H = 60° \qquad c_H = 10 \qquad RW = 0$$
$$\theta_S = 0° \qquad c_L = 0 \qquad r = .01$$

Using the quantum probabilities, the probability of observing a success if the agent works hard (shirks) are

$$p = \sin^2\left(\frac{60°}{2}\right) = \sin^2 30° = \left(\frac{1}{2}\right)^2 = \frac{1}{4}$$

$$q = \sin^2\left(\frac{0°}{2}\right) = 0$$

The two constraints are

$$\frac{1}{4}U(I_S) + \frac{3}{4}U(I_F) = U(10)$$
$$U(I_F) = U(0)$$

Solving for $U(I_S)$ yields

$$U(I_S) = -.619$$
$$I_S \cong 47.91$$

The expected payment made to the agent is

$$\frac{1}{4}I_S + \frac{3}{4}I_F = \frac{1}{4}(47.91) + \frac{3}{4}(0) = 11.98.$$

If the action angle θ_H were observable, then it would be possible to pay the agent a constant amount; in this example, the amount would be 10, the personal cost to the agent of working θ_H. The extra cost, risk premium, is the difference: 1.98 is the cost of supplying incentives to the agent. The risk premium borne by the agent is the additional social cost associated with publicly unobservable action.

In the next section the numerical example is augmented to include another agent. The issue is what happens to the risk premia when aggregate performance measures are employed for evaluating the agents. The general result is that, under conditions for positive synergy, the risk premia associated with aggregate performance measurement is less than that associated with individual performance measurement.

4.   COST OF CONTROL AND SYNERGISTIC EXPANSION OF THE FIRM

Continuing with the numerical example from the previous section, suppose two agents, both capable of delivering $\theta_H = 60°$, are combined into one firm. As before the personal cost of working hard is 10 for each agent, and each is capable of shirking ($\theta_S = 0°$) with personal cost of zero.

Design the optimal incentive contract for one agent under the assumption that the other agent is working hard, that is, working hard is a best response. Working and shirking success probabilities are calculated.

Work $$\sin^2\left(\frac{60° + 60°}{2}\right) = \sin^2 60° = (.866)^2 = \frac{3}{4}$$

Shirk $$\sin^2\left(\frac{0° + 60°}{2}\right) = \sin^2 30° = \left(\frac{1}{2}\right)^2 = \frac{1}{4}$$

The following control equations are implied.

$$\frac{3}{4}U(I_s) + \frac{1}{4}U(I_F) = U(10)$$

$$\frac{1}{4}U(I_s) + \frac{3}{4}U(I_F) = U(0)$$

The solution is $I_s \cong 15.40$ and $I_F \cong -4.65$. The expected payment is $\frac{3}{4}I_s + \frac{1}{4}I_F \cong 10.39$ so the risk premium is only .39. Notice this is well below the one agent firm control loss calculated in the previous section: 1.98. Since the same contract can be written for the other agent, the conclusion is that aggregate performance measurement lowers cost of control relative to individual performance measurement. With individual measures there are four possible realizations available for control purposes — two for each agent. Even though the number of possible realizations from the aggregate measurement system declines, the cost of control declines, as well.

While the contract is designed with working as a best response, there is no collusion problem in the sense that there does not exist a dominant sub-game accessible to the agents. If both agents shirk, then under the above contract both receive $U(I_F, 0) = U(-4.65) < U(0)$. That is, they are better off pursuing alternative employment than both shirking.

The point that the cost of control might decline as the size of the firm increases is illustrated by the numerical example. In the presence of quantum synergy, the effect is general. Synergy is positive whenever the sum of the angles is less than $180°$; the same condition on the angles which determined the demand for bundling activities together also implies the cost of control will decrease when aggregate performance measures are employed. Synergy and cost of control go hand in hand. A general result is stated in proposition 2; the proof is in appendix 2.

PROPOSITION 2.

If $0 < \sum_{j=1}^{n} \theta_j < 180°$, then $RP_j(\text{aggregate}) < RP_j(\text{individual}) \; \forall \, j$.

(RP_j is the risk premium for agent j.)

5. DISCUSSION OF INDIVIDUAL MEASUREMENT

In a multiple agent firm with control problems, a natural inclination is to attempt to obtain measures of each agent's action. When there is synergy, there is no benefit to obtaining additional measurements — two is enough: either success or failure for the firm as a whole. Simply measuring total firm output is the least cost way to control all agents in the firm.

Furthermore, it may not even be possible to acquire additional measures beyond the firm-wide measure without mitigating the synergy. The agents' behavior may change if they are aware they are being evaluated on individual rather than firm performance. In fact, in Nature that is exactly what happens. A mysterious aspect of quantum physics is that the interference in a system is destroyed whenever an outside observer takes a measurement of the system — this is the effect captured in the corollary. It is not clear why or how this works, but the experimental evidence is overwhelming that it does, indeed, work this way. (See, for example, the discussion of the two slit experiment in Feynman, 1963, pp. 37-7 to 37-10.)

It is plausible that economic synergies work similarly. When agents are aware that the individual activity will be scrutinized, they may emphasize the individual component of their activity at the expense of the synergistic component, much like an individual athlete in a team sport may emphasize individual statistics to the detriment of team welfare. If economic synergy follows quantum synergy, instituting individual measures, and basing rewards on them, may prove counterproductive.

It is not hard to find examples of organizations where generating excessive performance measures had apparently detrimental effects. Enron, for example, was seemingly generating synergies by combining physical pipelines and energy delivery capability with a vigorous trading activity. However, they insisted on compensation based on individual and divisional performance (see McLean and Elkind, 2004, pp. 63-4). A quote from *Conspiracy of Fools* by Kurt Eichenwald about reaction to individual performance reviews emphasizes the point.

> "Not surprisingly, the analysts were in open revolt. In written evaluations, they told Kaminski that forced ranking was destroying the company. If everyone did a good job, the only way to move ahead was by undermining a colleague, but analysts needed to work as a team to get the best answers. Rather than sabotaging each other, they verbally attacked Enron and Skilling for pushing an idea without understanding the consequences." Eichenwald, 2005, p. 462.

The University is another institution in which synergy is important and delicate. Idea creation in the community of scholars relies upon open communication and collegial support. The tendency seems to be, at least anecdotally, to emphasize individual achievement — number of publications, "top-tier" hits, teaching ratings, and so forth — at the expense of acknowledging the contributions of an academic discipline to the store of scholarly knowledge, and the important role of a synergistic environment for scholarly progress. Einstein remarked, "All education is the culmination of the knowledge of preceding generations. We achieve immortality by working together, learning together, and teaching each other. ... Bear in mind that the wonderful things you learn in schools are the work of many generations, produced by enthusiastic effort, and infinite legwork in every part of the world." (Eger, 2005, p.111) To the extent that quantum probabilities capture these interactions, reliance on individual measures is myopic.

A final speculation is the role of accounting as a measurement device. It appears to be appropriate in a quantum world in at least two ways. One is that quantum probabilities are binary, that is, they partition measurements into two possibilities: up or down spin, for example, or positive or negative charge, or the general "success" or "failure." Double entry accounting is designed to accommodate binary results: revenue is recognized or not, an expenditure is an asset or an expense, and so forth (Antle and Demski, 1989, Liang, 2000 and 2001, and Christensen and Demski, 2003, ch. 14–16).[13]

Another relevant property of double entry accounting is its ability to aggregate data across multiple activities. Suppose individual measurements, and the corresponding negative impact on synergy, are a concern. Double entry accounting can aggregate division (individual) results into firm-wide numbers for evaluation purposes. Of course, the mere existence of divisional numbers prior to aggregation might cause a problem, as divisions pay them too much attention and endanger synergy. Double entry enables a second means of rendering the division numbers less relevant. Accruals and allocations can be made at the firm-wide level only. Effectively, division numbers can be cash flow; only the firm-wide numbers include accrual components. Perhaps this can further reduce inappropriate divisional attention to local numbers. In summary, double entry might have two useful properties in a quantum probability environment: binary recognition, and the ability to employ accruals for appropriate firm-wide measures only.

6.   CONCLUDING REMARKS

The basic result is that the control problem is eased whenever the conditions are right for positive synergy. It is unnecessary to try to measure everything in sight in an attempt to evaluate multiple agents' actions; it is sufficient to restrict attention to an observed outcome for the combined firm

---

[13] The typical transactions-based approach to accrual accounting (a la cost accounting) encourages a wait-and-see approach while an assessment approach encourages peeking into the black box to see what lies ahead. While peeking may be viewed as proactive in some contexts, it is a malignancy in the present context – peeking destroys synergy.

as a whole. In fact, it is dangerous to measure individual agents, as that destroys synergy.

The result follows from the assumption that economic synergies behave like quantum physical interference. That, of course, is a big assumption, and no real justification is offered here. Nonetheless, it can be pointed out that for many years some prominent physicists resisted the implications of interference in quantum mechanics. Einstein, for example, was concerned about some of the implications including, as he put it, "spooky action at a distance." Also, there was the problem of explaining why the act of observing a quantum system destroys the interference. It was only after compelling experimental evidence that the theory gained acceptance.

At least in the business realm there is some inclination to accept the basic ideas, if not the details. For example, the phenomenon of synergy has been frequently discussed in an economic setting. While perhaps not well understood, particularly in a setting with uncertainty, it seems that its existence is acknowledged. Also, it is plausible that observation and compensation based on individual performance measures may reduce, destroy, or even create negative synergy in an organization.

Modeling probabilities in the quantum sense allows serious examination of the interplay among productive activities and measurement activities. In the quantum world synergy across productive activities is a first order effect of the inherent uncertainty. Furthermore, the productive and measurement activities are inextricably linked; it is not possible to talk about productive activities without explicit recognition of how the measurement activity occurs. Measurement activities, such as accounting, are at the center of the analysis.

Finally, we note that quantum probabilities are capturing apparently striking phenomena. It seems plausible that economic synergy effects are of lesser magnitude than those observed in Nature. The results with respect to the concurrent movement of synergy and control costs might not be so crisp. As opposed to the results offered in this paper, there may be interior solutions trading off the benefits of synergy with the costs of control. The optimality of aggregated (firm-wide) performance measures may be altered. That is an open question. Nonetheless, keeping in view at least some synergistic effects seems appropriate. Accounting takes place in firms, and firms are characterized by the (hopefully efficient) bundling of activities.

ACKNOWLEDGMENTS

We thank Anil Arya, Mark Bagnoli, Anne Beatty, John Christensen, Peter Christensen, Reining Chen, Joel Demski, Ron Dye, Tom Frecka, Hans

Frimor, Jonathan Glover, Yuji Ijiri, Pierre Liang, Scott Liao, Haijin Lin, John O'Brien, Sarah Rice, Reed Smith, Eric Spires, Rick Young, and workshop participants at the Ohio State Colloquium and the Purdue Summer Research Conference.

APPENDIX 1

This appendix contains an axiomatic development of the basic quantum probabilities used in the paper. There are two fundamental probabilities to derive: for individual activities (unbundled) and for a firm (bundled activities). For individual activities the probability of success will be derived as $\sin^2 \dfrac{\theta_j}{2}$, where the activity is a function of θ_j.

When n activities (functions of θ_i, where i goes from 1 to n) are bundled together in a firm, the success probability to be derived is $\sin^2 \displaystyle\sum_{j=1}^{n} \dfrac{\theta_j}{2}$.

Visually

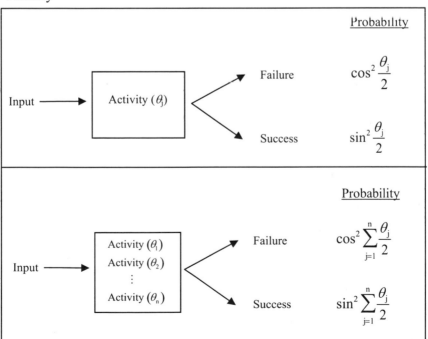

The probabilities are derived using an axiomatic development which follows Nielsen and Chuang (2002).

Axiom 1 — Superposition

A quantum unit (qubit) is represented by a two element vector $\begin{bmatrix} \alpha \\ \beta \end{bmatrix}$ where α and β are (possibly complex) numbers, known as amplitudes, such that $|\alpha|^2 + |\beta|^2 = 1$.

Dirac notation will ease the discussion. $|0\rangle = \begin{bmatrix} 1 \\ 0 \end{bmatrix}$ and $|1\rangle = \begin{bmatrix} 0 \\ 1 \end{bmatrix}$, so $\begin{bmatrix} \alpha \\ \beta \end{bmatrix} = \alpha|0\rangle + \beta|1\rangle$. The superposition axiom is required to capture the inherent uncertainty of quantum objects. That is, there exists a fundamental inability to predict the outcome of a quantum experiment; only probabilities can be specified. See, for example, Milburn (1998), especially chapter one.

Axiom 2 — Measurement

The probability that qubit $|\psi\rangle = \alpha|0\rangle + \beta|1\rangle$ will be measured as $|0\rangle$ is $\langle \psi | 0\rangle\langle 0 | \psi\rangle = |\alpha|^2$ (or measured as $|1\rangle$ is $\langle \psi | 1\rangle\langle 1 | \psi\rangle = |\beta|^2$).

Superposition collapses when an observation takes place. The probability of the measurement yielding a particular state is the square (of the modulus) of the amplitude of that state. See, for example, Feynman (1963).

Axiom 3 — Transformation

Evolution of the system or qubit transformation is accomplished by a linear operator – a unitary matrix.

A useful transformation matrix is $H = \dfrac{1}{\sqrt{2}}\begin{bmatrix} 1 & 1 \\ 1 & -1 \end{bmatrix}$. H has the unitary property; that is, after multiplication by H, the resulting qubit has amplitudes which, when squared, add to one. For example, $H|0\rangle = \dfrac{|0\rangle + |1\rangle}{\sqrt{2}}$ and

$H|1\rangle = \dfrac{|0\rangle - |1\rangle}{\sqrt{2}}$. The other unitary transformation used in the derivation is

$\Theta = \begin{bmatrix} e^{i\theta} & 0 \\ 0 & 1 \end{bmatrix}$ called a phase shifter. $\Theta|0\rangle = e^{i\theta}|0\rangle$ and $\Theta|1\rangle = |1\rangle$. The two

unitary transformation matrices are combined in an important quantum device called an interferometer (see Bouwmeester and Zeilinger, 2000).

Axiom 4 — Combination

Two (or more) qubits are combined into one system according to tensor multiplication of vectors.

Tensor multiplication is defined as follows.

$$\begin{bmatrix} \alpha_1 \\ \beta_1 \end{bmatrix} \otimes \begin{bmatrix} \alpha_2 \\ \beta_2 \end{bmatrix} = \begin{bmatrix} \alpha_1\alpha_2 \\ \alpha_1\beta_2 \\ \beta_1\alpha_2 \\ \beta_1\beta_2 \end{bmatrix}$$

Dirac (1958) notation simplifies tensor multiplication. For example,

$|0\rangle \otimes |0\rangle = |00\rangle$, where $|00\rangle = \begin{bmatrix} 1 \\ 0 \\ 0 \\ 0 \end{bmatrix}$. Also, $|0\rangle \otimes |1\rangle = |01\rangle$, $|1\rangle \otimes |0\rangle = |10\rangle$, and

so forth.

The most important two qubit operation is $\mathrm{CNOT} = \begin{bmatrix} 1 & 0 & 0 & 0 \\ 0 & 1 & 0 & 0 \\ 0 & 0 & 0 & 1 \\ 0 & 0 & 1 & 0 \end{bmatrix}$.

The first qubit is the control and the second qubit is the target such that

$\mathrm{CNOT}|00\rangle = |00\rangle$, $\mathrm{CNOT}|01\rangle = |01\rangle$, $\mathrm{CNOT}|10\rangle = |11\rangle$, and

$\mathrm{CNOT}|11\rangle = |10\rangle$.

An important two qubit state is called an "entangled" pair of qubits, so important it has its own conventional notation, denoted $|\beta_{00}\rangle$. Start with $|00\rangle$ and perform, in order, an H transformation on the first qubit (denote the operation H_1), and then a CNOT transformation on the pair.

$$|\beta_{00}\rangle = \text{CNOT } H_1 |00\rangle = \text{CNOT} \frac{|00\rangle + |10\rangle}{\sqrt{2}} = \frac{|00\rangle + |11\rangle}{\sqrt{2}}$$

The resulting two-qubit system is referred to as an entangled state; note that it cannot be created by the tensor combination of any two individual qubits (Azcel, 2001, Nielsen and Chuang, 2002, and Zeilinger, 2000). $|\beta_{00}\rangle$ is a Bell or EPR state and its orthogonal complements are $|\beta_{01}\rangle = \frac{|01\rangle + |10\rangle}{\sqrt{2}}$,

$|\beta_{10}\rangle = \frac{|00\rangle - |11\rangle}{\sqrt{2}}$, and $|\beta_{11}\rangle = \frac{|01\rangle - |10\rangle}{\sqrt{2}}$. Together, the four are said

to form the Bell basis (Bell, 1964).

Probability Derivations

For the single activity probability, use $|\beta_{00}\rangle$ as the input and $H_1 \Theta_1 H_1$ as the transformation activity.

The probability of the outcome $|\beta_{01}\rangle = \frac{|01\rangle + |10\rangle}{\sqrt{2}}$ increases in θ_1 (as long as the sum of angles is less than 180 degrees) so it is labeled as a "success" signal.

$$H_1\Theta_1H_1|\beta_{00}\rangle = H_1\Theta_1\frac{|00\rangle+|10\rangle+|01\rangle-|11\rangle}{2}$$

$$= H_1\frac{e^{i\theta_1}(|00\rangle+|01\rangle)+|10\rangle-|11\rangle}{2}$$

$$= \frac{e^{i\theta_1}(|00\rangle+|10\rangle+|01\rangle-|11\rangle)+|00\rangle-|10\rangle-(|01\rangle-|11\rangle)}{2\sqrt{2}}$$

$$= \frac{(e^{i\theta_1}+1)}{2}\left(\frac{|00\rangle+|11\rangle}{\sqrt{2}}\right)+\frac{(e^{i\theta_1}-1)}{2}\left(\frac{|10\rangle+|01\rangle}{\sqrt{2}}\right)$$

$$= \frac{(e^{i\theta_1}+1)}{2}|\beta_{00}\rangle+\frac{(e^{i\theta_1}-1)}{2}|\beta_{01}\rangle$$

Now, the probabilities are calculated as $\left|\dfrac{e^{i\theta_j}+1}{2}\right|^2 = \cos^2\dfrac{\theta_j}{2}$ and

$\left|\dfrac{e^{i\theta_j}-1}{2}\right|^2 = \sin^2\dfrac{\theta_j}{2}$. (The last step uses Euler's formula:

$e^{i\theta} = \cos\theta + i\sin\theta$; and the trigonometric identity:

$\cos^2\dfrac{\theta}{2} = \dfrac{1+\cos\theta}{2}$ (Nahin, 1998)).

Bundled activities probabilities are derived similarly to single activity probabilities.

$$H_1\Theta_1H_1H_2\Theta_2H_2|\beta_{00}\rangle = |\beta_{00}\rangle\left(\frac{e^{i(\theta_1+\theta_2)}+1}{2}\right)+|\beta_{01}\rangle\left(\frac{e^{i(\theta_1+\theta_2)}-1}{2}\right)$$

The probabilities are $\left|\dfrac{e^{i(\theta_1+\theta_2)}+1}{2}\right|^2 = \cos^2\dfrac{\theta_1+\theta_2}{2}$ and

$\left|\dfrac{e^{i(\theta_1+\theta_2)}-1}{2}\right|^2 = \sin^2\dfrac{\theta_1+\theta_2}{2}$.

Quantum probabilities can be extended to n-activity settings. First, we define n-qubit entangled inputs then we identify quantum probabilities associated with individual and bundled productive activities. The entangled input is $|\beta_{00\ldots0}\rangle = CNOT_{12}H_1\ CNOT_{23}H_2\ \ldots\ CNOT_{n-1,n}H_{n-1}\ |00\ldots0\rangle$ and its complement is $|\beta_{00\ldots1}\rangle = CNOT_{12}H_1\ CNOT_{23}H_2\ \ldots\ CNOT_{n-1,n}H_{n-1}\ |00\ldots1\rangle$, where the subscripts refer to the qubit to which the transformation applies; hence for $CNOT_{ij}$ i is the control qubit and j is the target qubit.

The results are summarized in the following observation.

OBSERVATION

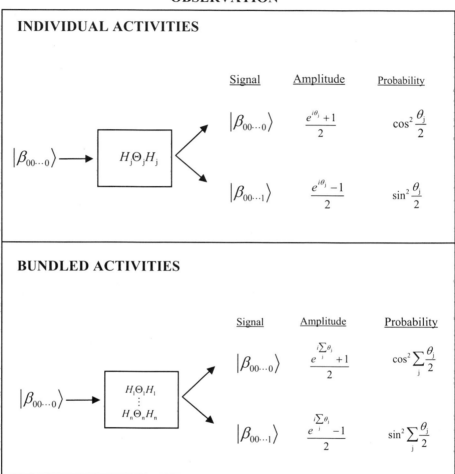

Expected value

Finally, expected value of quantum phenomena is defined relative to an observable, say O. An observable is a Hermitian operator; it has real eigenvalues that reflect possible realized values for a random variable. The observable in the present context is $O = s \, | \beta_{00\ldots 1} \rangle \langle \beta_{00\ldots 1} | + f \, | \beta_{00\ldots 0} \rangle \langle \beta_{00\ldots 0} |$.

For example, when n = 2

$$O = \frac{1}{2}\begin{bmatrix} f & 0 & 0 & f \\ 0 & s & s & 0 \\ 0 & s & s & 0 \\ f & 0 & 0 & f \end{bmatrix}$$

where s and f are the outcomes associated with success and failure (say, one and zero). The expected value of O is $E[O] \equiv \langle O \rangle = \langle \psi_k | O | \psi_k \rangle$ where $| \psi_b \rangle$ = $H_1\Theta_1H_1 \quad \ldots \quad H_n\Theta_nH_n | \beta_{00\ldots0} \rangle$ for bundled activities and $| \psi_j \rangle$ = $H_j\Theta_jH_j | \beta_{00\ldots0} \rangle$ for individual activities. Hence, by the measurement axiom $\langle O \rangle = P(s)\ s + P(f)\ f$ so that for bundled activities

$$\langle O \rangle = \sin^2 \sum_{j=1}^n \frac{\theta_j}{2}\ s + \cos^2 \sum_{j=1}^n \frac{\theta_j}{2}\ f = \sin^2 \sum_{j=1}^n \frac{\theta_j}{2},\ \text{and for individual activities}$$

$$\langle O \rangle = \sin^2 \frac{\theta_j}{2}\ s + \cos^2 \frac{\theta_j}{2}\ f = \sin^2 \frac{\theta_j}{2}\ \text{(where } s = 1 \text{ and } f = 0\text{)}.$$

APPENDIX 2

PROOF OF PROPOSITION 1

Let $S\left(\sum_{j=1}^n \theta_j\right) \equiv \sin^2 \sum_{j=1}^n \frac{\theta_j}{2} - \sum_{j=1}^n \sin^2 \frac{\theta_j}{2}$ denote synergy for the angles $\theta_1 \ldots \theta_n$. Let

$\omega_1 \equiv \sum_{j=1}^{n-1} \theta_j$ and $\omega_2 \equiv \theta_n$. Then $S\left(\sum_{j=1}^n \theta_j\right) = \sin^2 \frac{\omega_1 + \omega_2}{2} - \sin^2 \frac{\omega_1}{2} - \sin^2 \frac{\omega_2}{2}$

Using the identity $\sin^2 \frac{\theta}{2} = \frac{1 - \cos\theta}{2}$,

$$S\left(\sum_{j=1}^n \theta_j\right) = \frac{\cos(\omega_1) + \cos(\omega_2) - \cos(\omega_1 + \omega_2) - 1}{2}\ \text{and}$$

$$\frac{dS\left(\sum_{j=1}^n \theta_j\right)}{d\omega_2} = \frac{-\sin\omega_2 + \sin(\omega_1 + \omega_2)}{2}$$

For $0 < \theta_1 < 180°$, $S\left(\sum_{j=1}^n \theta_j\right)$ is continuous and equal to zero at $\omega_2 = 0$ and

$\omega_1 + \omega_2 = 180°$. $\dfrac{dS\left(\sum\limits_{j=1}^{n}\theta_j\right)}{d\omega_2}$ is positive at $\omega_2 = 0$ and negative at

$\omega_1 + \omega_2 = 180°$, and it equals zero at a unique point in between (from Figure

A2-1, $\dfrac{dS\left(\sum\limits_{j=1}^{n}\theta_j\right)}{d\omega_2} = 0$ when $\omega_2 = \dfrac{180° - \omega_1}{2}$). Therefore, $S\left(\sum\limits_{j=1}^{n}\theta_j\right)$ is

everywhere positive for $0 < \omega_1 + \omega_2 = \sum\limits_{j=1}^{n}\theta_j < 180°$, and negative when the sum

exceeds $180°$. (Throughout the paper the sum of angles never exceeds $360°$ by assumption.) This completes part (ii).

To finish part (i) assume $S\left(\sum\limits_{j=1}^{n-1}\theta_j\right) > 0$ for $0 < \sum\limits_{j=1}^{n-1}\theta_j < 180°$. Then

$$S\left(\sum_{j=1}^{n}\theta_j\right) = S\left(\sum_{j=1}^{n-1}\theta_j\right) + \sin^2\frac{\sum\limits_{j=1}^{n-1}\theta_j + \theta_n}{2} - \sin^2\frac{\sum\limits_{j=1}^{n-1}\theta_j}{2} - \sin^2\frac{\theta_n}{2} > 0.$$

Then (i) is true by induction.   ∨

PROOF OF COROLLARY

The proof follows directly from the definition of synergy and proposition 1.

PROOF OF PROPOSITION 2

First, for reference purposes, we state some relationships derived from the statement of the control problem.

$$E(\text{payment}) \equiv E[I] = \left(\frac{1 - \cos(\theta_{1H} + \theta_2)}{2}\right)I_S + \left(\frac{1 + \cos(\theta_{1H} + \theta_2)}{2}\right)I_F$$

$$I_S = -\frac{1}{r}\ln\left(-U(I_S)\right) \qquad I_F = -\frac{1}{r}\ln\left(-U(I_F)\right)$$

$$U(I_S) = \frac{\left(1 + \cos(\theta_{1L} + \theta_2)\right)U(RW + c_H) - \left(1 + \cos(\theta_{1H} + \theta_2)\right)U(RW + c_L)}{\cos(\theta_{1L} + \theta_2) - \cos(\theta_{1H} + \theta_2)}$$

$$U(I_F) = \frac{\left(\cos(\theta_{1L} + \theta_2) - 1\right)U(RW + c_H) + \left(1 - \cos(\theta_{1H} + \theta_2)\right)U(RW + c_L)}{\cos(\theta_{1L} + \theta_2) - \cos(\theta_{1H} + \theta_2)}$$

$$\frac{dI_s}{d\theta_2} = -\frac{1}{r}\frac{\frac{dU(I_s)}{d\theta_2}}{U(I_s)} \qquad \frac{dI_L}{d\theta_2} = -\frac{1}{r}\frac{\frac{dU(I_L)}{d\theta_2}}{U(I_L)}$$

$$\frac{dU(I_s)}{d\theta_2} = \frac{\left[\sin(\theta_{1H}-\theta_{1L})+\sin(\theta_{1H}+\theta_2)-\sin(\theta_{1L}+\theta_2)\right]}{\left[\cos(\theta_{1L}+\theta_2)-\cos(\theta_{1H}+\theta_2)\right]^2}\left[U(RW+c_L)-U(RW+c_H)\right]$$

$$\frac{dU(I_F)}{d\theta_2} = \frac{\left[\sin(\theta_{1H}-\theta_{1L})+\sin(\theta_{1L}+\theta_2)-\sin(\theta_{1H}+\theta_2)\right]}{\left[\cos(\theta_{1L}+\theta_2)-\cos(\theta_{1H}+\theta_2)\right]^2}\left[U(RW+c_L)-U(RW+c_H)\right]$$

The proof depends on how other agents' inputs θ_2 affects the informativeness of aggregate measures which has two parts: how feasibility of motivating θ_H depends on θ_2 and demonstrating that the derivative of expected payment with respect to θ_2 is negative (reduces cost of control).

It is feasible to motivate θ_H if $\dfrac{\text{probability(failure}|\theta_L)}{\text{probability(failure}|\theta_H)} > e^{r(c_H-c_L)}$ (see Christensen and Demski, 2003, pp. 250-1).

Since $\dfrac{1+\cos(\theta_{1L}+\theta_2)}{1+\cos(\theta_{1H}+\theta_2)} \geq \dfrac{1+\cos\theta_{1L}}{1+\cos\theta_{1H}}$ for $0 \leq \theta_j \leq \pi/2$ and $\theta_{1L} < \theta_{1H}$ (equal iff $\theta_2 = 0$), there exist values of θ_2 (associated with aggregate measures) when it is feasible to motivate θ_H while it is infeasible to motivate θ_H when it is infeasible using individual measures (there is no θ_2).

The proof then follows from the sign of the expression for the derivative of expected payment with respect to θ_2. Following considerable algebraic manipulation (see Fellingham and Schroeder, 2005, for details).

$$\frac{dE[I]}{d\theta_2} = \frac{1-\cos(\theta_{1H}+\theta_2)}{2}\frac{dI_s}{d\theta_2}+\frac{1+\cos(\theta_{1H}+\theta_2)}{2}\frac{dI_F}{d\theta_2}+\frac{\sin(\theta_{1H}+\theta_2)}{2}(I_s-I_F) < 0.$$

REFERENCES

Aczel, A. 2001. *Entanglement: The Greatest Mystery in Physics*. New York, NY: Four Walls Eight Windows.

Amershi, A., J. Demski and J. Fellingham. 1985. "Sequential Bayesian Analysis in Accounting Settings," *Contemporary Accounting Research*, Spring.

Antle, R. and J. Demski. 1989. "Revenue Recognition," *Contemporary Accounting Research*, Spring.

Arya, A., J. Glover, and S. Sunder. 1998. "Earnings Management and the Revelation Principle," *Review of Accounting Studies* 3, No. 1 and 2.

Arya, A. 2002. "Synergy Among Seemingly Independent Activities," *Contemporary Accounting Research*, Fall.

Bell, J. 1964. "On the Einstein-Podolsky-Rosen Paradox," *Physics*, Volume 1.

Bouwmeester, D. and A. Zeilinger. 2000. "The Physics of Quantum Information: Basic Concepts," in *The Physics of Quantum Information*, Dirk Bouwmeester, Artur Ekert, and Anton Zeilinger, (eds.). Berlin: Springer.

Christensen, J. and J. Demski. 2003. *Accounting Theory: An Information Content Perspective*. New York, NY: McGraw Hill-Irwin.

Datar, S., and M. Gupta. 1994. "Aggregation, Specification and Measurement Errors in Product Costing," *The Accounting Review* (October).

Davidovich, L. 2005. "Quantum Information," *MRS Bulletin*, February.

Demski, J. and H. Frimor. 2000. "Performance Measure Garbling Under Renegotiation in Multi-Period Agencies," *Journal of Accounting Research* (Supplement).

Dirac, P. 1958. *The Principles of Quantum Mechanics*. Oxford, UK: Oxford University Press.

Eger, J. 2005. *Einstein's Violin*. New York: Jeremy P. Tarcher/Penguin

Eichenwald, K. 2005. *Conspiracy of Fools*. New York, NY: Broadway Books.

Feller, W. 1950. *An Introduction to Probability Theory and Its Applictions*. New York: John Wiley & Sons.

Fellingham, J., P. Newman, and Y. Suh. 1985. "Contracts Without Memory in Multi-period Agency Models," *Journal of Economic Theory*, December.

Fellingham, J. and D. Schroeder. 2005. "Quantum Information and Accounting," *Journal of Engineering and Technology Management*, forthcoming.

Feynman, R., R. Leighton, and M. Sands. 1963. *The Feynman Lectures on Physics, volume 1*. Reading MA: Addison-Wesley Publishing Co.

Liang, P. 2000. "Accounting Recognition, Moral Hazard, and Communication," *Contemporary Accounting Research*, 2000.

Liang, P. 2001. "Recognition: An Information Content Perspective," *Accounting Horizons*, September.

McLean, B. and P. Elkind. 2004. *The Smartest Guys in the Room*. New York, NY: Penguin Books.

Milburn, G. 1998. *The Feynman Processor: Quantum Entanglement and the Computing Revolution*. Reading, MA: Perseus Books.

Nahin, P. 1998. *An Imaginary Tale: The Story of* $\sqrt{-1}$. Princeton, NJ: Princeton University Press.

Newman, P., and R. Sansing. 1993. "Disclosure Policies with Multiple Users," *Journal of Accounting Research* (Spring).

Nielsen, M. and I. Chuang. 2002. *Quantum Computation and Quantum Information*. Cambridge, UK: Cambridge University Press.

Nielsen, M. 2003. "Simple Rules for à Complex Quantum World," *Scientific American*, 288 (5).

Penrose, R. 2004. *The Road to Reality*. New York, NY: Random House, Inc.

Sunder, S. 1997. *Theory of Accounting and Control*. Cincinnati, OH: International Thomson.

Tegmark, M. and J. Wheeler. 2001. "As Quantum Theory Celebrates its 100th Birthday, Spectacular Successes are Mixed with Persistent Puzzles," *Scientific American* (February).

Zeilinger, A. 2000. "Quantum Teleportation," *Scientific American*, Volume 282 (4).

Zuric, W. 1991. "Decoherence and the Transition from Quantum to Classical," *Physics Today* (October).

Chapter 5

MORAL HAZARD WITH HIDDEN INFORMATION

Frøystein Gjesdal
Norwegian School of Economics and Business Administration

Abstract: Moral hazard with hidden information refers to a control problem where the agent's actions are observable, but not the information on which they are based. This paper analyses the case in which an agent (for example a subcontractor or a dealer) obtains perfect information before deciding on his action. The close relationship to adverse selection allows easy derivation of the set of feasible sharing rules. The optimal action (production plan) is then derived, and it is shown that action efficiency (and incentive power) is uniformly lower than first-best (except in the best and the worst state), but greater than efficiency in the corresponding adverse selection problem. It is shown that efficiency and incentive strength is decreasing uniformly in the agent's aversion to risk (properly defined). The level of risk may be endogenously as well as exogenously determined. Holding exogenous risk constant it is shown that risk averse agents tend to end up with more risky production plans. However, the effects of exogenous changes in risk are ambiguous. It is further demonstrated that the risk aversion of the principal will have the opposite effect as a more risk averse principal will tend to prefer more efficient (and less risky) production. Finally, it is argued that principals prefer agents to be informed before actions are taken, but after contracting. This information structure also represents a social optimum.

Key words: Incentives, risk sharing, moral hazard, outsourcing

1. INTRODUCTION

Many observers have noted that moral hazard may not only arise from unobservable actions. In fact actions taken by a decision maker on behalf of others may be readily observable. Still the moral hazard problem remains if decisions are based on the agent's private, non-verifiable information. To establish what the agent actually did is one thing, to determine whether the action was called for under the circumstances is quite a different matter.

Consider the level of production at a subcontractor (sales volume at a dealership). Production volume (sales) will in general be measurable. An audit may have established that actual quantity in a period was low. Still the subcontractor (dealer) may argue that low production (sales) was optimal due to high costs (low demand). Also consider a budget-controlled department in a larger organization. An audit may document how money has been spent without being able to draw strong conclusions about the effectiveness of the operations. If information about demand and costs is local, in the sense that it is hard to verify and communicate, there is no way of proving whether shirking is involved.

This paper will consider an organizational setting where production is outsourced to a subcontractor with private information about unobservable production costs. Regulating the relationship with spot contracting will not work well as the agent may take advantage of superior information. Nor will relational contracts work if the joint information is insufficient to sustain such contracts.[14] Hence long term (ex ante) contracts will be considered the instrument of control. Contracts may be fixed or variable. Contracts for a fixed quantity of the good at a fixed fee are feasible. Such contracts will avoid any incentive problems, but will impose risk on the agent. More importantly fixed contracts will not allow the parties to take advantage of variations in cost. Variable contracts, on the other hand, will allow principal and agent to fine tune production and improve risk sharing, at the cost of potentially serious incentive problems. Optimal contracting in such a setting is the topic of this paper.

The contracting problem referred to here has been termed "moral hazard with hidden information" (Arrow (1985), Hart and Holmstrom (1987), Rasmusen (1989)). In such an agency problem the action is the agent's strategy, i. e. a mapping from a set of information signals to a set of decisions. Several authors have noted that the problem of moral hazard with differential information may be analyzed by means of regular agency models with multidimensional actions (Gjesdal (1982), Hart and Holmstrom(1987), Holmstrom and Milgrom (1987), (1992)). However, the problem has a

---

[14] The terms "outsourcing", "spot contracting" and "relational contracting" follow the terminology of Baker, Gibbons and Murphy (2002). The alternative to outsourcing is integrated production where the principal covers (but does not necessarily observe) the cost of production, and the agent is uninformed.

special structure that may be exploited (preferences and costs are naturally additively separable).[15]

This paper studies a generic case of moral hazard with hidden, perfect information. This model is in many respects a polar opposite of the "classical" models of moral hazard (Holmstrom (1979), Shavell (1979)). In the classical models there are typically a large number of sharing rules implementing a given action. The analysis has primarily focused on locating the risk-minimizing scheme. In contrast, problems of moral hazard with hidden perfect information in general have unique incentive schemes (for each action), and the focus naturally shifts to identifying the optimal action.

The objective of this paper is to derive the optimal action (state contingent production plan) in a moral hazard problem with hidden, perfect information. The paper employs a standard, infinite state screening model that is familiar from adverse selection problems.[16] Indeed the relationship between the widely studied problem of adverse selection and moral hazard with hidden information is exploited to facilitate the analysis of the latter problem. The analysis focuses on the relationships among efficiency, incentive strength, risk and risk aversion. It is shown that efficiency and incentive strength are negatively related to the agent's risk aversion (the production plan under adverse selection is a limiting case when risk aversion approaches infinity).

Risk is endogenous as well as exogenous in problems of hidden information. Holding the exogenous risk constant, it is shown that the risk of the production plan is positively related to agents' risk aversion, and hence negatively related to efficiency and incentive strength. The principal's degree of risk aversion has the opposite effect. It is positively related to efficiency and incentive strength and negatively related to endogenous risk. On the other hand variations in exogenous risk have ambiguous effects. Changes in efficiency and incentive strength may differ from state to state. Thus qualitatively the results do not differ from those of "classical" models of moral hazard, but the difference in perspective brings novel insights.

---

[15] The particular structure of the Holmstrom and Milgrom (1992) multi-task model does not invite the hidden information interpretation.

[16] The point of view taken in this paper is that the nature of the voluntary participation constraints should distinguish between moral hazard and adverse selection. Here the agent's utility is constrained in ex ante (expected) utility terms. This is justified by the not altogether attractive assumption that principal and agent may enter into binding contracts before private information is received. The model is therefore one of moral hazard. The term adverse selection will be reserved for games in which the voluntary participation constraints are formulated state by state. Such formulations are reasonable if information is received before contracting, or if the agent may leave after becoming informed.

Finally, organizational issues related to the choice of information structure are addressed. It is shown that the principal prefers the agent to be informed, but not before he is contractually bound to perform his job. Better information improves decision making and risk sharing. Loss of control is not an issue although incentive compatibility concerns imply that information cannot be used (first-best) optimally. The agent may under certain circumstances prefer to collect information before contracting with the principal. However, this is not an efficient solution under the assumptions made here.

This paper generalizes early work by Hart (1983) and Holmstrom and Weiss (1985). It is also related to more recent papers by Prendergast (2002) and Baker and Jorgensen (2003). However, the analysis here fails to provide general support for Baker and Jorgensen's claim that a negative relationship between risk and incentive strength is reversed when moral hazard arises from hidden information. A paper that is particularly close to the present one is Salanié (1990). Under fairly restrictive assumptions with respect to preferences, beliefs and technology, he characterizes the optimal production plan and analyses its properties; in particular the effects of varying the agent's risk aversion are addressed. Propositions 3 – 5 below represent direct generalizations of Salanié's results in this area. Pre-decision information has also received considerable attention in the management accounting literature. The focus has primarily been on whether the agency is actually better off with an informed agent (see Baiman and Sivaramakrishnan (1992), Christensen (1981), Farlee (1998) and Penno (1984), (1989), as well as Cremer and Khalil (1992) in economics).

The paper is organized as follows: In section 2 the model is formulated and discussed. The set of feasible sharing rules is characterized on the basis of well-known results. In section 3 the optimal action (the contingent production plan) under moral hazard with hidden information is derived and evaluated. Section 4 focuses on the implications of risk and the agent's degree of risk-aversion for efficiency and incentive strength. The value of information is addressed in section 5. In sections 3 - 5 the principal is (for the most part) assumed to be risk neutral. Risk averse principals are introduced in section 6. Section 7 discusses possible extensions of the model and contains summary and conclusions.

2.   THE MODEL

The context of the model is that of production planning at a subcontractor. The principal receives revenue from the sale of x units of a product. Without loss of generality the price is set equal to 1. The agent incurs a private cost of production $W(x,\theta)$, where θ is the state variable. θ will be referred to as the productivity indicator. x is observable, θ and W are not. W is differentiable and satisfies the following, familiar regularity conditions (convex costs and "one-crossing property"):

$$\frac{\partial W}{\partial x} = W_x > 0, \frac{\partial W}{\partial \theta} = W_\theta < 0, \frac{\partial^2 W}{\partial x \partial \theta} = W_{x\theta} < 0, \frac{\partial^2 W}{\partial x^2} = W_{xx} > 0$$

The total cost as well as the marginal cost decrease in the productivity indicator θ. θ has a density function $f(\ )$, and distribution function $F(\ )$. The support of θ is the real interval $[\underline{\theta}, \overline{\theta}]$. It is assumed that $f(\theta) > 0$ for all θ[17].

The contract with the subcontractor specifies a conditional payment $S(x,\theta)$ from the principal to the agent. If the agent is a government agency, S may represent the budget.[18] The agent determines $x(\theta)$ after he has observed θ. The principal does not observe θ, and, as will become clear subsequently, in this model the only way for her to learn θ is through observation of x. Thus it is unnecessary to consider communication. However, it may be useful to interpret the model in the context of a revelation game where the principal determines the production plan and the payment after being told the true state by the agent. [19]

One set of constraints, referred to as incentive compatibility constraints, specify that agents choose production volumes x according to their own preferences. Expression (2) below captures incentive compatibility. A second constraint (expression (1) below) is the individual rationality (or voluntary participation) constraint, which specifies that the agent's expected utility of wealth should be larger than some specified constant U^*. $U(\ )$ and $V(\ )$ are the utility functions of agent and principal respectively. Both are differentiable and concave. [20]

---

[17] These are all assumptions that are commonly made in models of adverse selection (see references listed below).

[18] Indeed substituting variable for fixed budgets is a central feature of the reforms usually referred to as "new public management".

[19] Thus a "state-space" formulation is convenient in the hidden information model. This is in contrast to the classical models – see Hart and Holmstrom (1985).

[20] As the agent's decision is made under certainty, the model represents a degenerate version of a general principal-agent model. In fact it is a special case of two different models. The obvious interpretation is one of nonrandom output and random, unobservable costs. However, the model may also be viewed as a degenerate version of a more standard model with random output and nonrandom production costs. In the latter case the model requires a decision variable that is distinct from the output, and which the principal does not observe.

The principal chooses $S(x,\theta)$ to maximize her expected utility. Then the "moral hazard with hidden information" problem may be formulated as follows:

"MHHI problem":

$$\text{Max}_{S(x,\theta)} \int_{\underline{\theta}}^{\bar{\theta}} V(x - S(x,\theta))f(\theta)d\theta$$

subject to

$$\int_{\underline{\theta}}^{\bar{\theta}} U(S(x,\theta) - W(x,\theta))f(\theta)d\theta \geq U* \qquad (1)$$

$$x(\theta) = \arg\max_{\hat{x}(\theta)} \int_{\underline{\theta}}^{\bar{\theta}} U(S(\hat{x},\theta) - W(\hat{x},\theta))f(\theta)d\theta \qquad (2)$$

It is easy to see that the maximization in (2) is point-wise, and (2) may be transformed into the following set of separate constraints:

$$\forall\theta : x(\theta) = \arg\max_{\hat{x}(\theta)} \{S(\hat{x},\theta) - W(\hat{x},\theta)\} \qquad (2')$$

In an adverse selection problem the individual rationality constraints corresponding to (1) would look as follows:

$$\forall\theta : U(S(x,\theta) - W(x,\theta)) \geq U* \qquad (3)$$

However, under the assumption made on the cost function it is well known that only one of these restrictions is binding, and (3) simplifies to:

$$U(S(x,\underline{\theta}) - W(x,\underline{\theta})) \geq U* \qquad (3')$$

The programming problem, which results when (3') is substituted for (1), is an adverse selection problem, and will be referred to as the "adverse selection" problem (AS) corresponding to the MHHI problem.

The incentive constraints (2) (or (2')) are identical in the MHHI and the corresponding AS problems. The solution to the AS problem is well known. This may be exploited to characterize the set of feasible sharing rules in the MHHI problem. (2') determines the sharing rule $S(x,\theta)$ up to a constant. (1) will always hold as an equality and determines the constant. Thus the following result is immediate.

PROPOSITION 1. Assume that $x(\theta)$ is given. Then the set of sharing rules defined by (2) is nonempty if and only if $x(\theta)$ is non-decreasing. Moreover,

$$S(x(\theta),\theta) = W(x,\theta) + \bar{s} - \int_{\underline{\theta}}^{\theta} W_t(x,t)dt \qquad (4)$$

PROOF: See any decent treatment of adverse selection.[21]

The fact that the incentive compatibility constraints determine the sharing rule (budget function) up to a constant, contrasts quite sharply with the classical models of moral hazard.[22] There the possibility set generally contains many sharing rules, and the focus is on selecting the one which shares risk most efficiently. Increasing the dimensionality of the action space, shrinks the set of feasible sharing rules.[23] Ignoring the constant term, (4) will always have a unique solution. However, (4) is a necessary, but not sufficient condition for incentive compatibility.[24]

$S(x, \theta)$ is a function of θ. However, the partial derivative of $S(x,\theta)$ with respect to θ is zero. This implies that S does not vary with θ except through x. It follows that the total derivative of S with respect to x equals the partial derivate in the relevant state. If $x(\theta)$ is invertible this may be written as follows:[25]

$$\frac{dS}{dx} = W_x(x,\theta(x))$$

dS/dx is sometimes referred to as the incentive strength. $Z = S(x,\theta) - W(x,\theta)$ is the agent's profit. The profit may depend on the state as well as the output. The next proposition spells out some of the tradeoffs involved in providing

---

[21] For example Mussa and Rosen (1978), Baron and Myerson(1982), or Guesnerie and Laffont (1984). A model which is close to the present one in spirit is Sappington (1983).

[22] See e. g. Holmstrom (1979) and Shavel(1979).

[23] This argument has been made in general terms by Holmstrom and Milgrom (1987) and (1992). In the moral hazard problem with perfect hidden information, the dimensionality of the action space is higher than that of the outcome space.

[24] The fact that the set of feasible sharing rules (given an action $x(\theta)$) may be empty, is of relevance for the debate on the solution methods for moral hazard problems, such as the MHHI, where constraints appear in the form of maximization problems. The usual approach going back to Ross (1972) and Holmstrom (1979), has been to substitute the first order condition. Subsequently, the validity of this approach was investigated in some detail (see e.g. Grossman and Hart (1982), Rogerson(1987) and Jewitt (1988)). (4) is in fact derived from the first-order conditions of the maximization problem (2). The second order condition is satisfied if and only if $x(\theta)$ is non-decreasing. Hence the second-order condition cannot be ignored in the present case. However, if $x(\theta)$ is non-decreasing, the agent's maximization problem is properly convex, and any local optimum is a global optimum as well.

[25] If $x(\theta)$ is not invertible this derivative does not exist everywhere.

incentives in the MHHI models. These are quite similar to those encountered in the hidden action model.

PROPOSITION 2: Let $x_A(\theta)$ and $x_B(\theta)$ be two production plans such that $x_A(\theta) > x_B(\theta)$. Then the incentives schemes S_A and S_B that implement the respective production plans have the following properties:

(i) S_A provides stronger incentives than S_B

(ii) S_A is riskier than S_B

PROOF: Incentive strength is compared only where $x(\theta)$ is invertible. To prove (i) it is sufficient to note that $\theta_A(x) < \theta_B(x)$ implies $W_x(x,\theta_A(x)) > W_x(x,\theta_B(x))$. (ii) is proved by focusing on the profit functions. The following relationship holds between the profit shares Z_A and Z_B:

$$dZ_B\Big/d\theta = -W_\theta(x_B,\theta) < -W_\theta(x_A,\theta) = dZ_A\Big/d\theta$$

The inequality follows since $W_{x\theta}$ is negative by assumption, and $x_B(\theta)$ is smaller than $x_A(\theta)$. QED

3. THE OPTIMAL PRODUCTION PLAN

Proposition 1 implies that for a given production plan the sharing rule is uniquely determined. The principal's problem is to determine the production plan as a function of the state of nature. Looking at the programming problem it is clear that only the actors' risk aversion prevents the problem from unraveling completely; under risk neutrality it is a matter solving a set of independent, state-wise and trivial planning problems. Thus the principal faces a risk sharing problem. However, the sharing rule allows no degrees of freedom. Risk sharing must be accomplished via the real economy – the production plan.

In this section only the agent is assumed to be risk averse. The case of risk averse principal is discussed in section 6. The next proposition simply states the first-order condition for the principal's problem. The production plan which solves the first-order condition is an optimal solution if and only if it is increasing in the state of nature:

PROPOSITION 3: Assume that the production plan $x^{**}(\theta)$ satisfies the following condition.

$$(1 - W_x(x**,\theta)) + \frac{(1-F(\theta))}{f(\theta)} W_{x\theta}(x**,\theta)(1 - \lambda E\{U'()|t \geq \theta\}) = 0 \quad (5)$$

Then $x^{**}(\theta)$ is optimal in the MHHI problem with risk neutral principal if and only if $x^{**}(\theta)$ is weakly increasing in θ.

PROOF: Substituting (4) into the principal's problem, she maximizes her objective function subject to (1). The associated Langrangian is:

$$
\begin{aligned}
L = &\int_{\underline{\theta}}^{\bar{\theta}} [x - W(x,\theta) - \bar{s} + \int_{\underline{\theta}}^{\theta} W_\theta(x,t)dt] f(\theta)d\theta \\
&+ \lambda \int_{\underline{\theta}}^{\bar{\theta}} U(\bar{s} - \int_{\underline{\theta}}^{\theta} W_\theta(x,t)dt) f(\theta)d\theta
\end{aligned}
\tag{6}
$$

Differentiating with respect to $x(\hat{\theta})$ and $\bar{s}$ gives the first-order conditions for the optimal production plan. Note that $x(\hat{\theta})$ enters the (outer) integrands for every $\theta: \theta \geq \hat{\theta}$.

$$
\begin{aligned}
\frac{\partial L}{\partial x(\hat{\theta})} = &\, f(\hat{\theta}) - W_x(x,\hat{\theta})f(\hat{\theta}) + W_{x\theta}(x,\hat{\theta}) \int_{\hat{\theta}}^{\bar{\theta}} f(\theta)d\theta \\
&- \lambda W_{x\theta}(x,\hat{\theta})(1 - F(\hat{\theta})) \int_{\hat{\theta}}^{\bar{\theta}} U'() \frac{f(\theta)}{(1 - F(\hat{\theta}))} d\theta \\
= &\, (1 - W_x(x,\hat{\theta})) + \frac{1 - F(\hat{\theta})}{f(\hat{\theta})} W_{x\theta}(x,\hat{\theta})(1 - \lambda E\{U'()|\theta \geq \hat{\theta}\}) = 0
\end{aligned}
$$

$$
\frac{\partial L}{\partial \bar{s}} = -1 + \lambda E U'() = 0
\tag{7}
$$

Second order conditions are also satisfied under mild restrictions on third derivatives of the cost function.[26] A production plan $x(\theta)$ satisfying (5) is optimal if and only if it is feasible. It is feasible if and only if it is non-decreasing. QED.

The solution to (5) may not be feasible. Feasibility is particularly a concern in (bad) low-θ states when the agent is very risk averse. This issue will be addressed in the next section. For the remainder of this section it will be assumed that the solution to (5) is feasible and therefore optimal.

---

[26] If the solution to the first-order condition of the corresponding AS problem is a maximum, the solution to (5) is a maximum a fortiori.

(5) is perhaps best understood by referring to the solution of the corresponding AS problem and the first-best solution. The optimal adverse selection production plan will be denoted x*(θ) and solves[27]:

$$(1 - W_x(x^*, \theta)) + \frac{1 - F(\theta)}{f(\theta)} W_{x\theta}(x^*, \theta) = 0 \tag{8}$$

On the other hand the first-best solution denoted x***(θ) of course solves:

$$(1 - W_x(x^{***}, \theta)) = 0 \tag{9}$$

The second term in (8) is non-positive. For $\theta = \bar{\theta}$ it equals 0 since $F(\bar{\theta}) = 1$. It is strictly negative for all $\theta < \bar{\theta}$ Thus x* = x*** in the best state. In all other states x*< x***. The absolute value of the second term in (8) measures the difference between marginal cost and marginal revenue (which here equals 1) in the AS problem.

Comparing (5) and (8), the difference is that in (5) the last term is multiplied by 1 - H(θ) where H(θ) is defined by (the second equality follows from (7)):

$$H(\hat{\theta}) = \lambda E\{U'()|\theta \ge \hat{\theta}\} = \frac{E\{U'()|\theta \ge \hat{\theta}\}}{EU'()} \tag{10}$$

Since H is bounded, it follows that x**($\bar{\theta}$) = x***($\bar{\theta}$), and first-best obtains in the best state in the MHHI model as well. H > 0 implies that for all other states the difference between marginal revenue and marginal cost is less in the MHHI than in the corresponding AS problem. Thus x**(θ) > x*(θ) for θ < $\bar{\theta}$. Production is uniformly larger in the MHHI model than in the corresponding AS model.

Since the conditional expectation equals the unconditional expectation when θ = $\underline{\theta}$ it follows that H($\underline{\theta}$) = 1. Thus x**($\underline{\theta}$) = x***($\underline{\theta}$). Hence in the

---

[27] See e.g. Mussa and Rosen (1978), Baron and Myerson(1982), Guesnerie and Laffont (1984) or Sappington (1983).

MHHI model, unlike in the corresponding AS model, first-best production obtains in the worst state as well as in the best state.[28]

To maintain incentive compatibility the agent's profit $Z = S - W$ must be increasing in θ (see the proof of Proposition 2). It follows that $E\{U'()|\theta \geq \hat{\theta}\}$ $= H(\hat{\theta})/\lambda$ is decreasing in $\hat{\theta}$. Thus, $H(\theta) < 1$ for $\theta > \underline{\theta}$. This implies that when the principal is risk neutral $x^{**}(\theta) < x^{***}(\theta)$ for all $\underline{\theta} < \theta < \overline{\theta}$. The preceding arguments prove the next proposition.

PROPOSITION 4: Let $x^*(\theta)$, $x^{**}(\theta)$, and $x^{***}(\theta)$ be defined by (8), (5) and (9) respectively. If the principal is risk neutral and the agent is strictly risk averse, then for all $\underline{\theta} < \theta < \overline{\theta}$; $x^*(\theta) < x^{**}(\theta) < x^{***}(\theta)$

Intuitively, these results are not hard to understand. The marginal cost to the principal of increasing production in some state, say $\hat{\theta}$, is higher than the out-of-pocket cost in that state. To maintain incentive compatibility S( ) will have to increase by some amount not only in state $\hat{\theta}$, but in every state with higher productivity as well. Otherwise some higher productivity agents will pretend to be in $\hat{\theta}$. In the MHHI model, unlike in the corresponding AS model, the principal is able to recapture some (but not all) of this informational quasirent by charging the agent a higher fee $\overline{s}$ up front. Therefore the "virtual marginal cost" is strictly smaller in the MHHI model, and production will be more efficient.

The reason why the principal cannot recapture all of the informational quasirent, as would obviously be the case if the agent were risk neutral, can be explained as follows: Incentive compatibility requires that the profit Z is increasing in θ. Since the principal is risk neutral, this is contrary to first best risk sharing. Consider an increase of production in state $\hat{\theta}$. Then marginal informational quasirent must be paid in the states in which the agent is already relatively well off, namely all states which are preferable to $\hat{\theta}$. Because of risk aversion the marginal utility of money in these states is lower than average. The principal is only able to recapture some of the expected informational quasirent because the up front payment will be valued at average marginal utility. The exception occurs in the very worst state. When production increases in this state, informational quasirent is paid in all states. Then the principal may also recapture the quasirent in total.

Proposition 2 describes a general trade-off between incentives and risk sharing. (5) captures the same tradeoff in terms of the marginal cost of production. Increasing production in any state (with the exception of the

---

[28] At this point it is prudent to remind the reader that this production plan is *assumed* to be feasible. A production plan which calls for first-best production in the worst state may not always be feasible.

extreme states) entails a risk-increasing modification of the sharing rule. Ignoring the risk premium, this change is a mean preserving spread. H( ) captures the marginal increase in the risk premium which is part of the marginal (virtual) cost of production.[29]

(5) characterizes the solution to the MHHI problem, and it is useful for analyzing some of the properties of the solution. However, it does not provide a convenient way to derive the actual production plan. Salanié who brings heavy mathematical weaponry to bear on the special case of exponential utility, uniform distribution and quadratic objective function, concludes as follows: "…la resolution complete du programme (est) presque impossible".

4.   RISK AND THE AGENT'S RISK AVERSION

In the previous section it was shown that when the agent is risk averse the (contingent) production plan is less than first-best efficient. Of course when the agent is risk neutral, efficiency does obtain[30]. Demonstrating that efficiency is inversely related to the usual measure of (absolute) risk aversion will make the story complete.

Above it has been shown that production is greater in MHHI than in the corresponding AS problem. One might then conjecture that the solution under moral hazard approaches that under adverse selection when risk aversion approaches infinity. Indeed it will be shown that this is in fact the case.

In section 3 it was pointed out that the solution to (5) in general will equal first best in the state in which productivity is lowest. This level of production is strictly higher than production in the same state in the corresponding AS model. Moreover this result does not depend on the agent's level of risk aversion. This seems to contradict the convergence reported in the previous paragraph. The explanation to this apparent paradox

---

[29] The fact that efficiency obtains in the best and the worst state when the state space has interval support, does not imply that production would always be efficient in a two-state model. When the probability of every state is strictly positive, an increase in production in the worst state will make the agent strictly worse off in this state. His profit will increase in the good state and hence decrease in the bad. Thus there is an increase in risk for which the principal must compensate the agent. The reader is referred to the analysis by Holmstrom and Weiss (1985). Although not readily apparent, the discrete analogue of (5) is equivalent to the first-order condition derived by Holmstrom and Weiss.

[30] When the agent is risk neutral $H(\theta) = 1$ for all θ since U' is constant. This result holds irrespective of the principal's attitude towards risk.

is to be found in the fact that the solution to (5) is not always feasible in the MHHI problem because the production plan does not increase in θ. If so, the solution to (5) does not solve the principal's problem. In particular (5) is unlikely to provide a solution for small values of θ when the agent is sufficiently risk averse.

The solution $x(\theta)$ of (5) is decreasing in θ in some interval if the first order condition decreases in θ. For the corresponding AS problem this issue has been explored by many authors. Since $W_x(x,\theta)$ is assumed to be decreasing in θ, a sufficient condition for (8) to increase in θ is that $(1 - F) / f$ is non-increasing and $W_{\theta x}(x,\theta)$ is non-decreasing. In the MHHI model these conditions are no longer sufficient. The reason is that $1 - H(\theta)$ is increasing in θ. As argued previously this is the case because the agent's aversion to risk makes transfers of informational rent to the agent more costly in good states than in bad. In the MHHI model there is therefore one more reason to expect that the first-order condition may yield a production plan that is infeasible. The following proposition (part (b)) is a formal statement of this fact. It also indicates how and when this complication is likely to occur. Part (a) of the proposition deals with the issue of convergence. This part of the proposition does not require the principal to be risk neutral.

PROPOSITION 5: (proof available upon request)

(a) Let $R(\ )$ be the agent's Pratt-Arrow measure of absolute risk aversion. Then $EV(x^{**}(\theta)-S(x^{**})) \to EV(x^*(\theta)-S(x^*))$ as $R(\ ) \to \infty$.

(b) Let $x \cdot (\theta)$ be the solution to (5). Then regardless of W and F, $x \cdot (\theta)$ decreases for low θ if the agent is sufficiently risk averse.

When the production plan that solves (5) is infeasible, it must be "smoothed". For an interval containing $\underline{\theta}$ production will be constant. The optimal, minimal, "pooling" level of production must satisfy two conditions. First of all the integral of (5) over the relevant interval must be 0. Secondly, $x^{**}(\ )$ should be non-decreasing. The solution to this problem will not be pursued further here.[31]

If the optimal production plan specifies pooling in "bad states", production will necessarily be lower than first-best in the worst state. This follows from the "smoothing" procedure just described. In the corresponding AS problem pooling may be optimal in low-productivity states for a different reason also. Because of the high marginal virtual cost in these states, production may not be profitable at all. In such a corner solution $x(\theta)$

---

[31] How to modify the solution to the first-order condition to obtain the optimal solution, has been investigated in considerable detail (see e.g. Baron and Myerson (1982) and Bulow and Roberts (1989)).

will equal 0 in an interval including $\underline{\theta}$. This particular phenomenon is less likely to occur in the MHHI model.

One might also ask whether pooling in bad states will always occur in the MHHI problem. Indeed up to this point it has not been shown that the solution to (5) is ever an optimal solution. A closer look at the proof of Proposition 5 reveals, however, that such concerns are unwarranted. If risk aversion is small enough, the derivative of the production plan is positive at $\underline{\theta}$. Furthermore, it can be shown that for some probability distributions pooling because of risk aversion will only occur for low values of θ (for intervals containing $\underline{\theta}$). For other distributions this result does not hold. Finally, it should be pointed out that Proposition 4 holds even if $x^{**}(\theta)$ is different from $x\bullet(\theta)$.

The fact that adverse selection with perfect information may be regarded as a limiting case of moral hazard with hidden perfect information (Proposition 4a), is perhaps best regarded as a purely formal property[32]. At the intuitive level the two models are quite different. In AS the principal is only concerned with the agent's utility in the worst case. The reason is that the agent may always claim that this is the state, which actually obtains. Thus the agent will get his reservation utility in the worst state and strictly positive informational rent in all other states. When the agent is uninformed at the time of contracting, but infinitely risk averse, it is again the utility in the worst case that matters. Infinite risk aversion implies that no loss is tolerable. Hence the agent will insist upon his reservation level of utility even in the worst state. Consequently, he will obtain quasirent in every other state.

Above it was argued that increasing production in any state increases the risk imposed on the agent. Hence the marginal cost of production includes a risk cost. Intuitively this marginal risk cost should increase in risk aversion. Moreover the efficiency of the optimal production plan and the incentive strength should be inversely related to the agent's risk aversion as well. The next proposition demonstrates that this is indeed the case.

It will be assumed that the principal is risk neutral, and that the optimal production plan solves (5). Under these assumptions $1 - H(\theta)$ (see equation (10)) will be used as a measure of the marginal cost of risk. H may also be said to measure productive efficiency. $H = 0$ implies that production equals that of the AS problem. $H = 1$ implies first best production.[33] Since the

---

[32] It has not been shown that the production plan x^{**} converges to x^*. However, x^* is the uniquely optimal production plan given the restriction $U(\underline{\theta}) = U^*$. Hence when $U(\underline{\theta})$ is "close to" U^*, x^{**} must be "close" to x^*.

[33] A similar measure may be defined for intervals in which the optimal production plan is "smoothed".

marginal cost is measured given a sharing rule $Z(\theta)$, risk aversion is also measured given a sharing rule. Comparing two situations A and B, risk aversion is said to be (uniformly) higher in A than in B if,

$$\forall \theta; R_A(\theta) = -\frac{U_A''(Z_A(\theta))}{U_A'(Z_A(\theta))} > -\frac{U_B''(Z_B(\theta))}{U_B'(Z_B(\theta))} = R_B(\theta)$$

The following Proposition summarizes the results.

PROPOSITION 6: Assume two MHHI problems A) and B), where the principal is risk neutral. Then if for all θ: $R_A(\theta) > R_B(\theta)$, then $H_A(\theta) < H_B(\theta)$ for all θ.

PROOF: Assume without loss of generality that $EU_A'(\ ) = EU_B'(\ ) = 1$. Then $\lambda = 1$, and it is sufficient to show that:

$$\forall \theta; \theta > \underline{\theta} : J(\theta) = H_A(\theta) - H_B(\theta)$$
$$= E\{U_A'(t)|t > \theta\} - E\{U_B'(t)|t > \theta\} < 0 \tag{11}$$

Since $R_A(\theta) > R_B(\theta)$, it follows from the work of Pratt (1964) that,

$$\exists \hat{\theta} : \forall \theta \neq \hat{\theta} : (U_A'(\theta) - U_B'(\theta))(\theta - \hat{\theta}) < 0 \tag{12}$$

Thus clearly $J(\theta) < 0$ for $\theta > \hat{\theta}$. Moreover, by assumption, $J(\underline{\theta}) = 0$. Differentiating $J(\ )$ with respect to θ, using (12), yields the following:

$$\frac{dJ(\theta)}{d\theta} = \frac{f(\theta)}{1 - F(\theta)}\left[U_B'(\theta) - U_A'(\theta) + J(\theta)\right] < 0, \text{for } all\ \theta \leq \hat{\theta}$$

Thus $J(\theta) < 0$ for all $\theta > \underline{\theta}$ QED

Risk aversion in the sense of Proposition 6 will increase if the agent is involved in a more risky gamble, or if he is more risk averse to start with.[34] According to the proposition the virtual marginal cost of production increases uniformly in risk aversion. However, this does not imply that larger risk aversion makes production less efficient (and incentives weaker)

---

[34] Wilson(1968) employs the same concept of risk aversion (given a sharing rule) when he states that a syndicate member's marginal share of profits (his stock) equals the ratio of his risk tolerance to the sum of all members' risk tolerances (the syndicate's risk tolerance).

in optimum (unless risk aversion is independent of wealth).[35] All that may be concluded is that if risk-aversion is larger in optimum, then production is less efficient (ceteris paribus). The ceteris paribus assumption in this proposition should be clearly understood. $H(\theta)$ is a relative measure of efficiency. If the risk of the incentive scheme increases in optimum, this may be caused by changes in the production function or the probability distribution. These changes may also affect productive efficiency directly.

Proposition 6, despite its limitations, along with Proposition 2, provide evidence of a clear trade-off between risk-sharing and (action) efficiency/incentive strength. Similar trade-offs are not always that easy to discern in moral hazard problems unless strong restrictions are imposed on preferences and beliefs. For empiricists it may also be useful to note that the risk of the production plan is endogenous. For example the distribution of first-best output will have a more narrow support than the production plan under adverse selection (infinite risk aversion). Holmstrom and Weiss (1985) draw attention to this phenomenon in the two-state model. Thus data may exhibit a negative relationship between efficiency and incentive strength on the one hand and risk on the other. However, in this case low-powered incentives and high risk are both caused by risk aversion. Empirically there will also be positive correlation of risk and risk aversion across agents, which may be counterintuitive.

It is perhaps more interesting to study the effects of exogenous changes in risk. This is the concern of Baker and Jorgensen (2003). Exogenous risk is related to the variation in cost which depends on the distribution of the productivity parameter and the cost function. Here the focus will be on variations in the distribution of θ ordered by second-order stochastic dominance. Unfortunately the effects on efficiency and incentive strength are not clear cut. Although a uniformly positive relationship between risk and incentive strength can be ruled out under certain conditions, it is still possible that a decrease in risk may lead to weaker incentives for some values of θ. The results are summarized in the following proposition.

PROPOSITION 7: Assume that the production plan satisfies the first-order condition (5) and that the exogenous risk decreases, then if the Lagrange multiplier λ does not decrease,

    (a)   The incentive strength will not always increase uniformly

    (b)   The incentive strength cannot decrease uniformly

PROOF: The first order condition (5) may be written as follows:

---

[35] Holmstrom and Weiss(1985) show that in the two-state model increasing risk aversion implies lower production in the bad state. Salanié (1992) derives the same result assuming constant absolute risk aversion.

$$(1 - W_x(x,\theta)) + \frac{1-F(\theta)}{f(\theta)} W_{x\theta}(x,\theta)(1 - H(\theta)) = 0$$

If the first and the last factor in the second term both decrease for some value of θ, then the optimal x (and the incentive strength) increases. On the other hand if both terms increase, the optimal x (and the incentive strength) decreases. Let the two distributions that are compared be denoted F_A (the more risky) and F_B. Since F_A has more weight in the tails, the reciprocal of its hazard rate is smaller when θ is sufficiently small. Also assume that it is larger when θ is sufficiently large (this weak assumption simplifies the argument, but is not necessary).

To prove (b) assume that incentive strength does decrease uniformly in optimum such that $x^*_B(\theta) < x^*_A(\theta)$. It will be shown that this leads to a contradiction as H_B is then greater than or equal to H_A for large θ. This follows from the proof of Proposition 2 as Z_A (the profit function implementing $x^*_A(\theta)$) is steeper than Z_B (implementing $x^*_B(\theta)$). Since Z_A and Z_B have the same expected utility, they must cross once, and for sufficiently high θ, $Z_A(\theta)$ is greater than the maximum value of Z_B. It follows that for sufficiently high θ and independent of the probability distributions, the following relationship must hold (since λ_B is assumed at least as large as λ_A):

$$\lambda_B E_B \{U'(Z_B)|\theta \geq \hat{\theta}\}) > \lambda_A E_A \{U'(Z_A)|\theta \geq \hat{\theta}\})$$

For sufficiently high values of θ, the first and third factors in the last term of the first-order condition are both smaller when the distribution of θ is F_B. This contradicts the optimality of x^*_B.

(a) is proved by demonstrating that reduced environmental risk does not imply uniformly stronger incentives in the corresponding AS problem. Since H equals zero in the AS problem, it is sufficient to recall that the reciprocal of the hazard rate for F_B is higher for low values of θ. Hence in this region reduced risk implies weaker incentives.   QED

The assumption that the production plan is an interior solution is crucial. If the optimal production plan involves shutting down production when productivity is low and the risk is high, reducing risk cannot lead to weaker incentives in these states. The assumption on the Lagrange multiplier is awkward, but certainly not a necessary assumption. The point is that wealth effects should not be too large. There is no reason to expect strong wealth effects in this setting.

If nothing else Proposition 7 demonstrates the complexity of the relationship between risk and incentives. A reduction in exogenous cost risk may for example lead to greater variation in endogenous output. Hence discussing risk, it is not arbitrary which random variable is the focus of the analysis. It may be useful to keep in mind that the familiar hypotheses about the relationships among risk, risk aversion and incentive strength that are tested by empiricists are based on the very simplest forms of agency models. Assuming that risk and actions are independent is not uncommon.

5. VALUE OF INFORMATION

An issue which has received considerable attention in the literature on moral hazard with hidden information, is whether information is welfare improving. Christensen (1981) and Penno (1990) construct examples where pre-decision information has negative effects on efficiency because informed agents may circumvent controls. Penno (1984) and Baiman and Sivaramakrishnan (1992) provide conditions under which pre-decision information is actually helpful.

Although not his primary concern, Farlee (1998) shows that information about fixed costs received by risk-neutral agents before contracting harms efficiency particularly if the principal tries to elicit the information (screening). In a model similar to the one in this paper Cremér and Khalil (1992) postulate that a risk-neutral agent may acquire information at a cost before signing the contract. They show that the principal will always structure the contract to remove the incentive to collect information by making the agent better off in bad states. Production in the bad state increases weakly in the cost of information. x* and x*** are limiting cases. Cremér and Khalil also point out that information acquisition is less of a problem if the agent is risk averse (as he must be made relatively well off in bad states in any case). They do not consider the possibility of principals offering agents a "signing fee" for contracting before collecting information.

With perfect information and the further assumptions made in this paper, the value of information is unequivocally positive. The optimal arrangement is to have the agent informed after contracting but before decisions are made. The principal prefers informed agents because the value of information for decision making outweighs any loss of control. The information will also be used to obtain better risk sharing. Although the available information cannot be used fully because of risk sharing considerations, the no information solution (which involves constant production and constant budget) is likely to be far more risky for the agent. He will have to absorb all of the variation in costs.

It is easy to demonstrate these conclusions mathematically: With no information the principal will have to choose a fixed level of production.

This solution is also feasible when the agent is informed, but will never satisfy (5). Hence the principal is better off with an informed agent provided the agent is informed after contracting. Similarly the principal may choose $x^*(\theta)$ even when the agent is informed after contracting. (This particular plan will be less expensive in the MHHI problem.) However, it follows from Proposition 4 that she will never do so. Hence the principal is strictly better off when the agent is informed after contracting.

The agent is indifferent between becoming informed before making a decision and not receiving any information at all. However, he clearly prefers to contract on the basis of private information to obtain rent. Still it may be argued that it is socially optimal to postpone information acquisition until after it is too late for the agent to leave his employment (should information turn out to be unfavorable). To see this consider the following situation: Assume that the agent has a choice whether to obtain information early (before contracting) or later (after contracting, but before taking action); in both cases the cost is zero. This is the limiting case in the Cremér and Khalil (1992) setting. He could then suggest to the principal that he would postpone information gathering in return for a fee. The principal now has two options. It follows from Cremér and Khalil that she may choose the AS solution $x^*(\theta)$. This is the best she can do if the agent can check what state obtains and reject any "loss contract".

However, she can clearly do even better by proposing a contract giving the agent the same level of expected utility, but involving a different production plan - the MHHI solution for the relevant participation constraint. This plan is strictly preferable according to Proposition 4. It is also feasible if the agent signs the contract right away which eliminates the "loss contract" constraint. Hence both individuals would be better off if the agent chose to be informed later rather than sooner. In this sense the arrangement is socially superior and not only better for the principal. These arguments prove the following proposition.

PROPOSITION 8: Under outsourcing the principal prefers that the agent should be informed after contracting and before decision making. This arrangement is also socially efficient.

The value of information may change if the null information alternative changes. The proposition presumes that production is outsourced even when the agent is uninformed. As a consequence the agent may never escape the production cost risk. If the alternative is insourcing (which makes sense if the reason for outsourcing is to provide incentives for information collection), the value of information is necessarily smaller. If production is integrated in the principal's business, the principal will cover production cost, and the agent will not be exposed to any risk (he is reduced to implementing decisions made by the principal). This makes the null information alternative more attractive. Outsourcing is only optimal if the gross value of information is sufficient to cover the agent's total risk premium. This is a generalized version of the problem studied by Prendergast (1992)[36]. However, with risk averse agent the value of information and the risk premium may both be increasing in the risk of the venture. Analyzing this trade-off is left for future work.

This section will conclude with a brief look at the potential value of additional post-decision information. Post-decision information is any random variable that is observed publicly after the decision has been made. Holmstrom (1979) derived conditions under which additional post-decision information may be valuable by allowing stronger incentives or better risk sharing in the presence of pre decision information. Essentially any extra public information about the agent's action or his private information is valuable. As explained earlier (see footnote 7), the problem studied here may be viewed as a degenerate version of Holmstrom's problem. His conditions will, however, apply here as well. In the more obvious interpretation of the model (where there is no action variable) new information is valuable if and only if it is informative about the state.

6.   RISK AVERSE PRINCIPAL

This section explores the consequences of introducing a principal that is averse to risk. The sharing rule is not affected by the principal's attitude towards risk given the production plan. The production plan, however, does change. Formulating the Lagrangian of the MHHI problem using (4), and differentiating as in the proof of Proposition 3, yields the first-order condition of the optimal production plan.

PROPOSITION 9: Assume that the production plan $x^{a**}(\theta)$ satisfies the following condition:

$$(1 - W_x(x^a **, \theta)) =$$

$$-\frac{(1 - F(\theta))}{f(\theta)} W_{x\theta}(x^a **, \theta) \frac{E\{V'()|t \geq \theta\}}{V'()} [1 - \lambda \frac{E\{U'()|t \geq \theta\}}{E\{V'()|t \geq \theta\}}] \qquad (13)$$

---

[36] Prendergast assumes that the agent is risk neutral but that there are other costs of outsourcing that may make insourcing optimal unless the value of information is sufficiently high.

Then $x^{a**}(\theta)$ is optimal in the MHHI problem with risk averse principal if and only if $x^{a**}(\theta)$ is weakly increasing in θ.

Several observations can be made regarding (13):

Observation 1: The solution to the corresponding AS problem can be derived from (13) by setting $\lambda = 0$ (the participation constraint is satisfied by appropriately choosing $\bar{s}$):

$$(1 - W_x(x^a *, \theta) + \frac{(1 - F(\theta))}{f(\theta)} W_{x\theta}(x^a *, \theta) \frac{E\{V'()|t \geq \theta\}}{V'()} = 0 \tag{14}$$

Define for use below,

$$\frac{(1 - F(\theta))}{f(\theta)} W_{x\theta}(x, \theta) = D(x, \theta), \text{ and } \frac{E\{V'()|t \geq \theta\}}{V'()} = G(x, \theta) \tag{15}$$

Clearly $G(\ ) > 0$, and $x^a*(\ ) \leq x^{***}(\ )$. Equality is as usual obtained for $\theta = \bar{\theta}$. The principal's final wealth Y is equal to x - S. Differentiating, $dY/d\theta = (1 - W_x(\ )) dx/d\theta$ which is non-negative as long as x is increasing in θ. It follows that the conditional expected marginal utility is less than the marginal utility, and $G \leq 1$. The last term in (14) is therefore smaller when the principal is risk averse. This argument leads to the following conclusion:

$$x*(\theta) \leq x^a*(\theta) \tag{16}$$

(16) is easily explained. The optimal production plan under adverse selection involves trading off value in bad states against value in good states. A risk averse principal is less willing to reduce profits in low productivity states to obtain higher profits in states in which she is already well off. Therefore production will be strictly higher (closer to first best) when the principal is adverse to risk. Note that as far as the agent is concerned there is no risk in the adverse selection problem. Still the principal, who is uninformed, faces risk until the true state is revealed by the agent. Therefore the principal's attitude towards risk matters.

Observation 2: In MHHI with risk neutral agent first best is as usual obtained by "selling the firm to the agent". $x^{***}(\ )$ and $S = x^{***} - \bar{s}$ clearly solve (13). As $x^{***}(\ )$ is increasing this is the optimal solution to the principal's problem.

When principal and agent are both risk averse, the analysis of (13) parallels that of (5). First of all define,

$$H^a(\theta) = \lambda \left(E\{U'()|t \geq \theta\} \right) / \left(E\{V'()|t \geq \theta\} \right) \tag{17}$$

As before, $H^a > 0$. $H^a = 1$ when $\theta = \underline{\theta}$. Hence the solution to the MHHI problem is closer to first best than the solution to the corresponding AS problem. First best is attained in the best and the worst state assuming feasibility. It is also possible to show (proof available upon request) that $H^a \leq 1$. This proves the following analogue of Proposition 4.

PROPOSITION 10: Let $x^{a*}(\theta)$, $x^{a**}(\theta)$, and $x^{***}(\theta)$ be defined by (14), (13) and (9) respectively. Then,

For all $\underline{\theta} < \theta < \overline{\theta}$; $x^{a*}(\theta) < x^{a**}(\theta) < x^{***}(\theta)$

The (weak form) of the second inequality of proposition 10 may also be argued informally as follows: Propositions 4 and 10 imply that the agent's share $(S - W)$ of net profit $(x - W)$ is never greater than 1. At the margin the relative share may be calculated as follows:

$$\frac{d(S-W)}{d(x-W)} = \frac{d(S-W)\Big/d\theta}{d(x-W)\Big/d\theta} = \frac{-W_\theta}{(1-W_x)dx\Big/d\theta - W_\theta} \tag{18}$$

The agent's marginal profit share is never greater than one since W_x is between 0 and 1 (by proposition 10), and x is increasing in θ. This is in contrast to "classical moral hazard" where the marginal share may very well exceed 1 (see Holmstrom (1979)). In MHHI both risk sharing and production would be inefficient if the marginal share were greater than one.[37] (18) also implies that the marginal profit share is always strictly positive.

To be optimal the solution to (13) must also be feasible. This issue will not be explored in any detail here. The analysis will be limited to $x^{a*}()$ which solves (14). Above it was shown that agent risk aversion could by itself cause the solution to (5) to be infeasible. The following proposition shows that risk aversion on the part of the principal does not cause similar problems.

PROPOSITION 11: If $x^*()$ is feasible, then so is $x^{a*}()$.

PROOF: The assumption in the proposition implies that the partial derivative of (8) with respect to θ is always positive. Hence using the definitions in (15) the following condition holds at x^{a*}:

$$\forall x, \theta: -W_{x\theta}(x,\theta) + D_\theta(x,\theta) > 0 \tag{19}$$

---

[37] The relevant reference for this discussion is Wilson (1968)

Differentiating (14) partially with respect to θ yields,

$$
\begin{aligned}
&-W_{x\theta}(x,\theta) + D_\theta(x,\theta)G(x,\theta) + D(x,\theta)G_\theta(x,\theta) \\
&\geq -W_{x\theta}(x,\theta) + D_\theta(x,\theta)G(x,\theta) > 0
\end{aligned}
\tag{20}
$$

The first inequality follows since D and G_θ are both non-positive. G_θ is non-positive because the numerator is decreasing in θ since we may assume that x(t) is increasing in t for all $t > \theta$. Note also that the denominator in G does not depend on θ. The second inequality follows from (19) noting that $0 < G < 1$. Note also that the sign of D_θ is irrelevant for the argument. QED

The discussion in this section may be summed up as follows: Maximizing the principal's expected profit implies increasing risk as production in poor states is reduced; just like the agent's risk aversion, the principal's risk aversion has real effects. However, unlike risk averse agents principals' risk aversion has positive effects on efficiency. As risk increases with expected monopoly rent, the more risk averse principals will tend to sacrifice rent and choose more efficient production. Empirically this also implies that risk aversion tend to be negatively correlated with (endogenous) risk as would be expected intuitively.

7.   CONCLUDING REMARKS

This paper has provided an analysis of moral hazard when the action control problem arises from the agent's superior state information rather than because actions are unobservable. The agent's decision is itself readily observable, but there is no way to determine whether it is the right one under the circumstances. It is a moral hazard problem because it is sufficient for the principal to makes sure that the agent's minimum utility constraint holds in expectation.

The case of moral hazard with hidden information is of considerable interest in itself. The analysis also provides insight into the general problem of moral hazard. The focus is more on action incentives than risk sharing. The model's simple structure makes it comparatively easy to give an interpretation of the solution, and the tradeoff between action incentives and risk sharing is transparent. However, to actually calculate the optimal solution is hard.

Moral hazard with hidden information is quite closely related to adverse selection. Incentive compatibility constraints are identical - only individual participation constraints differ. The fact that the sets of feasible sharing rules have a similar structure in the two problems, allows considerable simplification.

However, the optimal production plans are different under moral hazard and adverse selection. It is shown that production plans are uniformly more efficient under moral hazard compared with corresponding adverse selection problems. Inefficiency will still obtain when the agent is risk averse since the production plan must be modified relative to first best to reduce risk imposed on the agent. In moral hazard with perfect hidden information revenue risk is endogenous. Surprisingly revenue risk will tend to increase in the agent's risk aversion as the second-best production plan has wider support.

The principal's aversion to risk is of interest as well. Unlike the agent's risk aversion the principal's aversion to risk may also affect the production plan under adverse selection since the principal faces uncertainty even when the agent is fully informed. In this paper it is demonstrated that efficiency is positively related to the principal's degree of risk aversion. The reason is that the principal faces a tradeoff between monopoly rent and risk.

The paper also shows that the relationship between risk and incentives is complex in hidden information models as in most other models of moral hazard (with the exception of the simplest ones). It is shown that the changes in exogenous risk have ambiguous effects on incentive strength and efficiency. Another feature is that the concept of risk is ambiguous. A reduction in exogenous cost risk may very well imply an increase in endogenous revenue (output) risk.

In the particular hidden information model studied in this paper, it is clear that the principal prefers an informed agent to an uninformed one. One reason is that an informed agent may be prevented from using his information to harm the principal. However, it is in the principal's best interest (and indeed a social optimum) that the agent does not obtain information until he is committed to completing his task.

A crucial, simplifying assumption is that agents obtain *perfect*, information before choosing their decisions. A relaxation of this assumption would provide a natural extension of the model. However, such an extension is in general nontrivial as demand for real communication may arise. Whether it is reasonable to label the resulting model a moral hazard model, is an open question.

This paper addresses outsourcing contracts assuming that outsourcing has been implemented. The outsourcing decision itself has not been subject to analysis. If insourcing is characterized by agents who are uninformed, protected from risk and tightly controlled, the outsourcing decision will involve a tradeoff between improved decision making and larger risk premia subject to incentive constraints. This interesting issue will be left for future research.

ACKNOWLEDGEMENTS

I am grateful for helpful comments on variously titled earlier versions of this paper from A. Ziv, J. Yost, J. Demski, B. Jorgenson and especially S. Wielenberg as well as seminar participants at University of Florida, New York University, Norwegian School of Economics and Business Administration, Carnegie Mellon University and the IV EIASM Workshop on Accounting and Economics in Copenhagen.

REFERENCES

Arrow, Kenneth, "The economics of agency", in Pratt, J. W. and Zeckhauser, R. J., *"Principals and Agents: The Structure of Business"*, Boston 1985.

Baiman, Stan. and Sivaramakrishnan, Konduru, "The Value of Private Pre-Decision Information in a Principal-Agent Context", *The Accounting Review*, Oct., 1991.

Baker, George. and Jorgensen, Bjorn, "Volatility, Noise and Incentives" working paper, 2003.

Baker, George, Gibbons, Robert and Murphy, Kevin J., "Relational Contracts and the Theory of the Firm", *The Quarterly Journal of Economics*, Feb. 2002.

Baron, David and Myerson, Roger, "Regulating a Monopolist with Unknown Costs", *Econometrica*, 1982.

Bulow, Jeremy and Roberts, John, "The Simple Economics of Optimal Auctions", *Journal of Political Economy,* 1989.

Christensen, John, "Communication in Agencies", *Bell Journal of Economics*, Autumn, 1981.

Cremer, Jacques and Khalil, Fahad, "Collecting Information before Signing a Contract", The American Economic Review, Vol. 82, no. 3 (Jun., 1992), 566-578.

Farlee, Mitchell A., "Welfare Effects of Timely Reporting", Review of Accounting Studies, 3, 289-320 (1998)

Gjesdal, Froystein, "Information and Incentives: The Agency Information Problem", *Review of Economic Studies*, 1982.

Grossman, Sanford and Hart, Oliver, "An Analysis of the Principal-Agent Problem", *Econometrica*, 1983.

Hart, Oliver, "Optimal Labour Contracts Under Asymmetric Information: An Introduction", *Review of Economic Studies*, 52, 1983.

Hart, Oliver and Holmstrom, Bengt, "The Theory of Contracts" in Bewley, T. F. (ed.) *"Advances in Economic Theory Fifth World Congress"*, Cambridge University Press, 1987.

Holmstrom, Bengt, "Moral hazard and Observability", *Bell Journal of Economics*, 1979.

Holmstrom, Bengt and Milgrom, Paul, "Aggregation and Linearity in the Provision of Intertemporal Incentives", *Econometrica*, 1987.

_____, "Multi-task Principal-Agent Analyses: Incentive Contracts, Asset Ownership and Job Design," *Journal of Law, Economics and Organization,* 1992.

Holmstrom, Bengt and Weiss, Laurence, "Managerial Incentives, Investment and Aggregate Implications: Scale Effects", *Review of Economic Studies*, 50, 1985.

Jewitt, Ian, "Justifying the First-Order Approach to Principal-Agent Problems", *Econometrica*, 1988.

Mussa, Michael and Rosen, Sherwin, "Monopoly and product quality", *Journal of Economic Theory*, 1978.

Myerson, Roger, "Incentive Compatibility and the Bargaining Problem", *Econometrica*, 1979.

_____, *"Game Theory: Analysis of Conflict"*, Harvard University Press, 1991.

Penno, Mark, "Asymmetry of of pre-decision information and managerial accounting" *Journal of Accounting Research*, Spring, 1984.

_____, "Accounting Systems, Participation in Budgeting, and Performance Evaluation", *The Accounting Review*, April, 1990.

Pratt, John W., "Risk aversion in the small and in the large", *Econometrica*, 1964.

Prendergast, Candice, "The Tenuous Trade-off Between Risk and Incentives", *Journal of Political Economy*, 2002.

Rasmusen, Eric, *"Games and Information: An Introduction to Game Theory"*, New York, 1989.

Rogerson, William, "The First-Order Approach to Principal-Agent Problems", *Econometrica*, 1985.

Ross, Steven, "The Economic Theory of Agency: The Principal's problem", *American Economic Review*, 1973.

Salanié, Bernard, "Selection adverse et aversion pour le risque", *Annalés d'Économie et de Statistique*, 18, 1990.

Sappington, David, "Limited Liability Contracts between Principal and Agent", *Journal of Economic* Theory, 1983.

Shavell, Steven, "Risk Sharing and Incentives in the Principal and Agent Relationship", *Bell Journal of Economics*, 1979.

Wilson, Robert B., "Theory of Syndicates", *Econometrica*, 1968.

Chapter 6

ON THE SUBTLETIES OF THE PRINCIPAL-AGENT MODEL

Thomas Hemmer
University of Houston

Abstract: In this essay I focus on the equilibrium relation between the "risk" in a performance measure and the "strength" of the controlling agent's "incentives." The main motivation is that a large (mainly empirical) literature has developed postulating that the key implication of the principal-agent model is that this relation be negative. I first show that a standard principal-agent model, e.g., Holmström (1979), offers no equilibrium prediction about the relation between "risk" and "incentives." Next, I show that except in the highly stylized limiting Brownian version of Holmström and Milgrom (1987), this model doesn't yield a directional prediction for the equilibrium relation between "risk" and "incentives" either. This is due to the general property that risk arises endogenously in such principal-agent models. This, in turn, establishes that while the mixed empirical evidence on this relation may be useful from a descriptive vantage point, it does not shed any light on the validity of the principal-agent theory.

Keywords: Agency Theory, Incentives, Risk.

1.   Introduction.

One of the key advances in modern accounting thought was due to the eventual realization that fully understanding accounting without understanding the nature of the demand for accounting is not a possibility. The move to build a new understanding of accounting practices and principles from rigorous theoretical models of settings in which accounting information has real economic implications was, to a large part, due the efforts of Joel Demski starting in the second half of the nineteen sixties. The formal foundation for much of his and related work is the principal-agent model. While seemingly simple, this model, even in its most basic form, has proven to contain enough richness to identify missed subtleties and other shortcomings of relying on common wisdom and/or (casual) economic intuition in developing accounting theory. This in turn has led to a much richer understanding of the role of accounting numbers in facilitating economic exchanges.

Unfortunately, however, as strands of the literature has moved away from its origin, the theory itself has been assigned attributes that originate in casual economic intuition - not in the model itself. This is particularly true for the empirical literature that has focused on testing the validity of the principal-agent theory. A key catalyst for the development of the empirical principal-agent literature was Jensen and Murphy (1990). In their study they documented an average pay-performance sensitivity for a sample of CEO's of only around 0.3%. This number, they concluded, is much too low to provide any significant incentives and, more importantly, not consistent with the levels predicted of principal-agent theory. Jensen and Murphy base this latter conclusion on the observation that in the case of a risk neutral agent, the pay-performance sensitivity predicted by agency theory is 100%. It is implausible, they argued, that the 99.7 percentage point difference between \first-best" and observed incentives can be accounted for by managerial risk-aversion.

In response to the conclusion of Jensen and Murphy (1990), Haubrich (1994) provided a calibration study based on the model developed formally by Holmström and Milgrom (1987). His numerical examples demonstrate that pay performance sensitivity of 0.3% may well arise in this model for plausible parameter values, thereby rendering this part of Jensen and Murphy's (1990) conclusion invalid. Haubrich's (1994) study also made it evident that attempts to assess the predictive ability of principal-agent theory based on the absolute strength of the pay-performance relation are unlikely to be fruitful. This in turn prompted Garen (1994) to develop and test a set of comparative statics predictions about the pay-performance relation of a model also based on Holmström and Milgrom (1987). Most notably for this study, Garen (1994) predicts an inverse relation between inherent risk and the strength of the incentives provided to the agent, a prediction for which he finds only weak support in the data.

The weak nature of the empirical evidence in studies such as that of Garen (1994) appears to have motivated others to reexamine the empirical relation between risk and incentives.[1] Aggarwal and Samwick (1999), for example, suggest that the weak results reported by prior studies could be due to econometric problems. Specifically, a failure to control for differences in variance across firms.[2] After including such a control they find a strong negative association between pay-performance sensitivity and stock return volatility as measured by its variance. Since they argue that \[i]n most principal-agent models, the pay-performance sensitivity will be decreasing in the riskiness or variance of the firm's performance," they, in turn, interpret their empirical findings as providing strong support for the principal-agent paradigm.

In a more recent paper, however, Core and Guay (2002) argues that the study by Aggarwal and Samwick (1999) itself suffers from a lack of controls in the empirical specification. As Core and Guay (2002) point out, empirically there is a strong positive correlation between both firm size and compensation and between firm size and the specific risk-measure used by Aggarwal and Samwick (1999). Failing to control for firm size, they argue, therefore introduces a spurious negative correlation into Aggarwal and Samwick's (1999) regression. Core and Guay (2002) indeed document empirically that when a control for firm size is included in the Aggarwal and Samwick (1999) regression, the positive relation between risk and pay-performance slope documented by studies such as (for example) Demsetz and Lehn (1985) reemerges.

As does Aggarwal and Samwick (1999), Core and Guay (2002) also argue that an inverse relation between risk and incentives is a key prediction of the standard principal agent model (Holmström (1979)) and back up this claim with reference to the linear principal agent model developed by Holmström and Milgrom (1987). Accordingly, where Aggarwal and Samwick (1999) interpreted their result as strong support for the principal-agent model, Core and Guay (2002) view their finding of a strong positive relation between risk and the strength of the pay-performance relation as a rejection of the standard principal-agent model.[3] In addition, they argue that their results can be taken as evidence in support of the validity of the \managerial discretion hypothesis" advanced by Prendergast (2002).

By its very nature, empirical research always leaves room for attributing the findings of any one specific study to the failure to control for some particular omitted correlated variable. At a minimum, though, it appears that the aggregate empirical evidence on the pay-performance relation is not particularly supportive of the above mentioned hypothesis attributed to principal-agent theory. The purpose of this essay, however, is neither to critique nor expand the empirical evidence on the pay-performance relation and its determinants. Rather its purpose is to demonstrate formally that whether the available evidence suggests a positive or a negative relation or even no relation at all between risk and incentives, it cannot be used as evidence for or against the principal-agent model.

The reason is surprisingly straightforward: despite the persistent claims in the empirical literature, the standard principal-agent model simply does not provide a general equilibrium prediction on the relation between risk and incentives; the model allows this relation to go either way. This is certainly true in the case of the basic model explored by Holmström (1979). Moreover, except for the very special and somewhat implausible limiting case of the continuous time Brownian model, this is also true for the linear variant of the principal-agent model developed by Holmström and Milgrom (1987).[4] Indeed, as I demonstrate here, it is true even with the assumption that all agents are identical or if differences in agents' preferences and abilities are distributed randomly across firms (and time) and thus not subject to self-selection, an assumption on which much of the empirical literature on the principal-agent paradigm seems to be based.

Some intuition for why a positive and a negative relation between risk and incentives are equally plausible in standard principal agent models can be extracted from the following technical constraint. Production functions of the form "effort plus noise," where the "noise" can be taken to be exogenous, generally do not lend themselves to the first-order approach. Indeed, many of the known probability distributions for which a solution to the principal's problem can actually be obtained and studied share the property that they have support which is bounded from below.[5] Improving such distributions in the sense of first-order stochastic dominance necessarily implies that several moments are changing at once. Increases in the mean for such distributions commonly result in increases in the variance also as the distribution is "stretched out." Changes in exogenous production parameters that lead to increases in the equilibrium level of effort may therefore also lead to increases in equilibrium "risk" or variance. In such cases the model predicts a positive relation between risk and incentives if achieving the higher effort level requires stronger incentives. A negative relation is predicted only if the higher effort can be achieved with weaker incentives.

In the special case of the linear principal-agent model, presumably the agent's control extends only to the mean and not to the second moment - the "risk" of a normal distributed variable. Accordingly, the technical constraint detailed above for the standard Holmström (1979) model appears to be completely absent here. Furthermore, the variance of the output does appear in the denominator of the expression for the optimal weight on the performance measure in the agent's (linear) contract. This too certainly gives the appearance that the optimal weight on the performance measure is indeed decreasing in the performance measure's variance. As (e.g.) Aggarwal and Samwick (1999) put it, "the important feature of this expression is that the manager's pay-performance sensitivity, α_1, is clearly decreasing in σ_ϵ^2."[6] It thus appears that the empirical evidence at least could be interpreted as evidence for or against that specific model.

To understand why that is not a valid conclusion either, notice that the expression for the pay-performance sensitivity derived by Holmström and Milgrom (1987) is not the optimal solution to the principal's problem in that model. Rather, Holmström and Milgrom (1987) derive a simple approximation to the optimal contract, only to be exact for the very particular Brownian model obtained as the limiting case of their discrete model. I demonstrate here using the simplest possible version of their discrete model (the binomial) that it indeed has the same basic property as the standard model: changes in the expected output caused by changes in exogenous production parameters and resulting changes in the optimal (equilibrium) effort also affect higher moments (such as the variance) of the outcome distribution.[7] Depending on the particular properties of the production function, eliciting higher effort in response to changes in the production environment may, as in the standard principal-agent model, lead to either stronger or weaker equilibrium incentives.

I proceeds as follows. In section 2, I provide a parametric representation of the standard principal-agent model based on a Gamma distribution and demonstrate that for the standard model a positive and a negative equilibrium relation between risk and incentives are indeed equally plausible. In section 3 I analyze the binomial version of the model developed by Holmström and Milgrom (1987) to show that except in the limiting case of a Brownian motion, even in this model a positive and a negative equilibrium relation between risk and incentives are equally plausible. A brief conclusion is offered in section 4.

2. The Standard Principal-Agent Model

In general, agency theory centers on a simple moral hazard problem that arises due to two individuals' differing preferences, information, property rights, and abilities. The term \the standard principal-agent model" typically refers to a particular model of such a problem with a structure similar to that analyzed by Holmström (1979). In this model the principal owns the right to an uncertain future cash-flow, x. A productive effort, a, which can only be provided by an independent (risk-averse) agent arguments the probability distribution $f(x, a)$ guiding the cash-flow realization. The distribution is assumed to be enhanced by increasing levels of effort in the sense of first-order stochastic dominance. Thus, ceteris paribus, the principal always prefers higher levels of effort. The agent, on the other hand, is assumed to incur a (convexly) increasing personal cost of effort, $c(a)$, and therefore to prefer exerting less to more effort all else equal.[8] The moral hazard problem then arises from the fact that this effort cannot be observed either directly or indirectly from any other publicly observable variable.

Given the principal's inability to observe the delivery of the good he is interested in purchasing from the agent (i.e., the agent's effort), the principal's problem is to structure a contract that makes it in the agent's self interest to accept the terms and subsequently deliver a predictable level of effort at a cost acceptable to the principal. While a feasible solution involves paying the agent simply a fixed price for the effort to be supplied, such an arrangement can only be detrimental to the principal since it is immediately clear that with no claim to the final cash-flow, the self interested agent will end up supplying zero effort. Thus, if the optimal solution entails anything but zero effort it involves paying the agent partly in the form of a claim to the terminal cash flow, i.e., performance pay.[9]

An alternative (also feasible) solution is to sell the right to the entire terminal cash-flow to the agent up front. Clearly, this would eliminate the moral hazard problem and at least some of its potentially unwarranted consequences. The downside of this is that the risk-averse agent is now exposed to all the risk, some of which should be borne by the principal in a first-best world.[10] The undesirable nature of both these extreme contractual arrangements highlights that finding the optimal sharing rule in a standard principal-agent relation clearly does involve trading-off losses from inefficient risk sharing with improved managerial incentives.

Assuming for simplicity that the principal is risk neutral[11] and that the so-called first order approach is valid, the central problem can be summarized by the following maximization problem:

$$max_{s(x)} \int [x - s(x)] f(x, a) \ dx \tag{P1}$$

$$\int U(s(x)) f(x, a) \ dx - c(a) \geq \underline{U} \tag{IR}$$

$$\int U(s(x)) f^a(x, a) \ dx - c'(a) = 0 \tag{IC}$$

This program states that the principal maximizes his own utility by choosing a level of effort, a to induce and a pay schedule, $s(x)$. This pay schedule, in turn, must guarantee that the agent's opportunity cost is covered ($\underline{U}$ in the IR-constraint), and reflect the incentive problem present in the problem courtesy of the incentive compatibility or IC-constraint. In $P1$ the latter is represented by the (necessary) first order condition to the agent's choice of an optimal effort level. Thus the use of the term \the first-order approach."

Holmström (1979) provides the following characterization of the contract that solves $P1$:

$$\frac{1}{U'(s(x))} = \lambda + \mu \frac{f^a(x, a)}{f(x, a)} \tag{1}$$

where the LHS is the ratio of the (here risk neutral) principal's to the agent's marginal utility for income, $f^a(x, a)$, the numerator of the so-called likelihood ratio, is the first derivative of $f(x, a)$ with respect to the agent's effort, and λ and μ are positive Lagrange-multipliers associated with the IR and the IC constraints respectively. Since it can be shown that an optimal risk sharing arrangement is characterized by the ratio of the two parties' marginal utilities being constant, μ positive taken together with $\frac{f^a(x,a)}{f(x,a)}$ being non-constant in x

reveals that the optimal contract here indeed deviates from optimal risk-sharing in order to provide the desired level of incentives.[12]

The notion that the design of the optimal contract involves trading of risk-sharing losses with incentive gains appears to imply that, empirically more risky environments should produce contracts with weaker incentives.[13] It doesn't. While perhaps somewhat subtle, the reason why such a relation is not predicted by the trade-off reflected in the properties of the optimal contract (1), is simply that for this particular model, the known conditions that validate the first-order approach also imply that \risk" is an endogenous, not an exogenous variable and thus chosen as part of the optimal solution. The equilibrium values of both the multiplier μ and the likelihood ratio $\frac{f^a(x,a)}{f(x,a)}$ depend on the level of effort optimally chosen in the specific production environment. Accordingly, differences in exogenous variables that result in stronger incentives and higher effort may also result in higher equilibrium risk. In such cases, clearly the model predicts a positive relation between risk and incentives.

To verify that a positive association between incentive strength and firm risk by no means is inconsistent with the standard model, it will suffice to show that the solution given by (1) actually has this very property for some \reasonable" representation of the problem summarized by $(P1)$. To be \reasonable," such a representation must, in addition to not being too special to be even remotely plausible, but as mentioned above also satisfy certain conditions to ensure that the optimal solution indeed can be derived relying on the first-order approach. There are several such candidate (sufficient) conditions. Probably best known are the \Monotone Likelihood Ratio Condition" (MLRC) and the \Convexity of the Distribution Function Condition" (CDFC) first proposed by Mirrlees (1974). As proven by Rogerson (1985), if these conditions, which are both properties of the production function $f(x,a)$, arc mct, (1) docs indccd yield the optimal solution to the principal's problem.

Unfortunately, taken together the MLRC and CDFC are so severe that not only is it hard to find standard probability distributions that satisfy these conditions, the properties of distributions that do are not very amenable to the objective at hand for at least two reasons. First, distributions that satisfy MLRC and CDFC, at least the ones I'm familiar with, are simply not very attractive from the perspective of modeling something like stock values that empirically have very different distributions. Secondly, they are not easily ranked in terms of \riskiness" based on a simple measure such as variance either.

The undesirable properties of distributions that satisfy both the MLRP and the CDFC led to the development of an alternative set of (sufficient) conditions due to Jewitt (1988) . By imposing what are arguably somewhat modest restrictions on the nature of the parties utility functions, Jewitt (1988) shows that a broad class of standard production functions that avoid the problems of in particular the CDFC can be studied using the first-order approach. Most significantly for this study, the overall nature of the type of distributions admitted by Jewitt (1988) seems quite well suited for modeling variables such as stock prices. The example that follows is therefore chosen to satisfy the sufficient conditions of Jewitt (1988).[14]

Let the end of period (terminal) value of the firm be given as:

$$X = \frac{x}{k^\rho},$$

(2)

where k, which is an integer greater than 1, and ρ, which can be any real number, are firm-, industry-, or economy-specific exogenous variables, and x is a random variable with a Gamma distribution given by[15]

$$f(x, a, k) = \frac{1}{a} e^{-(x/a)} \frac{(x/a)^{k-1}}{(k-1)!}$$

(3)

where the managerial effort $a \in \mathcal{R}^+$.

While clearly "risk" and "noise" are constructs that are hard to devise a simple preference-free measure of in general, for the sake of argument I will here follow much of the empirical literature and focus on the variance of the measure to which the agent's compensation presumably is tied.[16] In this case this would be the variance of X. Straight forward integration by parts yields the second moments of the distribution given by (2) and (3) as:

$$\sigma^2 \equiv E\left[(X - \overline{X})^2 | a, k, \rho\right] = a^2 k^{(1-2\rho)}.$$

(4)

It can be noted that σ^2 is increasing in the agent's effort (a) here. Again, this is the result of a key property of many of the known distributions for which the first-order approach is valid: they exhibit constant support which is bounded below. Improving the outcome distribution in the sense of first-order stochastic dominance therefore implies that all moments of the distribution changes. Increased effort thus often leads to a more "spread out" distribution and thus to higher variance.

Although on the surface this appears to suggest that there would always be a positive correlation between variance and incentives for production functions with this property, since eliciting higher (variance increasing) effort presumably requires stronger incentives, making this conclusion would be premature. The reason for this is that the (equilibrium) effort the principal choose to elicit with an incentive contract is going to be determined by the only exogenous variables here, k and ρ, that also appear in (4). Thus, making any specific statements about the (equilibrium) relation between the strength of the incentives provided to the agent in this production setting and the variance of X, requires knowledge of the equilibrium relation between k, ρ, and a. This in turn requires knowledge of the agent's specific preferences for risk and effort. To actually be able to solve for the optimal level of effort as a function of the exogenous variables k and ρ, I rely on the following assumption about the agent's utility function

$$U(s, a) = 2s(X)^{\frac{1}{2}} - a. \tag{5}$$

Based on the production function given by (3) I can calculate:

$$\frac{f^a(x, a)}{f(x, a)} = \frac{x - ka}{a^2}, \tag{6}$$

which is linearly increasing in x (and thus satisfies the MLRC). Also, given the above assumptions about the parties' preferences, further mathematical manipulations of the model yield[17]

$$\mu = \frac{a^2}{2k}, \tag{7}$$

and

$$\lambda = \frac{U + a}{2}. \tag{8}$$

Given (5) the optimal contract, which now can be obtained from (1), takes the form:

$$s(X) = (\alpha + \beta X)^2, \tag{9}$$

Using (2), (6), (7) and (9) now yield the following expression the \weight" placed on the observable performance measure X:

$$\beta \equiv \frac{1}{2k^{(1-\rho)}}.$$

Now, also using (8), it then follows that

$$\begin{aligned} \alpha &= \lambda - \mu \times \frac{ka}{a^2} \\ &= \frac{U + a}{2} - \frac{a^2}{2k} \times \frac{ka}{a^2} \\ &= \frac{U}{2}, \end{aligned}$$

and the sensitivity of the agent's pay to the value of the observable measure thus is

$$\begin{aligned} \frac{ds(X)}{dX} &= 2(\beta\alpha + \beta^2 X) \\ &= 2(\beta\frac{U}{2} + \beta^2 X). \end{aligned}$$

Accordingly, the pay-performance sensitivity is directly related to β in this model. Since $\underline{U}$ is exogenous, a higher value of β implies a higher sensitivity of the agent's pay to the performance measure of X for all values of X.

Finally, because for this particular parametric representation of the standard principal-agent model the equilibrium level of effort induced by the optimal contract is

$$a = \frac{2k^{(1-\rho)} - \underline{U}}{1 + 1/k},$$

I can obtain a closed form solution (using (4)) for the equilibrium value of the variance of X as:

$$\sigma^2 = k^{(1-2\rho)} \times \left(\frac{2k^{(1-\rho)} - \underline{U}}{1 + 1/k} \right)^2. \tag{10}$$

Based on these closed-form expressions for the pay-performance sensitivity measure β and the variance of X, I can then state the following proposition:

PROPOSITION 1 *There exists a $\widehat{\rho} < 1$, such that for $\rho \in (\widehat{\rho}, 1)$, an increase in k leads to a decrease in both β and σ^2.*

PROOF: Suppose $\rho = 1$. From (10), then $\sigma^2 = \frac{(2-\underline{U})^2}{k+2+1/k}$ which is strictly decreasing in k, while $\beta = \frac{1}{2}$. Since $d\beta/dk$ is strictly increasing in ρ, continuity of $d\sigma^2/dk$ in ρ establishes the result.

In sum, $d\left[ds\left(X\right)/dX\right]/d\sigma^2$ for the basic principal model does not have a general sign. It can be positive, negative or zero depending on the exogenous production parameters' distributions.

3.   The Linear (Holmström-Milgrom) Model

While the basic tension in the standard principal-agent model is that between optimal risk-sharing and incentives, the analysis in the preceding section makes clear this does not imply that the standard principal-agent model of the type analyzed by Holmström (1979) among others predicts an inverse relation between (equilibrium) risk and incentives. As such, identifying empirical correlation structures that do not exhibit such an inverse relation cannot be used as evidence against the validity of the standard principal-agent model. However, while the empirical literature on the relation between risk and incentives often makes casual reference to the standard principal-agent model, the key source of the prediction typically appears to be a somewhat different model. Specifically, the so-called "Linear Principal-Agent Model" developed by Holmström and Milgrom (1987).

The linear principal-agent model has achieved a high degree of popularity among theorists and empiricists alike. From a theoretical perspective, the model's tractability, which allows for simple closed form solutions to the central choice variable in the basic theory (the optimal contract and, thus, the effort choice(s)), has allowed for insights into more complex agencies than appears manageable with the general model structure of the standard principal agent model. From an empirical perspective, the linear principal-agent model appears to make direct predictions about the regression coefficient of a standard OLS-regression since the optimal contract is a linear function of a normal distributed performance measure.[18]

Under the linear principal-agent model framework, the closed-form expression for the optimal contract is given by:

$$
\begin{aligned}
s(X) &= \alpha + \beta X \\
&= \alpha + \frac{X}{1 + r\sigma^2 c''/K},
\end{aligned} \tag{11}
$$

where, as in the previous section, α is the constant element (the \intercept"), β is the weight on the performance measure X and, thus the measure of \incentive strength," r is the coefficient of absolute risk aversion for an agent with a multiplicatively separable (in monetary wealth and effort) negative exponential utility function, σ^2 is the variance of X, c'' is the second derivative of the agent's personal cost of effort, and K is the marginal effect of the agent's effort on the mean of X. Accordingly, with r, K, and c'' positive, the appearance of σ^2 in the denominator of the expression for β is what gives rise to the prediction of an inverse relation between risk (σ^2) and incentives (β).

While this logic appears to be straight forward and thus on sure footing, it is none the less incorrect. The problem is that generally, the above expression does not actually characterize the optimal contract for the type of models studied by Holmström and Milgrom (1987). Rather, except in the highly implausible limiting continuous time case of their model which itself is to be viewed as an approximation to the more reasonable discrete problem,[19] (11) is an approximate solution to a dynamic principal-agent problem the specific nature of which I will explore in more detail below. The approximate nature of (11) is apparent even from the most casual reading of Holmström and Milgrom (1987) (emphasis added):

\Thus, we have determined a simple *approximate* relation between the action p to be implemented and the unique rule that implements it with certainty equivalent w for the case where single period risk is small.\

and later,

\The *approximate* forms (20) and (21) will be exact for the Brownian model (after change of variables).

To derive a Brownian model that *approximates* some discrete time model, we change our notation and normalizations as follows:....\

Since approximations may only work well locally, one has to exhibit restraint so as not to mechanically project the properties of the approximation onto the phenomenon being approximated. To verify that this is indeed a concern with the approximation given by (11), in the next section I derive the optimal contract for the most basic version of the agency relation underlying the linearity result in Holmström and Milgrom (1987). I then proceed to show that, in contrast to the approximate contract (11), the regression coefficient for the optimal contract is not monotone decreasing in the variance of the outcome distribution. The problem is that while it may appear that at least for the case of the linear principal agent model that σ^2 is truly an exogenous variable, it isn't. As for the model in section 2 it is simply one of the moments of the outcome distribution to be determined by the equilibrium effort level which in turn is determined by the properties of the production function and the preferences of the contracting parties.

3.1   The Basic Discrete Model

Holmström and Milgrom (1987) study the design of optimal incentives in a discrete model where the agent acts multiple times during the contract horizon to alter the probabilities over the feasible outcomes of a (stationary) multinomially distributed production function. There are a number of critical features of the Holmström and Milgrom (1987) model responsible for their results. On the production side, the production function is assumed to be stationary and not to exhibit any correlation between sub-periods. Also crucial for the results is that the agent learns the outcome realization of each sub-period before choosing his action for the next sub-period. From a technical perspective, the effect of facing an agent with such rich information is that the set of IC-constraints the contract must satisfy grows very large. This in turn severely limits the contractual forms available to the principal.

With the stationarity and time-independence of the production function and with the reduction in options available to the principal caused by the richness of the information available to the agent, the linearity result then follows from a careful choice of preference. In particular, in this model individuals are assumed to exhibit constant absolute risk aversion and only to be concerned with terminal (net) wealth. Moreover, in the case of the agent, his personal cost of effort is increasing convex and additively separable in each sub-period's effort. However, unlike, e.g., the standard model presented in Holmström (1979), the agent's utility function is not additively separable in utility for income and disutility for effort here. Rather, the agent's net wealth, of which his utility is an increasing concave function, is defined as terminal wealth net of his accumulated dis-utility for effort. Stated differently, dis-utility for effort is here measured in monetary terms rather than in utiles as in the standard representation.

To develop the linearity result and a closed form solution for optimal linear contract in the discrete Holmström and Milgrom (1987) setting,[20] assume that in each of the n sub-periods that make up the contracting horizon, the agent controls the probability of success (and thus failure) with his effort, a. For simplicity, let $pr\,(success) = a$, let the value of a success (the terminal cash flow implied by each success) be $K > 0$, and the value of a failure be zero in each of the sub-periods.[21] Also in the interest of parsimony, assume that the principal is risk-neutral while the agent is risk-averse with a negative exponential utility function multiplicatively separable in utility of consumption and dis-utility of effort, a coefficient of constant absolute risk aversion of one, and a quadratic dis-utility of effort function with a second derivative in each sub-period also of one. More specifically, let the agent's preferences be represented by the following (utility) function:

$$
U(W, a) = -e^{-\left[W - \sum_{t=1}^{n} \frac{a_t^2}{2}\right]},
\tag{12}
$$

where W is the total wealth accumulated by the agent at the end of the contracting horizon and $a \in \mathcal{R}^+$ continues (as in section 2) to represent the agent's effort.

Now consider the agent's problem in any given period $t \in [1, n]$. Let Ω_h denote the h'th of the 2^n possible outcome histories. Further let $\Omega_{h \neg t}$ identify the outcome history that differs from outcome history h in (and only in) period t. For the sake of argument and without loss of generality, I also adopt the convention that ceteris paribus, $\Omega_h \succ \Omega_{h \neg t}$. Differently stated, the t'th outcome for history Ω_h is $K > 0$. Also, let $A_t\,(\Omega_h)$ be the history of the agent's actions, subsequent to period t when the outcome history is Ω_h.[22] Finally, let the agent's compensation derived from realized history Ω_h be denoted Z_h and define for simplicity $B_h t \equiv Z_h \neg t - Z_h$. In the last period $(t = n)$, then, the agent's problem can be written as follows:

$$
\max_{a_{ht}} a_{ht} U \left[Z_h - c\,(A_t\,(\Omega_h)) + B_{ht} - \frac{a_{ht}^2}{2} \right]
$$

$$
+ b_{ht} U \left[Z_h - c\,(A_t\,(\Omega_{h \neg t})) - \frac{a_{ht}^2}{2} \right],
$$

where $b_{ht} \equiv 1 - a_{ht}$. The first-order condition to this problem is:

$$
U \left[Z_h - c\,(A_t\,(\Omega_h)) + B_{ht} - \frac{a_{ht}^2}{2} \right] - U \left[Z_h - c\,(A_t\,(\Omega_{h \neg t})) - \frac{a_{ht}^2}{2} \right]
$$

$$+ a_{ht}^2 U \left[Z_h - c\left(A_t\left(\Omega_h\right)\right) + B_{ht} - \frac{a_{ht}^2}{2} \right]$$

$$+ a_{ht} b_{ht} U \left[Z_h - c\left(A_t\left(\Omega_{h\neg t}\right)\right) - \frac{a_{ht}^2}{2} \right] = 0, \tag{13}$$

where $c\left(A_t\left(\Omega_h\right)\right) = c\left(A_t\left(\Omega_{h\neg t}\right)\right) = 0$ since here $t = n$ and period n is the last period.

Given the specific form of the agent's utility function summarized by (11), the agent's first-order condition in the final period can be simplified to yield

$$U[B_{ht}] + 1 + a_{ht}^2 U[B_{ht}] - a_{ht} b_{ht} = 0,$$

or

$$-U[B_{ht}] = \frac{1 - a_{ht} b_{ht}}{1 + a_{ht}^2}.$$

This, in turn, implies that the following expression for B can be obtained:

$$B_{ht} = \ln \left(\frac{1 + a_{ht} b_{ht}}{1 - a_{ht}^2} \right). \tag{14}$$

Accordingly, the marginal cost to the principal of eliciting effort from the agent in the final period is independent of the particular history and the optimal period n level of effort is therefore history independent as well. Accordingly, the equilibrium cost of effort to the agent in the last period is also history independent.

Now using the result that in the second-last period, $c\left(A_t\left(\Omega_h\right)\right) = c\left(A_t\left(\Omega_{h\neg t}\right)\right) > 0, \forall h$, (13) also characterizes the agent's effort choice in period $n - 1$. Accordingly, (14) characterizes the relation between the additional compensation to the agent for an outcome of K in period $n - 1$ and the agent's effort. Again, since there is no reference to historical (or future) events in this expression, the optimal level of effort induced by the optimal contract in period $n - 1$ is the same for all histories and identical to the optimal level of effort induced in period n. Through continued such backward induction it can then be shown that the lowest cost contract that implements an outcome distribution with mean $E[X]$ is the contract for which $a_{ht} = E[X]/Kn, \forall t \in [1, n]$, and all h.[23] Stated differently, a key property of the optimal solution to the principal's problem is that the agent is made to exert the same amount of effort in each and every sub-period regardless of the specific outcome history. Accordingly, $B_h t = B = \ln \left(\frac{1 + a^2}{1 - ab} \right), \forall t \in [1, n]$, and all h.

Given the result that the optimal pair (a, B) is the same for all n subperiods, and using the simplifying assumption that the agent's reservation utility is $U[0]$, I can write the IR-constraint as,

$$\sum_{j=0}^{n} \frac{j!}{(n - j)} a^j b^{n-j} U \left[\alpha + jB - \frac{na^2}{2} \right] = U[0], \tag{IR'}$$

where α corresponds to the constant part of the agents compensation in (11).

By again relying on the specific properties of a negative exponential utility function, (IR') can be re-expressed as follows:

$$(-1)^{n-1}(aU[B]-b)^n = U\left[-\alpha + \frac{na^2}{2}\right]. \tag{IR''}$$

Using (11) I can rewrite the above expression further to obtain

$$U\left[-\alpha + \frac{na^2}{2}\right] = (-1)^{n-1}\left(-\frac{a-a^2b}{1+a^2} - \frac{b+a^2b}{1+a^2}\right)^n$$

$$= (-1)^{n-1}\left(\frac{-1}{1+a^2}\right)^n.$$

Accordingly, $\alpha - \frac{na^2}{2} = nln\left(\frac{1}{1+a^2}\right)$ and the principal's problem,

$$\max_a na[K-B] - \alpha \tag{P2}$$

can thus be expressed as

$$\max_a na\left[K - \ln\left(\frac{1+a^2}{1-ab}\right)\right] + n\ln(1+a^2) - \frac{na^2}{2}. \tag{P2'}$$

The first-order condition to this program is

$$nK + n\ln n(1-ab) - n\ln(1+a^2) - n\left[\frac{a+2a^2}{1-ab} - \frac{2ab}{1+a^2} + a\right] = 0, \tag{15}$$

or

$$K - B - \Delta = 0, \tag{16}$$

where $\Delta \equiv \frac{a-2a^2}{1-ab} - \frac{2ab}{1+a^2} + a$.

What is interesting about this expression is that it reveals that not only is the effort, a, in any given period independent of history, the optimal level of effort in each period and, thus, the optimal amount of outcome-dependent pay, B, is independent of the number of sub-periods covered by the contract. Moreover, the amount of fixed compensation in the optimal contract is simply the amount the principal would provide if the agency only lasts one (sub-) period times the number of sub-periods for which the agency actually lasts. In other words, the optimal contract for an agency covering n sub-periods can be completely characterized by solving the principal's problem assuming that the agency lasts only for one period. Only the minimum payment the agent can receive in the n-period setting is n times α in the single period setting.

Worth noting at this juncture is that every success yields a terminal cash-flow of K and since the agent for every K units of cash flow receives a bonus of $B < K$, the optimal contract can be implemented as the following simple linear function of terminal cash flow, X,

$$s(X) = \alpha + \frac{B}{K}X,$$

where B/K thus is the slope coefficient or, alternatively, the pay-performance sensitivity, to be approximated by the expression for β in (15). The equilibrium sensitivity of the agent's compensation to the performance measure then can be written as

$$\beta^* = \frac{1}{1 + \frac{\Delta}{B}}.$$

Accordingly, the relation between the (exogenous) productivity parameter K and the pay-performance sensitivity is given by:

$$\frac{d\beta}{dK} = -\frac{\frac{da}{dK}\frac{d\frac{\Delta}{B}}{da}}{\left(1 + \frac{\Delta}{B}\right)^2},$$

and because $\frac{da}{dK}$ can be shown to be positive, the sign of $\frac{d\beta}{dK}$ is determined exclusively by the sign of $\frac{d\frac{\Delta}{B}}{da}$. Using (15) and (16) I can now calculate

$$\frac{d\frac{\Delta}{B}}{da} = \frac{-ba(a(a^2-1)^2 - (2 - 2a - 4a^2 + 3a^3 - 7a^4 + a^5 - a^6)\ln\left(\frac{1+a^2}{1-ab}\right)}{(1+a^2)(1-ab)^2\ln\left(\frac{1+a^2}{1-ab}\right)^2}.$$

$$(17)$$

Since the denominator is always positive, the sign of (17) is determined by the numerator.

For the sake of argument suppose now that the actual value of K implies that the optimal effort level is $a^* = \frac{1}{2}$. Then I can calculate

$$\text{Sign}\left(\frac{d\frac{\Delta}{B}}{da}\right)\bigg|_{a=\frac{1}{2}} = \text{Sign}\left(-\frac{1}{4}\left(\frac{9}{32} + \left(\frac{3}{64}\right)\ln\left(\frac{1.25}{.75}\right)\right)\right) < 0.$$

Accordingly, at $a^* = \frac{1}{2}$, the incentive weight β assigned to the agent is increasing in K. Furthermore, since for the binomial distribution we have

$$\sigma^2 = (a - a^2)nK^2,$$

I can obtain the relation between the exogenous productivity parameter K and the variance of the (aggregate) cash flow X as:

$$\frac{d\sigma^2}{dK} = \frac{da}{dK}nK^2 - 2a\frac{da}{dK}nK^2 + 2anK - 2a^2nK,$$

or

$$\frac{d\sigma^2}{dK} = n\left(\frac{da}{dK}[K^2 - 2aK^2] + 2K[a - a^2]\right).$$

Thus

$$\left.\frac{d\sigma^2}{dK}\right|_{a=\frac{1}{2}} = \frac{1}{2}nK > 0.$$

This leads to the following proposition:

PROPOSITION 2 *There exists a non-empty set $\mathcal{K}$, such that for $K \in \mathcal{K}$, an increase in K leads to both an increase in β and σ^2.*

PROOF: Follows immediately from the derivations above.

Proposition 2 summarizes the main result of the analysis contained in this section. Namely, even in the setting analyzed by Holmström and Milgrom (1987) the optimal contract does not necessarily change as a function of variance the way inspection of the approximate solution given by (11) would suggest. Again, this follows since the σ^2 that appears in (11) is not an exogenous variable. Rather, it is determined in equilibrium by the agent's effort and, thus, itself a function of the strength of the equilibrium incentives as measured by β.

3.2 Measuring Incentive Strength

The purpose of the analysis in the prior section has been to establish that although in settings of the sort analyzed by Holmström and Milgrom (1987), the expression (11) provides a good approximation to the optimal contract, (11) does not suggest that empirically, there should exist a negative relation between σ^2 and β. This section makes a related but different point. Specifically, that a reduction in the pay-performance sensitivity as measured by β does not imply that incentives are weakened. Thus, even in the cases where an inverse relation between σ^2 and β is established empirically, it cannot be concluded that there also is an inverse relation between σ^2 and the strength of the incentives faced by agents operating in such environments.

To see why changes in β cannot be taken as evidence of changes in the strength of incentives in the same direction, note that in this model the incentives for the agent is actually provided by B, not by β. The pay-performance sensitivity measure β simply represents what fraction of K is offered to the agent as a bonus. Surely, B is increasing in the marginal product, K. However, unless B is increasing \fast enough" relative to K, $\frac{B}{K}$ ($\equiv \beta$) will still be declining even as the strength of the compensation based incentives provided to the agent are increased. Specifically, if $\frac{dB}{dK} < \frac{1}{K}$, then $\frac{d\beta}{dB}$ is negative. This being more than a hypothetical possibility can be seen again relying on (17). Specifically, since

$$Sign\left(\frac{d\frac{\Delta}{B}}{da}\right)\Bigg|_{a=\frac{1}{4}} = Sign\left(-\frac{3}{16}\left(\frac{900}{4096} - \left(\frac{5203}{4096}\right)\ln\left(\frac{1.25}{.75}\right)\right)\right) > 0.$$

Accordingly, $\frac{d\beta}{da}\Big|_{a=\frac{1}{4}} < 0$. With $\frac{da}{dB} > 0$, $a \in (0, 1)$, $\frac{d\beta}{dB}\Big|_{a=\frac{1}{4}} < 0$.

While clearly this inverse relation between the pay-performance sensitivity β and the strength of incentives, B, doesn't hold for all equilibrium values of a, the point here is that it holds for some. Unless, then, the outside observer knows the exact properties of the incentive problem at hand, it is thus impossible to discern the strengths of the incentives provided from the observed correlation between pay and performance.

4.   Conclusion

Through a couple of specific yet quite standard examples, I make a simple point: the principal-agent paradigm does not yield a directional prediction for the relation between risk and the sensitivity of pay-to-performance. This is true whether one subscribes to the standard one-period variant popularized by Holmström (1979) or the dynamic \linear principal-agent" version suggested by Holmström and Milgrom (1987). In either case, the reason is simply that risk generally (as is effort and thus the strength of the optimal incentives) is endogenous and determined by the agent's effort in both these models. Accordingly, the empirical predictions one can extract from the principal-agent paradigm are not as straightforward as the empirical literature suggests that they are.

At some level the results contained in this essay are not particularly constructive. At least not in the sense of providing readily testable empirical predictions. Certainly they are not meant to be. This does not, however, imply that the results are not significant and useful. Identifying what is not generally true is not inherently less significant than finding special conditions under which something is true. Pointing out what agency theory does not predict is indeed important and useful. If for no other reason because a vast empirical literature has evolved over the last decade or so based on the (invalid) idea that the validity of the principal-agent model hinges on finding a negative empirical association between risk and incentives. The empirical results being mixed at best seems to suggest that this type of exercise could well continue for some time to come.

I acknowledge that pointing out that the basic premise of the above-mentioned type of empirical studies of the validity of the principal agent model is inherently flawed is unlikely to completely halt their production. By demonstrating the disconnect between such studies and the theory used to justify them, this essay could, however, at least help slow this activity and, in turn, help put the resources expended to a better use. This hope is the central motivation for writing this essay. Moreover, using agency theory to point out a missed subtlety in the perceived implications of agency theory itself seems to be a fitting way of paying tribute to the contribution of Joel Demski.

Notes

1. See Prendergast (2000) for a comprehensive review of the evidence provided by the empirical literature on the relation between risk and incentives.

2. See Aggarwal and Samwick (1999), page 67 for the specific argument.

3. Aggarwal and Samwick (1999) interpreted their finding as providing strong support for the standard principal-agent model.

4. This is significant since this model plays a central role as a source for the hypothesized link between risk and incentives at the core of the empirical principal-agent literature.

5. See Jewitt (1988) for a discussion

6. In Aggrawal and Samwick (1999), α_1 denotes the optimal incentive weight, and σ_ϵ^2 the variance of the performance measure.

7. All conclusions apply equally well to other variants of multinomial distributions analyzed by Holmström and Milgrom (1987).

8. Both $f(x, a)$ and $c(a)$ are required to be twice differentiable w.r.t. a.

9. If the principal is risk averse, compensating the agent in form of a flat wage is not optimal simply due to risk-sharing considerations.

10. In the specific case presented here where the principal is risk neutral, none of the risk should be borne by the agent in the first-best case. This, again, is the central argument underlying Jensen and Murphy (1990),

11. The assumption of risk-neutrality on the part of the principal is maintained for the remainder of this paper.

12. That $\frac{f^a(x,a)}{f(x,a)}$ is non-constant in x follows from the assumption that the agent's effort is valuable.

13. This is certainly the maintained hypothesis in the empirical principal-agent literature.

14. The analysis in this section borrows heavily from Hemmer et. al. (2000).

15. For simplicity I will refer to (3) as $f(x, a)$ henceforth. An example of an empirical counterpart is that the manager can affect operations in such a way that the distribution of future stock prices, which has support from zero to plus infinity, is shifted to the right in the sense of first-order stochastic dominance.

16. The fundamental conclusions offered in this paper does not hinge on this choice. It is made for consistency with the empirical literature and, to some degree, for ease of presentation.

17. Details available upon request.

18. As evident from the analysis of Mirrlees (1974), settings where the agent simply controls the mean of a normal distribution do not sit well with the principal-agent paradigm and certainly not with the first-order approach. To see this suppose $x \sim N\left(a, \sigma^2\right)$ so that $f(x, a) = \frac{1}{\sigma\sqrt{2\pi}} exp\left[-\frac{1}{2}\left((x - \gamma a)/\sigma\right)^2\right]$. Then $\frac{f^a(x,a)}{f(x,a)} = \frac{\gamma(x-\gamma a)}{\sigma^2}$ which is inconsistent with $\mu \neq 0$ in (1). Indeed, as shown by Mirrlees, for this type of production function, the first-best can be approximated arbitrarily close.

19. See the Holmström and Milgrom (1987) quote below.

20. For the purpose of the analysis in this paper a closed form expression for the optimal contract is required. As the focus of their analysis is somewhat different, Holmström and Milgrom (1987) does not provide such an expression.

21. Thus, the agent here is assumed to control the simplest possible member of the multinomial distributions: the binomial.

22. At time t only the costs of the current and future actions matter to the agent since the cost of actions taken in periods prior to time t is sunk and, thus irrelevant for the choice of period t effort.

23. To see this, notice that a_t enters linearly into $E[X]$, but quadratically into the agent's utility.

References

Aggarwal, R., and A. Samwick, 1999, The Other Side of the Trade-Off: The Impact of Risk on Executive Compensation. The Journal of Political Economy 107, 65-105.

Core, J., and W. Guay, 2002, The Other Side of the Trade-Off: The Impact of Risk on Executive Compensation: a Comment. Forthcoming, The Journal of Political Economy.

Demsetz, H., and K. Lehn, 1985, The Structure of Corporate Ownership: Causes and Consequences. The Journal of Political Economy 93, 1155-1177.

Garen, J., 1994, Executive Compensation and Principal-Agent Theory. The Journal of Political Economy 102, 1175-1190.

Haubrich, J., 1994, Risk Aversion, Performance Pay, and the Principal-Agent Problem. The Journal of Political Economy 102, 258-276.

Hemmer, T, O. Kim, and R. Verrecchia, 2000, Introducing Convexity into Optimal Compensation Contracts. Journal of Accounting and Economics 28, 307-327.

Holmström, B., 1979, Moral Hazard and Observability. Bell Journal of Economics 10, 74-91.

Holmström, B., and P. Milgrom, 1987, Aggregation and Linearity in the Provision of Intertemporal Incentives. Econometrica 55, 303-28.

Jensen, M., and K. Murphy, 1990, Performance Pay and Top Management Incentives. The Journal of Political Economy 98, 225-264.

Jewitt, I., 1988, Justifying the First-Order Approach to Principal-Agent Problems. Econometrica 56, 1177-1190.

Mirrlees, J., 1974, Notes on Welfare Economics, Information and Uncertainty. In Balch, McFadden, and Wu, editors, Essays on Economic Behavior under Uncertainty, Amsterdam: North Holland.

Prendergast, C., 2000, What Trade-Off of Risk and Incentives. American Economic Review Papers and Proceedings, 421-425.

Prendergast, C., 2002, The Tenuous Trade-Off of Risk and Incentives. The Journal of Political Economy 110, 1071-1103.

Rogerson, W., 1985, The First-Order Approach to Principal-Agent Problems. Econometrica 53, 1357-1367.

PART II

APPLIED THEORY

Chapter 7

INCENTIVE PROBLEMS AND INVESTMENT TIMING OPTIONS

Rick Antle,[1] Peter Bogetoft,[2] and Andrew W. Stark[3]
[1]Yale School of Management, [2]The Royal Agricultural University (Denmark),
and [3]Manchester Business School (United Kingdom)

Abstract: We characterize optimal investment and compensation strategies in a model of an investment opportunity with managerial incentive problems, caused by asymmetric information over investment costs and the manager's desire to consume slack, and flexibility over the timing of its acceptance. The flexibility over timing consists of the opportunity to invest immediately, delay investment for one period, or not invest at all. The timing option provides an opportunity to invest when circumstances are most favorable. However, the timing option also gives the manager an incentive to influence the timing of the investment to circumstances in which he gets more slack.

Under the assumption that investment costs are distributed independently over time, the optimal investment policy consists of a sequence of target costs, below which investment takes place and above which it does not.

The timing option reduces optimal cost targets, relative to the case when no timing option is present. The first cost target is lowered because the compensation function calls for the payment of an amount equal to the manager's option to generate future slack, should investment take place. This increases the cost of investing at the first opportunity, thus reducing its attractiveness. In order to ease the incentive problem at the initial investment opportunity, the second target cost is also lowered, even though no further timing options remain.

Making the additional assumption that costs are uniformly distributed, we generate additional insights. First, circumstances are identified in which not only does the cost target for immediate investment exceed that for delayed investment but also the probability of immediate investment exceeds the conditional probability of delayed investment, results impossible in the first-best context. Here, relatively speaking, incentive problems shift the probability of investment away from delayed investment towards immediate investment. Second, incentive problems are generally thought to reduce target costs, relative to opportunities with no incentive problems, in order to limit the manager's slack on lower cost projects. Incentive problems, however, have more complex effects in the opportunity analyzed here. As a result, we are able to identify circumstances under which the target cost for immediate investment may be increased by incentive effects, relative to the target cost that exists in the absence of incentive problems.

Keywords: Capital budgeting, Incentives, Investment Options

1.   Introduction

There is an extensive theoretical literature in accounting on resource allocation decisions in organizations, the ultimate goal of which is to understand the role of accounting information and its alternatives.[1] Motivated by work on capital rationing and organizational slack, Antle and Eppen [1985] - AE - offer a simple model of investment under uncertainty and dispersed information. They show how an owner's optimal response to a manager's superior information and desire for slack consumption leads to a hurdle rate contract that balances, *ex ante*, the *ex post* costs of underinvestment (capital rationing) against organizational slack.

AE study a simple, one-shot investment opportunity with one manager and a given information structure. Many variations of this model have been explored, and usually show that inefficiencies in resource allocation can be reduced in a number of ways. Most obviously, the production of information about costs can improve decisions (Antle and Fellingham [1990] and Antle, Bogetoft and Stark [2001]). Less obvious are the improvements brought about by restructuring the resource allocation decisions themselves. For example, Antle and Fellingham [1990], Arya, Fellingham and Young [1994], and Fellingham and Young [1990] show that there are beneficial incentive effects of tying together the analysis of a sequence of otherwise unrelated resource allocation decisions. Arya, Glover and Young [1996] show that it can be beneficial to tie together the resource allocation decisions affecting multiple managers, regardless of whether the dispersed information arrives before or after the investment decisions. Antle, Bogetoft and Stark [1999] and Arya and Glover [2001] show how bundling projects and considering them at the same time can ease incentive problems.

The purpose of this paper is to explore the effects on resource allocation decisions of another possibility - opening an option to delay the decision. The economics and finance literatures have emphasized the importance of options to delay. For example, Ross [1995] states that '... when evaluating investments, optionality is ubiquitous and unavoidable.' Dixit and Pindyck [1994] argue that '... irreversibility and the possibility of delay are very important characteristics of most investments in reality.' We explore the effects of opening an option to delay the decision by expanding the model of AE such that the investment opportunity can be accepted, if desirable at one of two points in time, but not both. As in AE, the source of information asymmetry between owner and manager relates to the cost of investment at each point in time.

If the owner can commit to an investment strategy, opening an option to delay cannot result in a net harm to him. In particular, he can always commit to forego investment in the future and reduce the investment opportunity to a one-shot chance. Opening an option to delay, however, does not produce all favorable effects. While it gives the owner a chance to invest under more favorable cost circumstances, it complicates incentive problems by giving the manager a valuable option on future slack consumption.

The main intended contribution of the paper is in investigating in detail the form of the optimal contracting and investment strategies when there is an option to delay. We also study the effects of the option to delay on the probability of investing at various points in time, and produce some comparative statics for specific classes of cost distributions.

The remainder of the paper is organized as follows. Section 2 presents the basic model involving independent costs. Section 3 analyzes its solution. Section 4 produces some comparative statics that illustrate the effects of the incentive problems on investment strategy. Section 5 provides provides concluding remarks and directions for additional research.

2. Model

A risk neutral owner can invest in a project with a present value of \$1 when undertaken, excluding managerial compensation. The project can be started immediately, or it can be delayed one period. There is only one project, so the opportunities to invest now or later are mutually exclusive.[2]

The investment must be implemented by a manager.[3] The manager knows the investment required if the project is started immediately, and he will learn the investment required if the project is delayed one period.[4] The owner knows the joint distribution governing the investment costs in both periods. We assume that the cost if the project is implemented now is independent of the cost if implemented one period from now. Also, the owner and the manager agree on the distribution of future costs. We assume the owner can commit to long-term contracts.

To formalize these ideas, let the two points in time at which an investment can take place be denoted by t_0 and t_1, where t_0 is 'now'. Let c_0 and c_1 be the costs required to produce the project if the investment occurs at t_0 or t_1, respectively. If implemented, the project has a present value of \$1 at the time of implementation.

At t_0, the manager knows c_0. The owner believes c_0 is drawn from a probability distribution on $[c_0^L, c_0^U]$. Let $F_0(c_0)$ and $f_0(c_0)$ denote the cumulative distribution and density functions, respectively, of the probability measure. At t_0, both the owner and manager believe c_1 is distributed on $[c_1^L, c_1^U]$, with cumulative distribution $F_1(c_1)$ and density $f_1(c_1)$, independent of c_0. At t_1, the manager observes c_1. We assume that $\frac{F_0(c_0)}{f_0(c_0)}$ and $\frac{F_1(c_1)}{f_1(c_1)}$ are increasing in c_0 and c_1 over their respective supports. For simplicity, we omit subsequently the subscripts on the probabilities, and let their argument identify the distribution. Thus, from now on, $F_0(c_0) = F(c_0)$ and $F_1(c_1) = F(c_1)$.

The owner must transfer to the manager the funds required to carry out the investment. Let y denote the total amount the owner turns over to the manager. To create an incentive issue in the model, we first assume the manager can consume any funds transferred from the owner in excess of those required to carry out the investment. For example, if the investment is to be made at t_0 with attendant cost c_0 and the owner provides resources of y_0, the manager consumes the excess, y_0 - c_0. This excess is 'slack'. Second, we assume the owner cannot monitor the manager's slack consumption. Further, slack must always be non-negative, implying that the manager is not allowed to fund investment from his or her own resources.

It will be useful for us to decompose the resources the owner provides to the manager at time t into the cost of the investment, c_t, and the manager's slack, $s_t = y_t - c_t$. Slack plays the role of compensation in our model, and we refer to slack as compensation from now on.[5]

At t_0, the owner asks the manager to report the cost that would be incurred if the investment were to be undertaken now. The owner also asks the manager to report the cost of the investment at t_1, after he learns it. We assume the owner can commit to contracts, so he can carry out the resource allocation decision by constructing a menu of contracts from which the manager must choose.[6] The menu gives the resources allocated and whether the investment is to be undertaken at each point in time as a function of the manager's communication about cost.[7] Without loss of generality, the menu is designed to induce the manager to communicate truthfully the cost.[8]

The owner's objective is to maximize the expected net present value of the opportunity. His cost of capital is $\rho \geq 0$, with corresponding discount factor $k = 1/(1 + \rho) \leq 1$. The choice variables are the functions describing the manager's compensation and whether the investment is undertaken depending on the manager's cost report. Let s_0 be a function mapping the set of possible costs at t_0, $[c_0^L, c_0^U]$, into the non-negative reals; i.e., $s_0 \colon [c_0^L, c_0^U] \to \Re^+$. s_0 gives the manager's t_0 compensation as a function of his cost message. Let s_1 be a function mapping the set of possible pairs of costs, $[c_0^L, c_0^U] \times [c_1^L, c_1^U]$, into the non-negative reals; i.e., $s_1 \colon [c_0^L, c_0^U] \times [c_1^L, c_1^U] \to \Re^+$. s_1 gives the manager's time t_1 compensation as a function of his t_0 and t_1 cost reports.

We model the decision to undertake the investment with an indicator function. Let d_0 be a function mapping $[c_0^L, c_0^U]$ into $\{0, 1\}$, with $d_0(c_0) = 0$ representing no investment at t_0 and $d_0(c_0) = 1$ representing investment at t_0. Let d_1 be a function mapping $[c_0^L, c_0^U] \times [c_1^L, c_1^U]$ into $\{0, 1\}$, with $d_1(c_0, c_1) = 0$ representing no investment at t_1 and $d_1(c_0, c_1) = 1$ representing investment at

t_1. The mutually exclusive nature of the investment implies the decision rules must satisfy the constraint $d_0(c_0) + d_1(c_0, c_1) \leq 1 \ \forall c_0, c_1$.

Using this notation, the owner's problem is to choose $d_0(\cdot), d_1(\cdot, \cdot), s_0(\cdot)$, and $s_1(\cdot, \cdot)$ to maximize his objective function:

$$\int_{c_0^L}^{c_0^U} \int_{c_1^L}^{c_1^U} [d_0(c_0)(1 - c_0) - s_0(c_0) + k(d_1(c_0, c_1)(1 - c_1) - s_1(c_0, c_1))]$$

$$f(c_0)f(c_1)dc_0dc_1$$

subject to constraints guaranteeing:

1 The manager's compensation is non-negative:[9]

$$s_0(c_0) \geq 0 \ \forall c_0 \tag{1}$$

and

$$s_1(c_0, c_1) \geq 0 \ \forall c_0, c_1. \tag{2}$$

We assume that the manager requires the present value of slack received across the two periods to be non-negative (i.e., the manager's two-period reservation utility is zero). Constraints (1) and (2) assure that this is the case and, hence, no separate constraint is required to ensure that the manager is willing initially to accept employment from the owner.[10]

2 The manager has incentives to report truthfully the cost at each point he may be required to report:[11]

$$s_1(c_0, c_1) \geq s_1(c_0, \hat{c}_1) + d_1(c_0, \hat{c}_1)(\hat{c}_1 - c_1) \ \forall c_0, c_1, \hat{c}_1 \tag{3}$$

and

$$s_0(c_0) + k \int_{c_1^L}^{c_1^U} s_1(c_0, c_1)f(c_1)dc_1 \geq s_0(\hat{c}_0) + d_0(\hat{c}_0)(\hat{c}_0 - c_0) +$$

$$k \int_{c_1^L}^{c_1^U} s_1(\hat{c}_0, c_1)f(c_1)dc_1 \ \forall c_0, \hat{c}_0. \tag{4}$$

3 The decision function respects the invest/do not invest nature of the problem:

$$d_0(c_0) \in \{0, 1\} \ \forall c_0 \tag{5}$$

and

$$d_1(c_0, c_1) \in \{0, 1\} \ \forall c_0, c_1. \tag{6}$$

4 The decision function respects the mutual exclusion of investing at t_0 or t_1:

$$d_0(c_0) + d_1(c_0, c_1) \leq 1 \ \forall c_0, c_1. \tag{7}$$

Except for the last two sets of constraints reflecting the integral nature of the project and the mutual exclusivity of investment at t_0 and t_1, this model is the same as that analyzed in Antle and Fellingham [1990]. They emphasized the improvements that could be made by tying the terms of the second investment decision to the outcome of the first, which we will see is not possible with mutually exclusive investments. As we establish in the next section, the mutual exclusivity constraints dramatically affect the optimal investment and compensation policies.

3.   Analysis

The optimal investment strategy takes the form of target costs, c_0^* and c_1^*, below which the project is undertaken and above which it is not. The optimal target cost at t_1 is independent of the cost outcome at t_0. Given this optimal investment strategy, it is straightforward to establish the optimal compensation policy. The optimal compensation policy gives zero compensation at any time the project is not undertaken, and provides slack when the project is taken. If the project is taken at t_1, this amount of slack is the difference between the target cost and the actual cost. If the project is taken at t_0, the amount of slack is the difference between the target cost and the actual cost, plus the expected present value of the slack the manager would have received at t_1 if the investment decision had been postponed.

The following proposition formalizes this investment strategy and the associated optimal compensation policy.

PROPOSITION 1 *The optimal investment strategy, should it exist, has target costs at t_0 and t_1, c_0^* and c_1^* respectively, such that:*

$$d_0^*(c_0) = \begin{cases} 0 \ \forall c_0 > c_0^* \\ 1 \ \forall c_0 \leq c_0^* \end{cases}$$

$$d_1^*(c_0, c_1) = \begin{cases} 0 \ \forall c_0 \leq c_0^*; \forall c_0 > c_0^* \ and \ c_1 > c_1^* \\ 1 \ \forall c_0 > c_0^* \ and \ c_1 \leq c_1^* \end{cases}$$

An optimal compensation schedule for the optimal pair of target costs (c_0^*, c_1^*) is:

$$s_0^*(c_0) = \begin{cases} (c_0^* - c_0) + k \int_{c_1^L}^{c_1^*} (c_1^* - c_1) f(c_1) dc_1 \ if \ c_0 \leq c_0^* \\ 0 \ otherwise \end{cases}$$

and

$$s_1^*(c_0, c_1) = \begin{cases} (c_1^* - c_1) \; if \; c_0 > c_0^* \; and \; c_1 \leq c_1^* \\ \qquad 0 \; otherwise. \end{cases}$$

The manager's compensation at t_0 deserves more comment. As indicated above, if the reported cost is such that investment takes place, the manager's compensation reflects two effects. One, $(c_0^* - c_0)$, compensates the manager for his knowledge of c_0. The other, $k \int_{c_1^L}^{c_1^*} (c_1^* - c_1) f(c_1) dc_1$, compensates him for foregoing the expected present value of slack at t_1. This latter effect arises from the mutual exclusivity constraints, and is the main force in the model that both complicates its solution and differentiates it from earlier analyses.

Proposition 1, by establishing the form of the optimal decision and compensation policies, provides a major assistance in exploring their levels. In particular, Proposition 1 allows us to reduce the owner's problem to one of choosing the target costs, c_0^* and c_1^*, to maximize:

$$F(c_0^*)(1-c_0^*)+k(1-F(c_0^*))F(c_1^*)(1-c_1^*)-kF(c_0^*)\int_{c_1^L}^{c_1^*}(c_1^*-c_1)f(c_1)dc_1. \quad (8)$$

After some manipulation and rearrangement, the first-order conditions for optimal (interior) solutions are:

1 The partial derivative with respect to c_0^* equals 0, which produces:

$$c_0^* = 1 - \left(\frac{F(c_0^*)}{f(c_0^*)} \right) - k \int_{c_1^L}^{c_1^*} (1 - c_1) f(c_1) \, dc_1. \quad (9)$$

2 The partial derivative with respect to c_1^* equals 0, which produces:

$$(1 - F(c_0^*)) (1 - c_1^*) = \frac{F(c_1^*)}{f(c_1^*)}. \quad (10)$$

We examine these first-order conditions to gain insight into the effects of the timing option and the incentive problem on the target costs. It is well-known (see, for example, Antle and Fellingham [1997]) that the optimal interior target cost, c^{OS}, if there is only one opportunity to invest is the solution to:

$$c^{OS} = 1 - \left(\frac{F(c^{OS})}{f(c^{OS})} \right). \quad (11)$$

Comparing equation (9) and (10) to (11) shows how mutual exclusivity ties together the choices of the optimal cutoffs. Both the value of the option and the necessity of compensating the manager for foregoing future expected slack show up in (9) in a term subtracted from the right-hand side: $k \int_{c_1^L}^{c_1^*} (1 - c_1) f(c_1) \, dc_1$.

The effects of the probability of delaying investment are reflected in (10) by the scaling of $\left(\dfrac{F(c_1^*)}{f(c_1^*)}\right)$ by $(1 - F(c_0^*))$. Proposition 2 reports that these effects imply the optimal cutoffs when there is the possibility of delaying the investment are below the respective cutoffs with a one-shot opportunity.

PROPOSITION 2 *Assuming that c_0^*, and c_1^* solve the first-order conditions:*

1. *The target cost at t_0, c_0^*, is less than or equal to the target cost, c_0^{OS}, if the opportunity at t_0 is a one-shot opportunity to invest with incentive problems:*

$$c_0^* \leq c_0^{OS}.$$

   Further, if $c_1^* > c_1^L$, the inequality is strict.

2. *The target cost at t_1, c_1^*, is less than or equal to the target cost, c_1^{OS}, if the opportunity at t_1 is a one-shot opportunity to invest with incentive problems:*

$$c_1^* \leq c_1^{OS}.$$

Further, if $c_0^* < c_0^U$, the inequality is strict.

Proposition 2 establishes that the target costs at each time are never greater than their one-shot counterparts. The conditions that yield strict inequality are rather mild. The condition $c_1^* > c_1^L$ simply asserts that c_1^* is greater than the minimum possible level of c_1^L. The condition $c_0^* < c_0^U$ asserts that c_0^* is strictly less than its maximum possible level of c_0^U. Both conditions simply avoid an extreme solution and guarantee that there is some chance that investment will take place at t_1. Some investment will take place at t_1 whenever the option to wait is valuable to the owner.

Lowering c_0^* relative to the one-shot cutoff reflects two effects. In the absence of incentive problems, the owner has to balance off the net present value (NPV) of investing at t_0 against the expected net present value of waiting and making the decision to invest at t_0. As a consequence, whereas the NPV hurdle for a one-shot deal is zero, for a timing option it is the expected NPV of waiting to invest. The first of the two effects comes from observing that this structure carries over to analyzing a timing option in the presence of incentive problems, with one interesting twist. Relative to the form for a one-shot deal, the cost target is reduced by $k \int_{c_1^L}^{c_1^*} (1 - c_1) f(c_1) \, dc_1$. This expression represents the sum of the values of the option to wait *to both the owner and the manager*, as opposed to merely the value to the owner, as in the absence of incentive problems. That it also contains the value of the timing option to the manager entirely reflects the compensation for foregoing the expected present value of slack at t_1 that has to be incorporated into total compensation when investment takes place at t_0. The second of the two effects comes from noting that the manager's compensation for foregoing future slack is only relevant if the investment is undertaken at t_0. Everything else equal, this will push the owner to delay investment.

The presence of the timing option at t_0 has an impact on the optimal target cost at t_1. This impact comes from the favorable effect lowering c_1^* has on the incentive problem at t_0. The manager's compensation for foregoing future expected slack depends on the cutoff at t_1, c_1^*, both through the amount of slack the manager would get for any specific cost realization, $(c_1^* - c_1)$, and through the probability of getting this slack.[12] Both effects work in the same direction, so that the higher c_1^*, the larger must be the manager's compensation for foregoing expected future slack. Lowering c_1^* reduces the manager's temptation to report a high cost at t_0, forego investment at t_0, and preserve the option on his compensation at t_1. Everything else equal, this will push the owner to invest less at t_1.

Overall, at the optimum, as in other contexts, the owner will balance the savings in investment cost and managerial compensation achieved by reducing investment against the lost expected profits from foregoing a valuable project. Nonetheless, this balancing act is more complex with mutually exclusive investments, in part because of the effects that the investment and compensation policies at one time have on the situation at the other time.[13]

4.   Comparative Statics

We now examine a class of special cases in which costs are uniformly distributed. The previous analysis leaves us unable to describe generally the effect of changing cost distributions at either t_0 or t_1 on target costs. Further, it leaves open how the presence or absence of an incentive problem affects target costs at t_0 when a timing option exists. Assuming costs are uniformly distributed allows us to gain insight into these issues. It also allows us to further highlight some of the economic tensions in our analysis.

We begin by examining the effects of changing cost distributions on the optimal target costs at t_0 and t_1. We then compare these effects with those that occur in the absence of incentive problems. By so doing, we are able to identify the important economic forces that incentive problems add to investment decision-making in the presence of a timing option.

The following proposition contains the results of this analysis.

PROPOSITION 3 *Assuming $c_0 \sim U[0, \hat{c}_0]$ and $c_1 \sim U[0, \hat{c}_1]$, with $\hat{c}_0 > 1 - \frac{k}{2\hat{c}_1}$ and $\hat{c}_1 \geq 1$,[14] then (i) c_0^* decreases and c_1^* increases as $\hat{c}_0$ increases; (ii)*

c_0^* *increases and* c_1^* *decreases as* $\hat{c}_1$ *increases; and (iii)* c_0^* *decreases and* c_1^*
increases as k *increases.*

These comparative statics illustrate nicely the way the incentive problems
and timing options interact to affect investment strategy. By way of contrast,
with no incentive problems, the optimal investment strategy is to invest at t_1 for
any cost realization less than 1 and invest at t_0 for any cost less than $1 - \frac{k}{2\hat{c}_1}$.[15]
With no incentive problems, therefore, the optimal investment strategy at t_1 is
unaffected by changes in any of $\hat{c}_0$, $\hat{c}_1$, or k, and the optimal investment strategy
at t_0 is unaffected by changes in $\hat{c}_0$. For a further contrast, with incentive
problems but no timing options, the optimal cost targets, c_0^{OS} and c_1^{OS}, are
unaffected by changes in $\hat{c}_0$ and $\hat{c}_1$, respectively. Therefore, the effects observed
in Proposition 3 are primarily a result of the *interaction* between incentive
problems and the timing option.

We now illustrate a set of conditions involving the upper bounds of the
cost supports at t_0 and t_1 under which $c_0^* > c_1^*$. This result is of interest because
it is not possible for the t_0 cost target to be higher than that at t_1 under first-best
conditions if $\hat{c}_1 \geq 1$. The following proposition illustrates these conditions.

PROPOSITION 4 *If* $c_0 \sim U[0, \hat{c}_0]$ *and* $c_1 \sim U[0, \hat{c}_1]$, *with* $\hat{c}_0$ *and* $\hat{c}_1(\geq 1)$
parameterized such that:

$$\hat{c}_0 = \frac{c^*(1 - c^*)}{(1 - 2c^*)} \tag{12}$$

$$\hat{c}_1 = \frac{kc^*(2 - c^*)}{2(1 - 2c^*)}, \tag{13}$$

with $2 - \sqrt{3} < c^* < .5$, *then* $c_0^* = c_1^* = c^*$. *By Proposition 3, an increase in
the upper bound of the cost support at* t_1, *or a decrease in the lower bound of
the cost support at* t_0 *relative to those indicated in equations (12) and (13) will
produce circumstances under which* $c_0^* > c_1^*$.

This proposition specifically illustrates the potential for the incentives
problem to shift the *relative* balance of investment from one point in time to
the other, as captured by the relationship between cost targets at the two points
in time. In the first-best case, it is not possible for the t_0 target cost to equal
or exceed that for t_1. In the second-best case, the *relative* balance shifts in
favour of earlier rather than later investment, in the sense that the probability of
investment at t_0 is higher, relative to the *conditional* probability of investment
at t_1, in the second-best than in the first-best case.

To illustrate, initially we can observe that the conditions of the proposition
guarantee that the target cost in the absence of incentive problems, $1 - \frac{k}{2\hat{c}_1}$,
is interior. Further, under the conditions of the proposition, the ratio of the

probability of investment at t_0 to the conditional probability of investment at t_1 is $\left((1 - \frac{k}{2\hat{c}_1})\frac{\hat{c}_1}{\hat{c}_0}\right)$ in the first-best case, whereas it is merely $\left(\frac{\hat{c}_1}{\hat{c}_0}\right)$ in the second-best case.[16]

Indeed, under certain circumstances, the ratio of these two probabilities in the second-best case can exceed 1 when both $\hat{c}_0$ and $\hat{c}_1$ are equal and exceed 1. This, again, is something that cannot happen in the absence of incentive problems. Initially, working within the assumptions of Proposition 4, let the discount factor be given by:

$$k = \frac{2(1 - c^*)}{(2 - c^*)}$$

with $\frac{3 - \sqrt{5}}{2} < c^* < .5$. If the discount factor is parameterized in this way, then:

$$\hat{c}_0 = \hat{c}_1 = \frac{c^*(1 - c^*)}{(1 - 2c^*)}$$

Then, both $\hat{c}_0$ and $\hat{c}_1$ exceed 1, the conditions on $\hat{c}_0$ and $\hat{c}_1$ in Proposition 4 are satisfied, and, hence, $c_0^* = c_1^* = c^*$. In this case, the probability of investment at t_0 clearly equals the conditional probability of investment at t_1. By Proposition 3, a small decrease in k will produce an outcome where $c_0^* > c_1^*$. Given that $\hat{c}_0$ and $\hat{c}_1$ remain fixed and equal, the probability of investment at t_0, $\frac{c_0^*}{\hat{c}_0}$, will now strictly exceed the conditional probability of investment at t_1, $\frac{c_1^*}{\hat{c}_1}$.

A further question can now be asked. Can the *relative* balance of investment shift enough towards t_0 to raise c_0^* above the target cost which holds in the absence of incentive problems? This is a possibility that does not exist for one-shot investment decisions. The next proposition illustrates our results on this issue.

PROPOSITION 5 *Assume that* $c_0 \sim U[c_0^L, c_0^U]$, $c_0^L < 1 - \frac{k}{2\hat{c}_1} < c_0^U$, *and* $c_1 \sim U[0, \hat{c}_1]$, $\hat{c}_1 > 1$. *Let* $r = \frac{k}{2\hat{c}_1}$. *Define* $f(r)$ *by:*

$$f(r) = \frac{(c_0^U - 1 + r)(3c_0^U - 1 + r - 2c_0^L)}{(2c_0^U - 1 + r - c_0^L)^2}$$

Now consider only those $\{c_0^L, c_0^U\}$ *pairs that satisfy:*

$$1 - c_0^L = r(2 - f(r)) \tag{14}$$

Then, for a fixed $r = \frac{k}{2\hat{c}_1}$, $c_0^* > c_0^{NI}$ *if (i)* c_0^*, c_1^* *and the target cost at* t_0 *in the absence of incentive problems are determined by the appropriate first-order conditions; and (ii)* $c_0 \sim U[c_0^L, b]$, *where* $[c_0^L, b] \subset [c_0^L, c_0^U]$ *for some* $\{c_0^L, c_0^U\}$ *pair that satisfy equation (14) and* $b \geq c_0^* > c_0^L$.

This proposition thus defines conditions under which the existence of incentive problems increases the probability of investing at t_0. Essentially, it defines the trade-offs that are possible between the upper and lower bounds of the support of c_0 which allow for the equality of c_0^* and c_0^{NI} via equation (14). Hence, equation (14) defines a curve in (c_0^L, c_0^U) space, for a given distribution of c_1, such that points below the curve define lower and upper bounds of the uniform support of c_0 that, as long as c_0^* and c_1^* are identified as a result of the first-order conditions, produce the outcome: $c_0^* > c_0^{NI}$.

We illustrate $\{c_0^L, c_0^U\}$ pairs which satisfy equation (14) for a particular value of r for which $k = .9$ and $\hat{c}_1 = 1$. Thus, $r = .45$. Here, $c_0^{NI} = 1 - .45 = .55$. Table 1 illustrates a number of such pairs. Table 1 suggests that situations in which $c_0^* = c_0^{NI}$ for $k = .9$ and $\hat{c}_1 = 1$ are characterized by lower uncertainty at t_0 relative to t_1, as characterized by the relative spread of costs. Nonetheless, the mean expected cost at t_0 can be lower or higher than the mean expected cost at t_1 without the result becoming impossible. As a consequence, it is difficult to say much about the likelihood of the types of situations illustrated by Proposition 5 occurring in empirical situations. All that can be said is that such situations are not impossible *a priori*.[17]

Table 7.1.   Upper and Lower Bounds on the Support of First Period Costs That Allow $c_0^* > c_0^{NI}$

c_0^L	c_0^U
.404	1.00
.399	.95
.393	.9
.384	.85
.371	.8
.35	.75
.318	.7
.268	.65
.194	.6

5.   Conclusion

We characterize the optimal investment and compensation strategies in a model of an investment opportunity with managerial incentive problems and flexibility over the timing of its acceptance. Acceptance is possible at two points in time. In the first-best world, such flexibility is viewed as potentially providing real economic benefits. The investment opportunity has a real option embedded within it - the opportunity to wait to invest.

In the second-best world, as in the first-best world, the optimal investment policy consists of target costs, below which investment takes place and above which it does not. We show how timing and incentive effects interact to affect these target costs. The interaction of these effects is fairly intricate. The existence of the timing option reduces optimal cost targets at both points in time. The t_0 target is lowered because the compensation function at t_0 calls for the payment of an amount equal to the manager's option to generate slack at t_1, should investment take place. This increases the cost of investing at t_0, thus reducing its attractiveness. The target cost is also lowered at t_1 when no further timing options remain. Lowering the target cost in the final period reduces the value of the agent's option on slack, which eases the incentive problem at t_0.

By making the assumptions that costs are uniformly distributed, we are able to generate additional insights. First, circumstances are identified in which not only does the cost target at t_0 exceed that at t_1 but also the probability of investing at t_0 exceeds the conditional probability of investing at t_1, results impossible in the first-best context. Here, relatively speaking, incentive problems shift the probability of investment away from t_1 towards t_0. Second, incentive problems are generally thought to reduce target costs, relative to opportunities with no incentive problems, in order to limit the manager's slack on lower cost projects. Incentive problems, however, have more complex effects in the opportunity analyzed here. As a result, we are able to identify circumstances under which the target cost at t_0 may be increased by incentive effects, relative to the target cost that exists in the absence of incentive problems.

Acknowledgments

We thank Anil Arya, Stan Baiman, John Fellingham, Hans Frimor, Will Goetzmann, David Green, Mike Maher, Steve Ross, Martin Walker, Mark Wolfson, Rick Young and workshop participants at Columbia University, the Copenhagen Business School, Glasgow University, the University of Manchester, Northwestern University, Ohio State University, Stanford Summer Research Camp, University of Waterloo, the Yale School of Management for helpful comments on earlier versions of this paper. Earlier versions have also been entitled 'Managerial flexibility, Incentive Problems and the Timing of Investment', and 'Incentive Problems and the Timing of Investment'.

Appendix

Proof of Proposition 1

First, we prove that if investment takes place at t_1 for a cost c_1 then it will also take place if the cost is $\hat{c}_1 < c_1$. Assume $\exists\, c_0, \hat{c}_1$, and c_1 with $\hat{c}_1 < c_1$ such that $d_1(c_0, \hat{c}_1) = 0$ while $d_1(c_0, c_1) = 1$.[18] Then the constraint in the second set under (2) that guarantees c_1 will be reported instead of $\hat{c}_1$ when the cost is $c_1 \Longrightarrow$

$$s_1(c_0, c_1) \geq s_1(c_0, \hat{c}_1).$$

But the constraint under (2) that guarantees $\hat{c}_1$ will be reported instead of c_1 when $\hat{c}_1$ is the true cost provides:

$$s_1(c_0, \hat{c}_1) \geq s_1(c_0, c_1) + (c_1 - \hat{c}_1).$$

Collecting these results and using that $\hat{c}_1 < c_1$ gives:

$$s_1(c_0, c_1) \geq s_1(c_0, \hat{c}_1) \geq s_1(c_0, c_1) + (c_1 - \hat{c}_1) > s_1(c_0, c_1),$$

- a contradiction.

Second, we prove that if investment takes place at t_0 for a cost c_0 then it will also take place if the cost is $\hat{c}_0 < c_0$. Assume $\exists\ c_0$ and $\hat{c}_0$ with $\hat{c}_0 < c_0$ such that $d_0(\hat{c}_0) = 0$ while $d_0(c_0) = 1$. Then the constraint in the second set under (2) that guarantees $\hat{c}_0$ will be reported instead of c_0 when the true cost is $\hat{c}_0$ implies:

$$
\begin{aligned}
s_0(\hat{c}_0) \ &+\ k \int_{c_1^L}^{c_1^U} s_1(\hat{c}_0, c_1) f(c_1) dc_1 > s_0(c_0) \\
&+\ (c_0 - \hat{c}_0) \\
&+\ k \int_{c_1^L}^{c_1^U} s_1(c_0, c_1) f(c_1) dc_1.
\end{aligned}
$$

Because $\hat{c}_0 < c_0$, we have:

$$
\begin{aligned}
s_0(c_0) \ &+\ (c_0 - \hat{c}_0) \\
&+\ k \int_{c_1^L}^{c_1^U} s_1(c_0, c_1) f(c_1) dc_1 > s_0(c_0) \\
&+\ k \int_{c_1^L}^{c_1^U} s_1(c_0, c_1) f(c_1) dc_1.
\end{aligned}
$$

The constraint in (2) that guarantees c_0 will be reported instead of $\hat{c}_0$ when c_0 is the true cost gives:

$$s_0(c_0) + k \int_{c_1^L}^{c_1^U} s_1(c_0, c_1) f(c_1) dc_1 \geq s_0(\hat{c}_0) + k \int_{c_1^L}^{c_1^U} s_1(\hat{c}_0, c_1) f(c_1) dc_1.$$

Collecting the inequalities produces:

$$s_0(\hat{c}_0) + k \int_{c_1^L}^{c_1^U} s_1(\hat{c}_0, c_1) f(c_1) dc_1 > s_0(\hat{c}_0) + k \int_{c_1^L}^{c_1^U} s_1(\hat{c}_0, c_1) f(c_1) dc_1.$$

- a contradiction.[19]

The results above imply that there is a single cost target at t_0, c_0^T, and a possible range of cost targets at t_1 contingent on the cost reported at t_0. We denote this range by $c_1^T(c_0)$. We start by deriving some results about the properties of the compensation payments, $s_0(.)$ and $s_1(.,.)$. We begin the argument at t_1. Suppose $c_0 > c_0^T$ and c_1, $\hat{c}_1 \leq c_1^T(c_0)$. The truthtelling constraints at t_1 imply:

$$s(c_0, c_1) \geq s(c_0, \hat{c}_1) + (\hat{c}_1 - c_1);$$

and

$$s(c_0, \hat{c}_1) \geq s(c_0, c_1) + (c_1 - \hat{c}_1).$$

Taken together, these constraints imply:

$$s(c_0, c_1) - s(c_0, \hat{c}_1) = (\hat{c}_1 - c_1).$$

Therefore, the contract can be written as:

$$s(c_0, c_1) = a(c_0) + (c_1^T(c_0) - c_1) \ \forall c_0 > c_0^T \text{ and } c_1 \leq c_0^T(c_0).$$

Now suppose $c_0 > c_0^T$ and $c_1 > c_1^T(c_0)$. The truthtelling constraints for c_1 and $c_1^T(c_0)$ yield:

$$s(c_0, c_1) \geq a(c_0) + (c_1^T(c_0) - c_1);$$

and

$$a(c_0) \geq s(c_0, c_1).$$

This implies:

$$a(c_0) \geq s(c_0, c_1) \geq a(c_0) + (c_1^T(c_0) - c_1) \ \forall c_0 > c_0^T \text{ and } c_1 > c_1^T(c_0).$$

Taking the limit as c_1 approaches $c_1^T(c_0)$, we have:

$$s(c_0, c_1) = a(c_0) \ \forall c_0 > c_0^T \text{ and } c_1 > c_1^T(c_0).$$

Constraints (3), which require that all resources come from the owner, imply:

$$a(c_0) \geq 0 \ \forall c_0 > c_0^T.$$

Now consider the case when $c_0 \leq c_0^T$. By the similar use of truthtelling constraints, it can be shown that:

$$s(c_0, c_1) = b(c_0) \ \forall c_0 \leq c_0^T, c_1.$$

Now turn to the truthtelling constraints at t_0 for two costs, c_0, $\hat{c}_0 \leq c_0^T$. We have:

$$s(c_0) + kb(c_0) \geq s(\hat{c}_0) + (\hat{c}_0 - c_0) + kb(\hat{c}_0);$$

and

$$s(\hat{c}_0) + kb(\hat{c}_0) \geq s(c_0) + (c_0 - \hat{c}_0) + kb(c_0).$$

Taken together, these constraints imply:

$$s(c_0) + kb(c_0) - s(\hat{c}_0) - kb(\hat{c}_0) = (\hat{c}_0 - c_0).$$

Because this equation must hold for all pairs of costs no greater than the target, we have for some constant, e:

$$s(c_0) + kb(c_0) = e + (c_0^T - c_0).$$

The truthtelling constraints for a cost greater than the target, $c_0 > c_0^T$, and the target cost, c_0^T, itself give:

$$s(c_0) + k[a(c_0) + \int_{c_1^L}^{c_1^T(c_0)} (c_1^T(c_0) - c_1)f(c_1)dc_1] \geq e + (c_0^T - c_0);$$

and

$$e \geq s(c_0) + k[a(c_0) + \int_{c_1^L}^{c_1^T(c_0)} (c_1^T(c_0) - c_1)f(c_1)dc_1].$$

Taken together, these constraints imply:

$$e \geq s(c_0) + ka(c_0) + k\int_{c_1^L}^{c_1^T(c_0)} (c_1^T(c_0) - c_1)f(c_1)dc_1 \geq e + (c_0^T - c_0).$$

Taking the limit as the cost, c_0, approaches the target, c_0^T, from above, we have:[20]

$$e = s(c_0^T) + ka(c_0^T) + k\int_{c_1^L}^{c_1^T(c_0^T)} (c_1^T(c_0^T) - c_1)f(c_1)dc_1.$$

Using these results allows the objective function to be written as:

$$\int_{c_0^L}^{c_0^T} (1 - c_0^T)f(c_0)dc_0$$

$$- F(c_0^T)\left(s(c_0^T) + ka(c_0^T) + k\int_{c_1^L}^{c_1^T(c_0^T)} (c_1^T(c_0^T) - c_1)f(c_1)dc_1 \right)$$

$$+ k\int_{c_0^T}^{c_0^U} \left(\int_{c_1^L}^{c_1^T(c_0)} (1 - c_1^T(c_0))f(c_1)dc_1 \right) f(c_0)dc_0$$

$$- \int_{c_0^T}^{c_0^U} (s(c_0) + k(a(c_0))) f(c_0)dc_0.$$

The first two lines of this formulation of the objective function express the probability-weighted value of investing at t_0 whereas the second two lines represent the probability-weighted value of investing at t_1.

Now suppose we set

$$s(c_0) = a(c_0) = 0 \; \forall c_0 > c_0^T \text{ and } a(c_0^T) = 0.$$

To maintain incentives to tell the truth at t_0, we must have that $c_1^T(c_0)$ is a constant with respect to c_0 which we shall denote by c_1^T. Further, set $c_1^T(c_0^T) = c_1^T$. Is this optimal? Any increase in $s(c_0)$ or $a(c_0)$ must be associated with a reduction in $c_1^T(c_0)$ below c_1^T to maintain truth-telling constraints. But, as long as $c_1^T \leq 1$, reducing $c_1^T(c_0)$ below c_1^T is not in the interests of the owner because the owner values additional production. Hence, setting $s(c_0) = a(c_0) = 0$ $\forall c_0 > c_0^T$ and having a single cost target at t_1 is optimal from the owner's point of view. Further, it is clearly optimal to set $a(c_0^T) = 0$ as the economizing solution.

In addition, $b(c_0)$ does not appear in the objective function and, hence, can be arbitrarily set equal to 0. Given the above, we get:

$$s(c_0, c_1) = (c_1^T - c_1) \; \forall c_1 \leq c_1^T \text{ and } \forall c_0 > c_0^T;$$

and

$$s(c_0, c_1) = 0 \; \forall c_1 > c_1^T \text{ and } \forall c_0 > c_0^T;$$

and

$$s(c_0, c_1) = 0 \; \forall c_0 \leq c_0^T \text{ and } c_1;$$

and

$$s(c_0) = (c_0^T - c_0) + k \int_{c_1^L}^{c_1^T} (c_1^T - c_1) f(c_1) dc_1 \; \forall c_0 \leq c_0^T.$$

These are the forms of the optimal compensation functions given in the proposition.[21]

Given that these compensation functions must hold for arbitrary c_0^T and c_1^T, they must also hold for the optimal target costs, c_0^* and c_1^*.

Proof of Proposition 2

For c_0^* and c_1^* derived from the appropriate first-order conditions, c_1^* is determined by solving:

$$(1 - F(c_0^*))(1 - c_1^*) = \left(\frac{F(c_1^*)}{f(c_1^*)} \right).$$

An interior c_1^{OS} is determined by solving:

$$1 - c_1^{OS} = \left(\frac{F(c_1^{OS})}{f(c_1^{OS})} \right).$$

For an optimal c_0^* derived from the first-order conditions:

$$1 - F(c_0^*) \leq 1.$$

Given that $\frac{F(c_1)}{f(c_1)}$ is increasing in c_1 it must be the case that $c_1^* \leq c_1^{OS}$. Further, unless $F(c_0^*) = 0$ or, equivalently, $c_0^* = c_0^L$, then $c_1^* < c_1^{OS}$.
c_0^* is determined by solving:

$$c_0^* = 1 - \left(\frac{F(c_0^*)}{f(c_0^*)}\right) - k \int_{c_1^L}^{c_1^*} (1 - c_1) f(c_1) \, dc_1.$$

An optimal c_0^{OS} derived from first-order conditions is determined by solving:

$$c_0^{OS} = 1 - \left(\frac{F(c_0^{OS})}{f(c_0^{OS})}\right).$$

$c_1^* \geq c_1^L$, therefore:

$$k \int_{c_1^L}^{c_1^*} (1 - c_1) f(c_1) \, dc_1 \geq 0.$$

Given that $\frac{F(c_0)}{f(c_0)}$ is increasing in c_0 it must be the case that $c_0^* \leq c_0^{OS}$. Further, unless $c_1^* = c_0^L$, $c_0^* < c_0^{OS}$.

Proof of Proposition 3
        Under the specified distributional assumptions, the first-order conditions for c_0^* and c_1^* reduce to:

$$2\hat{c}_1(1 - 2c_0^*) - kc_1^*(2 - c_1^*) = 0 \tag{7.A.1}$$

and

$$\hat{c}_0(1 - 2c_1^*) - c_0^*(1 - c_1^*) = 0 \tag{7.A.2}$$

respectively.
        We wish to identify the effects of varying $\hat{c}_0$, $\hat{c}_1$ and k on the target costs. Let z represent an arbitrarily chosen parameter from the previously mentioned three. Let the left hand sides of equations $(7.A.1)$ and $(7.A.2)$ be represented by the functions $A(c_0^*(z), c_1^*(z), z)$ and $B(c_0^*(z), c_1^*(z), z)$ respectively. Then, matrix equation $(7.A.3)$ provides the basis for identifying the effects of varying $\hat{c}_0$, $\hat{c}_1$ and k on the target costs:

$$\begin{bmatrix} \frac{dc_0^*}{dz} \\ \frac{dc_1^*}{dz} \end{bmatrix} = \frac{1}{|J|} \begin{bmatrix} B_2 & -A_2 \\ -B_1 & A_1 \end{bmatrix} \begin{bmatrix} -A_3 \\ -B_3 \end{bmatrix} \tag{7.A.3}$$

where

$$J = \begin{bmatrix} A_1 & A_2 \\ B_1 & B_2 \end{bmatrix}$$

and A_i (B_i) is the partial derivative of A (B) with respect to the i'th argument of the function.

We have:

$$\frac{dc_0^*}{dz} = \frac{1}{|J|}(-B_2 A_3 + A_2 B_3)$$

and

$$\frac{dc_1^*}{dz} = \frac{1}{|J|}(B_1 A_3 - A_1 B_3)$$

where A_3 and B_3 are the partial derivatives of $A(c_0^*(z), c_1^*(z), z)$ and $B(c_0^*(z), c_1^*(z), z)$ with respect to the parameter of interest, z. We now prove that $|J| > 0$. From the first order conditions:

$$A_1 = -4c_1^U$$
$$A_2 = -2k(1 - c_1^*)$$
$$B_1 = -(1 - c_1^*)$$
$$B_2 = (c_0^* - 2c_0^U)$$

Therefore, using the first-order conditions, we get:

$$|J| = 2c_1^U(4c_0^U - 1) - k(2 - 6c_1^* + 3c_1^{*2})$$

Using differentiation, it can be shown that $|J|$ is increasing in c_1^* for $c_1^* < 1$. Evaluating $|J|$ at $c_1^* = 0$ suggests that $|J| > 0$ if:

$$c_0^U > \frac{1}{4} + \frac{k}{4c_1^U}$$

Given that $k \leq 1$ and $c_1^U \geq 1$,

$$c_0^U > \frac{1}{2}$$

is sufficient to ensure that $|J|$ is positive. Note that the requirement in the proposition that:

$$c_0^U > 1 - \frac{k}{2c_1^U}$$

ensures that this is the case.

Given that $\mid J \mid > 0$, we have:

$$Sgn[\frac{dc_0^*}{dz}] = Sgn[-B_2 A_3 + A_2 B_3]$$

and

$$Sgn[\frac{dc_1^*}{dz}] = Sgn[B_1 A_3 - A_1 B_3]$$

As a preliminary, note that for c_0^{OS} and c_1^{OS} derived from first-order conditions, $.5 = c_0^{OS} > c_0^*$ and $.5 = c_1^{OS} > c_1^*$. Now, the expressions for the signs of the various derivatives produces:

$$Sgn[\frac{dc_0^*}{dc_0^U}] = Sgn[-2k(1 - c_1^*)(1 - 2c_1^*)] = -ve$$

$$Sgn[\frac{dc_1^*}{dc_0^U}] = Sgn[4c_1^U(1 - 2c_1^*)] = +ve$$

$$Sgn[\frac{dc_0^*}{dc_1^U}] = Sgn[-2(-2c_0^U + c_0^*)(1 - 2c_0^*)] = +ve$$

$$Sgn[\frac{dc_1^*}{dc_1^U}] = Sgn[-2(1 - c_1^*)(1 - 2c_0^*)] = -ve$$

$$Sgn[\frac{dc_0^*}{dk}] = Sgn[-c_1^*(2c_0^U - c_0^*)(2 - c_1^*)] = -ve$$

and

$$Sgn[\frac{dc_1^*}{dk}] = Sgn[c_1^*(1 - c_1^*)(2 - c_1^*)] = +ve$$

This establishes the results in the Proposition.

Proof of Proposition 4

Equations (12) and (13) straightforwardly arise from setting $c_0^* = c_1^* = c^*$ in equations (7.A.1) and (7.A.2) and solving. For an interior t_0 cost target in the absence of incentive problems, we require $1 - \frac{k}{2\hat{c}_1} < 1$, or $k > 2\hat{c}_1$. Using this inequality produces the condition that $0 > c^{*2} - 4c^* + 1$ or $(c^* - (2 - \sqrt{3}))(c^* + (2 - \sqrt{3})) < 0$. Thus, we require that $c^* > 2 - \sqrt{3}$.

Proof of Proposition 5

If $c_0 \sim U[c_0^L, c_0^U]$ and $c_1 \sim U[0, \hat{c}_1]$, $\hat{c}_1 \geq 1$, then the first-order condition for c_1^* suggests that:

$$c_1^* = \frac{(c_0^U - c_0^*)}{(2c_0^U - c_0^* - c_0^L)}$$

Using this expression in the first-order condition for c_0^* produces:

$$2c_0^* = 1 + c_0^L - \left[\frac{k}{2\hat{c}_1}\right]\left[\frac{(c_0^U - c_0^*)(3c_0^U - c_0^* - 2c_0^L)}{(2c_0^U - c_0^* - c_0^L)^2}\right]$$

Let

$$r = \frac{k}{2\hat{c}_1}$$

Then

$$c_0^{NI} = 1 - r$$

If we require

$$c_0^* = c_0^{NI}$$

then using $c_0^* = 1 - r$ on both sides of the equation for c_0^* above produces an equation relating values of r, c_0^L and c_0^U that result in the equality of c_0^* and c_0^{NI}. Letting

$$f(r) = \frac{(c_0^U - 1 + r)(3c_0^U - 1 + r - 2c_0^L)}{(2c_0^U - 1 + r - c_0^L)^2}$$

this equation is:

$$1 - c_0^L = r(2 - f(r))$$

Using the same methods as in Proposition 4, we can then demonstrate that reducing c_0^U will result in an increase in c_0^* but not c_0^{NI}, thus producing the result.

Notes

1. See Antle and Fellingham [1997] for a selective review of this literature.

2. Implicit in this assumption is the constraint that the project cannot be undertaken, abandoned, then restarted. We assume the abandonment value of the project is so low that abandonment is never optimal after an investment has been made.

3. Because there is only one manager, coordination problems do not arise. See Kanodia [1993] for an analysis of a model involving coordination.

4. Implicitly, we assume that the manager has unique skill in implementing the project, and cannot be profitably replaced. See Section 6 below for a discussion of this issue. This assumption precludes any meaningful analysis of the assignment of decision rights, as in Baiman and Rajan [1995].

We also assume that the manager knows the cost at the time of any communication instead of simply being better informed that the owner but still uncertain. For analyses where communication takes place without the manager being completely informed, see Christensen [1982] and Kirby et al [1991].

5. Although slack consumption is the source of the incentive problem in the model, similar results can be obtained by assuming the manager has direct preferences for more investment (as in Harris and Raviv [1996]) or has a preference for the use of specific technologies.

6. The owner's ability to commit and the absence of a moral hazard problem on his part imply he cannot benefit by assigning the rights to decide on the project entirely to the manager. For an analysis of the problem of assigning decision rights, see Baiman and Rajan [1995].

7. We assume the manager will always turn over to the owner the proceeds of the investment if it is undertaken.

8. The owner's ability to commit allows the application of the Revelation Principle (see Harris and Townsend [1981] and Myerson [1979]).

9. These constraints also can be interpreted as implying that limited liability holds at both t_0 and t_1. An alternative set of constraints is:

$$s_0(c_0) \geq 0; \text{ and}$$
$$s_0(c_0) + s_1(c_0, c_1) \geq 0.$$

We do not use this formulation for two reasons. First, we regard slack as only consumable at the time it is provided - it is not storable. Interpreting slack as a lack of effort is consistent with this view. Second, as indicated above, we require that at no point in time can the owner insist that the manager use personal resources to fund investment. Hence, the manager always needs the owner to fund investment.

10. The general constraint that ensures that the manager's compensation is sufficient to overcome his opportunity cost of working for the owner is;

$$s_0(c_0) + k \int_{c_1^L}^{c_1^U} s_1(c_0, c_1) f(c_1) dc_1 \geq \bar{U} \; \forall c_0,$$

where we assume that $\bar{U}$ is the reservation utility of the manager for a two-period contract. If $\bar{U} = 0$ then, clearly, requiring that $s_0(c_0) \geq 0$ and $s_1(c_0, c_1) \geq 0$ is sufficient to ensure this is so.

We assume that the manager's reservation utility is zero because if, alternatively, the manager's opportunity cost is very high, just fulfilling it would require all the benefits from the investment be given to the manager. In such a case, the manager internalizes all the externalities associated with the effects of his cost message on investment, and there are no incentive issues. We concentrate on cases in which there is a costly incentive problem by restricting $\bar{U}$ to be equal to zero. The solution will then reflect a costly tradeoff between distribution and efficiency, i.e., a costly incentive problem.

The same is true for the resource allocation models in AE and Antle and Fellingham [1990, 1995]. For example, in AE's one investment model, there is no rationing or slack if the manager's opportunity cost is so high as to require he get all the rents. For an extensive discussion of the tradeoff between distribution and efficiency in a one period model, see Antle and Fellingham [1995].

We assume the manager's discount rate is the same as the owner's. This assumption implies neither party has a comparative advantage in storage, and helps isolate the effects of incentives and timing options.

11. The first set of constraints ensures that the manager will report truthfully at t_1 regardless of his t_0 report. The second set of constraints ensures that the manager will report truthfully at t_0, assuming the manager reports truthfully at t_1. These two sets of constraints are equivalent to the full set of constraints guaranteeing that the truthful reporting strategy is optimal for the manager.

12. The effect on the probability comes through the upper limit in the integral.

13. We could relax some of the key assumptions of the analysis above. For example, we could assume that owner and manager are not tied together over both periods. Therefore, suppose the owner commits to dismiss the incumbent manager at t_0 if the cost report leads to the deferral of the investment decision to t_1. He then will hire another manager to provide a cost report at t_1. We can demonstrate that a target cost strategy is still optimal. Letting the target cost solutions to this problem be denoted by c_0^{NC} and c_1^{NC} we can demonstrate that

$$c_0^* \leq c_0^{NC} \leq c_0^{OS}$$

Note that, in this case, the owner commits to fire the manager and not to rehire him with any positive probability. The rationality of this commitment relies heavily upon the existence of a rich and frictionless market in ready-made replacements for the incumbent manager. If the incumbent can only be replaced at a cost or, alternatively, has a skill advantage over competing managers, it would be difficult to sustain a commitment to fire and not to rehire the incumbent.

If the manager expects to be retained or rehired with any positive probability, the incentive problems caused by his expected slack at t_1 will remain. The analysis in our primary model could be adapted to consider the possibility that the manager's tenure will end after t_0, but we would expect the qualitative features of Propositions 1 and 2 will remain, as long as the probability that the manager's tenure extents to t_1 is not zero.

We can also consider the possibility of renegotiation prior to the investment decision being made at t_1 if investment has not taken place at t_0. We assume the renegotiation would take place after the manager has acquired information about the cost of investing at t_1. It can be shown that the optimal target costs would be those that would survive a renegotiation; that is, the optimal targets will be "renegotiation-proof." The optimal renegotiation-proof target cost at t_1, c_1^{RP}, equals the target cost that would hold if the project were a one-shot deal at t_1. As a consequence, the owner picks the optimal renegotiation-proof t_0 target cost, c_0^{RP}, to maximize:

$$F(c_0^*)(1 - c_0^*) + k(1 - F(c_0^*))F(c_1^{OS})(1 - c_1^{OS}) - kF(c_0^*) \int_{c_1^L}^{c_1^{OS}} (c_1^{OS} - c_1)f(c_1)dc_1,$$

resulting in the following first-order condition for c_0^{RP}:

$$c_0^{RP} = 1 - \left(\frac{F(c_0^{RP})}{f(c_0^{RP})} \right) - k \int_{c_1^L}^{c_1^{OS}} (1 - c_1)f(c_1)\, dc_1.$$

We can then show that: $c_0^{RP} \le c_0^*$.

Allowing renegotiation helps the manager and hurts the owner. The manager gets more slack at t_1 through the renegotiation, and this complicates the incentive problem at t_0. The owner has incentives to find ways to prevent renegotiation, such as engaging a third party to impose a fine on him should renegotiation take place.

There are some commonalities involved in the effects of relaxing the assumption of commitment, whether it is the commitment of the owner and the manager to their relationship or their commitment not to renegotiate. First, the t_0 target cost is reduced relative to that in the one-shot deal. Second, the target cost at t_1 is that which would obtain for a one-shot investment opportunity at that time.

14. The lower bounds on $\hat{c}_0$ and $\hat{c}_1$ ensure that c_0^{OS} and c_1^{OS} are both determined by the appropriate first-order conditions and, hence, so are c_0^* and c_1^*.

15. This can be shown by noting that in the absence of incentive problems, the project should surely be taken at t_1. Using this result in the owner's problem with constraints (3) and (4) removed gives the optimal cost cutoff at t_0.

16. Naturally, the absolute size of the probabilities might be decreased in the second-best relative to the first-best case.

17. A more dramatic result arises when incentive problems cause the owner to forego an otherwise valuable option to wait. The conditions for this are rather severe — it cannot occur when the solution to the target costs are given by the first order conditions, but the possibility is more than a knife-edge result. For example, let $c_0 \sim U[.7, .8]$, $c_1 \sim U[0, 1\frac{2}{3}]$, and $k = 1$. With no incentive problems, the optimal investment policy is to invest if $c_0 \le 0.7$ and $c_1 \le 1$. In the presence of an incentive problem, $c_0^* = .8$, and the option to invest at t_1 is shut down.

18. The assumption that $d_0(c_0) = 0$, i.e., with c_0 the investment is not undertaken in the first period, is implicit in the assumption $d_1(c_0, c_1) = 1$.

19. The independence assumption is implicit in the densities under the integrals. Independence is used for the last weak inequality in the proof.

20. We define $a(c_0^T)$ as the limit of $a(c_0)$ as c_0 tends to c_0^T from above and $c_1^T(c_0^T)$ as the limit of $c_1^T(c_0)$ as c_0 tends to c_0^T from above.

21. Because of the arbitrary choice of $b(c_0)$, they are not unique.

References

Antle, R., P.Bogetoft and A.W.Stark. "Selection from Many Investments with Managerial Private Information," *Contemporary Accounting Research* (1999): 397-418.

Antle, R., P.Bogetoft and A.W.Stark. "Information Systems, Incentives and the Timing of Investments." *Journal of Accounting and Public Policy* (2001): 267-294.

Antle, R. and G.D.Eppen. "Capital Rationing and Organizational Slack in Capital Budgeting." *Management Science* (1985): 163-174.

Antle, R. and J.Fellingham. "Resource Rationing and Organizational Slack in a Two-Period Model." *Journal of Accounting Research* (1990): 1-24.

Antle, R. and J.Fellingham. "Information Rents and Preferences among Information Systems in a Model of Resource Allocation." Supplement to the *Journal of Accounting Research* (1995): 41-58.

Antle, R. and J.Fellingham. "Models of Capital Investments with Private Information and Incentives: A Selective Review," *Journal of Business Finance and Accounting* (1997)*:* 41-58.

Arya, A., J.Fellingham and R.Young. "Contract-based Motivation for Keeping Records of a Manager's Reporting and Budgeting History," *Management Science* (1994): 484-495.

Arya, A, J. Glover and R.Young. "Capital Budgeting in a Multidivisional Firm," *Journal of Accounting, Auditing and Finance* (1996): 519-533.

Arya, A. and J.Glover. "Option Value to Waiting Created by a Control Problem." *Journal of Accounting Research* (2001): 405-415.

Baiman, S. and M.Rajan. "Centralization, Delegation, and Shared Responsibility in the Assignment of Capital Investment Decision Rights." Supplement to the *Journal of Accounting Research* (1995): 135-164.

Christensen, J. "The Determination of Performance Standards and Participation." *Journal of Accounting Research* (1982): 589-603.

Dixit, A. and R.S.Pindyck. *Investment Under Uncertainty*, Princeton: Princeton University Press, (1994).

Fellingham, J. and R.Young. "The Value of Self-Reported Costs in Repeated Investment Decisions," *The Accounting Review* (1990) .

Harris, M. and A.Raviv. "The Capital Budgeting Process, Incentives and Information." *Journal of Finance* (1996): 1139-1174.

Harris, M. and R.Townsend. "Resource Allocation Under Asymmetric Information." *Econometrica* (1981): 33-64.

Kanodia, C. "Participative Budgets as Coordination and Motivational Devices." *Journal of Accounting Research* (1993): 172-189.

Kirby, A., S.Reichelstein, P.Sen and T.Y.Paik. "Participation, Slack, and Budget-Based Performance Evaluation." *Journal of Accounting Research* (1991): 109-127.

Myerson, R. "Incentive Compatibility and the Bargaining Problem." *Econometrica* (1979): 61-74.

Ross, S. "Uses, Abuses, and Alternatives to the Net-Present-Value Rule." *Financial Management* (1995): 96-102.

Chapter 8

ALIGNING INCENTIVES BY CAPPING BONUSES

Anil Arya[1], Jonathan Glover[2], and Brian Mittendorf[3]
[1]Ohio State University, [2]Carnegie Mellon University, and [3]Yale School of Management

Abstract: A puzzling feature of many incentive compensation plans is the practice of capping bonuses above a certain threshold. While bonus caps are often justified on the grounds of keeping pay levels in check, it has also been argued that such caps can wreak havoc on a firm's incentive problems. In this paper, we study a setting in which bonus caps can actually help align incentives. When a CEO is impatient, she may be tempted to take a hardline stance with a privately-informed manager in project selection: if she places little weight on future flows, she is fixated on cost-cutting and curtailing budget padding. A bonus cap can soften the CEO's posture by inducing risk aversion and thus creating a preference for a middle ground. We show that this force can enable a judiciously chosen cap to achieve goal congruence between shareholders and a CEO.

Key words: Bonus caps, hierarchies, incentives

1.   INTRODUCTION

The centerpiece of most incentive compensation plans is the use of performance bonuses as a "carrot" to encourage performance. Typically, however, incentive plans place a cap on bonuses once performance exceeds a certain threshold (ceiling). The prevalence of bonus caps is something of a puzzle.

Bonus caps have been criticized as having significant downsides. Limits on bonuses can encourage earnings management, foster a reluctance to take risks and enact change, and create a general atmosphere in which attention is diverted from undertaking value-enhancing activities to gaming the reward system (Healy 1985; Jensen 2003). The fatalistic view of bonus caps is summarized by Colvin (2001), who decrees "[w]hen a company caps bonuses, something is wrong. Somehow leadership, organization, measurement, decision-making, and incentives are not aligned with shareholder value. If they were, limiting bonuses would be foolish (p. 58)."

In this paper, we revisit the issue of bonus caps and find that when a firm's hierarchy embeds several layers of incentive concerns, a pay ceiling can serve a useful role. While the conventional wisdom is that "purely linear compensation formulas provide no incentives to lie, or to withhold and distort information, or to game the system (Jensen 2003, p. 379)," this setting highlights a circumstance in which linear pay schemes introduce distortions. And, these distortions can be eliminated by introducing a simple bonus cap.

To elaborate, we consider a situation in which shareholders entrust a CEO with running a firm. The CEO, in turn, relies on a manager to assist in project implementation. The manager, having specific expertise and being proximate to operations, holds advance knowledge of the costs of a new project. In reporting this cost, the manager is tempted to overstate (pad) his budget in order to introduce some slack in the arrangement. In eliciting and utilizing the manager's cost report, the CEO's interests are also potentially misaligned from the shareholders. In particular, a common complaint is that CEOs exhibit a short-term orientation/impatience, reflected in the model by the CEO discounting at a rate that may be higher than the shareholders' discount rate.[38] The problem with an overly impatient CEO is that she is excessively aggressive in setting the bar for project approval, since she doesn't value the future cash inflows as much as do shareholders.

If the CEO's precise impatience level (her discount rate) is known to the shareholders, a linear contract can be used to achieve goal congruence. Unfortunately, the linear scheme loses its bite when the shareholders are not fully aware of the degree of CEO impatience; a scheme that works well at some discount rates is sure to fail at another discount rate. Our main result is that introducing a pay ceiling on the simple linear scheme, a bonus cap, restores the correct incentives for the CEO irrespective of the rate at which she discounts. A cap on the CEO's compensation serves as a cap on her aggressiveness.

Since the concern is the CEO undervaluing the project, it would appear that adding a cap to bonuses could only make matters worse. However, a

---

[38]   The CEO's shorter horizon is consistent with such discounting. That is, suppose the CEO and shareholders both discount future cash flows at the rate r, but the manager retains his job in the next period only with probability p. Then the manager effectively discounts future compensation (associated with retaining his job) at a rate of $(1+r)/p - 1$, which is greater than r.

cap also serves to induce risk aversion on the CEO's part: since a big success is not rewarded extra anyway, she is more willing to trade the rewards from setting a more stringent hurdle for the increased likelihood of a bonus that comes with a relaxed hurdle. In fact, a judiciously chosen bonus ceiling can ensure the shareholders' desired strategy will be followed regardless of the CEO's discount rate.

The induced risk aversion arising in our setting is akin to that studied by Fellingham and Wolfson (1985) in the context of progressive taxes. With progressive taxes, the higher an individual's income, the higher the faction of income she gives up to the tax authority. The induced concavity (decreasing marginal utility for wealth) makes even an individual with risk-neutral preferences in after-tax income act as is she were risk-averse in before-tax income.[39] Roughly stated, a bonus cap in our setting corresponds to a dramatic introduction of concavity: above the cap, the CEO loses all incremental gains.

Our result has a similar flavor as Dutta and Reichelstein (2002), which demonstrates that overcoming multiple incentive problems can be accomplished via residual income with appropriate depreciation and capital charge choices. In our particular setup, where incentive problems are spread out among multiple layers of a hierarchy, it turns out that capping a simple linear pay relationship can align incentives without placing demands on depreciation or capital charge rates.

Incentive problems stemming from hierarchies have been extensively studied (e.g., Baron and Besanko 1992; Demski and Sappington 1987, 1989; McAfee and McMillan 1995; Melumad et al. 1992, 1995). Given the variety of pay schemes analyzed in the streams of related literature, it seems apropos to stress that the objective of the paper is not to conduct a "horse race" between capped linear pay and other pay arrangements that too may achieve goal congruence. Rather, our goal is more modest: to highlight a benefit of placing bonus caps on simple pay schedules which may counteract the well-known costs of doing so. As such, the broader point of the paper is that bonus caps, even when unable to achieve perfect goal congruence, can serve to shift a manager's focus toward longer-term objectives. If a manager is inclined to concentrate on short-term self interest, putting a cap on annual

---

[39] In this vein, Arya et al. (2005) demonstrate benefits of progressive taxes stemming from reducing the aggressiveness of a buyer who contracts with a privately-informed seller. By smoothing after-tax payouts, the taxing authority is able to shift the buyer's focus away from cutting seller rents towards overall efficiency. The resultant gains can be shared among all parties with appropriate tax rates.

pay can help remove blinders and bring long-term interests, and those of the organization as a whole, to the fore.

2.   MODEL

A firm faces a long-term project which, if accepted, yields cash flows (revenues) of x_t, $x_t \geq 0$, at the onset of period t, t $= 1, 2, \ldots, n$. To reflect the project's long-term nature, assume $x_t > 0$ for some t > 1. The project requires an investment (cost) at t $= 1$ of I, I $\in [0, \bar{I}]$. Depending on the value of I, the project's net present value (NPV) can be either positive or negative.

That is, $0 < \sum_{t=1}^{n} \frac{x_t}{(1+\rho)^{t-1}} < \bar{I}$, where ρ, $\rho \geq 0$, is the firm shareholders' discount rate. The common knowledge beliefs over I are represented by the probability density function f(I), with the associated cumulative distribution function F(I).[40] We assume f(I) is differentiable and positive throughout its support. Also, as is standard, we assume the distribution satisfies the monotone hazard rate condition, H'(I) ≥ 0, where $H(I) = \frac{F(I)}{f(I)}$. Besides this project under consideration, the firm's other operations yield net cash flows of π_t in period t.

An incentive problem arises in our setting because the firm's manager is privy to the investment cost up front. Such an information advantage may be a consequence of the manager's expertise and/or his proximity to operations. The manager must be reimbursed for implementation costs incurred and can consume as slack any excess funds. Since the manager privately knows the investment cost, his temptation to overstate cost is clear.

One possibility is for shareholders to directly contract with the manager (as in Antle and Eppen 1985). This approach is implicitly costly, since a diverse set of shareholders are, by nature, difficult to coordinate. Typically, firms are characterized by a separation of ownership and operational control with shareholders leaving operational dealings to other parties, say the appointed CEO. The problem is that the CEO's objectives may also be misaligned with the shareholders' goals.

A frequently discussed reason for shareholders-CEO goal incongruence is referred to as the horizon problem: relative to shareholders,

---

[40]   Here, we model uncertainty as arising in the initial period. The results are unaltered if there is also uncertainty in cash flows of subsequent periods.

CEOs tend to take a more short-term view in making decisions. We model such relative impatience by assuming the CEO discounts cash flows at the rate λ, where $\lambda \geq \rho$. Though the CEO is, of course, cognizant of her precise discount rate, the firm's shareholders are not.

In this setup, in a spirit similar to Rogerson (1997), we look for an incentive scheme that can achieve goal congruence. That is, we ask whether the shareholders can specify CEO compensation so that the CEO's contracting with the manager results in the same project approval and funding decisions that would have been achieved had the shareholders directly dealt with the manager. To ensure solidified goal congruence, we seek a contract in which the CEO has strict incentives to do as intended; and, if the CEO is indifferent between choices, we assume she makes the decision that pleases the manager.

3. RESULTS

The setting studied here is one in which conflicts of interest on two tiers of hierarchy are compounded. To highlight the role played by the confluence of incentive problems, we present solutions that address the incentive problem from the bottom tier up.

3.1 Both I and λ are publicly observed

If both sources of incentive conflict are removed, the firm's project acceptance rule is straightforward: the project is accepted if and only if it provides positive NPV to the shareholders. In this case, the present value of project revenues is $\sum_{t=1}^{n} \frac{X_t}{(1+\rho)^{t-1}}$. Since the investment cost is I, the project is accepted only for $I \leq \sum_{t=1}^{n} \frac{X_t}{(1+\rho)^{t-1}}$. As we next confirm, a similar rule applies when I is privately observed, except the cutoff is more stringent to account for the manager's information rents.

3.2 Only λ is publicly observed

If λ but not I is public, the firm faces a problem of adverse selection at the managerial level but not a pressing horizon problem at the CEO level. The firm's optimal project acceptance mechanism in this case has an intuitive feel. The project is accepted if and only if the manager's investment cost report is below a pre-specified hurdle. And, to restrain budget padding, the firm promises to pay the manager the hurdle amount when the project is accepted. The hurdle rate characterization is a consequence of the manager's rent-seeking desire and the fact that the manager must be reimbursed for costs he incurs in project implementation (see, for example, Antle and Eppen 1985).

Given this characterization, the shareholders' net present value of the project given a hurdle, k, is:

$$F(k)\left[\sum_{t=1}^{n}\frac{\pi_t + x_t}{(1+\rho)^{t-1}} - k\right] + [1 - F(k)]\left[\sum_{t=1}^{n}\frac{\pi_t}{(1+\rho)^{t-1}}\right] \qquad (1)$$

Taking the first-order condition of (1), the optimal k, denoted k^*, is the unique k-value that satisfies (2):

$$k^* + H(k^*) = \sum_{t=1}^{n}\frac{x_t}{(1+\rho)^{t-1}} \qquad (2)$$

(2) states that the traditional NPV rule is adjusted to include not just the investment cost (k) but also the cost associated with the payment of managerial information rents (H(k)). Because of the latter, the project is accepted less often when I is private than when it is public. Though this more stringent acceptance criteria is the shareholders' preferred project adoption rule, the question remains whether the CEO would be willing to implement it when the decision is delegated to him. As it turns out, with λ known, a simple pay scheme for the CEO achieves the desired result.

PROPOSITION 1.
   If λ is publicly observed, a compensation scheme that is linear in cash flows achieves goal congruence.

PROOF.
   Denote a linear pay scheme by $\alpha_t + \beta_t CF_t$, where α_t is the period-t intercept, β_t is the period-t slope, and CF_t is the period-t net cash flow. Let $\beta_t = \beta\left[\dfrac{1+\lambda}{1+\rho}\right]^{t-1}$, where $\beta > 0$. The CEO's present value of pay for a given k is:

$$\sum_{t=1}^{n}\frac{\alpha_t}{(1+\lambda)^{t-1}}+\beta F(k)\left[\sum_{t=1}^{n}\frac{\pi_t+x_t}{(1+\lambda)^{t-1}}\frac{(1+\lambda)^{t-1}}{(1+\rho)^{t-1}}-k\right]$$

$$+\beta[1-F(k)]\left[\sum_{t=1}^{n}\frac{\pi_t}{(1+\lambda)^{t-1}}\frac{(1+\lambda)^{t-1}}{(1+\rho)^{t-1}}\right] \qquad (3)$$

(3) is a positive linear transformation of (1). Hence, k^*, the maximizer of (1) is also the maximizer of (3). ■

Intuitively, the linear scheme achieves goal congruence by assuring that the differential in discounting between the parties is offset by a concurrent rise in the bonus slope over time. The result is consistent with the reasoning in Jensen (2003). As long as the conflict of interest between the shareholders and CEO is well-defined, a linear pay scheme does best in aligning their interests. However, if λ is also unknown, aligning interests is more precarious. We next layer in the issue of λ being only privately known to the CEO.[41]

3.3   Neither I nor λ is publicly observed

When the confluence of incentives is considered, the usual means of achieving goal congruence falls short. Intuitively, the linear scheme in Proposition 1 cannot be implemented since λ is unknown. Any linear payment schedule that works for one λ value is sure to fail for another. However, it turns out a simple contract in which payments are linear in cash flows up to a ceiling above which bonuses are capped can resolve the problem.

Consider a two-period example in which $\pi_1 = \pi_2 = 0$, $\rho = 0$, $x_1 = 25$, $x_2 = 5$, and $I \sim U[0,40]$. In this case, with I privately observed, the shareholders' preferred project assignment rule, by (2), sets $k^* = 15$; for the uniform distribution, the left-hand-side of (2) is 2k and the right-hand-side is 30, the sum of the revenues. Here, the project is accepted if and only if the manager's cost budget is at or below 15. Moreover, if the project is accepted, 15 is transferred to the manager to cover his implementation cost. The question is if and how the shareholders can design compensation so that the CEO is eager to implement this rule.

---

[41]   A private λ suggests that keeping a linear arrangement but basing it on residual income with appropriately chosen depreciation and capital charges can align incentives. In our setting, however, the presence of an initial cash inflow, x_1, can disable the use of residual income. That is, the project's residual income at t = 1, x_1, is necessarily free of depreciation and capital charges.

With linear pay (and no bonus caps), the CEO's expected present value of pay for a given k is:

$$\alpha_1 + \frac{\alpha_2}{1+\lambda} + \frac{k}{40}\left[\beta_1(25-k)+\beta_2\frac{5}{1+\lambda}\right] \tag{4}$$

Taking the derivative of (4) yields the CEO's chosen k-cutoff:

$$k = \frac{25}{2} + \frac{\beta_2}{\beta_1}\frac{5}{2(1+\lambda)} \tag{5}$$

Clearly, for a given λ, β's can be chosen to assure k = 15. However, with λ unknown and only the β_2/β_1 ratio at the shareholders' disposal, assuring goal congruence is impossible. In particular, to achieve goal incongruence requires setting $\beta_2/\beta_1 = 1+\lambda$. Thus, if β_2/β_1 is chosen to work for one λ value it will not work for all other λ values.

As alluded to previously, however, hope is not lost. Consider a contract that specifies pay that is linear in cash flows but places a cash flow ceiling, above which bonuses are capped. In particular, let the CEO's period t compensation be:

$\alpha + \beta CF_t$ for $CF_t \leq 10$ and
$\alpha + \beta 10$ for $CF_t > 10$.

With capped bonus, the CEO's expected present value of pay for a given k is:

$$\alpha\left[\frac{2+\lambda}{1+\lambda}\right] + \beta\frac{k}{40}\left[\text{Min}\{(25-k),10\} + \frac{5}{1+\lambda}\right] \tag{6}$$

The CEO's unique maximizer of (6) is k = 15 for any $\lambda \geq 0$. To see this, consider the two cases corresponding to whether the minimum in (6) is 25 - k or 10, i.e., whether k > 15 or k < 15. In the k > 15 case, the derivative of (6) with respect to k is:

$$\frac{\beta}{40}\left[25 + \frac{5}{1+\lambda} - 2k\right] \tag{7}$$

For k >15, (7) is negative for all $\lambda \geq 0$. Hence, the CEO strictly prefers k = 15 to any k > 15. For k < 15, the derivative of (6) is:

$$\frac{\beta}{40}\left[10 + \frac{5}{1+\lambda}\right] \tag{8}$$

Since (8) is positive, the CEO also strictly prefers k = 15 to any k < 15. Hence, the proposed bonus-cap contract achieves goal congruence for any $\lambda \geq 0$. Before elaborating on the intuition behind the result, we first confirm this benefit of bonus caps holds more generally.

PROPOSITION 2.
    If λ and I are both privately observed,
    (i)   a linear compensation scheme cannot achieve goal congruence.
    (ii)   a compensation scheme which is linear up to a bonus cap can achieve goal congruence.

PROOF.
    (i) With a linear pay schedule, the CEO's expected present value of pay for a given k is:

$$\sum_{t=1}^{n} \frac{\alpha_t}{(1+\lambda)^{t-1}} + F(k)\left[\beta_1(\pi_1 + x_1 - k) + \sum_{t=2}^{n} \frac{\beta_t(\pi_t + x_t)}{(1+\lambda)^{t-1}}\right]$$
$$+ [1 - F(k)]\left[\sum_{t=1}^{n} \frac{\beta_t \pi_t}{(1+\lambda)^{t-1}}\right] \tag{9}$$

Assuming $\beta_1 \neq 0$, taking the derivative of (9) with respect to k yields the CEO's chosen cutoff, the unique k-value that satisfies (10):

$$k + H(k) = \sum_{t=1}^{n} \frac{\beta_t x_t}{\beta_1 (1+\lambda)^{t-1}} \tag{10}$$

To achieve goal congruence, the right hand side of (10) must equal the right hand side of (2) for all $\lambda \geq 0$. Clearly, since the pay scheme only has n-1 degrees of freedom (β_t/β_1 for t = 2,...,n) and λ can take on infinitely many values, goal congruence cannot be assured. The remaining possibility is $\beta_1 = 0$. Here, the CEO will choose a corner solution, either k = 0 or k = $\bar{I}$. Since k^* is interior, goal congruence cannot be achieved under any linear pay arrangement.

(ii) Consider the analog to the contract in the example: $\alpha_1 = ... = \alpha_n = \alpha$, $\beta_1 = ... = \beta_n = \beta$, and a cash flow ceiling of $\pi_1 + x_1 - k^*$. We next confirm this contract achieves congruence for any $\lambda \geq \rho$. The CEO's discounted present value of pay for a given k is:

$$\sum_{t=1}^{n} \frac{\alpha}{(1+\lambda)^{t-1}} + \beta F(k) Min\{\pi_1 + x_1 - k, \pi_1 + x_1 - k^*\}$$

$$+ \beta F(k) \sum_{t=2}^{n} \frac{Min\{\pi_t + x_1, \pi_1 + x_1 - k^*\}}{(1+\lambda)^{t-1}}$$

$$+ \beta[1 - F(k)] \sum_{t=1}^{n} \frac{Min\{\pi_t, \pi_1 + x_1 - k^*\}}{(1+\lambda)^{t-1}} \tag{11}$$

For $k > k^*$, the derivative of (11) with respect to k is:

$$\beta f(k) \left[\pi_1 + x_1 - k + \sum_{t=2}^{n} \frac{Min\{\pi_t + x_1, \pi_1 + x_1 - k^*\}}{(1+\lambda)^{t-1}} \right]$$

$$- \beta f(k) \sum_{t=1}^{n} \frac{Min\{\pi_t, \pi_1 + x_1 - k^*\}}{(1+\lambda)^{t-1}} - \beta F(k) \tag{12}$$

Dividing (12) by $\beta f(k)$ yields:

$$\pi_1 + x_1 - k + \sum_{t=2}^{n} \frac{Min\{\pi_t + x_1, \pi_1 + x_1 - k^*\}}{(1+\lambda)^{t-1}}$$

$$- \sum_{t=1}^{n} \frac{Min\{\pi_t, \pi_1 + x_1 - k^*\}}{(1+\lambda)^{t-1}} - H(k) \tag{13}$$

For $k > k^*$, $\lambda \geq \rho$, and $x_t \geq 0$, tedious comparison reveals (13) is (weakly) less than:

$$\sum_{t=1}^{n} \frac{x_t}{(1+\rho)^{t-1}} - H(k) - k \tag{14}$$

By the monotonicity of H(k) and the condition for k^* in (2), (14) is negative for $k > k^*$. That is, the CEO's discounted present value of pay is decreasing in k beyond k^*. Hence, the CEO strictly prefers k^* to any $k > k^*$.

For $k < k^*$, the derivative of (11) with respect to k is:

$$\beta f(k)\left[\pi_1 + x_1 - k^* + \sum_{t=2}^{n} \frac{\text{Min}\{\pi_t + x_t, \pi_1 + x_1 - k^*\}}{(1+\lambda)^{t-1}}\right]$$

$$-\beta f(k)\sum_{t=1}^{n} \frac{\text{Min}\{\pi_t, \pi_1 + x_1 - k^*\}}{(1+\lambda)^{t-1}} \qquad (15)$$

If $x_1 - k^* > 0$, (15) is positive. If $x_1 - k^* \le 0$, (15) is nonnegative; since the manager prefers the added slack that comes with a higher k, any points of CEO indifference would support her choosing a higher k. Thus, the CEO prefers k^* to any $k < k^*$. Hence, the CEO opts to follow the shareholders' desired strategy, regardless of λ. ■

The reason bonus caps work so effectively in aligning incentives is that they restrain excessive rationing by the CEO. To elaborate, in contracting with the privately informed manager, the CEO chooses a project acceptance hurdle by weighing the likelihood of accepting a positive NPV project with the information rents handed to the manager. Since the CEO is relatively more impatient than shareholders, a plain (time invariant) linear pay arrangement would translate into her placing a lower weight on the project value and thus opting to limit rents more than the shareholders would like. Keeping a linear arrangement but placing a higher weight on future streams in pay does not solve the problem, since this runs the risk of swinging the pendulum too far–the increasing weights can induce overweighting of project revenues (for some λ-values) and, thus, an excessive k.

By capping bonuses, however, the shareholders are able to achieve the best of both worlds. In particular, they can use a plain linear pay arrangement while simply picking a bonus cap so that the CEO does not get any added benefits from cutting k below k^*. In effect, the bonus cap induces risk aversion on the CEO's part and encourages her to follow a "safer" approach by choosing a less aggressive k–the specific ceiling chosen serves to center her attention on k^*.[42]

Notice that not only does a simple bonus cap achieve goal congruence, but it does so using time invariant α's and β's. It is straightforward to show it can achieve the same outcome for any choice of α's and for a variety of β's. Furthermore, it is the use of a bonus cap which proves critical, not the form of the compensation arrangement up to the cap (i.e., it need not be

---

[42] This effect of ceilings in discouraging risk-taking is a counterpart to the oft-discussed effect of options (floors) in encouraging risk-taking. While intuitive, both interpretations are subject to the caveat in Ross (2004): adding convexity (concavity) to an incentive schedule does not necessarily encourage (discourage) risk-taking for all utility functions.

linear). In fact, a bang-bang contract in which the CEO's bonus is not only capped but is constant also works in this scenario. In other words, the goal congruence benefits of a bonus cap are achieved while keeping several degrees of freedom in contracting.

The degrees of freedom permitted by the bonus cap arrangement can prove useful in the face of other incentive issues in the organization including when the CEO's differential discounting problem is more severe.

PROPOSITION 3.

Even when it is not known whether the CEO is more or less impatient than the shareholders, a simple perturbation of the contract presented in Proposition 2 assures goal congruence.

PROOF.

Consider a variant of the contract in Proposition 2: $\alpha_1 = \ldots = \alpha_n = \alpha$, $\beta_t = \dfrac{\beta}{(1+\rho)^{t-1}}$, and a cash flow ceiling of $\pi_1 + x_1 - k^*$. In this case, the CEO, in effect, discounts at the rate $(1+\lambda)(1+\rho)-1 = \rho+\lambda(1+\rho)$, which exceeds ρ, the shareholders discount rate. Hence, the differential discounting problem reduces to a one-sided problem of impatience, and Proposition 2's arguments apply. ■

Intuitively, by using the time-variant bonus coefficients the shareholders ensure that, even if the CEO is inherently more patient than they are, she will behave as if she is less patient–the CEO's future pay is scaled down by the shareholders' discount rate, so any discounting by the CEO will translate into her behaving in a more impatient manner. And, of course, if the CEO is more impatient to begin with, this will only magnify the impatience.

Although CEO impatience is, by itself, not a desirable trait, guaranteeing impatience allows the shareholders to make use of a bonus cap to achieve goal congruence. The shareholders design the bonus coefficients, the β_ts, to ensure the CEO is impatient. Knowing where the CEO stands enables shareholders to use bonus caps to neutralize the problem.[43]

---

[43]   The benefits of knowing what one is up against have been stressed elsewhere. As George W. Bush emphasized in pushing his case for a second American Presidency: "[e]ven when we don't agree, at least you know what I believe and where I stand."

4.   CONCLUSION

Bonus caps in pay arrangements have proved resilient in the face of persistent criticism. While the typical view of aligning incentives through the elimination of non-linearities in pay is appealing, the fortitude of bonus caps suggests exceptions to the rule may be commonplace. This paper examines one such exception. In the presence of incentive concerns dispersed among multiple layers of a firm's hierarchy, we show that placing a cap on traditional linear pay arrangements can help align incentives.

In particular, the setting studied herein is one with a hierarchy of incentive problems. Shareholders contract with a CEO who, in turn, contracts with a manager; the CEO's impatience and the manager's penchant for budget padding lead to compounded incentive problems. By rewarding the CEO a performance bonus, the shareholders are able to incentivize the CEO to take the reigns of capital allocation to balance benefits of project acceptance with costs of budget padding.

If the CEO is impatient, however, she may undervalue projects and set higher project hurdles than shareholders would like. Fortunately, the shareholders can assure that the CEO will enact a reasonable project hurdle rate simply by placing a cap on her bonus. The cap induces risk aversion on the CEO's part and forces her to seek a middle ground in which she is willing to tolerate some budget padding in order to increase the likelihood of project acceptance.

REFERENCES

Antle, R. and G. Eppen. 1985. Capital rationing and organizational slack in capital budgeting. *Management Science* 31: 163-174.

Arya, A., J. Glover, and B. Mittendorf. 2005. Taxes and the efficiency-rent extraction tradeoff. Forthcoming, *Journal of Public Economic Theory*.

Baron, D. and D. Besanko. 1992. Information, control and organizational structure. *Journal of Economics and Management Strategy* 1: 367-384.

Colvin, G. 2001. Earnings aren't everything. *Fortune* 144 (5): 58.

Demski, J. and D. Sappington. 1987. Hierarchical regulatory control. *RAND Journal of Economics* 18: 369-383.

Demski, J. and D. Sappington. 1989. Hierarchical structure and responsibility accounting. *Journal of Accounting Research* 27: 40-58.

Dutta, S. and S. Reichelstein. 2002. Controlling investment decisions: depreciation- and capital charges. *Review of Accounting Studies* 7: 253-281.

Fellingham, J. and M. Wolfson. 1985. Taxes and Risk Sharing. *The Accounting Review* 60: 10-17.

Healy, P. 1985. The effect of bonus schemes on accounting decisions. *Journal of Accounting and Economics* 7: 85-107.

Jensen, M. 2003. Paying people to lie: the truth about the budgeting process. *European Financial Management* 9: 379-406.

McAfee, P. and J. McMillan. 1995. Organizational diseconomies of scale. *Journal of Economics and Management Strategy* 4: 399-426.

Melumad, N., D. Mookherjee, and S. Reichelstein. 1992. A theory of responsibility centers. *Journal of Accounting and Economics* 15: 445-484.

Melumad, N., D. Mookherjee, and S. Reichelstein. 1995. Hierarchical decentralization of incentive contracts. *RAND Journal of Economics* 26: 654-672.

Rogerson, W. 1997. Inter-temporal cost allocation and managerial investment incentives: A theory explaining the use of economic value added as a performance measure. *Journal of Political Economy* 105: 770-795.

Ross, S. 2004. Compensation, incentives, and the duality of risk aversion and riskiness. *Journal of Finance* 59: 207-225.

Chapter 9

THE CONTROLLABILITY PRINCIPLE IN RESPONSIBILITY ACCOUNTING: ANOTHER LOOK

Anil Arya[1], Jonathan Glover[2], Suresh Radhakrishnan[3]

[1]The Ohio State University, [2]Carnegie Mellon University, [3]Univeristy of Texas, Dallas

Abstract: In this paper, we illustrate some subtleties related to responsibility accounting by studying two settings in which there are interactions among multiple control problems. In the first setting, two agents are involved first in team production (e.g., coming up with ideas) and then in related individual production (e.g., implementing the ideas). We provide conditions under which the agents are not held responsible for the team performance measure, despite each agent conditionally controlling it. The conditions ensure the incentive problem related to individual production is so severe it drives out any demand for the team performance measure. The team incentive problem is not binding because of the large "spillback" from the individual problem to the team problem.

In the second setting, we provide conditions under which an agent is held responsible for a variable he does not conditionally control. Conditional controllability is a notion derived for one-sided moral hazard. Our model is instead one of two-sided moral hazard. Under two-sided moral hazard, it can be optimal for an agent's pay to depend on variables conditionally controlled by the principal. This serves as a substitute for commitment by the principal.

Key words: Responsibility Accounting and Controllability

1.   INTRODUCTION

A basic premise of responsibility accounting is managers should be held accountable for variables they control. There is some ambiguity about the definition of the word "control." A casual notion of control, which we refer to as controllability, is a manager's pay should depend on variables whose (marginal) distribution he can affect by his supply of inputs. Antle and

Demski (1988) use a principal-agent model to make the notion of control more precise. A manager conditionally controls a variable if, conditioned on other information present, the manager's input influences the distribution of the variable. This definition is referred to as conditional controllability or informativeness. Antle and Demski highlight the pitfalls of not distinguishing between the two notions of controllability: controllability does not imply conditional controllability, nor is it implied by conditional controllability.

Conditional controllability helps explain why certain measures are included in a manager's performance evaluation and reward system, even though the manager might not have direct control over the measures. For example, consider the practice of relative performance evaluation. Suppose a CEO's actions do not influence the S&P 500. However, given the stock price of the company the CEO runs, the S&P 500 can be informative of the CEO's actions. The CEO's performance is viewed as better when his stock price goes up by 10% and the S&P 500 remains unchanged compared to a situation in which the index also goes up by 10%. The use of relative performance evaluation helps sort out the noise introduced by shocks to the economy affecting both the performance of the CEO and the S&P 500. Relative performance evaluation is a fairly intuitive application of informativeness. In other settings (e.g., insulating vs. non-insulating cost allocations or choosing to designate a division as a revenue, cost, profit, or investment center), the implications of conditional controllability can be subtler.

While the relationship between controllability and conditional controllability is well established, less is known about the circumstances in which a variable is valuable in contracting. Conditional controllability is a necessary but not a sufficient condition for a variable to be valuable. For example, numerous operational measures such as number of patents obtained, customer satisfaction scores, warranty claims, etc. are often not included in the manager's performance evaluation even though the manager might conditionally control them. In this paper, we focus on the value of information.

In the first setting we study, the agents each take multiple actions, sequentially. The first act is taken in a team project. The second act is taken in an individual project. There is a spillover from the team project to the individual project--the first act of the agent influences not only the team output but also his individual output. Such a spillover may occur, for example, if a team is used to come up with project ideas, with individuals subsequently implementing various components of the projects. In this case, the individual output depends not only on the effort the agent exerts in the implementation stage but also on the effort the agents exert in developing project ideas. Another case in which such a spillover may occur is if by working hard on a joint project an agent learns and is better able to implement a subsequent individual project.

In our model, both individual and team performance measures are available for contracting, and both measures are informative of the agents' actions. Yet, it is sometimes optimal to use only the individual performance measures in compensating the agents. The reason is the only informative variable for the second act is the individual performance measure. If the second control problem is severe enough, the incentives provided to motivate the second action spillover ("spillback") and also motivate the first action. When there is no incremental cost to motivating the first act once the second act is motivated, the team performance measure is not used even though it is informative of the first act.

Our purpose of studying the team setting is to emphasis the distinction between necessary and sufficient conditions for information to have value becomes important with multiple acts and interdependencies in performance measures. This point is also emphasized in Demski (1994, Ch. 22) in the context of a task assignment example. Demski refers to problems such as ours as examples in which bad performance measures drive out good ones.

The standard principal-agent model is one in which the principal has full powers of commitment and does not supply a productive input; the agent supplies the only productive input and has no powers of commitment. The second setting we consider is again one of multiple acts, but the acts are supplied by both the agent and the principal. The principal's and the agent's acts are substitutes. The principal can intervene and supply her act after observing the agent's act. In our model, neither the principal nor the agent is assumed to be able to commit to an action. The model is one of double moral hazard.

In our double moral hazard setting, we show a variable uninformative of the agent's act is nevertheless valuable in determining his compensation. The payment from the principal to the agent is used not only to motivate the agent but also to dissuade the principal from intervening and bailing the agent out. Because a lack of intervention makes it (ex ante) easier to motivate the agent, a variable uninformative of the agent's act is useful in contracting with him. Although the notion of conditional controllability is derived in a model of one-sided moral hazard, the use of an uninformative variable in contracting with the agent can be reconciled with conditional controllability; the variable is informative of the principal's act.

The common thread linking the two settings is the interaction between multiple control problems. It is in such settings the distinction between informativeness and the value of information becomes subtle. Determining the informativeness of a variable is a statistical exercise of checking whether or not the agent can affect the probability distribution of the variable conditioned on the other information present. Determining the value of a variable requires one to consider the contracting problem in the absence of the variable. If the variable is informative of the act(s) associated with the binding incentive compatibility constraints, it is valuable in contracting. Finding the value of information is a contextual exercise.

The remainder of the paper is organized into two sections. Section 2 studies a team setting in which an informative team performance measure is not valuable. Section 3 studies a double moral hazard setting in which the agent's optimal contract compensation depends on a variable uninformative of his act.

2. INFORMATIVE BUT NOT VALUABLE

2.1 Model

A risk-neutral principal contracts with two risk-neutral agents, A and B. Each agent is involved first in a team production process and then in an individual production process. The team output, T, depends on agent A's effort, a_I, agent B's effort, b_I, and a random productivity parameter, θ^T, $a_I \in \{a_L, a_H\}$, $b_I \in \{b_L, b_H\}$, $T \in \{T_L, T_H\}$, $0 \leq T_L < T_H$. The output of agent A's individual production process, I^A, depends on agent A's first effort a_I, on his second effort, a_2, and another productivity parameter, θ^A, $a_2 \in \{a_L, a_H\}$, $I^A \in \{I_L, I_H\}$, $0 \leq I_L < I_H$. Agent B runs a similar individual production process--his acts, productivity parameters, and individual performance measure are denoted by b_I, b_2, θ^B, and I^B. Note the spillover effect. Agent i's individual performance measure depends on his first act. Efforts are subject to moral hazard. Agent i's effort is not observed by either agent j or by the principal, $i, j = A, B$; $i \neq j$.

We assume θ^T, θ^A, and θ^B are uncorrelated. Throughout the remainder of the paper, we suppress these productivity parameters and concentrate directly on the (common knowledge) probability distribution over the outputs. Also, we assume the agents are ex ante symmetrical and focus on only one of the agents, say agent A. We suppress superscripts whenever convenient.

Let $Pr(T_m | a_I, b_I)$ denote the probability $T = T_m$, $m = L, H$, given the agents' acts a_I and b_I. Similarly, let $Pr(I_n | a_I, a_2)$ denote the probability $I = I_n$, $n = L, H$, given agent A's first act a_I and second act a_2. We assume both probability distributions satisfy first order stochastic dominance (FOSD) in each of the acts. For example, in the case of the individual performance measure, FOSD implies $Pr(I_H|a_H,a_2) \geq Pr(I_H|a_L,a_2)$ and $Pr(I_H|a_1,a_H) \geq Pr(I_H|a_1,a_L)$.

The only variable informative of agent A's second act is his individual performance measure: $Pr(I|T,a_1,a_2)$ depends nontrivially on a_2. Both I and T are assumed to be informative of a_1: $Pr(I|T,a_1,a_2)$ and $Pr(T|I,a_1,b_1)$ depend nontrivially on a_1.

Denote by s_{mn} the payment the principal makes to agent A if $T = T_m$ and $I = I_n$. Agent A's utility is $s - a_1 - a_2$ and the principal's utility is $T + I^A + I^B - s^A - s^B$. With a slight abuse of notation, a_1 and a_2 denote the effort level and the disutility associated with the effort level: $0 \leq a_L < a_H$. It is assumed T_H and I_H are sufficiently greater than T_L and I_L, respectively, it is optimal for the principal to induce the agents to choose high effort in both the production processes they are involved in.

The question we address is as follows: since agent A has to be motivated to set $a_1 = a_H$ and the team output is informative of a_1, should agent A's compensation depend on the team output?

The optimal payments for agent A are found by solving program (P1). In program (P1), the principal's objective is to minimize the expected payments to agent A subject to (Nash) individual rationality and incentive compatibility constraints. Agent A's individual rationality constraint (IR) ensures, given agent B joins the firm and chooses $b_1 = b_2 = b_H$, agent A (at least weakly) prefers to join the firm and choose $a_1 = a_2 = a_H$ as opposed to going elsewhere and earning his reservation utility, $\bar{U}, \bar{U} \geq 0$. Agent A's incentive compatibility constraint (IC$_{mn}$) ensures, given agent B joins the firm and chooses $b_1 = b_2 = b_H$, agent A prefers to choose $a_1 = a_H$ and $a_2 = a_H$ rather than $a_1 = a_m$ and $a_2 = a_n$, $m,n = L,H$. Finally, the payment s must be nonnegative (NN); the principal makes payments to the agent, not the other way around.[44]

$$\underset{s}{Min} \ \underset{m}{\Sigma} \ \underset{n}{\Sigma} \ Pr(T_m|a_H,b_H)Pr(I_n|a_H,a_H)s_{mn} \qquad \text{(P1)}$$

$$\text{s.t.} \ \underset{m}{\Sigma} \ \underset{n}{\Sigma} \ Pr(T_m|a_H,b_H)Pr(I_n|a_H,a_H)s_{mn} - a_H - a_H \ \geq \ \bar{U} \qquad \text{(IR)}$$

---

[44] The use of nonnegativity (or bankruptcy) constraints is a common way to motivate contracting frictions when all parties are risk neutral (e.g., Antle and Eppen 1985; Sappington 1983). An alternative is to assume the agent is risk averse. While the characterization of optimal payments is somewhat more tedious (because of the nonlinear formulation of the program), our results can be obtained in the risk-averse setting as well.

$$\sum_m \sum_n Pr(T_m|a_H,b_H)Pr(I_n|a_H,a_H)s_{mn} - a_H - a_H \geq$$

$$\sum_m \sum_n Pr(T_m|a_L,b_H)Pr(I_n|a_L,a_L)s_{mn} - a_L - a_L \qquad (IC_{LL})$$

$$\sum_m \sum_n Pr(T_m|a_H,b_H)Pr(I_n|a_H,a_H)s_{mn} - a_H - a_H \geq$$

$$\sum_m \sum_n Pr(T_m|a_L,b_H)Pr(I_n|a_L,a_H)s_{mn} - a_L - a_H \qquad (IC_{LH})$$

$$\sum_m \sum_n Pr(T_m|a_H,b_H)Pr(I_n|a_H,a_H)s_{mn} - a_H - a_H \geq$$

$$\sum_m \sum_n Pr(T_m|a_H,b_H)Pr(I_n|a_H,a_L)s_{mn} - a_H - a_L \qquad (IC_{HL})$$

$$s_{mn} \geq 0 \qquad (NN)$$

If I alone is used to determine agent A's compensation, the optimal contract can be found by solving a variant of program (P1). The new program (P2) differs from (P1) only in being more constrained. The added constraint is $s_{Ln} = s_{Hn}$, i.e., the constraint reflects payments to agent A which do not depend on the team performance measure (the first subscript) but only on the individual performance measure (the second subscript).

2.2   Result

The solution to programs (P1) and (P2) are presented in Table 1 for two numerical examples. In Example 1, the optimal payments for agent A depend on both the team and individual outputs, while in Example 2 the payments depend only on the individual output.

Table 9-1. Example 1

Parameters	$a_L = b_L = 0$, $a_H = b_H = 1$. $\bar{U} = 0$. $Pr(I_H\|a_L,a_L) = 0.2$, $Pr(I_H\|a_L,a_H) = 0.4$, $Pr(I_H\|a_H,a_L) = 0.5$, $Pr(I_H\|a_H,a_H) = 0.9$. $Pr(T_H\|a_I,b_I) = Pr(I_H\|a_I,a_2)$.
Solution to (P1)	$s_{LL} = 0$, $s_{LH} = 0$, $s_{HL} = 0$, $s_{HH} = 25/9 \approx 2.778$. Expected payment = 2.25.
Solution to (P2)	$s_{LL} = s_{HL} = 0$, $s_{LH} = s_{HH} = 20/7 \approx 2.857$. Expected payment= $18/7 \approx 2.571$.

Table 9-2. Example 2

Parameters	$a_L = b_L = 0$, $a_H = b_H = 1$. $\bar{U} = 0$. $Pr(I_H\|a_L,a_L) = 0.2$, $Pr(I_H\|a_L,a_H) = 0.4$, $Pr(I_H\|a_H,a_L) = 0.6$, $Pr(I_H\|a_H,a_H) = 0.9$. $Pr(T_H\|a_I,b_I) = Pr(I_H\|a_I,a_2)$.
Solution to (P1) and (P2)	$s_{LL} = s_{HL} = 0$, $s_{LH} = s_{HH} = 10/3 \approx 3.333$. Expected payment = 3.

The intuition for when agent A's payments depend on the team output and when they do not can be found by focusing on the binding incentive compatibility constraint in program (P2). There are two control problems associated with agent A--the agent has to be motivated to choose $a_I = a_H$ (the first control problem) and also motivated to choose $a_2 = a_H$ (the second control problem). The only informative variable regarding a_2 is the individual performance measure which depends on both a_I and a_2. The effect of the spillover from the team project into the individual project results in an interaction between the two control problems. If the second control problem is severe enough, there is no use for any informative variable in the first control problem. In this case, the I-contingent bonus needed to motivate a_2 is large enough it motivates a_I at no extra cost. The team output is of no use even if it were a perfect proxy for a_I.

In our numerical examples, when payments are conditioned only on I, the (IC$_{LL}$) constraint binds in Example 1, while (IC$_{HL}$) binds in Example 2. In Example 1, the control problem causing a friction is the one in which the agent chooses $a_I = a_2 = a_L$ instead of $a_I = a_2 = a_H$. Here, the team output is valuable since it can reduce the cost of motivating a_I. In contrast, in

Example 2 the control problem causing a friction is the one in which the agent chooses $a_1 = a_H$ and $a_2 = a_L$ instead of $a_1 = a_H$ and $a_2 = a_H$. Since T is not informative of a_2, the team performance measure does not help with this control problem--agent A's payments depend only on I.

In Proposition 1, we present a sufficient condition under which the team output is not valuable in contracting with the agent. (C.1) ensures the binding incentive compatibility constraint in program (P2) is (IC_{HL})--motivating $a_2 = a_H$ is the source of the contracting friction.

$$(C.1) \quad Pr(I_H|a_H,a_H) - Pr(I_H|a_H,a_L) \leq Pr(I_H|a_H,a_m) - Pr(I_H|a_L,a_m), \quad m = L,H$$

(C.1) is satisfied by the parameters chosen in Example 2 but not by the parameters in Example 1. Intuitively, (C.1) states the marginal impact of the second act (given a high first act) is smaller than the marginal impact of the first act (irrespective of the second act). (C.1) implies a big spillover effect of the first act on the individual performance measure. A big spillover implies the incremental effect of the second act on the individual performance is small: given $a_1 = a_H$, I is a poor proxy for the observability of a_2. Since it is difficult to measure the impact of a_2 motivating $a_2 = a_H$, requires a large bonus. The bonus is so large it automatically also motivates $a_1 = a_H$.

PROPOSITION 1. The team performance measure, T, which is informative of the agent's first act, is not valuable for contracting with the agent if (C.1) holds.

The informativeness condition, as derived in Holmstrom (1979), is a necessary condition for a variable to be valuable in our sequential multi-act setting. It is not sufficient. The purpose of Proposition 1 is to emphasize interactions between control problems of varying severity with the same agent can make determining the sufficient conditions for an informative signal to be valuable (and to be not valuable) subtle.[45]

In the next section, we study a double moral hazard setting in which a variable uninformative of the agent's act is valuable in contracting with him. This might seem to violate the notion informativeness is a necessary condition for a variable to be valuable. However, recall the assumptions under which this necessary condition is derived. One assumption is the productive input is supplied only by the agent. If the principal also supplies a

---

[45] If $\bar{U} = a_L = 0$, (C.1) is both necessary and sufficient for the team performance measure to be not valuable.

productive input and both the principal's and the agent's effort choices are subject to moral hazard, a signal may be valuable for contracting with the agent even if it is not informative of the agent's act. A variable informative of the principal's act can be useful in contracting with the agent because it serves as a substitute for the principal's commitment.

The common threads linking sections 2 and 3 is the focus on (1) the interaction between different control problems, i.e., the interplay between different incentive compatibility constraints and (2) using the binding incentive compatibility constraint(s) to determine the value of information.

3. UNINFORMATIVE BUT VALUABLE

3.1 Model

A risk-neutral principal owns a production technology. The output of the technology is denoted by x, $x \in \{x_L, x_H\}$, $0 \le x_L < x_H$, and is consumed by the principal. The principal can run the technology herself. The principal's effort b, $b \in \{b_L, b_H\}$, influences the distribution over x as follows. If b_L is chosen, $x = x_L$ with probability 1. If b_H is chosen, $x = x_H$ with probability 1.

Alternatively, the principal can hire an agent to help her run the technology. When the agent is hired, his effort a, $a \in \{a_L, a_H\}$ and the principal's effort, b, influences the distribution over x as follows: $Pr(x_H | a_L, b_L) < Pr(x_H | a_H, b_L)$ and $Pr(x_H | a_L, b_H) = Pr(x_H | a_H, b_H) = 1$. If the principal chooses b_H, $x = x_H$ with probability 1, irrespective of whether or not the agent is hired and irrespective of the agent's act. We interpret b as the principal's intervention decision; b_L is "not intervening" and b_H is "intervening."

The principal's effort also influences the distribution of a second variable y, $y \in \{y_L, y_H\}$. The probability $y = y_H$ is $Pr(y_H | b_L)$ if b_L is chosen and $Pr(y_H | b_H)$ if b_H is chosen. The signal y is assumed to be informative of the principal's act, i.e., $Pr(y_H | b_L) \ne Pr(y_H | b_H)$, but uninformative of the agent's act, i.e., $Pr(y | x, b, a) = Pr(y | b)$.

Both parties observe each other's acts, but neither act is contractible. A contract contingent on the effort levels cannot be enforced (verified) by a third party. The contractible variables are x and y. Denote by s_{mn} the payment the principal makes to the agent if $x = x_m$ and $y = y_n$, $m, n = L, H$. The agent's utility is $s - a$ and the principal's utility is $x - s - b$. The disutility of acts are ordered: $0 \le a_L < a_H$ and $0 \le b_L < b_H$.

The sequence of events is as follows. First, the principal decides whether or not to hire the agent to run the production process. Second, if the principal chooses to hire the agent, she offers him a contract. Third, assuming the contract is accepted, the agent chooses his productive act. Fourth, the principal observes the agent's act and decides whether or not to intervene, i.e., she chooses her own productive act: $b(a)$ denotes the principal's act choice as a function of the agent's act choice. Fifth, the outcome x and the signal y are realized and the contract is settled. The question is as follows: since the variable y is uninformative of the agent's act, should the agent's compensation depend on it?

The optimal payments for the agent are found by solving program (P3). The principal's objective is to maximize her expected utility subject to the following constraints. The first constraint (IR^A) ensures the contract is individually rational: the agent must receive an expected utility of at least $\bar{U}$, which is the expected utility of his next best opportunity. The second constraint (IC^A) ensures a is incentive compatible for the agent: a is a best response to s and b. The third constraint (IC^P) ensures b is incentive compatible for the principal: b is a best response to s and a. The (IC^P) constraint is needed because the principal cannot commit ex ante to an effort level. Finally, the payments s must be nonnegative (NN).

$$\underset{s\ a\ b(a_L)\ b(a_H)}{Max} \quad \underset{m}{\Sigma}\ \underset{n}{\Sigma}\ Pr(x_m|a,b(a))\ Pr(y_n|b(a))[x_m - s_{mn} - b(a)] \qquad \text{(P3)}$$

$$\text{s.t.}\ \underset{m}{\Sigma}\ \underset{n}{\Sigma}\ Pr(x_m|a,b(a))\ Pr(y_n|b(a))s_{mn} - a \geq \bar{U} \qquad \text{(IR}^A\text{)}$$

$$\underset{m}{\Sigma}\ \underset{n}{\Sigma}\ Pr(x_m|a,b(a))\ Pr(y_n|b(a))s_{mn} - a \geq$$

$$\underset{m}{\Sigma}\ \underset{n}{\Sigma}\ Pr(x_m|a',b(a'))\ Pr(y_n|b(a'))s_{mn} - a' \quad \forall\ a' \qquad \text{(IC}^A\text{)}$$

$$\underset{m}{\Sigma}\ \underset{n}{\Sigma}\ Pr(x_m|a,b(a))\ Pr(y_n|b(a))\ [x_m - s_{mn} - b(a)] \geq$$

$$\underset{m}{\Sigma}\ \underset{n}{\Sigma}\ Pr(x_m|a,b'(a))\ Pr(y_n|b'(a))[x_m - s_{mn} - b'(a)] \quad \forall\ b' \qquad \text{(IC}^P\text{)}$$

$$s_{mn} \geq 0 \qquad \text{(NN)}$$

If only x is used in determining the agent's compensation, the optimal payments can be found by solving a variant of program (P3). The new program (P4) differs from (P3) only in being more constrained: $s_{mL} = s_{mH}$.

Before proceeding, we impose some restrictions on our setting for expositional convenience: $\bar{U} = x_L = a_L = b_L = Pr(x_H|a_L,b_L) = 0$. In the next section, we present a numerical example and provide a sufficient condition under which the agent's optimal payments depend on y.

3.2   Result

In Table 2, we present the parameters and solutions to programs (P3) and (P4) for a numerical example. In Example 3, y, which is uninformative of a, is valuable in contracting with the agent.

Table 9-3. Example 3

Parameters	$a_L = 0$, $a_H = 1$. $b_L = 0$, $b_H = 5$. $x_L = 0$, $x_H = 7$. $\bar{U} = 0$.
	$Pr(x_H|a_L,b_L) = 0$, $Pr(x_H|a_H,b_L) = 0.75$, $Pr(x_H|a_L,b_H) = 1$, $Pr(x_H|a_H,b_H) = 1$.
	$Pr(y_H|b_L) = 0.40$, $Pr(y_H|b_H) = 0.50$.
Solution to (P3)	$a = a_H$, $b(a_L) = b(a_H) = b_L$.
	$s_{LL} = s_{LH} = s_{HL} = 0$, $s_{HH} = 4$.
	Principal's expected payoff $= 4.05$.
Solution to (P4)	$a = a_H$, $b(a_L) = b(a_H) = b_L$.
	$s_{LL} = s_{LH} = 0$, $s_{HL} = s_{HH} = 2$.
	Principal's expected payoff $= 3.75$.

The intuition for why y is valuable in contracting with the agent can be found by focusing on the binding incentive compatibility constraint in program (P4). The incentive compatibility constraints in (P4) reflect two control problems: (1) the agent has to be motivated to choose the appropriate act and (2) the agent has to be convinced the principal will not bail him out if he shirks--convincing the agent of this is problematic because, if the principal does not rescue the agent, the principal suffers herself as well (the output is x_L rather than x_H). To elaborate, consider the optimal contract with the agent based on x alone. The alternatives available to the principal are as follows.

(i) The principal can run the firm herself. In this case, the principal chooses b_H and her expected payoff is $x_H - b_H = 2$.

(ii) The principal can hire the agent and motivate him to choose a_L. The agent can be motivated to choose a_L by setting all payments equal to 0 (since

$\bar{U} = a_L = 0$). When the agent chooses a_L, the principal has two choices. She can intervene (choose b_H) and obtain $x_H - b_H = 2$ or she can refrain from intervening (choose b_L) and obtain 0. The principal prefers to intervene and her payoff is again $x_H - b_H = 2$.

(iii) The principal can hire the agent and motivate him to choose a_H. In our risk-neutral setting, the optimal contract can be characterized so the only non-zero payment made is when $x = x_H$. Denote this payment by s_H. If the agent believes the principal will intervene when he chooses a_L, he will always choose a_L. By choosing a_L rather than a_H, the agent saves on the disutility of effort as well as obtains s_H with probability 1. Hence, in order to motivate a_H, the principal must convince the agent ex ante (before the agent chooses his act) she will not intervene ex post (after the agent has chosen his act).

It is in the principal's own best interest not to intervene when the agent chooses a_L if $x_H - s_H - b_H \leq 0$; this is (IC^P). Recall, if the principal does not intervene and the agent chooses a_L, the output is $x_L (= 0)$ and she makes a payment of 0. If the principal does not intervene, it is in the agent's own best interest to choose a_H if $0.75s_H - a_H \geq 0 \cdot s_H - a_L = 0$; this is ($IC^A$). The ($IC^A$) constraint implies $s_H \geq 4/3$ and the (IC^P) constraint implies $s_H \geq 2$. The (IC^P) constraint dominates the (IC^A) constraint and determines the payment. The principal's expected payoff is $(0.75)[7 - 2] = 3.75$.

Comparing the principal's expected payoff in (i) through (iii), the principal's optimal strategy is to hire the agent, motivate him to choose a_H, and not to intervene. This is the solution to program (P4) presented in Table 2.

Since (IC^P) binds under the solution to program (P4), y is valuable, since it is informative of the principal's act. To see how y is optimally used, consider the following contract: $s_{HH} = 4$ and all other payments are zero. Under this contract (IC^P) is satisfied as an equality: by intervening, the principal obtains $7 - (0.5)4 - 5 = 0$; by not intervening, she obtains 0 also.

Given the principal does not intervene, the contract also satisfies (IC^A): if the agent chooses a_L, he obtains 0; if the agent chooses a_H, he obtains $(0.75)(0.4)(4) - 1 = 0.2$. The principal's expected payoff is $(0.75)7 - (0.75)(0.4)4 = 4.05$. This is the solution to program (P3) in Table 2.

The role of the payments from the principal to the agent is twofold. One, the payments are used to motivate the agent to choose a_H. Two, the payments are used to deter the principal from choosing b_H. When the second role dominates the first role, the incentive compatibility constraint for the principal rather than the incentive compatibility constraint of the agent binds. In this case a variable informative of the principal's act helps with contracting with the agent since it relaxes (IC^P). In particular, $y = y_H$ is informative of the principal's intervention. By ex ante promising to pay the agent a large amount when $y = y_H$ the principal makes it ex post self enforcing for her to not intervene.

Building on the above intuition, the proof of Proposition 2 shows condition (C.2) is sufficient for y to be useful in contracting with the agent. The lower bound on b_H ensures the disutility of b_H is sufficiently large, the principal prefers to hire an agent and motivate him to choose a_H rather than run the technology herself. The upper bound on b_H ensures the disutility of b_H is sufficiently small, she prefers to intervene when the payments are as specified by (IC^A) and the agent shirks. These conditions ensure the source of the contracting friction is (IC^P).

$$(\text{C.2}) \quad \frac{x_H}{1 + Pr(x_H|a_H)} < b_H < x_H - \frac{a_H}{Pr(x_H|a_H)}$$

PROPOSITION 2. The variable y, which is uninformative of the agent's act, is valuable for contracting with the agent if (C.2) holds.

APPENDIX

PROOF OF PROPOSITION 1.

The optimal payments for agent A as a function of I alone are determined by solving program (P2). Denote $s_{Ln} = s_{Hn}$ by s_n. In our risk-neutral setting, where the risk premium (and, hence, the spread in payments) is not an issue, the optimal contract can always be characterized with $s_L = 0$. Making this substitution and writing all constraints in terms of how large s_H should be, program (P2) can be written as follows.

$$\underset{s}{Min} \quad Pr(I_H|a_H, a_H)s_H \tag{P2}$$

$$\text{s.t.} \quad s_H \geq \frac{\bar{U} + a_H + a_H}{Pr(I_H|a_H, a_H)} \tag{IR}$$

$$s_H \geq \frac{a_H - a_L + a_H - a_L}{Pr(I_H|a_H, a_H) - Pr(I_H|a_L, a_L)} \tag{IC_{LL}}$$

$$s_H \geq \frac{a_H - a_L}{Pr(I_H | a_H, a_H) - Pr(I_H | a_L, a_H)} \qquad (IC_{LH})$$

$$s_H \geq \frac{a_H - a_L}{Pr(I_H | a_H, a_H) - Pr(I_H | a_H, a_L)} \qquad (IC_{HL})$$

$$s_H \geq 0 \qquad (NN)$$

The (IR) constraint dominates the (NN) constraint, since the reservation utility and disutility of effort are nonnegative. Also, (C.1) implies the (IC_{HL}) constraint (at least weakly) dominates the (IC_{LH}) and the (IC_{LL}) constraints. The former follows from $Pr(I_H | a_H, a_H) - Pr(I_H | a_H, a_L) \leq Pr(I_H | a_H, a_H) - Pr(I_H | a_L, a_H)$. To show ($IC_{HL}$) dominates ($IC_{LL}$), we need to show

$$\frac{a_H - a_L}{Pr(I_H | a_H, a_H) - Pr(I_H | a_H, a_L)} \geq \frac{a_H - a_L + a_H - a_L}{Pr(I_H | a_H, a_H) - Pr(I_H | a_L, a_L)} \; .$$

This is equivalent to showing

$$\frac{1}{Pr(I_H | a_H, a_H) - Pr(I_H | a_H, a_L)} \geq \frac{2}{Pr(I_H | a_H, a_H) - Pr(I_H | a_L, a_L)}$$

$$\Rightarrow 2[Pr(I_H | a_H, a_H) - Pr(I_H | a_H, a_L)] \leq Pr(I_H | a_H, a_H) - Pr(I_H | a_L, a_L)$$

$$\Rightarrow Pr(I_H | a_H, a_H) - 2Pr(I_H | a_H, a_L) \leq - Pr(I_H | a_L, a_L)$$

$\Rightarrow Pr(I_H | a_H, a_H) - Pr(I_H | a_H, a_L) \leq Pr(I_H | a_H, a_L) - Pr(I_H | a_L, a_L)$, which is true from (C.1).

Hence, under (C.1), s_H is determined either by the (IR) constraint or by the (IC_{HL}) constraint. If the (IR) constraint holds as an equality, then the principal's expected payments are first-best and she can do no better with additional information. If the (IC_{HL}) constraint holds as an equality, it implies the control problem of motivating $a_2 = a_H$ is the one causing the contracting friction. Additional information is useful if and only if it is informative of a_2. Since T is not informative of a_2, it does not help in reducing the principal's expected payments to the agent. ∎

PROOF OF PROPOSITION 2.

Under (C.2), the optimal contract with the agent based on x alone has the following features: (1) the principal hires the agent and motivates a_H and (2) the binding incentive compatibility constraint is the one ensuring it is self enforcing for the principal not to intervene even if the agent chooses a_L. The optimal contract based on x is determined in Step 1 below. Given Step 1, y is valuable because it is informative of the principal's act and using it helps reduce the cost of satisfying the principal's incentive compatibility constraint. This is shown in Step 2.

In the proof, we denote $Pr(x_H|a_H, b_L)$ by p_H, $Pr(y_H|b_L)$ by q_L, and $Pr(y_H|b_H)$ by q_H. Recall $Pr(x_H|a_L, b_L) = 0$ and $Pr(x_H|a_L, b_H) = Pr(x_H|a_H, b_H) = 1$.

Step 1. The alternatives available to the principal are as follows.

(i) The principal can run the firm herself. In this case, the principal chooses b_H and her expected payoff is $x_H - b_H$. From (C.2), the upper limit on b_H implies $x_H - b_H > a_H/p_H > 0$.

(ii) The principal can hire the agent and motivate him to choose a_L. The agent can be motivated to choose a_L by setting $s_{mn} = 0$ for all m, n (since $\bar{U} = a_L = 0$). When the agent chooses a_L the principal has two choices. She can intervene (choose b_H) and obtain $x_H - b_H$ or she can refrain from intervening (choose b_L) and obtain U. Since $x_H - b_H > 0$, she intervenes. The principal's payoff is again $x_H - b_H$.

(iii) The principal can hire the agent and motivate him to choose a_H. In our risk-neutral setting the optimal contract can be characterized so $s_{Ln} = 0$ and $s_{Hn} = s_H > 0$. If the agent believes the principal will intervene when he chooses a_L, he will always choose a_L. By choosing a_L rather than a_H, the agent saves on the disutility of effort as well as obtains s_H with probability 1. Hence, in order to motivate a_H, the principal must convince the agent ex ante (before the agent chooses his act) she will not intervene ex post (after the agent has chosen his act).

The principal's incentive compatibility constraint (IC^P) ensures, under the contract, it is in the principal's own best interest not to intervene if the agent chooses a_L. (Satisfaction of (IC^P) also implies the principal will not intervene if the agent chooses a_H.) Hence, (IC^P) requires $x_H - s_H - b_H \leq 0$. Recall, if the principal does not intervene and the agent chooses a_L, the output is x_L $(= 0)$ and she makes a payment of 0. The agent's incentive compatibility constraint (IC^A) ensures, under the contract and given the principal will not intervene, it is in the agent's own best interest to choose a_H. Hence, (IC^A) requires $p_H s_H - a_H \geq 0 \cdot s_H - a_L = 0$. The ($IC^A$) constraint implies $s_H \geq a_H/p_H$ and the (IC^P)

constraint implies $s_H \geq x_H - b_H$. From the upper limit on b_H, it follows the (IC^P) constraint dominates the (IC^A) constraint: $s_H = x_H - b_H$. The principal's expected payoff is $p_H[x_H - (x_H - b_H)] = p_H b_H$.

Finally, compare the principal's expected payoff in (i) through (iii). The lower limit on b_H implies the principal's optimal strategy is to hire the agent, motivate him to choose a_H, and not to intervene.

Step 2.

Given (IC^P) binds under the optimal contract determined in Step 1, it follows y, a variable informative of the principal's act, is valuable. To see how y is optimally used assume, without loss of generality, $q_H > q_L$. Consider the following contract: $s_{HH} = k_1 = (x_H - b_H)/q_H$ and all other payments are zero. Under this contract (IC^P) is satisfied. By intervening, the principal obtains $x_H - q_H k_1 - b_H = 0$; by not intervening, she obtains 0.

Given the principal does not intervene, we next check to see if the contract satisfies (IC^A). If the agent chooses a_L, he obtains $0 \cdot k_1 - a_L = 0$. If the agent chooses a_H, he obtains $p_H q_L k_1 - a_H$. There are two cases to consider.

Assume $p_H q_L k_1 - a_H \geq 0$. In this case (IC^A) is satisfied and the principal's expected payoff is $p_H x_H - p_H q_L (x_H - b_H)/q_H$. Since $q_H > q_L$, this is greater than $p_H x_H - p_H (x_H - b_H)$, the principal's expected payoff when the contract is based on x alone.

Assume $p_H q_L k_1 - a_H < 0$. This implies $a_H/(p_H q_L) > (x_H - b_H)/q_H$. Denote the LHS of the inequality by k_2 (note the RHS is k_1). In this case use the following contract: $s_{HH} = k_2$ and all other payments are zero. Since $k_2 > k_1$, (IC^P) is satisfied (now as a strict inequality). Also, now (IC^A) is satisfied as an equality. The principal's expected payoff is $p_H x_H - p_H q_L k_2 = p_H x_H - a_H$. From the upper bound on b_H, this is greater than $p_H x_H - p_H (x_H - b_H)$, the principal's expected payoff based on x alone. ∎

REFERENCES

Antle, R., and J. Demski. 1988. The controllability principle in responsibility accounting. *The Accounting Review* 63: 700-718.

Antle, R., and G. Eppen. 1985. Capital rationing and organizational slack in capital budgeting. *Management Science* 31: 163-174.

Demski, J. 1994. *Managerial Uses of Accounting Information*. Norwell, MA: Kluwer Academic Publishers.

Holmstrom, B. 1979. Moral hazard and observability. *Bell Journal of Economics* 10: 74-91.

Sappington, D. 1983. Limited liability contracts between principal and agent. *Journal of Economic Theory* 29: 1-21.

Chapter 10

PUBLIC DISCLOSURE OF TRADES BY CORPORATE INSIDERS IN FINANCIAL MARKETS AND TACIT COORDINATION

Steven Huddart,[1] John S. Hughes,[2] and Carolyn B. Levine[3]

[1]*Pennsylvania State University,* [2]*University of California at Los Angeles,*
[3]*Carnegie Mellon University*

Abstract: We consider the consequences of public disclosure of insider trades on trading costs and price discovery in financial markets. Similar to Cournot competition in product markets, corporate insiders with common private information have incentive to trade more aggressively than a monopolist with the same information. Since, given periodic financial corporate reporting, insiders routinely have access to information in advance of the market, it is reasonable to expect them to seek ways to limit trades and, thereby, increase profits. Public reporting of insider trades may have the unintended effect of furthering tacit coordination by allowing insiders to monitor each others' trades. Moreover, even without such reporting, we show how insiders may be able to sustain coordinated behavior depending on the distribution characterizing liquidity trading. Thus, competition among corporate insiders may be less influential in price discovery than previously thought.

Keywords: Public Disclosure, Insider Trading, Tacit Coordination

Introduction

A common perception of regulation which requires public disclosure of trades by corporate insiders, well expressed by Carlton and Fischel (1983), is that "The greater the ability of market participants to identify insider trading, the more information such trading will convey." In this paper, we suggest that public disclosure of insider trades per se may actually inhibit the price discovery process by dampening competition among insiders as they seek to exploit their information advantage.

The notion that competition among insiders with common private information serves to advance price discovery is based on an analogy to Cournot behavior in product markets. As in that setting, Cournot insiders trade more aggressively on their private information than a monopolist would trade, thereby causing more of their private information to become impounded in price. However, this effect of competition presumes a static trading environment in which insiders lack the means to coordinate their demands.

It seems clear that officers, directors, and other corporate insiders routinely have information about earnings, dividend changes, contract awards, order backlogs, product approvals, appraisal values, research discoveries, litigation outcomes, and other recurring events in advance of public announcements.[1] Accordingly, a more suitable environment in which to analyze their behavior is a dynamic setting involving repeated episodes of private information arrival, opportunities to trade, and public release of that information. From a modeling standpoint this recommends characterization as a repeated game.

Our approach is based on one-period models of monopoly and Cournot competition by Kyle (1985) and Admati and Pfleiderer (1988), respectively. The extension to multiperiod play involves simple trigger strategies analogous to those of Green and Porter (1984). To capture the impact of public disclosure of insider trades, we consider scenarios in which insiders are able through such reports to perfectly monitor each others' trades or are able to only imperfectly monitor trades by observing the aggregate order flow. The former scenario involves a straightforward application of the Folk Theorem. The latter scenario is broken down into special cases wherein noise from liquidity demands has either bounded (moving) or unbounded support. Distributional assumptions range over the error class, which encompasses symmetric distributions distinguished by a shape parameter that determines kurtosis. This class includes the normal along with its limiting families, the uniform and Laplace. Dutta and Madhavan (1997) independently consider repeated insider trading assuming the normal and apply optimal strategies described by Abreu (1988). Their results are qualitatively similar to ours in that case. By departing from optimal trigger strategies and imposing some further structure, we obtain simple and intuitive characterizations of equilibria for a variety of cases. This, in turn, allows us to portray the significant role played by the kurtosis of liquidity demands.

Holden and Subrahmanyan (1992) and Foster and Viswanathan (1993) consider the effects of competition among identically informed insiders in a context of long-lived information. They find that price discovery is accelerated in comparison to Kyle's monopolist case. Foster and Viswanathan (1996) extend the analysis to the case of heterogeneously informed insiders and show that the degree of competition depends upon the correlation structure of insiders' private signals. In contrast, we suppress the longevity of information and focus on the scope for tacit coordination as the insider trading game is repeated. The analysis is eased substantially by assuming one round of trade between public announcements, which reveal previously private information. We conjecture that allowing multiple rounds prior to each public announcement would not alter the qualitative conclusion that the coordination sustained by repeated play damps competition among insiders and impedes price discovery, especially when insiders can perfectly monitor each others' trades.

Our principal results are (i) mandated public disclosure of insider trading facilitates coordination by insiders in extracting monopoly rents to their private information, implying less price discovery rather than more as regulators might intend; (ii) in keeping with Fudenberg et al. (1994), moving support for liquidity demands may allow insiders to extract full monopoly rents even in the absence of public disclosure of their trades; and (iii) more platykurtic distributions of liquidity demands imply greater prospects for insiders to improve upon Cournot behavior in extracting rents. One further result establishes the ability of insiders receiving different private signals to act as a monopolist with all the signals given perfect monitoring. The most notable policy implication of these results is that private disclosure of insiders' trades might dominate public disclosure. That way, regulators can enforce restrictions on insider trading but preserve the benefits of competition among the insiders.

The remainder of this paper is organized as follows: section 1 on background relates our model to the empirical evidence; section 2 presents the basic model for a single period; section 3 analyzes the case of perfect monitoring; section 4 considers imperfect monitoring, including cases in which the Folk Theorem does or does not apply; section 5 extends the case of perfect monitoring to allow for imperfect private information; and section 6 offers some conclusions.

1.   Background

Regulations governing insider trading in the U. S. include Section 16(d) of the Securities Exchange Act of 1934 which requires corporate insiders (i.e., officers, directors, and principal owners of equity securities) to file statements of their holdings and reports of changes in those holdings. the Sarbanes-Oxley Act amended Section 16(a) by accelerating the filing deadline for Section 16 insider transaction reports to two business days after the transaction occurs. These statements are public records. As well, insider trades are disclosed in the SEC News Digest daily and by commercial data services. Section 16(b) requires insiders to disgorge profits from "short-swing" trading.[2] Rule 10b-5 from Section 10 of the Act requires insiders refrain from trading on material non-public information such as an impending takeover bid.

Notwithstanding the above restrictions, there is considerable empirical evidence that insider trading is abnormally profitable. For example, Seyhun (1986 and 1992b) finds that open market purchases and sales by corporate insiders predict up to 60 percent of the variation in one-year-ahead aggregate stock returns. Similarly, Pettit and Venkatesh (1995) report a strong tendency for insiders' net purchases to be significantly above and below normal between one and two years in advance of long horizon returns that are above and below normal, respectively. Damodaran and Liu (1993) find insiders of REITs buying (selling) after they receive favorable (unfavorable) appraisal news and before its public release.

Whereas, as noted by Seyhun (1992a), insider trading litigation has evolved to discourage trade in advance of material earnings and merger announcements, insiders are rarely prosecuted for trading on other kinds of information. Even if corporate insiders cannot profit from their private information through trades covered by regulation, they may be able to profit from unregulated Over the Counter Swaps of the return on their firm's shares for the return on some other asset.[3] Moreover, even earnings releases afford scope for front-running by insiders, provided they exercise some discipline in the timing of their trades.[4] For example, Penman (1982) finds that insiders tend to buy (sell) stock before the release of earnings forecasts that caused an increase (decrease) in share price. Similarly, Elliot et al. (1984) finds decreased selling and increased buying in advance of a variety of announcements including earnings releases.

While we are unaware of large scale data analyses pointing to widespread coordinated behavior has yet to unfold, there are any number of anecdotes suggesting that the trading decisions of insiders at the same firm are not independent. In fact, it is commonplace at some companies for the same group of insiders to trade together and in the same direction. For instance, among the fifty most active issues recently listed by Corporate Ownership Watch, corporate insiders, including officers and large shareholders, at LHS Group sold roughly proportionate quantities of stock in three of the first seven months of 1998 (see Figure 10.1). In another example, EDS officers and directors collectively sold nearly a half-million shares in weeks preceding a stock price drop of 30 percent and, as reported in the *Wall Street Journal*, "Two previous rounds of insider sales were followed by stock-price reductions in the 30 percent range in 1996 and 1997."[5] The company reported "worse-than-expected" earnings approximately a month and a half later. In a case involving non-earnings information, eight executives of Curative sold shares in advance of an FDA warning letter judged by Curative's CFO not to be material and, hence, not in violation of restrictions on insider selling.[6]

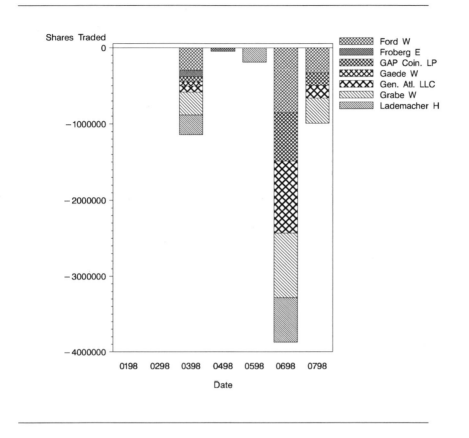

Figure 10.1. Pattern of Insider Trading. The trading activity of insiders at LHS Group for the first half of 1998. Vertical axis plots the number of shares traded. Negative figures are sales. Data are from Form 4s filed with the Securities and Exchange Commission. Trades are grouped by the month in which the form is filed. Trades by insiders of less than 40,000 shares in any month are omitted.

Stepping back to consider the consequences of a tightening of US filing rules since the early 1980s when "many [insiders] were barely aware of the rules," one observer describes the response by insiders as moving toward more "orchestration" of their trades to "paint the insider tape." The observer goes on to suggest that only a small handful seem to engage in this activity, but that the companies of these traders "seem to stand out the most," at least with respect to insider buying.[7] Whether a desire by insiders to avoid costly competition underlies such orchestration is an open question.

2.   Basic Model

We assume a single asset is traded over a countably infinite time horizon, $T = \{1, 2, ...\}$. The asset's value at time t is

$$v_t = p_0 + \sum_{s=1}^{t} \delta_s,$$

where p_0 is an initial known price and δ_t is a Bernoulli distributed innovation; i.e.,

$$\delta_t = \begin{cases} \sigma & \text{with probability } \frac{1}{2}, \text{ and} \\ -\sigma & \text{with probability } \frac{1}{2}. \end{cases}$$

The variance of δ_t is σ^2. Although the Bernoulli distribution is chosen for analytic convenience in cases with imperfect monitoring, it is not unrealistic. Many pieces of information that plausibly affect firm value are binary, for example, the award of a contract, a legal judgment, or a regulatory decision such as the award of a patent or the permission to market a drug.

There are N insiders each of whom receives a private signal $\theta_{jt}, j \in J = \{1, ..., N\}$, at the start of every period. Initially we assume that all insiders receive identical and perfect information, or $\theta_{jt} = \delta_t$. After trading in that period is completed, δ_t is revealed at the end of period t.[8] Insiders' trading strategies, $x_j = \{x_{jt}(\theta_{jt})\}_{t \in T}$, are functions of their signals. Denote the set of such strategies X and define $X_{-j} = \{x_i\}_{i \in J, i \neq j}$. Remaining players in our game include liquidity traders whose demands, u_t, are exogenously generated and distributed uniformly on the interval $[-b, b]$ independent of δ_t and a market maker. One could interpret the bounded support as a stylized proxy for resource constraints and other frictions that mitigate arbitrarily large positions. We relax this assumption later by assuming unbounded support for the case with imperfect monitoring. Moreover, similar to the binary support for innovations in firm value, bounded support for liquidity demands is not crucial for the case with perfect monitoring.

Given the market orders of all traders, the net order flow, y_t, is given by

$$y_t = \sum_{j=1}^{N} x_{jt} + u_t.$$

Conditional on the observed order flow, the market maker sets price equal to the expected value of the asset. The breakeven price, p_t, is

$$p_t = p_t(y_t, v_{t-1}) = E[v_t \mid y_t, v_{t-1}] = \begin{cases} v_{t-1} + \sigma, & \text{if} \quad y_t > \bar{y}, \\ v_{t-1}, & \text{if} \quad -\bar{y} < y_t < \bar{y}, \quad (1) \\ v_{t-1} - \sigma, & \text{if} \quad y_t < -\bar{y} \end{cases}$$

where $\bar{y} = b + \sum_{j \in J} x_{jt}(-\sigma)$ and $-\bar{y} = -b + \sum_{j \in J} x_{jt}(\sigma)$ are the critical thresholds such that, in equilibrium, more extreme aggregate order flows reveal insiders' private information, σ (respectively, $-\sigma$). Thus, if $y \in [-\bar{y}, \bar{y}]$ then the market maker infers an insider's information is σ or $-\sigma$ with equal probability and hence does not adjust the price from its initial value. Outside this range, the market maker infers δ from the order flow and set price equal to v. [9] Figure 10.2 depicts the order of events in a representative trading round. Figure 10.3 depicts the distributions of order flow, conditioned on the insiders' information.

The objective of each risk-neutral insider is to maximize the net present value of expected profits over time horizon $\mathcal{T}$. The one-period discount factor is $\gamma \in (0, 1)$. An equilibrium has the insiders choosing the expected profit maximizing demand given price, and the market maker choosing the breakeven (in expectation) price. These conditions are given below:

For all $j \in J$ and $t \in \mathcal{T}$, for all realizations of θ_{js} and any $\hat{x}_{js}$,

$$\sum_{s=t}^{\infty} \gamma^{s-t} E\left[\pi_s\left(x_{js}(\theta_{js})\right) \mid \bar{y}, X_{-j}\right)\right] \geq \sum_{s=t}^{\infty} \gamma^{s-t} E\left[\pi_s\left(\hat{x}_{js}(\theta_{js})\right) \mid \bar{y}, X_{-j}\right)\right], \quad (2)$$

where $E[\pi_s(x_{js}(\theta_{js}) \mid \bar{y}, X_{-j})] \equiv E[x_{js}(\theta_{js})(v_s - p_s)]$.

Consider the one-shot game, $\mathcal{T} = \{1\}$. Here, insider j seeks to maximize the single-period expected profits conditional on his private information and his conjectures about the strategic choices of other insiders and the market maker. Suppose the insider's signal is $\theta_{j1} = \sigma$. [10] Then, suppressing time subscripts when no confusion can result and writing $x_{j1}(\sigma)$ as simply x_j, expected profits are:

$$\begin{aligned}
&E[\pi_j\left(x_j(\sigma) \mid \bar{y}, X_{-j}\right)] \\
=\quad &E[x_j(v_1 - p_1) \mid \bar{y}, X_{-j}] \\
=\quad &x_j(v_1 - p_0 - \sigma)\Pr(p_1 = p_0 + \sigma) + x_j(v_1 - p_0)\Pr(p_1 = p_0) \\
&+ x_j(v_1 - p_0 + \sigma)\Pr(p_1 = p_0 - \sigma), \quad (3) \\
=\quad &\sigma x_j \Pr(p_1 = p_0) \\
=\quad &\sigma x_j \Pr(-\bar{y} \leq y_1 \leq \bar{y}) \\
=\quad &\sigma x_j \int_{-\bar{y}}^{\bar{y}} \frac{1}{2b} du \\
=\quad &\sigma x_j \left(1 - \frac{x_j + \sum_{\substack{i \neq j \\ i \in N}} x_i}{b}\right).
\end{aligned}$$

In (3), the first term in the sum is zero because the market maker adjusts price to equal the expected value of the firm, so insiders cannot profit. The third term in the sum is zero because, conditional on $\theta_{jt} = \sigma$, insiders buy, and thus order flow cannot fall in the range where the market maker lowers the stock price.

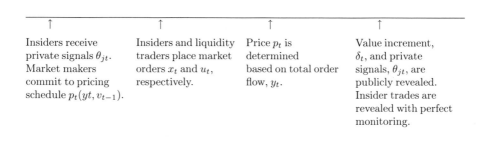

Figure 10.2.   Timeline for Period t

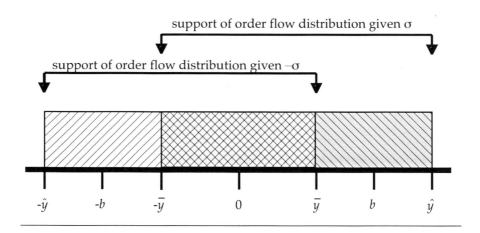

Figure 10.3.   Conditional Distributions of Orderflow. This figure plots the distribution of the order flow conditional on insiders receiving (i) signal $-\sigma$, in which case the order flow is distributed uniformly on $[-\hat{y}, \bar{y}]$ or, (ii) signal σ, in which case the order flow is distributed uniformly on $[-\bar{y}, \hat{y}]$. The two distributions overlap in the cross-hatched region. For any realized order flow in the cross-hatched region, the market maker correctly assesses that it is equally likely that the insiders' information about fundamental value is σ or $-\sigma$. Hence, there is no revision in the price of the stock. If the order flow is less than $-\bar{y}$, then the insiders' information is that the stock is overvalued, and the market maker reduces the current period price by σ. If the order flow exceeds $\bar{y}$, then the insiders' information is that the stock is undervalued, and the market maker increases the current period price by σ.

An equilibrium in this case is a set of strategies for the insiders and the market maker such that

$$E\left[\pi_j\left(x_j(\sigma) \mid \bar{y}, X_{-j}\right)\right] \geq E\left[\pi_j\left(\hat{x}_j(\sigma) \mid \bar{y}, X_{-j}\right)\right],$$

for all $\hat{x}_j, j \in J = \{1, 2, ..., N\}$, and $\bar{y}$ satisfies (1). It follows from Admati and Pfleiderer (1988) that an equilibrium has

$$x_j = x^c = \frac{b}{N+1}, \quad \text{for } j \in J,$$
$$\bar{y} = \bar{y}^c = \frac{b}{N+1}, \quad \text{and}$$
$$E(\pi_j(x_j)) = E(\pi^c) = \frac{b\sigma}{(N+1)^2}, \quad \text{for } j \in J,$$

where we use the superscript c to denote Cournot behavior. When $N = 1$, the solution collapses to Kyle's (1985) monopolist case, denoted with superscript k:

$$x^k = \frac{b}{2},$$
$$\bar{y}^k = \frac{b}{2}, \quad \text{and}$$
$$E(\pi^k) = \frac{b\sigma}{4}.$$

Were each insider to trade quantity x^k/N, the expected profits of each would be

$$\frac{E(\pi^k)}{N} = \frac{b\sigma}{4N} > \frac{b\sigma}{(N+1)^2}, \quad N \geq 2.$$

Thus, there are benefits to coordination, provided self-enforcing strategies can be found such that insiders cooperate in setting their demands at least some of the time.

3. Perfect Monitoring

We begin our analysis of the repeated insider trading game with a setting in which insiders report their trades following each trading round and those reports are publicly disclosed.

Consider the strategy in which each insider chooses x^k/N in every period unless the publicly-revealed trades from the previous round indicate that an insider has defected. The incentive to defect in the first period is characterized by the following optimization:

$$\max_{x_j} E\left[\pi_j\left(x_j(\sigma)\mid \bar{y}, X_{-j} = \{b/2N\}_{i\in J, i\neq j}\right)\right]$$

$$= \max_{x_j} \sigma x_j \left(1 - \frac{x_j + (N-1)b/2N}{b}\right),$$

where, again, we write $x_j(\sigma)$ as simply x_j. It follows from the first-order condition that

$$x_j = \frac{b(N+1)}{4N}.$$

Expected first-period profit given defection is, therefore,

$$E(\pi^d) = \frac{b\sigma(N+1)^2}{16N^2},$$

and the expected first-period gain from defection is

$$E(\pi^d) - \frac{E(\pi^k)}{N} = b\sigma\frac{(N-1)^2}{16N^2}. \tag{4}$$

If a defection occurs, then by self-enforcing preplay agreement insiders choose the Cournot demands for all future periods. The present value of expected future losses from playing the Cournot solution rather than the Kyle solution is

$$\sum_{t=1}^{\infty} \gamma^t \left(\frac{E(\pi^k)}{N} - E(\pi^c)\right) = \frac{\gamma}{1-\gamma} b\sigma \frac{(N-1)^2}{4N(N+1)^2}. \tag{5}$$

Comparing the above with the present value of the expected gain and losses from defection, it is evident that the credible threat to play Cournot in future periods is sufficient to sustain an equilibrium in which insiders collectively behave as a single Kyle monopolist in the current and all future periods for all γ such that the right-hand side of (4) is less than that of (5) or, upon rearranging terms,

$$\gamma > \frac{(N+1)^2}{(N+1)^2 + 4N}, \quad \text{for } N \geq 2. \tag{6}$$

PROPOSITION 1 *Assume public reporting of insider trades, perfect private information, and uniformly distributed liquidity demands. For any number of insiders, $N \geq 2$, and a sufficiently large discount factor, γ, there exists an equilibrium to the infinitely-repeated insider trading game such that aggregate insider demand and expected insider profits in each period correspond to the Kyle monopolist solution.*

PROOF: For all $N \geq 2$, (6) implies $\gamma \in (0, 1)$. Accordingly, a γ can be found such that $x_{jt} = x^k/N$ is a best response to $x_{it} = x^k/N$, for all $i \in J, i \neq j$, and $p_t = E(v_t \mid y_t, v_{t-1})$ defined by (1) for all $t \in T$. Thus, both conditions for an equilibrium are met.

4.   Imperfect Monitoring

In this section, we assume insiders' trades are not publicly reported *ex post*. In this case, aggregate order flow serves as the only signal that may be used to implement coordinated strategies among corporate insiders, all of whom receive perfect private information.

4.1   Bounded (Moving) Support

Recall that the order flow is comprised of both insiders' demands and the random demands from uninformed traders. We define trigger strategies as a pair of critical values, $(-\hat{y}, \hat{y})$, of the order flow conditioned on the realization of the private signal that is publicly observed *ex post*. Set $\hat{y}$ equal to the upper end of the support of the order flow distribution given aggregate insider demand corresponding to the Kyle monopolist solution. Correspondingly, set $-\hat{y}$ equal to the lower end of the support of the order flow distribution given the Kyle solution.[11]

Since choosing the Cournot demands, x^c, along with the price $p_t = E(v_t \mid y_t, v_{t-1})$, is a subgame perfect equilibrium for all $t \in \mathcal{T}$, cooperative strategies in the repeated game exploit the threat of Cournot play to enforce a Pareto-preferred (by insiders) equilibrium. For the remainder of this section, we suppress the time subscript, t. Below, we consider the case $\delta = \sigma$. The case $\delta = -\sigma$ is symmetric. Consider a candidate equilibrium in which each insider's choice of quantity traded is x^k/N, $\hat{y} = b + x^k$, and $T = \infty$. It is sufficient for this to be an equilibrium that no insider has incentive to defect unilaterally from this quantity choice given the threat of Cournot play forever in the event the defection is detected. An insider who contemplates increasing the quantity he trades by d increases his profits by $d\sigma$ per unit traded in the event the market maker does not update the price given the order flow, but he also decreases the probability the price is not updated by $d/(2b)$ and increases the probability he is detected and punished with Cournot play forever by $d/(2b)$. The optimal defection is

$$
\underset{d}{\arg\max} \quad \sigma\left(\frac{x^k}{N} + d\right)\left(1 - \frac{x^k/N + d + (N-1)x^k/N}{b}\right)
$$
$$
- \sigma\left(\frac{x^k}{N}\right)\left(1 - \frac{x^k/N + (N-1)x^k/N}{b}\right)
$$
$$
- \frac{\gamma}{1-\gamma}\left(\frac{E(\pi^k)}{N} - E(\pi^c)\right)\left(\frac{d}{2b}\right).
$$

The first line of this expression is the expected profit in the first period for an insider who defects from the equilibrium to trade $x^k/N + d$ for some $d > 0$.

The second line is the expected profit that an insider would earn in the current period if he did not defect. Hence, the difference of these terms is the payoff to defection in the current period. The third line is expected present value of the reduction in future profits from Cournot rather than monopolistic choices of quantities traded, multiplied by the probability of this outcome.

This expression is strictly concave in d and hence has a unique maximum. The maximizing value of d, from the first-order condition is

$$d = \frac{b(N-1)}{4N}\left(1 - \frac{\gamma}{1-\gamma}\cdot\frac{N-1}{4(N+1)^2}\right).$$

A defection is worthwhile in this equilibrium only if $d > 0$. The discount factor can always be chosen large enough to discourage defection. The critical value of the discount factor is

$$\gamma = \frac{4(N+1)^2}{4(N+1)^2 + N - 1} > \frac{(N+1)^2}{(N+1)^2 + 4N} \quad N \geq 2.$$

The right-hand side of the above inequality is the critical value of the discount rate in the case of perfect monitoring. As we would anticipate given a positive probability that a defection is not detected under imperfect monitoring, the critical discount factor in this case is strictly greater than the critical discount factor with perfect monitoring.

Accordingly, we have shown the following proposition and corollary.

PROPOSITION 2 *Assume no public reporting of insider trades, perfect private information, and uniformly distributed liquidity demands. For any number of insiders, $N \geq 2$, and a sufficiently large discount factor, γ, there exists an equilibrium to the infinitely-repeated insider trading game such that aggregate insider demand and expected insider profits in each period correspond to the Kyle monopolist solution.*

COROLLARY 1 *Under the same assumptions as those in Proposition 2, the critical discount factor for implementing the Kyle monopolist solution, as an equilibrium in every period of the infinitely-repeated insider trading game, through the trigger strategy defined by critical values $(-\hat{y}, \hat{y})$, is strictly greater than the critical discount factor for implementing the Kyle monopoly solution in the case of publicly reported insider trades.*

The moving support plays an obvious role in driving the above results. We interpret bounds on liquidity demands as a stylized reflection of market frictions which preclude unlimited buying and selling by unmodeled liquidity traders. Interestingly, the critical discount factor for this case does not depend on the bounds of this distribution implying robustness with respect to the parameterization.

4.2   Unbounded Support

We now assume that the distribution of liquidity demands extends over the entire real line. This condition implies that defection is never detected with certainty. By assuming normality one might appeal to the optimal strategies of Abreu (1988) (e.g. Dutta and Madhavan, 1997). Instead, we gain some flexibility in choosing distributions by retaining simple trigger strategies and assuming that market makers commit to linear pricing schedules, $p(y_t, v_{t-1}) = \lambda y_t + v_{t-1}$.[12] The ability to demonstrate how the shape of distributions contributes to implementability of coordinated play outweighs the disadvantages of imposing this structure.[13]

We consider the error distribution class for which the Laplace, normal, and uniform are special cases. These three distributions are distinguished by the values of a shape parameter, which governs the degree of kurtosis. Generally speaking, we show that the more platykurtic (i.e., closer to uniform) the distribution, the easier it is to sustain coordination. Coordination is easier to sustain because the sensitivity of our Green and Porter-type trigger strategy to a true defection (rather than a spurious liquidity demand shock) becomes greater implying a higher likelihood of triggering a penalty only if a defection has occurred.

Suppose the insiders' information is $\theta_{jt} = \sigma$.[14] Again, we suppress the time subscript, t. In the first period and any later cooperative period an insider's problem is:

$$\max_{xj} W_j$$

where

$$
\begin{aligned}
W_j &= E\left[\pi_j(\sigma) \mid \lambda, X_{-j}\right] + F(\hat{y} \mid \sigma, X)\gamma W_j \\
&+ (1 - F(\hat{y} \mid \sigma, X))\left(\sum_{s=1}^{T-1} \gamma^s E[\pi^c] + \gamma^T W_j\right), \quad (7)
\end{aligned}
$$

$$
E\left[\pi_j(x_j(\sigma) \mid \lambda, X_{-j})\right] = E\left[x_j\left(\sigma - \lambda\left(\sum_{i \in J} x_i + u\right)\right)\right],
$$

$$
E[\pi^c] = \frac{\sigma \sigma_u}{(N+1)\sqrt{N}},
$$

and the function $F(\hat{y} \mid \sigma, X)$ is the cumulative distribution function (CDF) of the order flow, y, evaluated at the critical value $\hat{y}$.[15] The CDF is conditioned on private information $\delta = \sigma$ and insiders choosing demands X. Specifically, for the error distribution

$$F(y \mid \sigma, X) = \int_{-\infty}^{y} \frac{\exp \dfrac{-\left| z - \sum_{j=1}^{N} x_j \right|^{\frac{2}{\alpha}}}{2\sigma_u^2}}{\sqrt{\sigma_u} 2^{1+\frac{\alpha}{2}} \Gamma(1 + \frac{\alpha}{2})} \, dz. \tag{8}$$

The first term on the right-hand side of (7) is the profit insider j expects in the current period given the quantities traded by the other insiders. The probability that insiders will continue to play cooperatively is $F(\hat{y} \mid \sigma, X)$, where X denotes $\{s_i\}_{i \in J}$. The second term is the present value of insider j's future profits given the order flow, y, is less extreme than the critical value $\hat{y}$ times the probability that order flow is less extreme than the critical value. The third term is the present value of insider j's future profits given the order flow is more extreme than $\hat{y}$ times the probability that order flow exceeds the critical value. The probability that the order flow will be greater than the critical value $\hat{y}$ given δ equals σ is $1 - F(\hat{y} \mid \sigma, X)$, in which event a penalty phase of duration $T - 1$ begins, followed by a return to cooperative play.

Recursive equation (7) can be solved for W_j:

$$\begin{aligned} W_j &= \frac{E(\pi^c)}{1 - \gamma} + \frac{E\left[\pi_j(\sigma) \mid \lambda, X_{-j}\right] - E(\pi^c)}{1 - \gamma^T - (\gamma - \gamma^T) F(\hat{y} \mid \sigma, X)} \\ &= \frac{E(\pi^c)}{1 - \gamma} + \frac{E\left[\pi_j(\sigma) \mid \lambda, X_{-j}\right] - E(\pi^c)}{1 - \gamma + (\gamma - \gamma^T) F(-\hat{y} \mid -\sigma, X)} \end{aligned} \tag{9}$$

where, by symmetry, $F(\hat{y} \mid \sigma, X) = 1 - F(-\hat{y} \mid -\sigma, X)$. The right-hand side of (8) is easy to interpret. The first term is the present value of expected profits assuming Cournot behavior over an indefinite time horizon, and the second term is the present value of the expected gains to cooperative behavior taking into account penalty phases during which insiders do not play cooperatively. If the probability of entering a penalty phase is large, then the second term will be small, consistent with less frequent cooperative behavior.

The first-order conditions are met if $\partial W_j / \partial x_j = 0$ for all $j \in J$, which implies

$$\frac{\partial E\left[\pi_j(\sigma) \mid \lambda, X_{-j}\right]}{\partial x_j(\sigma)} = \frac{E\left[\pi_j(\sigma) \mid \lambda, X_{-j}\right] - E(\pi^c)}{\frac{1-\gamma}{\gamma - \gamma^T} + F(-\hat{y} \mid -\sigma, X)} \cdot \frac{\partial F(-\hat{y} \mid -\sigma, X)}{\partial x_j(\sigma)} \tag{10}$$

for all $j \in J$.

Linearity of prices and Bernoulli private information imply insider demands can be written in the form $x_j(\theta) = \beta_j \theta$, which is familiar from Kyle (1985). Invoking symmetry in choices of β_j (i.e., $\beta_1 = \beta_2 = \ldots = \beta_N = \beta$)

and a choice of λ that yields zero expected profits for the market maker leads to

$$\frac{\partial E\left[\pi_j(\sigma) \mid \lambda, X_{-j}\right]}{\partial x_j(\sigma)} = \left(1 - \frac{N(N+1)\beta^2\sigma^2}{\sigma_u^2 + N^2\beta^2\sigma^2}\right)\sigma^2, \tag{11}$$

for all $j \in J$. For convenience, we make the further transformation of variables

$$k_1 = \beta\frac{N\sigma}{\sigma_u},$$
$$k_2 = \beta^c\frac{N\sigma}{\sigma_u},$$

where k_1 becomes the control variable in the insider's problem and k_2 is a constant entering into the determination of $E[\pi^c]$; i.e., $E[\pi^c] = (\beta^c\sigma^2)/(N+1)$, $\beta^c = \sigma_u/(\sqrt{N}\sigma)$.

We begin with the Laplace distributions for which the shape parameter is $\alpha = 2$. Integrating (8) for this choice of α we obtain

$$F(-y \mid \delta = -\sigma, X) = \frac{1}{2}\exp\left(-\frac{\sqrt{2}}{\sigma_u}(\hat{y} - \sigma\beta)\right), \tag{12}$$

Hence,

$$\frac{\partial F(-y \mid \delta = -\sigma, X)}{\partial \beta} = \frac{\sqrt{2}}{\sigma_u}F(-y \mid \delta = -\sigma, X). \tag{13}$$

Substituting from (12) and (13) into the right-hand side of (10) and equating with the right-hand side of (11) leads to the following necessary condition for a solution other than Cournot behavior in every period:

$$\frac{(N - k_1^2)(1 + k_2^2)}{(k_1k_2 - 1)(k_2 - k_1)} = \frac{\sqrt{2}}{\sigma_u}\frac{F(-\hat{\sigma} \mid \delta = -\sigma, X)}{\frac{1-\gamma}{\gamma-\gamma^T} + F(-\hat{y} \mid \delta = -\sigma, X)}$$

Since, for $T = \infty$ and γ close to 1, the right-hand side approximates but does not exceed $\sqrt{2}$, and the left-hand side exceeds $\sqrt{2}$ for $N \geq 2$, then we arrive at the following result:

PROPOSITION 3 *Assume no public reporting of insider trades, perfect private information, and Laplace distributed liquidity demands. For any number of insiders, $N \geq 2$, and discount factor γ, there does not exist a trigger strategy $(\hat{y}, T)$ equilibrium to the infinitely-repeated insider trading game under which insiders improve upon expected profits from Cournot behavior.*

In the case of normally distributed liquidity demands, further analysis implies

$$
\frac{\partial F(-\hat{y} \mid -\sigma)}{\partial \beta_i} = \frac{\sigma}{\sqrt{2\pi}\sigma_u} \exp\left(-\frac{1}{2}\left(\frac{-\hat{y} + N\beta\sigma}{\sigma_u}\right)^2\right)
$$

$$
= \frac{\sigma}{\sqrt{2\pi}\sigma_u} \exp\left(-\frac{1}{2}\left(\frac{-\hat{y} + k_1\sigma_u}{\sigma_u}\right)^2\right).
$$

Thus, after rearrangement and simplification, the first-order conditions obtained by equating the right-hand sides of (10) and (11) can be re-expressed as follows:

$$
\frac{(N - k_1^2)(1 + k_2^2)}{(k_1 k_2 - 1)(k_2 - k_1)} =
$$

$$
\sigma_u \frac{\frac{1}{\sqrt{2\pi}\sigma_u} \exp\left(-\frac{1}{2}\left(\frac{-\hat{y}+k_1\sigma_u}{\sigma_u}\right)^2\right)}{\frac{1-\gamma}{\gamma-\gamma^T} + \int_{-\infty}^{-\hat{y}} \frac{1}{\sqrt{2\pi}\sigma_u} \exp\left(-\frac{1}{2}\left(\frac{-z+k_1\sigma_u}{\sigma_u}\right)^2\right) dz}. \tag{14}
$$

When penalty phases are characterized by Cournot play, $k_2 = \sqrt{N}$, condition (14) becomes

$$
\frac{(N - k_1^2)(1 + N)}{(k_1\sqrt{N} - 1)(\sqrt{N} - k_1)} = \frac{\sigma_u f(\hat{y} \mid \delta = \sigma)}{\frac{1-\gamma}{\gamma-\gamma^T} + (1 - F(\hat{y} \mid \delta = \sigma))}, \tag{15}
$$

where we have exploited $f(-\hat{y} \mid \delta = -\sigma) = f(\hat{y} \mid \delta = \sigma)$ and $F(-\hat{y} \mid \delta = -\sigma) = 1 - F(\hat{y} \mid \delta = \sigma)$. Writing the first-order-conditions in this manner contributes to the proof of the proposition below:

PROPOSITION 4 *Assume insiders possess perfect private information and liquidity demands are normally distributed. For any number of insiders, $N \geq 2$, and sufficiently large discount factor, γ, there exists a trigger strategy $(\hat{y}, T)$ that satisfies the first-order-conditions for an equilibrium to the infinitely-repeated insider trading game, and under which aggregate expected insider profits exceed those from Cournot behavior.*

PROOF: The left-hand side of (14) is positive and finite for all $k_1 \in (1, \sqrt{N})$. The right-hand side is increasing in the hazard rate, $f/(1 - F)$, which, in turn is increasing in critical value, $\hat{y}$. The hazard rate for a normal distribution is strictly monotone increasing over the real line (Bagnoli and Bergstrom, 1989). Set the duration of the penalty phase $T = \infty$. A discount factor, γ, can always be found sufficiently close to 1 such that $(1 - \gamma)/\gamma$ becomes arbitrarily small, thereby allowing the effect of the hazard rate to dominate in determining the magnitude of the right-hand side.

The second-order conditions are more difficult to assess. Unfortunately, convexity of the distribution function F is not sufficient in itself to ensure that the value function W given by (8) is concave.[16] However, numerical examples display at least quasi-concavity, implying in those examples, that first-order-conditions are sufficient as well as necessary in characterizing an equilibrium.[17]

Proposition 4 demonstrates the existence of a cooperative equilibrium when liquidity traders' demands are normally distributed and the discount factor is sufficiently high. Figure 10.3 depicts the right-hand side of (14) as a function of the critical value, $\hat{y}$, for a series of three discount factors γ_1, γ_2, and γ_3, which, moving to the left, become closer to 1. The remaining parameters are $N = 2, \sigma_u^2 = \sigma^2 = 1, k_2 = \sqrt{2}$. Also, k_1 is fixed at slightly less than k_2. These values imply a left-hand side of approximately 8.5. Hence, as the graph shows, a $\hat{y}$ close to -2.25 for $\gamma = \gamma_3$ will satisfy the first-order-condition for a cooperative equilibrium. Figure 10.4 depicts the natural log of the value function (8) for values of $\beta_1 \in (.3, 1.3)$, given $\beta_2 = .704 < 1/\sqrt{2} \approx .707, \gamma = \gamma_3$, and N, σ_u^2, and σ^2 as above.[18] The optimum at $\beta_1 = \beta_2 = .704$ confirms the existence of a cooperative equilibrium in which demands are less than those under Cournot competition (Figure 10.5).

A comparison of results for Laplace and normally distributed liquidity demands suggests the kurtosis of the distribution is crucial to the existence of cooperative equilibria. The intuition for this observation is that platykurtic (closer to uniform) distributions offer more scope for detecting defections (i.e., over-aggressive trading) by insiders which shift the location parameter. By choosing an error distribution that is sufficiently platykurtic, the hazard rate increases at an increasing rate. For instance, we employ the following distribution function in developing the right-hand side of (14) (i.e., a shape parameter $\alpha = \frac{1}{4}$):

$$F(-\hat{y} \mid -\sigma, X) = \int_{-\infty}^{-\hat{y}} \frac{\exp \frac{|y+k_1\sigma_u|^8}{2\sigma_u}}{\sqrt{\sigma_u}2^{\frac{9}{8}}\Gamma\left(\frac{9}{8}\right)} \, dy,$$

Figure 10.6 depicts the new right-hand side of (14). Given an infinite penalty phase duration $(T = \infty)$, discount factor γ close to one, and k_1 close to $\sqrt{2}$, then the right-hand side will equal the left-hand side for some $\hat{y}$ greater than 2. Setting $\hat{y} = 2.4$, we find equilibrium values of $\beta_1 = \beta_2 = 0.576$ which are closer to the shared monopoly demand of $\frac{1}{2}$ than under the earlier normality assumption.

4.3 General Imperfect Monitoring

Although trigger strategies have the advantage of simplicity, they are not optimal (from the insider's point of view) for inducing cooperative behavior. Abreu et al. (1986) show that optimal strategies are bang-bang in the sense that

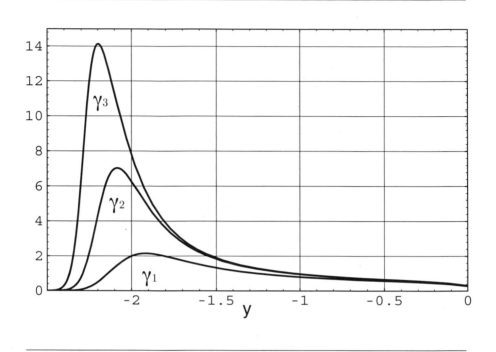

Figure 10.4. First Order Condition as a Function of y and γ. This figure plots the right-hand side of the first order condition, $\dfrac{\sigma_u f(y)}{\frac{\gamma}{1-\gamma}+1-F(y)}$ as a function of the order flow, y, for discount factors $\gamma_1 = .9$, $\gamma_2 = .99$, and $\gamma_3 = .999$.

either the best cooperative solution or the non-cooperative solution is played each round in equilibrium. The process governing which solution is played is Markov. Since noise in the monitor under imperfect information implies non-degenerate transition probabilities, then the cooperative solution cannot be achieved in every period even when our restriction to trigger strategies is removed. This, in turn, suggests that, qualitatively, there is little to be gained from solving for optimal strategies even if that were feasible for non-normal cases.

5.   Imperfect Private Information

We can generalize our earlier results with perfect monitoring by assuming that private information is imperfect and insider trades are publicly disclosed *ex*

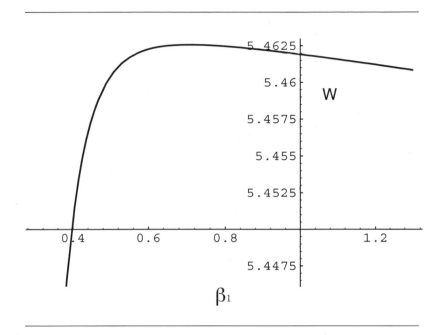

Figure 10.5. Value function for $\beta_2 = 0.704$. This figure plots the natural log of the value function, W, as a function of $\beta_1 \in (0.3, 1.3)$, given $\beta_2 = 0.704$.

post. These conditions approximate analysts' trades on their earnings forecast before they are publicly announced.[19]

Specifically, we assume that liquidity demands are normally distributed and private signals have the following structure:

$$\theta_{jt} = \delta_t + e_{jt} , \ e_{jt} \sim NID(0, \sigma_e^2).$$

The one-shot Cournot and Kyle monopolist solutions, where the monopolist observes all of the signals, are now

$$\beta^c = \frac{\sigma_u}{\sqrt{N}(\sigma_e^2 + \sigma^2)^{\frac{1}{2}}},$$

$$\lambda^c = \frac{\sigma^2}{2\sigma_e^2 + (N+1)\sigma^2} \frac{\sqrt{N}(\sigma_e^2 + \sigma^2)^{\frac{1}{2}}}{\sigma_u},$$

$$E(\pi^c) = \frac{\sigma^2}{2\sigma_e^2 + (N+1)\sigma^2} \frac{\sigma_u(\sigma_e^2 + \sigma^2)^{\frac{1}{2}}}{\sqrt{N}},$$

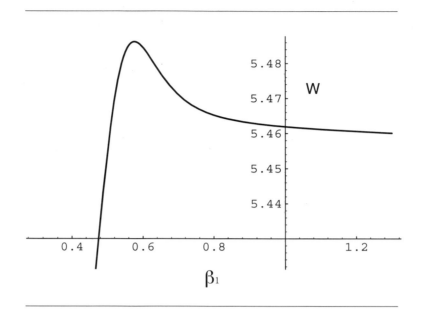

Figure 10.6. Value function for $\beta_2 = 0.576$. This figure plots the natural log of the value function, W, as a function of $\beta_1 \in (0.4, 1.2)$, given $\beta_2 = 0.576$.

and

$$\beta^k = \frac{\sqrt{N}\sigma_u}{(\sigma_e^2 + N\sigma^2)^{\frac{1}{2}}},$$

$$\lambda^k = \frac{\sqrt{N}\sigma^2}{2\sigma_u(\sigma_e^2 + N\sigma^2)^{\frac{1}{2}}},$$

$$E(\pi^k) = \frac{\sqrt{N}\sigma^2\sigma_u}{2(\sigma_e^2 + N\sigma^2)^{\frac{1}{2}}},$$

respectively. Hence,

$$\frac{1}{N}E(\pi^k) = \frac{\sqrt{N}\sigma^2\sigma_u}{2N(\sigma_e^2 + N\sigma^2)^{\frac{1}{2}}}.$$

Similar to the perfect information case, $E(\pi^k)/N > E(\pi^c)$ implying that insiders can implement the monopoly solution for values of γ close to one.

PROPOSITION 5 *Assume public reporting of insider trades and imperfect private information. For any number of insiders, $N \geq 2$, and a sufficiently large* *discount factor, γ, there exists an equilibrium to the infinitely-repeated insider trading game such that aggregate demand and expected insider profits in each period correspond to the Kyle monopolist solution.*

PROOF: As in the case with perfect information, the expected gain from defection in any given period is finite, while expected future losses from henceforth playing the Cournot solution can be made arbitrarily large by setting γ sufficiently close to 1.[20]

Tacit coordination in this case has two consequences: a reduction in demand by eliminating the effects of competition, and constructive sharing of information. Interestingly, in the absence of tacit coordination, insiders prefer not to share information. Analogous to product market games, there is more to gain from having rivals trade less intensely when extreme signals are realized than to lose from having rivals trade more intensely when non-extreme signals are realized. However, once the effects of competition are mitigated, then insiders jointly benefit from more precise private information.

To better understand how insiders benefit from information sharing without exchanging signals, suppose one insider gets a high private signal realization and another gets a low realization. The first trader would go too far long and the second too far short relative to demands based on both signals. However, the price adjustment would tend to be lower than that based on the first insider's demands and higher than that based on the second insider's demands. The first (second) insider loses from having set her demands too high (low), but benefits from the smaller price adjustment. The net result is that expected profits match the expected profits of a single insider with both signals who chooses the monopoly demand. Hence, if a strategy can be found which induces each insider to select a demand equal to half the intensity a monopolist who receives both signals would choose, then the total profits to insiders would equal a monopolist's profits based on all of the information.

6. Conclusion

In this paper, we consider how insiders in a financial market may tacitly coordinate trades to their mutual benefit to limit the aggregate quantities they trade. Analogous to tacit coordination to reduce output in oligopolistic product markets, we show that traders benefit when they trade less intensely on their private information. Whether insiders can achieve the full Kyle monopoly solution depends upon the extent to which they can monitor each other's trades. Given public reporting of insider trades, we demonstrate implementability of the monopoly solutions for sufficiently large discount factors. Even without public reporting, moving support for the aggregate order flow may suffice to implement the monopoly solution, albeit for discount factors strictly larger than the critical discount factor for the case with public reporting. Working within the error class of distributions, we show that some gains to tacit coordination are also achievable for sufficiently large discount factors when there is unbounded support and, hence, no positive probability of certain detection of defections. While the restrictions to linear price schedules and simple trigger strategies limit the generality of our results in this last case, it seems reasonable to conclude that (i) some degree of tacit coordination is achievable by corporate insiders with common and repeated access to private information, and (ii) public reporting of insider trades exacerbates the problem of such coordination.

Our principal findings that corporate insiders may benefit (at the expense of liquidity traders) from regulations that require *ex post* reporting of their trades run contrary to the intent of insider trading regulations. Given repeated rounds of trading, mandatory public reporting of insider trades improves insiders' ability to monitor each other's demand, thereby facilitating tacit coordination. This is especially true when private signals relate to information routinely revealed through public announcements, such as earnings releases, and the cohort of insiders remains stable for many periods, as is often the case with corporate officers, directors and principal stock holders. Relaxing the assumption of perfect information, we also consider settings in which insiders, say financial analysts, have imperfect information. The results are qualitatively similar, although an added feature in this setting is that insiders, constructively, behave as if they were able to pool their private signals.

The Sarbanes-Oxley Act does not change the definition of an insider or the types of transactions which must be reported; however, the Act shortens the filing deadline for Forms 4 from the tenth of the month following the trade to the second business day after a reportable transaction occurs. Also, the types of transactions for which delayed reporting on Form 5 is allowed is narrowed. While the shortening of the reporting interval may in effect reduce the liquidity available to disguise insiders demands in the sense of Kyle's multi-round trading model, it also may have made it easier to coordinate trades. In addition, pre-planned trading programs under Rule 10b5-1 may facilitate trade coordination by insiders. The effects of this rule on the abnormal returns and profitability of insider trade are analyzed by Jagolinzer (2004).

Similar to Fishman and Hagerty (1995) and John and Narayanan (1997), our results contribute to a deeper understanding of the potential consequences of regulations that require the public reporting of insider trades. Although our analysis abstracts away from manipulation in the sense of the above studies, it reinforces the view that, *ceteris paribus*, public reporting of insiders' trades may be counter-productive. Of course, insider trading regulations are not limited to public reporting of insiders' trades, e.g., disgorging profits on short-swing transactions pursuant to section 16(b) of the Securities and Exchange Act, 1934. However, this requirement could be enforced without making reported trades publicly available to other insiders and market makers.[21] Since the short-swing profit rule is itself controversial,[22] then our results also add to the debate on the merit of that regulation.

Finally, we observe that the impact of insider trading in the price discovery process depends on the degree of competition among corporate insiders. In turn, this degree of competition depends on the availability of a public record of insider trades, and the nature of other market participants' liquidity demands. Our results suggest that, ceteris paribus, public disclosure of insider trades, paradoxically, inhibits rather than advances price discovery.

Notes

1. See Hoskin et al. (1986) for a description of information typically disclosed concurrent with periodic earnings announcements.

2. Under this requirement insiders must hold their positions following the purchase or sale of shares in their firm for a minimum of six months to exploit their information advantage.

3. We are indebted to David Hsieh for this observation.

4. Companies frequently set blackout periods prior to earnings announcements during which corporate insiders are not permitted to trade. for example, trading may only be allowed on the twenty days beginning three days after an earnings announcement. However, this does not preclude trading on information expected to surface in the next earnings announcement. In fact, limiting the window for insider trading may enhance tacit coordination by clustering insider trades.

5. Laura Saunders Egodigwe, "EDS insiders unloaded $22.7 million worth of stock in 6-week span," *Wall Street Journal* (May 6, 1998), p. C1.

6. Laura Saunders Egodigwe, "Curative insiders sell stock before warning by FDA is disclosed," *Wall Street Journal* (April 22, 1998), p. C1.

7. Bob Gabele. "The inside story: Increased scrutiny makes interpreting their trades tougher" *Barron's* (April 6, 1998), p. 20.

8. To ease the analysis, we rule out multiple rounds of trading between public revelation of inside information. In so doing, we suppress an interesting issue concerning the effect of public disclosing of insider trades before such revelation. Huddart et al. (1998) show the existence of a mixed strategy equilibrium in which insiders add noise to their information-based demands to preserve some of their private information for future rounds of trade.

9. Recall that private information is short-lived implying no scope for strategic behavior in the sense of manipulating prices for future trading advantage by going contrarian. Hence, an insider can only profit from private information by trading in the same direction as the private signal.

10. The case $\theta_{j1} = -\sigma$ is symmetrical.

11. We provide conditions under which these trigger points yield monopoly profits to insiders in aggregate. When this choice of trigger points yields monopoly profits to insiders in aggregate, then no alternative strategy can do better. In particular, other choices of trigger points are dominated. Choosing trigger points less in absolute value than $\hat{y}$ implies that sometimes a penalty phase is entered when no deviation has occurred. Since monopoly profits can be implemented with zero probability of falsely triggering a penalty phase, trigger points less in absolute value than $\hat{y}$ are dominated. Choosing trigger points greater in absolute value than $\hat{y}$ implies defections resulting in order flows greater in absolute value than $\hat{y}$ go unpunished. Since such defections can be punished without falsely triggering a penalty phase by using trigger points $(-\hat{y}, \hat{y})$, then trigger points greater in absolute value than $\hat{y}$ are dominated.

12. Note that λ replaces $\bar{y}$ as the endogenous parameter defining the market maker's strategy.

13. In the absence of commitment, *ex post*, a breakeven market maker would have incentive to deviate from a linear price schedule unless the distributional assumptions support expectations that are linear in order flow. Our assumption allows us to consider a family of distributions for liquidity demands. Varying the

kurtosis of liquidity demands illustrates the sensitivity to an insider's defection of the probability realized demand, y, falls outside the critical order flow values.

14. The case $\theta_{jt} = -\sigma$ is symmetric.

15. See Admati and Pfleiderer for a derivation of $E[\pi^c]$.

16. Porter (1983) claims that convexity of the distribution function is sufficient for concavity of the value function. However, it can be shown by counterexample that a ratio of concave and convex functions need not be concave. Green and Porter (1984) do not address the issue of existence and do not report on second-order conditions.

17. A qualitatively similar case would be to assume that insiders' trades are reported, but that private signals contain additive noise. Since the characterizations of demands and price adjustments are more complex and no new insights appear to be present, we do not extend our analysis to this case.

18. The log transformation is useful to demonstrating concavity and ensuring numerical precision.

19. See Abdel-khalik and Ajinka (1982) for discussion and analysis of returns in this case. Their findings suggest that profitable trading strategies can be found based on advance knowledge of forecast revisions and abnormal returns cannot be earned shortly after their public release.

20. Details are available from the authors upon request.

21. Fishman and Hagerty (1995) make a similar point, and cite the reporting of futures positions to the Commodities Futures Trading Commission (CFTC).

22. See Fishman and Hagerty (1995), pp. 665-666, for a discussion of this debate.

References

Abreu, D., 1988, "On the Theory of Infinitely Repeated Games with Discounting," *Econometrica,* 80, 383–396.

Abreu, D., D. Pearce, and E. Stacchetti, 1986, "Optimal Cartel Equilibria with Imperfect Monitoring," *Journal of Economic Theory,* 39, 251–269.

Abdel-khalik, A. R., and B. B. Ajinkya, 1982, "Returns to Informational Advantages: The Case of Analysts' Forecast Revisions," *The Accounting Review,* 57, 661–680.

Admati, A., and P. Pfleiderer, 1988, "A Theory of Intraday Patterns: Volume and Price Variability," *Review of Financial Studies,* 1, 3–40.

Bagnoli, M., and T. Bergstrom, 1989, "Log-concave Probability and Its Applications," Working Paper No. 89-23, University of Michigan.

Carlton, D., and D. Fischel, 1983, "The Regulation of Insider Trading," *Stanford Law Review,* 35, 857–895.

Damodaran, A., and C. Liu, 1993, "Insider Trading as a Signal of Private Information," *Review of Financial Studies,* 6, 79–119.

Dutta, P., and A. Madhavan, 1997, "Competition and Collusion in Dealer Markets," *Journal of Finance,* 52, 245–276.

Fishman, M., and K. Hagerty, 1995, "The Mandatory Disclosure of Trades and Market Liquidity," *Review of Financial Studies,* 8, 637–676.

Foster, F. D., and S. Viswanathan, 1993, "The Effect of Public Information and Competition on Trading Volume and Price Volatility," *Review of Financial Studies,* 6, 23–56.

Foster, F. D., and S. Viswanathan, 1996, "Strategic Trading when Agents Forecast the Forecasts of Others," *The Journal of Finance,* 51, 1437–1478.

Fudenberg, D., D. Levine, and E. Maskin, 1994, "The Folk Theorem with Imperfect Public Information," *Econometrica,* 62, 997–1039.

Green, E. J., and R. H. Porter, 1984, "Noncooperative Collusion under Imperfect Price Information," *Econometrica,* 52, 87–100.

Holden, C., and A. Subrahmanyam, 1992, "Long-lived Private Information and Imperfect Competition," *The Journal of Finance,* 47, 247–270.

Hoskin R. E., Hughes, J. S., and Ricks, W. E., 1986, "Evidence on the Incremental Information Content of Additional Firm Disclosures Made Concurrently with Earnings," *Journal of Accounting Research,* 24, 1–36.

Huddart, S., Hughes, J. S., and C. B. Levine, 1998," Public Disclosure of Insider Trades, Trading Costs, and Price Discovery," Working paper, Duke University.

Jagolinzer, A. 2004, An empirical analysis of insider trade within Rule10b5-1. *Unpublished Ph.D. Thesis,* Pennsylvania State University.

John, K., and R. Narayanan, 1997, "Market Manipulation and the Role of Insider Trading Regulations," *Journal of Business,* 70, 217–247.

Kyle, A., 1985, "Continuous Auctions and Insider Trading," *Econometrica,* 53, 1315–1335.

Penman, S., 1982, "Insider Trading and the Dissemination of Firms' Forecast Information," *Journal of Business,* 55, 479–503.

Pettit, R. R., and P. C. Venkatesh, 1995, "Insider Trading and Long-run Return Performance," *Financial Management,* 24, 88–104.

Porter, R. H., 1983, "Optimal Cartel Trigger Price Strategies," *Journal of Economic Theory,* 29, 313–338.

Seyhun, H. N., 1986, "Insiders' Profits, Costs of Trading, and Market Efficiency," *Journal of Financial Economics,* 16, 189–212.

Seyhun, H. N., 1992a, "The Effectiveness of Insider Trading Sanctions," *Journal of Law and Economics,* 35, 149–182.

Seyhun, H. N., 1992b, "Why Does Aggregate Insider Trading Predict Future Stock Returns?" *Quarterly Journal of Economics,* 107, 1303–1331.

PART III

CONNECTIONS TO PRACTICE

Chapter 11

THE STRUCTURE OF PERFORMANCE-VESTED STOCK OPTION GRANTS

Joseph J. Gerakos[1], Christopher D. Ittner[1], David F. Larcker[2]
[1]University of Pennsylvania, [2]Stanford University

Abstract: U.S. executive compensation traditionally relies on stock options that vest over time. Recently, however, a growing number of institutional investors have called for the use of performance-vested options that link vesting to the achievement of performance targets. We examine the factors influencing the structure of performance-vested stock option grants to U.S. CEOs. We find that performance-vested options comprise a greater proportion of equity compensation in firms with lower stock return volatility and market-to-book ratios, and in those with new external CEO appointments, providing some support for theories on the options' incentive and sorting benefits. However, firms with larger holdings by pension funds are less likely to completely replace traditional options with performance-vested options, and make traditional options a greater percentage of option grants, suggesting that token performance-vested option grants may also be used to placate pension funds that are calling for their use. In addition, our exploratory examination of performance-vesting criteria finds similarities and differences to prior studies on the choice of performance measures in compensation contracts.

Key words: Compensation, stock options, performance measurement, incentives

1.   INTRODUCTION

Two issues that have received considerable attention in the accounting and economics literatures are the use of stock option grants and choice of performance measures in executive compensation contracts. U.S. firms traditionally grant options with vesting conditional on elapsed time alone (e.g., 25% of the options vest in each of the four years after the grant).

However, an increasing number of institutional investors are calling for "traditional" options to be replaced by "performance-vested" options.[46] In contrast to traditional options, performance-vested options link vesting not only to elapsed time, but also to improvements in stock market, accounting, or other performance measures.   According to proponents, these options only reward executives when they achieve superior economic performance and not when performance merely mirrors competitors or follows market trends, thereby providing stronger incentives to maximize shareholder value. Yet, despite these claims and extensive international use of performance-vested options, theoretical and empirical research on performance-vested options is extremely limited.

The objective of this study is to provide a rich description of the structure of performance-vested option grants made by U.S. firms, and to offer exploratory evidence on some of the factors influencing variations in the magnitude of these grants, the mix between traditional and performance-vested options, and the performance measures used for vesting purposes. In doing so, we hope to foster additional research on a compensation component that many expect to see widely adopted by U.S. firms (e.g., Tully, 1998; Frieswick, 2003), as it already has been by many of their international counterparts.

We explore these issues using a sample of 128 U.S. firms that initially granted performance-vested options to their CEOs between 1993 and 2002. Two of the strongest determinants of performance-vested option grant design are the firm's stock return volatility and market-to-book ratio, with lower volatility and market-to-book ratios associated with greater use. New CEO appointments also appear to have some influence on the mix of options and the choice of performance objectives for vesting. Moreover, we find that firms with larger holdings by pension funds are less likely to completely replace traditional options with performance-vested options, and make traditional options a greater percentage of option grants. We conclude our exploratory analysis with suggestions for future research.

---

[46] Among the U.S. institutional investors or investment advisors calling for the use of performance-vested or other performance-based options (e.g., premium or indexed) are the AFL-CIO (2003), CalPERS (2003), and Institutional Shareholder Services (2004). In the U.K., institutional pressure from organizations such as the Association of British Insurers and the National Association of Pension Funds have led the vast majority of British firms to include performance-vesting criteria in their option grants. Similarly, a survey by Towers Perrin finds significant use of performance-vested options in other countries (http://www.towers.com/towers/locations/germany/pdfs/(20.pdf)), which they attribute to differences in tax and legal systems and in the role of institutional investors.

2.   LITERATURE REVIEW

2.1   Background

Performance-vested options can serve as complements or substitutes for traditional options in compensation contracts. Performance-vested option grants typically are made at market price, with vesting based on the achievement of stock market, accounting, or other performance targets. Options with vesting linked to stock price generally identify a target price and a minimum number of trading days the closing price must be above the target for the option to vest. When vesting is based on stock returns, the firm usually specifies a minimum level of cumulative annual returns over a set period. Accounting-based vesting typically is linked to cumulative EPS growth. Vesting can also be contingent on non-financial performance, but details on the specific non-financial performance criteria or targets (e.g., improvements in some type of non-financial metric or achievement of a strategic milestone) frequently are not provided in the proxy statement.

Performance can be measured on a relative or absolute basis. When performance is measured on a relative basis, the firm identifies an index or comparison group for performance evaluation. Vesting is then based on the achievement of a minimum performance level compared to this group (e.g., performance in the top 20%). When performance is measured on an absolute basis, the firm targets a specific performance level or improvement rate. Appendix A provides examples of the performance objectives used by firms in our study.

During the sample period, U.S. firms generally accounted for executive stock options under APB No. 25. Executive option grants under APB No. 25 are subject to either fixed or variable accounting, depending upon the date the number of options received and their corresponding exercise price become known (hereafter denoted "measurement date"). If the measurement date occurs after the grant date, the grant is subject to variable accounting and the firm must expense, on an ongoing basis, the difference between the current value of the options and the value of the options on the grant date. If the measurement date is the same as the grant date, the grant is subject to fixed accounting rules and the firm does not incur this adverse accounting treatment.

Performance-vested options can require a charge against income because the measurement date, which is contingent on the achievement of performance targets, differs from the grant date. To avoid this accounting expense, most firms using performance-vested options include cliff-vesting provisions in their compensation plans. Under these provisions, 100 percent of the options vest at one point in time (typically at or during the ninth year after the grant) regardless of performance. However, vesting is accelerated if the pre-established performance targets are met. Under APB No. 25, the measurement date does not change when options vest on an accelerated basis if the vesting terms are explicitly stated in the compensation plan. Consequently, performance-vested options with cliff vesting provisions do not require a charge against income.[47]

2.2 Economic Justifications

The use of performance-vested options typically is justified in terms of incentive effects. According to many institutional investors and other proponents, performance-vested options provide stronger incentives for executives to outperform competitors, rather than rewarding them for stock price increases solely due to general market improvements (e.g., AFL-CIO, 2003; CalPERS, 2003). Firms frequently offer similar explanations when justifying their use of performance-vested options. For example, Conoco's 1999 proxy statement notes that:

> It is the Committee's policy that the vesting schedule for option grants be predominantly performance-based, with appropriately aggressive vesting targets. When structured this way, the Committee believes that the options properly align the interests of management and shareholders by rewarding management only for exceptional business performance.

Theoretical support for the incentive benefits from performance-vested options, on the other hand, is limited. Johnson and Tian (2000) compare the valuation of traditional options relative to various types of non-traditional options. Holding the Black-Scholes value of the option grant constant, their results indicate that performance-vested options (which they assume to be tied to stock market performance and to have no cliff-vesting provisions)

---

[47] In our sample, 74 percent of the firms using performance-vested options include cliff-vesting provisions. Capital One's options, for example, vested in three years if the stock price increased at a compound annual rate of at least 20 percent over the next three years. However, if they did not vest in three years, they would eventually vest in nine years regardless of stock price performance. In response to criticism of this feature, the company's compensation committee chairman explained (Westreich, 1999):

> That feature is necessary so that the company is not required to take a significant expense against earnings in its reported income statement, as a result of the aggressive performance features built into the plan. ... Capital One's directors believe it would clearly not be in our stockholders' interests to burden the company's results with an accounting charge that companies without performance-based options would not have to take.

provide stronger incentives to increase stock price than traditional options (i.e., larger option *deltas*), as well as stronger incentives to increase return volatility (i.e., larger option *vegas*). The increase in risk-taking incentives is greatest at low volatility levels, but continues to be greater than traditional options at higher volatility levels. They conclude that firms with stronger motivations to increase stock price and stock volatility, along with those having risk-averse executives and under-developed but risky positive net present value investment opportunities, benefit the most from granting performance-vested options.

Camara (2001) builds on their analysis to examine the incentive effects of options that link vesting to performance relative to a comparison group. His model indicates that performance-vested options with relative performance hurdles do not provide stronger incentives than traditional options for improving shareholder wealth, but do provide stronger incentives to undertake risky capital investment projects and increase stock volatility.

Arya and Mittendorf's model (2004) suggests that performance-based options can also be used for gauging new managerial talent. For example, the firm can offer performance-vested stock options that require superior performance to generate a payment to a new CEO. Since firm value and the likelihood of option exercise are contingent on managerial ability, only high talent managers will accept this type of risky compensation contract.

Together with the claims of performance-vested option proponents, these models suggest that firms desiring to increase incentives to improve stock market performance by taking on more risky capital investments that increase volatility, or those attempting to use riskier compensation to sort new CEO candidates based on talent, will (contingent upon adoption) make performance-vested options a larger component of option grants.

2.3   Institutional Pressure

An alternative explanation for the use of performance-vested options is that they are granted to placate institutional investors. Many (activist) pension funds are among the strongest proponents of performance-vested options, and many have sponsored proxy resolutions calling for firms to adopt performance-vested options, or have issued proxy voting guidelines that call for shareholders to withdraw support for stock option plans that are not performance-based. CalPERS (2003), for example, states that it will not support any executive compensation plan that does not include a significant proportion of performance-based (i.e., performance-vested, premium, or indexed) options.

Symbolic management and institutional theories argue that firms often adopt token compensation elements (or "window-dressing") that are desired by external stakeholder groups in order to protect the organization from having its compensation decisions questioned (e.g., Meyer and Rowan, 1977; Westphal and Zajac, 1994, 1998; Zajac and Westphal, 1995). Similarly, critics charge that external pressure from pension funds or other institutional investors has led firms to incorporate performance-vested options into their compensation plans, with no expectation that these options will improve incentives or performance (Morgenson, 2003, 2004). By including a relatively small number of performance-vested options in the compensation plan or using performance-vested options as "add-ons" to large traditional option grants, firms may be able to reduce pension funds' or other institutional investors' criticism of compensation practices while limiting the actual impact of performance-vested options on the firms' internal compensation practices (Zajac and Westphal, 1995; Conyon et al., 2001). Consistent with this prediction, Westphal and Zajac (1998) find that minimal adoption of long-term incentive plans in U.S. firms interacts with institutional ownership to limit subsequent governance changes, suggesting that the minimal adoption satisfies institutional investors' calls for governance reforms.

3.   SAMPLE

We conduct our exploratory analysis using a sample of firms that made initial performance-vested option grants to their CEOs between 1993 and 2002. We identify a preliminary sample of performance-vested option adopters through extensive keyword searches of LiveEdgar, Dow Jones Interactive, and the comment field of ExecuComp. We supplement these search results with performance-vested option users identified in research reports by The Corporate Library (Hodgson, 2001) and F.W. Cook (Kim, 2002).

We confirm the use and initial adoption date of performance-vested options by examining the firm's proxy statements. To obtain a clean sample of firms where the observed adoption of performance-vested options for CEOs represents a shift in compensation policy, we exclude firms where: (1) the use or initial adoption date of performance-vested options could not be verified, (2) performance-vested options had previously been granted to other members of the executive team, or (3) the options related to a new corporate entity (e.g., an IPO or a spin-off).

Our final sample consists of 128 observations. Table 1 provides the distribution of observations by industry and adoption date. The sample firms operate in 38 different two-digit SIC codes. The largest representation is found in business services, utilities, depository institutions, electrical equipment, and chemical and allied products. No other industry comprises more than 6 percent of the sample. Relative to the population on Compustat, our sample has substantially more utilities, wholesalers of nondurable goods, food stores, insurance carriers, and business service firms. The percentage representation of firms in other industries is within two percent of their representation in Compustat. The most frequent adoption years are 1997 (14.8%), 1999 (12.5%), 2000 (11.7%), 1995 (11.9%), and 1994 (10.2%).

4. VARIABLES

4.1 Option Grant Characteristics

We use several variables to measure the relative use and magnitude of traditional and performance-vested option grants. The first two variables represent the mix of traditional and performance-vested options. REPLACE equals one when performance-vested options completely replace traditional options, else zero. %PERFORMANCE equals the number of performance-vested options granted to the CEO divided by the total number of options granted to this executive in the adoption year.

Our second set of variables examines the magnitude of option grants relative to those made in the past two years. Two limitations of the %PERFORMANCE measure are that it does not distinguish between performance-vested option grants that are complements or substitutes for traditional options, and does not provide information on whether option grants have increased or decreased relative to the past. Consider, for example, three firms that historically have granted 100 options per year to their CEOs. The first replaces 50 traditional options with performance-vested options, but continues to grant 100 options. The second continues to grant 100 traditional options, but supplements these with 100 performance-vested options. The third increases all types of options, granting 200 traditional options and 200 performance-vested options. %PERFORMANCE has the same value for each of these firms, despite the significant differences in their use of performance-vested options.

In order to distinguish these differences, we develop two additional measures. TRADITIONAL/PAST is the ratio of the number of traditional options granted to the CEO in the grant year to the average number of traditional options granted to the CEO in the prior two years. Similarly, PERFORMANCE/PAST is the ratio of the number of performance-vested options granted to the CEO in the grant year to the average annual grant of traditional options to the CEO in the prior two years.[48] If the CEO is new, we use option grants made to the previous CEO for the denominators of these two measures.

We use the number of options for these variables because it is unclear how to value performance-vested options that include cliff-vesting provisions but accelerate vesting if performance targets are achieved. However, since the value of performance-vested options is lower than that for traditional options, any increase in the number of stock options granted when performance-vested options are included in the compensation plan may simply be due to more options being required to meet the agent's reservation wage. We investigate this possibility by repeating the analyses using the option *values* reported in the firm's proxy statements rather than the number of options. The correlation between the change in the number of options and the change in reported option values is 0.73, indicating that changes in the number of options are also picking up compensation changes. Our results are nearly identical using these alternative measures.

4.2   Predictor Variables

- Past Performance

If boards of directors grant performance-vested options because they are unhappy with the incentives provided by the existing compensation plan, we would expect more extensive use of these options when past performance has been lower. We use two variables to measure past performance. RETURNS is the annual raw stock return for the year prior to the grant, minus the median annual stock return for all firms in the same two-digit SIC code. Returns are continuous and cumulated monthly.

RISING TIDE examines the common claim that performance-vested options are most beneficial when they prevent executives from benefiting from general stock market improvements while under-performing their competitors. This variable equals zero if the firm's stock market returns in the year prior to the grant were negative or REL RETURNS were positive. If stock market returns were positive but the firm under-performed its competitors (i.e., RETURNS were negative), RISING TIDE equals RETURNS (i.e., the extent to which the firm under-performed its competitors). If performance-vested options are used to prevent CEOs from benefiting from general market gains without improving firm performance,

---

[48] Some firms did not grant options in the prior two years. We exclude these firms from our statistical tests.

more extensive use of performance-vested options is expected when the firm has previously under-performed in a rising market.

- Relative Investment

We use the level of investment relative to competitors to examine theories that performance-vested options are more beneficial when the executive has greater opportunity to increase firm value by increasing investments in profitable, but risky, long-term projects. If firms in the same industry face similar investment opportunities, those that are currently investing less than competitors should receive the greatest benefit from the risk-taking incentives provided by performance-vested options, while those that are currently investing more than competitors may actually experience negative returns from greater risk-taking incentives.

We use two variables to test these incentive implications. The firm's INVESTMENT LEVEL is computed using the sum of capital expenditures, advertising, and research and development (R&D), deflated by total assets, for the year prior to the grant minus the median of this ratio for firms in the same SIC code.[49] If the relative investment level is negative, NEG_INVESTMENT equals INVESTMENT LEVEL, and zero otherwise; if the relative investment level is positive, POS_INVESTMENT equals INVESTMENT LEVEL, and zero otherwise. Johnson and Tian's (2000) work suggests that the use of performance-vested options should be negatively associated with both NEG_INVESTMENT and POS_INVESTMENT (i.e., greater adoption and use when investment levels are lower than competitors, and lower adoption and use when investment levels are greater than competitors).

- Market-to-Book Ratio

We also include the firm's market-to-book ratio at the beginning of the adoption year (denoted MTB) in our tests. If firms with greater growth opportunities(as reflected in higher market-to-book ratios) use performance-vested options to foster greater risk-taking in order to exploit these opportunities, MTB will be positively associated with their use. Conversely, if a low market-to-book ratio is an indication that the firm's stock market performance is unsatisfactory, and that greater incentives are needed to increase risk-taking and boost share price, MTB will be negatively associated with performance-vested option use.

---

[49] If capital expenditures, advertising, and R&D are missing in Compustat, we set these values equal to zero.

- Stock Volatility

The option valuation models of Johnson and Tian (2000) and Camara (2001) suggest a negative association between stock return volatility and the emphasis on performance-vested options. VOLATILITY is measured using the standard deviation of continuous daily returns for the year prior to the grant.

- New CEO

Indicator variables for new CEOs are used to examine Arya and Mittendorf's (2004) claim that performance-based options can be used for sorting new managerial talent. Since new CEOs who are promoted from within typically possess significant stock holdings in the company prior to their promotion (and are likely to be well-known by the firm, minimizing any sorting benefits), performance-vested option grants may have different incentive effects on internally-promoted CEOs than on CEOs hired from outside. We therefore examine these two groups separately. NEW CEO_IN is an indicator variable coded one if the firm appointed a new CEO from inside, and zero otherwise. NEW CEO_OUT is an indicator variable coded one if the firm appointed a new CEO from outside, and zero otherwise.

- Institutional Pressure

The variable PENSION is used to investigate the influence of institutional investors on the structure of performance-vested option grants. PENSION equals the percentage of outstanding shares held by pension funds (obtained from CDA/Spectrum). We also examined total institutional holdings and holdings by the activist pension funds identified by Wahal (1996). The results for these two alternative measures yield almost identical results. Since pension funds have been the strongest proponents of performance-vested options, we report results using PENSION. However, the consistent findings using the alternative measures indicate that our results using pension fund holdings more broadly reflect the influence of institutional (and activist) investors on the structure of performance-vested option grants.

4.3   Descriptive Statistics

Table 2 summarizes the characteristics of performance-vested option grants. Sixty-nine percent of firms granting performance-vested options also grant traditional options to the CEO. Over half (61%) grant performance-vested options on an on-going basis, with these options representing 71 percent of total grants on average (median = 78%). In the adoption year, the mean (median) firm grants total options (traditional plus performance-vested) that are 5.35 (1.38) times greater than the average number of grants made over the past two years. The mean number of traditional options granted in the adoption year is 2.03 times past grants (significantly different than one [p < 0.01, two-tailed]), while the median is 0.76 times past grants (not significantly different than one [p = 0.53, two-tailed]). Thus, the number of traditional options granted in the adoption year tends to be similar to or larger than prior traditional option grants. Mean and median performance-vested option grants are 3.13 and 1.67 times the total number of options granted in the past, respectively (both significantly different than one [p < 0.01, two-tailed]).

For comparison purposes, the mean (median) firm in a sample of non-adopters matched on size and industry (not reported in the tables) granted 2.32 (0.74) times the number of options granted in the past. Neither mean nor median traditional option grants (relative to past grants) are significantly different in performance-vested option adopters and their matched control firms. The mean and median numbers of total options granted, on the other hand, are significantly higher in performance-vested option adopters (p < 0.01, two-tailed). This evidence indicates that performance-vested options tend to be granted *on top of* existing traditional option grants.

Roughly half (50.78%) of performance-vested option adopters use absolute stock returns as their sole performance target, 27.34 percent use absolute accounting performance alone, and 15.63 percent use only non-financial performance. Relative performance targets, such as those examined in Camara's (2001) model, are rarely used by firms in our sample, with only 4.69 percent of adopters linking vesting to relative accounting or stock performance.

5.   RESULTS

5.1   Number and Mix of Options

Table 3 investigates both the mix of performance-vested and traditional options in the adoption year and the magnitude of option grants relative to past grants.[50] The pseudo or adjusted R^2s range from 0.20 to 0.31. VOLATILITY is negatively associated with the proportion of options that are performance-vested and the number of performance-vested options relative to the number of past option grants. Moreover, the number of traditional options granted relative to the past is not significantly related to

---

[50] Sample sizes vary in our tests due to missing data for some of our variables.

volatility, suggesting that the larger performance-vested option grants are "add-ons" to rather than replacements for traditional option grants. These results are consistent with the models by Johnson and Tian (2000) and Camara (2001), which indicate that the incentive benefits from performance-vested options are higher at low volatility levels. Differences in stock volatility, on the other hand, are not significantly associated with the *complete* replacement of traditional options with performance-vested options.

Performance-vested options represent a smaller proportion of option grants when the firm has a larger market-to-book ratio and when holdings by pension funds are larger. MTB is negative and significant using either REPLACE or %PERFORMANCE as the dependent variable, suggesting that firms that have already been recognized by the market as undertaking risky investments with significant growth opportunities may be less inclined to use performance-vested options to achieve these objectives. Alternatively, firms with low market-to-book ratios that wish to expand their growth opportunities in the future may make more extensive use of performance-vested to provide incentives to take on greater risk and increase stock volatility and returns.

Larger holding by pension plans are also negatively associated with the proportion of options that are performance-vested, consistent with firms using token grants to placate institutional investors who are calling for the use of performance-vested options. The appointment of a new CEO from outside tends to be accompanied by larger traditional *and* performance-vested option grants than those made to the previous CEO. Inside CEO appointments are associated with larger traditional option grant. However, they are not significantly associated with differences in performance-vested option grants, and are negatively associated with the proportion of options that are performance-vested. This evidence suggests that performance-vested options may be more effective in providing incentives and gauging managerial talent when the new CEO is hired from outside, rather than being a known quantity who already has an equity stake in the firm.

Finally, relative investment levels appear to play some role in the mix of options. As expected, POS INVESTMENT is negatively related to %PERFORMANCE, indicating that firms that are already investing more than their industry counterparts are likely to include fewer performance-vested options in the grant mix. Surprisingly, the coefficient on NEG INVESTMENT is positive and significant in the REPLACE model. This result implies that performance-vested options are less likely to completely replace traditional options when investment levels are below those of competitors, a finding somewhat inconsistent with analytical results indicating that these options are more valuable when the firm seeks to increase investments in risky but positive net present value projects.

5.2   Vesting Criteria

Table 4 provides exploratory evidence on the determinants of vesting criteria. We examine three categories of performance measures: (1) stock levels or returns, (2) accounting results, and (3) non-financial performance. Each category is coded one if vesting is based partially or completely on that type of measure, and zero otherwise.

Performance-vested option proponents and theoretical studies provide little guidance on the choice of vesting criteria. However, the performance measurement literature indicates that some of the factors influencing the use of stock, accounting, or non-financial measures are the measures' informativeness (typically examined using proxies for the measures' noise), regulation, and firm strategy or growth opportunities (e.g., Lambert and Larcker, 1987; Smith and Watts, 1992; Bushman et al., 1996; Ittner et al., 1997, among others). Given our limited understanding of the factors influencing the choice of vesting criteria, we estimate our models using the predictor variables from the earlier tests. Consistent with prior performance measurement studies, VOLATILITY proxies for the noise in stock return measures, and MTB proxies for growth opportunities (or an innovation strategy). In addition, we add two new variables. SDROA equals the standard deviation in return on assets over the past five years, a proxy for the noise in accounting measures. REGULATED is an indicator variable for firms in regulated industries and equals one for utilities and telecommunications firms, and zero otherwise.

As with our earlier results, we find that stock return volatility is a significant predictor of option plan design. Consistent with prior studies, VOLATILITY is negatively associated with the use of stock measures, reflecting the lower use of measures with greater noise. Instead, firms with higher stock volatility tend to make greater use of non-financial measures as performance criteria.

Holdings by pension funds are positively associated with the use of accounting measures. Firms in regulated industries are also more likely to use accounting criteria for vesting. However, they are no more likely to use non-financial measures. The latter result differs from those of Bushman et al. (1996) and Ittner et al. (1997), who found greater use of individual and non-financial measures in CEO bonus contracts when the firm operated in a regulated industry. We also find no evidence that the standard deviation in ROA or market-to-book ratio, which other studies have found to be associated with compensation performance measure choices, influence the choice of vesting criteria.

The performance measures used for new CEOs vary depending upon whether the CEO was appointed from inside or outside. Performance-vested option grants to outside appointments tend to make greater use of stock measures, while those to inside appointment focus more on accounting measures. These differences may reflect the (sometimes substantial) equity incentives already provided by insiders' existing stock and option holdings, reducing the need for market-based performance criteria.

6. SUMMARY AND CONCLUSIONS

Our exploratory analysis of initial performance-vested option grants to CEOs of 128 U.S. firms finds that the majority of firms grant these options together with traditional options, and that the number of performance-vested options and total options tend to be substantially larger than the number of options granted in the past. Supplemental analysis (not reported in the tables) indicates that these results hold even when the option values reported by the firms replace the number of options. Firms with higher market-to-book ratios and stock return volatility tend to make performance-vested options a smaller component of option grants, as do firms with larger pension holdings. The appointment of a new CEO from outside, on the other hand, is positively associated with the number of traditional and performance-vested grants relative to the number of options granted in the past. Finally, our examination of the performance criteria used for vesting identifies both similarities and differences between the performance measure determinants for this type of option and the performance measure determinants found in studies examining other compensation components.

As with all compensation studies, our analysis has a variety of limitations. First, our predictor variables are likely to be endogenous to some extent and our coefficient estimates will have some degree of inconsistency. We attempt to minimize endogeneity problems by focusing on the initial adoption of performance-vested options, with our predictor variables relating to the period prior to adoption. If the predictor variables are predetermined or exogenous, our estimation results will not be affected by endogeneity. This scenario will apply if all of our predictor variables are fixed before selection of the compensation contract. Even if this is not true, Larcker and Rusticus (2005) show that it is quite likely that ordinary least squares (or logistic) estimates are better specified than the traditional instrumental variable estimates that are typically used to address endogeneity problems in empirical research. Consequently, it is unlikely that a simultaneous equations approach would reduce potential endogeneity issues. Second, our analysis almost certainly has a number of model misspecifications such as measurement error in the constructs, correlated omitted variables, and other similar problems. It is difficult to judge the severity of the econometric problems caused by these misspecifications.

Despite these limitations, our study provides new insights into compensation plan design choices and identifies a number of opportunities for future research. Perhaps the most important is the effects of performance-vested options on managerial actions and firm performance. In particular, it would be useful to examine whether firms that adopt performance-vested options for incentive reasons improve performance, while those that adopt them to placate institutional investors do not. Similarly, to what extent are incentive and performance changes associated with the structure of performance-vested option grants (e.g., the number and mix of options, the choice of performance criteria, the achievability of performance targets, or cliff vesting provisions)? Future theoretical research can also move beyond the option valuation models used in prior analytical studies (in which stock price is not a function of agent actions) to develop principal-agent models in which the actions of the agent can affect the distribution of stock prices (e.g., Lambert and Larcker, 2005). Finally, the effects of accounting changes on the use of performance-vested options can be investigated. Currently, firms using performance-vested options must include cliff-vesting provisions to avoid incurring an accounting expense, but these provisions have been criticized for breaking the link between pay and performance. Mandatory expensing of stock options can eliminate the disparity in accounting treatments that exist between traditional options and performance-vested options, and therefore the relative costs and benefits from their use.

ACKNOWLEDGMENT

We thank seminar participants at The Wharton School for their comments on an earlier draft of the paper. The financial support of Ernst & Young is greatly appreciated.

APPENDIX A: EXAMPLES OF PERFORMANCE OBJECTIVES USED IN PERFORMANCE-VESTED STOCK OPTION GRANTS

- **Accounting Performance**

Options granted by the company ... are performance based ... Vesting is accelerated if the following targets are met: Three (3) consecutive years of 15% growth in EPS or 50% cumulative growth in EPS in two (2) years or less over base year 1998 (adjusted for impact from acquisitions and divestitures). (Perkin Elmer's 2000 Proxy Statement)

- **Stock Performance**

To ensure that Mr. Lay's interests remain properly aligned with shareholder interests, the Committee granted a total of 1,275,000 stock options, 50% granted in December, 1996 and 50% granted in January, 1997, at market value on each grant date. The stock options will be fully vested on November 1, 2003. However, the vesting schedule may be accelerated if Enron's total shareholder return equals or exceeds 120% of the S&P 500 in calendar years 1997, 1998 and 1999. (Enron's 1996 Proxy Statement)

- **Non-Financial Performance**

The exercisability of the options with an expiration date of August 5, 2008 can accelerate upon approval of Dermagraft® for the treatment of diabetic foot ulcers by the U.S. Food and Drug Administration. (Advanced Tissue Sciences' 1998 Proxy Statement)

REFERENCES

AFL-CIO. 2003. Exercising authority, restoring accountability. AFL-CIO.

Arya, A. and Mittendorf, B. 2004. Offering stock options to gauge managerial talent. Working paper, Ohio State University and Yale School of Management.

Bushman, R.; R. Indjejikian; and A. Smith. 1996. CEO Compensation: The Role of Individual Performance Evaluation. Journal of Accounting and Economics (April): 161-93.

CalPERS, 2003, Investment Committee Agenda, Sacramento, CA.

Camara, A. 2001. The pricing of relative performance based incentives for executive compensation. Journal of Business Finance & Accounting 28 (9 & 10): 1149-1191.

Conyon, M., Peck, S., Read, L., and Sadler, G. 2000. The structure of executive compensation contracts: UK evidence, Long Range Planning 33, 478-503.

Frieswick, K. 2003. Better options. CFO.com, May 1 (http://www.cfo.com/article/1,5309,9415|0|BS|12|141,00.html).

Hodgson, P. 2002. Applying Performance Conditions to Stock Options (The Corporate Library, Portland, Maine).

Institutional Shareholder Services 2004. http://www.amerindo.com/pdfs/2004CondensedUSGuidelines.pdf

Ittner, C.D.; D.F. Larcker; and M.V. Rajan.1997. The Choice of Performance Measures in Annual Bonus Contracts. *The Accounting Review* (April): 231-55.

Johnson, S. and Tian, Y. 2000. The value and incentive effects of nontraditional executive stock option plans, Journal of Financial Economics 57, 3-34.

Kim, J. 2002. The 2002 Top 250: long-term and stock-based grant practices for executives and directors (Frederic W. Cook & Co., Inc., New York, New York).

Lambert, R.A.; and D.F. Larcker. 1987. An Analysis of the Use of Accounting and Market Measures of Performance in Executive Compensation Contracts. Journal of Accounting Research (Supplement): 179-203.

Lambert, R. and Larcker, D. 2005. Stock options, restricted stock, and incentives. Working paper, University of Pennsylvania and Stanford University.

Larcker, D. and Rusticus, T., 2005. On the use of instrumental variables in accounting research. Working paper, University of Pennsylvania.

Meyer, J. and Rowan, B. 1977. Institutional organizations: formal structure as myth and ceremony. American Journal of Sociology 83: 340-363.

Morgenson, G. 2003. Greed is still good at some companies. New York Times, June 14, Section 3, 1, 5.

Morgenson, G. 2004. Bubble lives on at Broadcom, where options still rain down. New York Times, April 18: Section 3, 1, 9.

Smith, C.; and R. Watts. 1992. The Investment Opportunity Set and Corporate Financing, Dividend, and Compensation Policies. Journal of Financial Economics (December): 263-92.

Tully, S. 1998. Raising the bar. Fortune 137(11), June 8: 272-275.

Wahal, S. 1996. Pension fund activism and firm performance, Journal of Financial and Quantitative Analysis 31, 1-23.

Westphal, J. and Zajac, E. 1994. Substance and symbolism in CEOs' long-term incentive plans. Administrative Science Quarterly 39: 367-390.

Westphal, J. and Zajac, E. 1998. The symbolic management of stockholders: corporate governance reforms and shareholder reactions. Administrative Science Quarterly 43: 127-153.

Westreich, S.I. 1999. Letter to the editor: performance-vested options best for shareholders. Wall Street Journal, June 7: A23.

Zajac, E. and Westphal, J. 1995. Accounting for the explanations of CEO compensation: substance and symbolism. Administrative Science Quarterly 40: 283-308.

Table 11-1. Distribution of Performance-Vested Option Users by Industry and Adoption Date

Panel A: Industry

		Sample Number	Percentage	Compustat Percentage
1	Agricultural production - crops	1	0.78%	0.20%
10	Metal mining	1	0.78%	1.23%
13	Oil and gas extraction	1	0.78%	2.95%
20	Food and kindred products	1	0.78%	1.76%
22	Textile mill products	1	0.78%	0.49%
24	Lumber and wood products	1	0.78%	0.39%
26	Paper and allied products	1	0.78%	0.81%
27	Printing and publishing	2	1.56%	1.09%
28	Chemicals and allied products	8	6.25%	5.93%
29	Petroleum and coal products	1	0.78%	0.43%
30	Rubber and misc. plastics products	2	1.56%	0.97%
32	Stone, clay and glass products	3	2.34%	0.59%
33	Primary metal industries	1	0.78%	1.16%
34	Fabricated metal products	1	0.78%	1.09%
35	Industrial machinery and equipment	7	5.47%	5.28%
36	Electronic and other electric equipment	9	7.03%	5.95%
38	Instruments and related products	7	5.47%	5.26%
39	Misc. manufacturing industries	2	1.56%	1.01%
48	Communications	3	2.34%	3.20%
49	Electric, gas and sanitary services	10	7.81%	2.74%
50	Wholesale trade - durable goods	2	1.56%	2.17%
51	Wholesale trade - nondurable goods	5	3.91%	1.29%
53	General merchandise stores	1	0.78%	0.52%
54	Food stores	4	3.13%	0.53%
56	Apparel and accessory stores	2	1.56%	0.64%
57	Furniture and home furnishing stores	1	0.78%	0.44%
58	Eating and drinking places	1	0.78%	1.42%
59	Misc. retail	2	1.56%	1.58%
60	Depository institutions	10	7.81%	9.31%
61	Non-depository institutions	3	2.34%	1.24%
62	Security and commodity brokers	2	1.56%	0.96%
63	Insurance carriers	7	5.47%	2.36%
70	Hotels and other lodging places	1	0.78%	0.48%
73	Business services	17	13.28%	10.18%
75	Auto repair, services and parking	1	0.78%	0.21%
80	Health services	2	1.56%	1.76%
87	Engineering & management services	3	2.34%	1.70%
99	Other	1	0.78%	1.23%

Table 11-2. (continued)

<u>Panel B: Adoption Year</u>

1992	3	2.34%
1993	9	7.03%
1994	13	10.16%
1995	14	10.94%
1996	11	8.59%
1997	19	14.84%
1998	10	7.81%
1999	16	12.50%
2000	15	11.72%
2001	11	8.59%
2002	7	5.47%
	128	100.00%

Compustat percentages based on the distribution of publicly traded companies as of 1997.

Table 11-2. Descriptive Statistics for the Sample of Performance-Vested Stock Option Users

Panel A: Distribution of Performance Measures in Performance-Vested Option Grants

Performance Measures	Distribution
Absolute accounting performance	27.34%
Absolute stock performance	50.78%
Non-financial performance	15.63%
Absolute stock and accounting performance	1.56%
Relative stock performance	3.13%
Relative accounting performance	1.56%

Panel B: Grant Characteristics and Predictor Variables

	N	MEAN	STDDEV	Q1	MEDIAN	Q3
Grant Characteristics						
REPLACE	128	0.41	0.49	0.00	0.00	1.00
%PERFORMANCE	128	0.71	0.30	0.49	0.78	1.00
TRADITIONAL/PAST	90	2.03^*	3.76	0.00	0.76^{NS}	1.56
PERFORMANCE/PAST	90	3.13^*	3.43	0.83	1.67^*	4.00
TOTAL/PAST	90	5.35^*	6.39	1.38	2.61^*	5.61
MULTIPLE	128	0.61	0.49	0.00	1.00	1.00
Predictor Variables						
RETURNS	110	0.04	0.46	-0.24	0.04	0.27
RISING TIDE	126	-0.02	0.07	0.00	0.00	0.00
NEG INVESTMENT	125	-0.02	0.04	-0.04	0.00	0.00
POS INVESTMENT	128	0.03	0.08	0.00	0.00	0.03
MTB	113	3.11	4.41	1.36	2.52	4.41
VOLATILITY	114	0.03	0.02	0.02	0.03	0.04
NEW CEO_IN	128	0.10	0.30	0.00	0.00	0.00
NEW CEO_OUT	128	0.10	0.30	0.00	0.00	0.00
PENSION	128	0.01	0.02	0.00	0.01	0.02

[*] Ratio of the number of options of this type granted in the adoption to the average number of total options granted in the past two years is greater than one at the one percent level (two-tailed). Signed rank test for medians and t-tests for means.

[NS] Ratio of the number of options of this type granted in the adoption to the average number of total options granted in the past two years is not significantly different than one at the ten percent level (two-tailed signed rank test).

Option grant characteristics relate to the initial year performance-vested options are granted to the CEO. REPLACE is coded one if performance-vested options completely replaced traditional options in CEO compensation grant during the adoption year, else zero. %PERFORMANCE equals the number of performance-vested options granted to the CEO in the initial grant year, divided by the total number of option granted to the CEO that year. PERFORMANCE/PAST is the ratio of the number of performance-vested options granted to the CEO to the average of annual number of options granted to the CEO in the prior two years. TRADITIONAL/PAST is the ratio of the number of traditional options granted to the CEO to the average of annual number of options granted to the CEO in the prior two years. TRADITIONAL/PAST is the ratio of the total number of options (traditional and performance-vested) granted to the CEO to the average of annual number of options granted to the CEO in the prior two years. MULTIPLE GRANTS equals one if performance-vested options are granted more than once (i.e., are not one-time grants), and zero otherwise.

RETURNS is the annual buy and hold return for the year prior to the grant year minus the median annual buy and hold return over the same period for the firm's in the same two-digit SIC code. RISING TIDE is the interaction between RETURNS and a dummy variable coded as one if the firm's unadjusted stock returns for the year prior to granting were positive and the industry adjusted returns were negative, and zero otherwise. NEG INVESTMENT is the minimum of zero and the sum for the year prior to the grant year of capital expenditures, advertising, and R&D (deflated by total assets) minus the median of this ratio for the firm's industry as defined by two-digit SIC. POS INVESTMENT is the maximum of zero and the sum for the year prior to the grant year of capital expenditures, advertising, and R&D (deflated by total assets) minus the median of this ratio for the firm's industry as defined by two-digit SIC. MTB is the firm's market-to-book ratio in the year prior to the grant. VOLATILITY is the standard deviation of the firm's continuous daily returns for the year prior to the grant year. NEW CEO_IN equals one if the firm appointed a new CEO from inside either in the year prior to the grant year or in the grant year, else zero. NEW CEO_OUT equals one if the firm appointed a new CEO from outside either in the year prior to the grant year or in the grant year, else zero. PENSION is the percentage of shares outstanding held by pension funds at the beginning of the grant year.

Table 11-3. Determinants of Performance-Vested Option Grant Mix and Magnitude

	REPLACE	%PERFOR-MANCE	PERFOR-MANCE /PAST	TRADITIONAL /PAST
Intercept	1.39**	0.98***	3.30***	-0.54
	(4.91)	(15.15)	(3.57)	(-0.59)
RETURNS	0.45	0.08	-0.63	-0.60
	(0.58)	(1.23)	(-0.69)	(-0.65)
RISING TIDE	1.17	-0.06	-2.91	1.77
	(0.16)	(-0.19)	(-0.56)	(0.34)
NEG	12.02*	0.67	-5.37	-6.49
INVESTMENT	(2.92)	(0.91)	(-0.54)	(-0.66)
POS	-4.65	-0.66#	5.66	4.64
INVESTMENT	(1.08)	(-1.61)	(0.95)	(0.78)
MTB	-0.15**	-0.02***	0.05	0.05
	(5.27)	(-3.38)	(0.64)	(0.49)
VOLATILITY	-19.03	-3.07*	-47.42**	25.43
	(1.33)	(-1.91)	(-2.18)	(1.17)
NEW CEO_IN	-0.70	-0.21**	-0.38	3.55***
	(0.85)	(-2.43)	(-0.31)	(2.87)
NEW	0.05	-0.03	4.80***	3.24**
CEO_OUT	(0.00)	(-0.36)	(3.65)	(2.46)
PENSION	-23.37#	-3.07*	20.66	38.02
	(2.46)	(-1.89)	(0.72)	(1.33)
Pseudo or Adj. R2	0.20	0.21	0.21	0.31
n	108	108	83	83

***, **, *, # significantly different from zero at the 1%, 5%, 10%, and 15% levels respectively (two-tailed test). Logit estimates for REPLACE and ordinary least squares estimates for other dependent variables; Chi-square or t-statistics in parentheses.

Option grant characteristics relate to the initial year performance-vested options are granted to the CEO. REPLACE is coded one if performance-vested options completely replaced traditional options in CEO compensation grant during the adoption years, else zero. %PERFORMANCE equals the number of performance-vested options granted to the CEO in the initial grant year, divided by the total number of option granted to the CEO that year. PERFORMANCE/PAST is the ratio of the number of performance-vested options granted to the CEO to the average of annual number of options granted to the CEO in the prior two years. TRADITIONAL/PAST is the ratio of the number of traditional options granted to the CEO to the average of annual number of options granted to the CEO in the prior two years. See Table 2 for other variable definitions.

Table 11-4. Logit Models Examining the Determinants of Performance Measures Used in Performance-Vested Option Grants

	Stock Measures	Accounting Measures	Non-financial Measures
Intercept	1.88**	-1.93***	-2.43***
	(6.00)	(8.39)	(7.87)
RETURNS	-0.66	-0.11	0.81
	(1.41)	(0.04)	(1.68)
RISING TIDE	-4.95	0.31	--- [a]
	(1.05)	(0.01)	
NEG INVESTMENT	-8.08	4.66	9.72
	(1.50)	(0.45)	(1.22)
POS INVESTMENT	-1.69	-0.82	0.93
	(0.18)	(0.06)	(0.04)
MTB	-0.01	0.05	0.04
	(0.02)	(0.66)	(0.29)
VOLATILITY	-54.35**	5.60	49.50**
	(5.59)	(0.11)	(4.08)
NEW CEO_IN	-0.98	1.07#	-0.09
	(1.68)	(2.23)	(0.01)
NEW CEO_OUT	1.50*	-0.74	-1.56
	(2.80)	(0.66)	(1.61)
PENSION	-11.00	32.38**	-27.47
	(0.46)	(4.77)	(1.51)
REGULATED	-0.90	1.09#	-0.46
	(1.59)	(2.30)	(0.16)
SDROA	0.87	1.26	-2.50
	(0.34)	(0.81)	(1.17)
Pseudo. R^2	0.25	0.21	0.21
n	108	108	108

a. RISING TIDE equals zero for all firms using non-financial measures, , resulting in quasi-complete separation in the logit model. Consequently, this variable is not included in the reported results.

***, **, *, # significantly different from zero at the 1%, 5%, 10%, and 15% levels respectively (two-tailed test). Chi-square statistics in parentheses.

Option grant characteristics relate to the initial year performance-vested options are granted to the CEO. Stock measures is coded one if vesting is based all or in part on stock market returns or stock price, else zero. Accounting measures is coded one if vesting is based all or in part on accounting criteria (e.g. EPS). Non-financial measures is coded one if vesting is based on non-financial measures or milestones. REGULATED equals one if the firm operates in regulated utilities or telecommunications industries. SDROA equals the standard deviation in return on assets over the past five years. See Table 2 for other variable definitions.

Chapter 12

THE LCAMR MISSILE
A Case Study

William P. Rogerson
Northwestern University

Abstract: This paper presents a fictional case study of an aerospace firm's analysis of whether to undertake a new missile program for sale in foreign markets. The adoption of this new program will affect fully allocated accounting costs on all of its programs. The issue explored is whether and how the firm ought to take into account the fact that the prices it receives on many of the products it sells to the U.S. government are based on fully allocated accounting costs and how this potentially affects the firm's incentives to produce as efficiently as possible

Key words: Cost allocation, cost-based pricing, defense procurement, overhead

1.   INTRODUCTION

This is a purely fictional case study that I originally prepared in 1992, to teach to senior executives of Lockheed as part of a one-week executive education course that they attended at the Kellogg Graduate School of Management. It is designed to illustrate the main conclusions that I reached in an article published in *The Accounting Review* (Rogerson 1992), on how overhead allocation rules used by defense contractors distort their incentives to produce as efficiently as possible when the prices they are allowed to charge the Department of Defense are based on these fully allocated costs. Although I never attempted to formally publish this case, over the years a number of professors have asked me for permission to use it in MBA cost accounting courses, and I am delighted to be given the opportunity to make this case available to a wider audience by including it in this volume in honour of Joel Demski on the occasion of his 65th birthday. Joel has published research related to this subject that I highly recommend to the reader (Christensen and Demski 1997, 2003). A more comprehensive overview of the entire subject of cost allocation is contained in chapter 6 of Demski(1994).

Although the data in the case is purely fictional, the cost structure of Advanced Missiles is based upon actual cost data for four major aerospace contractors described in a report prepared by the Institute for Defense Analysis (McCullogh and Balut, 1990). Therefore, the cost data is representative of that exhibited by real aerospace firms. However, other than for the fact that the AMRAAM missile exists, all circumstances in this case are fabricated and are not based upon any particular firm or project.

The nature of the contracting procedures and cost allocation rules used in defense procurement have not changed substantially in the thirteen year period since this case was written, so the incentive effects identified in this case are still as real and important as they were when the case was first written.

2.   BACKGROUND: GENERAL

In January 1991, Sandy Crosberg, manager of financial analysis at Advanced Systems Corporation, told a case writer, "What I learned about incremental analysis at Business School doesn't always apply in the defense contracting arena. Although plenty of our program costs are sunk, revenues on our government programs are largely based on costs and therefore sunk costs are hardly irrelevant." He was convinced that some sort of full-allocation approach to project analysis was required in this environment. Crosberg used the LCAMR (pronounced *el-cam'-er*) project as an example. The LCAMR (Low Cost Advanced Medium Range) missile was a new air-to-air missile designed exclusively for foreign sales. It was essentially a less sophisticated and therefore cheaper version of the very successful AMRAAM (Advanced Medium Range Air-to-Air Missile) which Advanced had just begun full-rate production on for the US Government.

3.   BACKGROUND: ADVANCED SYSTEMS

Advanced Systems Corporation was a large aerospace firm primarily engaged in the business of being a prime contractor and major subcontractor on aerospace systems for the US Government. It was organized into two divisions, the Advanced Aircraft Company and the Advanced Missiles Company.

Advanced Missiles' business over the next ten years was projected to fall into five main programs or areas. First, was the new TSSCM, the Tri-Service Stealth Cruise Missile. Full-scale development was currently underway with low-rate production scheduled for mid-1993 and full-rate production scheduled for 1995. The second program was the AMRAAM. Full-rate production had begun in 1990 and was scheduled to continue for at least another 12 years. The AMRAAM was an extremely sophisticated missile designed to possess beyond-visible-range and fire-and-forget capabilities. That is, the pilot could fire the missile at an enemy aircraft prior to actually being close enough to see it. The missile's sophisticated radar would then lock onto the target and home in on it without further involvement of the pilot. The TSSCM and AMRAAM were the crown jewels of Advanced Missiles and promised to insulate it from the hard times that many defense contractors seemed likely to experience over the next few years. In both cases it was the sole source producer of a state-of-the-art system highly desired by the military services.

The third program, the Thunderbolt missile, was more troubled because of dual-sourcing. Production was currently underway and scheduled for completion in 1998. Advanced Missiles was initially chosen as the lead contractor on the program due to its preeminent R&D capability. Its competitor on the program, while not possessing nearly the R&D capability of Advanced Missiles, was extremely good at keeping production costs low. Thus, Advanced Missiles had been earning profit margins of between negative 10 percent and negative 5 percent and had been winning on average only 30 percent of each annual buy. This situation was projected to continue.

The fourth area of activity for Advanced Missiles was purely commercial business. This consisted of a range of subcontracts for commercial aircraft producers. While not extremely profitable, this business made use of otherwise idle capacity.

Advanced Missiles' fifth area of activity was a range of R&D contracts with the US Government. This activity was largely carried out under cost-type contracts and involved improving and upgrading current products as well as more speculative projects designed to result in entirely new weapons further in the future.

Advanced Missiles used a relatively typical cost accounting system to accumulate and allocate costs. There were four major direct cost pools: manufacturing labor, engineering labor, material (including subcontracts), and miscellaneous direct costs (the largest element of which was directly charged special tools and test equipment). There were three major indirect cost pools: manufacturing overhead, engineering overhead, and general and administrative (G&A) overhead.[51] Direct costs were accumulated by the contract and indirect costs were allocated in proportion to direct costs. Manufacturing and engineering overhead were allocated using bases of, respectively, direct manufacturing labor, and direct engineering labor. G&A was allocated in proportion to total cost input (which is the cost when all costs except G&A have been allocated).

For purposes of cost estimation, Advanced Missiles maintained a cost model which predicted how overhead would respond to changes in the level of direct costs. The prescribed method for estimating the cost of a project was to directly estimate the direct costs and then use the cost model to estimate the incremental effects on overhead. The cost-model currently used by Advanced Missiles aggregated overhead into two pools, G&A and M&E (which was the sum of manufacturing and engineering overhead). G&A was estimated to be 100 percent fixed. M&E was estimated by the formula

$$y = 90.3 + .95x$$

where y denotes M&E overhead in millions of 1990 dollars and x denotes direct labor (manufacturing and engineering) in millions of 1990 dollars. (In 1990 M&E overhead was equal to $261.4 million. According to the above formula, $90.3 million of M&E overhead is fixed. Therefore, the M&E pool was estimated to be 35 percent fixed.)

Cost projections were initially made in real dollars. Then inflation was accounted for by using a general company-wide inflation projection unless special circumstances on a particular project argued for a different inflation projection. The current company-wide inflation projection was 4 percent per year.

Table 11-1[52] displays Advanced Missiles' cost projections by program for the next 11 years using the previously described estimation methodology under the assumption that LCAMR would not be undertaken. Lines 1-14 display direct cost estimates. Then lines 15-17

---

[51] Advanced Missiles also had a number of smaller direct and indirect pools such as material handling and pools created for off-site-work. The aggregate value of these pools was insignificant and had no impact on any of the issues discussed in this case. Therefore for purposes of expositional simplicity these have been ignored.

[52] To fit the page size, all tables in this case have been divided into two parts where Part I presents the data for 1991-1996 and Part II presents the data for the remaining years (1997-2001 or 1997-2002, depending upon the table). References to tables in the text that do not specify a particular part are referring to the entire table, consisting of both parts.

display overhead projections calculated using the cost model. The projected overhead allocations to each program are shown in lines 18-24.[53] The sum of direct and indirect costs (which yield total cost by program) are presented in lines 25-31. Lines 32-33 report the projected overhead rates. Lines 34-39 report projections for various values associated with facilities capital.

4.   BACKGROUND: LCAMR

The major problem with the AMRAAM for foreign sales was that its formidable list of capabilities was matched by an equally formidable price tag, about $800,000. Although Advanced Missiles would certainly sell some AMRAAM's to well-heeled foreign buyers, Advanced Missiles' foreign marketing group estimated that an essentially separate market existed for a much cheaper missile with somewhat reduced performance capabilities. In December 1989 a research team began design work on such a missile and LCAMR was the result.

LCAMR was a variant of the AMRAAM that incorporated identical form, factor, platform integration, and engagement envelope parameters. Its seeker was significantly less complex and expensive than the AMRAAM's by: (1) incorporating state-of-the-art VLSI technology which significantly decreased the cost of production; (2) operating in semiactive mode only (permitting deletion of active radar components from the seeker); and (3) foregoing certain aspects of multimode operation (details classified). In operation, the LCAMR would be utilized similarly to the currently deployed AIM-7M Sparrow, i.e., the engaging aircraft would have to illuminate the target in the final stages of engagement. Unlike the Sparrow, however, the LCAMR could operate semi-autonomously, which means that the missile could be fired using only search radar parameters, and fly most of the way to the target. The illuminator needed to be turned on only during the last few seconds, and the fire control system did this automatically. Thus the LCAMR was considerably more effective than the Sparrow, not only in terms of the AMRAAM platform's range and low-level engagement parameters, but also in terms of not alerting target aircraft of their impending engagement.

According to the marketing plan which had been developed, finalization of design parameters and establishment of the production line would occur

---

[53] Since Advanced Missiles projected M&E overhead as a single pool it projected allocations of this pool by assuming that it was allocated using a base of total direct labor.

in 1991 with placement of orders and production beginning in 1992. Deliveries would then commence in 1993. (Production of each missile would require approximately one year from start to finish. Thus deliveries would lag about one year behind placement of orders and commencement of production.)[54]

According to the marketing plan, 350 missiles would be produced each year for a period of 10 years. At this point the missile would be technologically outdated and production would cease. Total projected deliveries of 3,500 missiles constituted approximately 10 percent of the total projected foreign demand for medium priced air-to-air missiles during this period. The marketing plan was based on an initial selling price of $371,400 per missile. The real selling price would remain constant and only be adjusted to reflect the inflation rate.

Costs of production were projected as follows. Total development costs incurred to date were $20 million. (Most of these were incurred during 1989.) Completion of full-scale development and establishment of the production line during 1991 was projected to cost $20 million in direct labor, $16 million in other direct costs, and an investment of $100 million in special test equipment for the new seeker. No expansion of floor space or significant purchases of general-purpose capital equipment was necessary due to existing excess capacity. The first year of production in 1992 was projected to require $19 million in direct labor and $39.7 million in other direct costs. The real direct labor cost was projected to follow a learning rate of 82 percent (i.e., every time output doubled, price would decline by 18 percent). Approximately 66.5 percent, or $26.4 million, of the other direct costs corresponded to complex subcontracted items which would also experience learning. It was projected that the price paid by Advanced Missiles for these subcomponents would experience a learning rate of 90 percent (i.e., every time output doubled, price would decline by 10 percent). The other direct costs corresponded to simpler or standard items and the real price of these items was projected to remain constant.

5.   ALTERNATIVE PRODUCTION METHODS

As part of the initial design phase, a working group had been created to identify possibilities for reducing production costs. They had come up with two possibilities.

---

54   All of the dollar figures for costs and revenues are expressed in 1991 dollars unless otherwise stated.

The first possibility was to produce the phased array antenna and its associated electronics in-house. It was normal practice for Advanced Missiles to subcontract this component and the estimated costs reported above were for the case where the antenna was subcontracted. In the first year of production, the antennas would cost $17.5 million if purchased from a subcontractor. In-house production would require an additional $6 million in direct labor and $5.2 million in purchased material during the first year. No significant investment would be required.

The second possibility was to purchase significantly cheaper, less automated, test equipment for the seeker. The cost projections outlined in the previous section had been prepared under the assumption that a highly automated and integrated testing suite similar to that used for the AMRAAM would be purchased. The US Government had, of course, paid for this test equipment as a direct charge on the first contract. The working group argued that a less automated approach was more appropriate in a purely commercial effort like the LCAMR where cost was of primary importance. The same levels of reliability could be achieved by using more off-the-shelf equipment, running more tests at intermediate stages, and testing more times using less accurate methods. This alternative approach would require an investment of only $50 million instead of $100 million. However, because it was less automated, more direct labor would be required. In the first year of production an extra $7 million in direct labor would be required.

6. CAPITAL BUDGETING AT ADVANCED SYSTEMS

Advanced Systems' recently revised financial handbook described a "textbook perfect" capital budgeting system. A company-wide cost of capital was calculated using the CAPM and the weighted cost of capital approach. This cost of capital was to be used for project analysis unless it could be convincingly argued that the project under consideration exhibited a beta considerably different than the company-wide beta (which was approximately equal to 1). The prescribed procedure was to calculate incremental after-tax nominal cash flows and then calculate an NPV at the appropriate cost of capital and also calculate the IRR. In order to be accepted a project had to exhibit a positive NPV (or, equivalently, an IRR greater than the cost of capital).

Total incremental costs were to be calculated by directly estimating incremental direct costs and using the current cost model to project incremental overhead costs. The current company projections for inflation rates were to be used unless specific circumstances argued for use of a different rate for a particular project.

The current cost of capital used by Advanced Systems was 18 percent. The projected inflation rate was 4 percent per year. The current cost model used to project overhead within Advanced Missiles was described above.

7.   CROSBERG'S ANALYSIS: THE INCREMENTAL APPROACH

Following Advanced Systems' manual, Crosberg calculated the incremental after-tax nominal cash flows for the project. Table 11-2A outlines the major steps and results of this calculation. In particular, note that incremental overhead costs were included. Using the cost model, these were estimated to be 95 percent of direct labor costs. In order to evaluate the alternative production possibilities, Crosberg performed precisely the same analysis for three other cases in addition to the base case. Table 11-2B displays the results for the alternative of producing the phased array antennas in-house which Crosberg labelled the "reduced subcontracting case." Table 11-2C displays the results for the alternative of using less automated test equipment which Crosberg labelled the "reduced automation case." Finally, table 11-2D displays the results of simultaneously adopting both alternatives. Crosberg called this the "reduced subcontracting/automation case."

The results of Crosberg's analysis are summarized below in exhibit 1.

Exhibit 1

The NPV and IRR of LCAMR Under the Incremental Approach

Case	NPV at 18% (*millions of 1991 $*)	IRR (%)
A. Base	21.7	20.1
B. Reduced subcontracting	25.3	20.5
C. Reduced automation	26.0	21.0
D. Reduced subcontracting/automation	29.6	21.4

The project yielded a positive NPV under all production scenarios. Each of the alternatives suggested by the working group increased NPV. Therefore, the highest NPV resulted when both alternatives were adopted. This yielded an NPV of $29.6 million and an IRR of 21.4 percent.

8. CROSBERG'S ANALYSIS: THE FULL ALLOCATION APPROACH

Crosberg felt uncomfortable with his analysis. His own gut feeling was that his incremental analysis was understating the cost of LCAMR to Advanced Missiles. The accounting system would allocate a share of fixed overhead (G&A and the fixed portion of M&E) to LCAMR and incremental analysis ignored this. Crosberg summarized his feelings as follows.

I understand the logic behind incremental analysis and it may well be perfectly correct in a purely commercial environment. However, things are different in the defense contracting arena. Revenues on government programs are largely based on costs. If LCAMR was a government project we would recover 100% of our costs, whether fixed, sunk, or whatever. Therefore these costs would be relevant and we would consider them. It doesn't seem consistent to me to ignore them simply because LCAMR happens to be commercial. Let me put this another way. If we used the same assets on government programs, we would be entitled to reimbursement for the fixed and sunk portions. It doesn't seem reasonable to settle for less when we transfer these assets to commercial use. I doubt that 35% of our M&E or 100% of our G&A overhead is truly fixed in the long run. If we consistently adopt projects that don't cover their share of these costs we're likely to simply end up not covering them in the long run.

Because of his concerns, Crosberg recalculated the profitability of LCAMR under assumption that all of the overhead allocated to LCAMR was a cost of LCAMR. Once again, he the performed the analysis for all four production alternatives. First he projected the share of overhead that LCAMR would be allocated each year by recalculating the cost projections in table 11-1. The results for all four cases are presented in tables 11-3A to 11-3D. Line 23 of these tables displays the overhead allocated to LCAMR. Then Crosberg recalculated his cash flow analysis by replacing the incremental overhead values with the fully-allocated overhead values. The results are presented in tables 11-4A to 11-4D (i.e., tables 11-4A to 11-4D are exactly the same as tables 11-2A to 11-2D except that fully-allocated overhead has replaced incremental overhead.)

The results of this analysis are presented below in exhibit 2.

Exhibit 2
The NPV and IRR of LCAMR Under the Full Allocation Approach

Case	NPV at 18% (*millions of 1991 $*)	IRR (%)
A. Base	-25.8	15.6
B. Reduced subcontracting	-28.9	15.3
C. Reduced automation	-30.1	14.8
D. Reduced subcontracting/automation	-33.0	14.5

The project yielded a negative NPV under all production scenarios. Furthermore, both alternative production methods reduced NPV. Therefore, the lowest NPV resulted when both alternatives were adopted. Even under the most favorable case (the base case) the project yielded in NPV of −$25.8 million and an IRR of only 15.6 percent.

9.   CROSBERG'S CONCLUSIONS

Crosberg drafted a memo to the chief comptroller summarizing the conclusions of both the incremental and full allocation analysis. He noted that the approaches disagreed on the desirability of the project and also disagreed on whether the alternative production methods would increase or decrease profitability. He argued that the full allocation approach was more appropriate given the cost-based nature of the bulk of Advanced's business. He also suggested that consideration be given to revising the financial handbook in light of the lessons learned from this project.

10.   QUESTIONS

Why did the full-allocation approach yield lower NPVs?

Why did the full-allocation approach reverse the relative rankings of the four alternative production methods?

Suppose that Advanced had been a purely commercial firm. Would Crosberg's incremental analysis have been correct? Does anything change because most of Advanced's business is with the government? Why?

"Erosion" is defined to be a reduction in an existing product's revenues due to the introduction of a new product. Should Crosberg have considered the effects of erosion? If so, on which products?

Which approach should Crosberg have used? If neither approach is correct, what is the correct approach?

Suppose that most of Advanced's business had been purely commercial and the LCAMR project was to be sold to the government. How would your answer to question 5 change? Why?

REFERENCES

J. Christensen and J. Demski, Product Costing in the Presence of Endogenous Subcost Functions, *Review of Accounting Studies*, 2(1), 65-87, (1997).

J. Christensen and J. Demski, Factor Choice Distortion Under Cost-Based Reimbursement , *Journal of Management Accounting Research*, 15, 145-160, (2003).

J. Demski, *Managerial Use of Accounting Information* (Kluwer Academic Publishers, Norwell, MA, 1997).

J. McCullough and S. Balut, Cost Trends in the Aircraft Industry, Institute for Defense Analysis Report D-764, May 1990.

W. Rogerson, Overhead Allocation and Incentives for Cost Minimization in Defense Procurement, *The Accounting Review*, 67(4), 671-690, (1992).

Table 12-1. - Projected Costs by Program if LCAMR is not Undertaken

PART I (1991-1996) – in millions of then-year dollars

DIRECT LABOR:	1991	1992	1993	1994	1995	1996
1 TSSCM	20	42	50.1	100	85.3	79
2 AMRAAM	120	102.3	94.8	90.8	88.5	87.4
3 THUNDERBOLT	18.9	18.7	18.6	18.6	18.7	18.9
4 COMMERCIAL	20.2	21	21.8	22.7	23.6	24.5
5 R&D	11.4	11.9	12.4	12.9	13.4	13.9
8 LCAMR	0	0	0	0	0	0
7 ALL PROGRAMS	190.5	195.9	197.7	245	229.5	223.7
OTHER DIRECT COSTS:						
8 TSSCM	0	300	300	220	217.4	219.4
9 AMRAAM	262	258.9	261.3	266	272.1	279.2
10 THUNDERBOLT	41.6	42.8	44	45.4	46.9	48.4
11 COMMERCIAL	63.2	65.7	68.3	71	73.8	76.8
12 R&D	2.8	2.9	3	3.1	3.2	3.3
13 LCAMR	0	0	0	0	0	0
14 ALL PROGRAMS	369.6	670.3	676.6	605.5	613.4	627.1
OVERHEAD BY TYPE:						
15 M&E	274.7	283.5	289.1	338.1	327.6	326.5
16 G&A	60	62.4	64.9	67.5	70.2	73
17 TOTAL	334.7	345.9	354	405.6	397.8	399.5
OVERHEAD BY PROGRAM:						
18 TSSCM	32.4	82.6	96.9	164	147.2	141
19 AMRAAM	212.9	175.7	166.2	152.7	155.5	158.2
20 THUNDERBOLT	33.6	31.9	32.2	30.8	32.2	33.5
21 COMMERCIAL	37.2	36.7	38.7	38.4	41.5	44.3
22 R&D	18.6	19	20	19.7	21.3	22.6
23 LCAMR	0	0	0	0	0	0
24 ALL PROGRAMS	334.7	345.9	354	405.6	397.8	399.5
TOTAL COST:						
25 TSSCM	52.4	424.6	447	484	449.9	439.4
26 AMRAAM	594.9	536.9	522.3	509.5	516.1	524.8
27 THUNDERBOLT	94.1	93.4	94.8	94.8	97.8	100.8
28 COMMERCIAL	120.6	123.4	128.8	132.1	138.9	145.6
29 R&D	32.8	33.8	35.4	35.7	37.9	39.8
30 LCAMR	0	0	0	0	0	0
31 ALL PROGRAMS	894.8	1212.1	1228.3	1256.1	1240.7	1250.3
OVERHEAD RATES:						
32 M&E RATE	1.44	1.45	1.46	1.38	1.43	1.46
33 G&A RATE	0.07	0.05	0.06	0.06	0.06	0.06
CAPITAL:						
34 NBV LAND	10.3	10.3	10.3	10.3	10.3	10.3
35 NBV BUILDINGS	53	71.3	83.6	78.3	73.9	69.5
36 NBV EQUIPMENT	86.9	143.9	206.9	197.1	187.2	177.5
37 NBV TOTAL	150.2	225.5	300.8	285.7	271.4	257.3
38 INVESTMENT	12	90.3	97.9	15	14.3	13
39 DEPRECIATION	16.2	15	22.6	30.1	28.6	27.1

Table 12-1. - Projected Costs by Program if LCAMR is not Undertaken

PART II (1997-2001) – in millions of then-year dollars

DIRECT LABOR:	1997	1998	1999	2000	2001	AVG.
1 TSSCM	75.6	73.8	72.8	72.5	72.5	67.6
2 AMRAAM	87	87.1	87.5	88.3	89.4	93
3 THUNDERBOLT	19.1	19.4	0	0	0	13.7
4 COMMERCIAL	25.5	26.5	27.6	28.7	29.8	24.7
5 R&D	14.5	15.1	15.7	16.3	17	14
8 LCAMR	0	0	0	0	0	0
7 ALL PROGRAMS	221.7	221.9	203.6	205.8	208.7	213.1
OTHER DIRECT COSTS:						
8 TSSCM	223.3	228.5	234.4	241	248.2	221.1
9 AMRAAM	287.1	295.6	304.8	314.5	324.8	284.2
10 THUNDERBOLT	50	51.7	0	0	0	33.7
11 COMMERCIAL	79.9	83.1	86.4	89.9	93.5	77.4
12 R&D	3.4	3.5	3.6	3.7	3.8	3.3
13 LCAMR	0	0	0	0	0	0
14 ALL PROGRAMS	643.7	862.4	629.2	649.1	670.3	619.7
OVERHEAD BY TYPE:						
15 M&E	329.2	334.1	321.7	329	337.1	317.3
16 G&A	75.9	78.9	82.1	85.4	88.8	73.6
17 TOTAL	405.1	413	403.8	414.4	425.9	390.9
OVERHEAD BY PROGRAM:						
18 TSSCM	138.4	137.9	145.1	146.9	149.1	125.6
19 AMRAAM	161.2	164.4	176	180.4	185.2	171.7
20 THUNDERBOLT	34.6	35.7	0	0	0	24
21 COMMERCIAL	47	49.6	54.8	57.7	60.7	46.1
22 R&D	24	25.4	27.9	29.4	31	23.5
23 LCAMR	0	0	0	0	0	0
24 ALL PROGRAMS	405.1	413	403.8	414.4	425.9	390.9
TOTAL COST:						
25 TSSCM	437.3	440.2	452.3	460.4	469.8	414.3
26 AMRAAM	535.3	547.1	568.3	583.2	599.4	548.9
27 THUNDERBOLT	103.7	106.8	0	0	0	71.5
28 COMMERCIAL	152.4	159.2	168.8	176.3	184	148.2
29 R&D	41.9	44	47.2	49.4	51.8	40.9
30 LCAMR	0	0	0	0	0	0
31 ALL PROGRAMS	1270.5	1297.3	1236.6	1269.3	1304.9	1223.7
OVERHEAD RATES:						
32 M&E RATE	1.48	1.51	1.58	1.6	1.62	1.5
33 G&A RATE	0.06	0.06	0.07	0.07	0.07	0.1
CAPITAL:						
34 NBV LAND	10.3	10.3	10.3	10.3	10.3	10.3
35 NBV BUILDINGS	65.6	61.8	57.7	55	55.6	65.9
36 NBV EQUIPMENT	168.8	160.6	151.5	145.2	146.7	161.1
37 NBV TOTAL	244.7	232.7	219.5	210.5	212.6	237.4
38 INVESTMENT	13	12	10	14	23.1	28.6
39 DEPRECIATION	25.6	24	23.2	23	21	23.3

Table 12-2A. - Projected Incremental Cash-Flows for LCAMR: Base Case

PART I (1991-1996) in millions of then-year dollars

	1991	1992	1993	1994	1995	1996
1 FACILITIES CAPITAL:	-100	0	0	0	0	0
OPERATING COST:						
2 DIRECT LABOR (1)	-20	-19.8	-16.9	-15.6	-15	-14.6
3 OVERHEAD (2)	-19	-18.8	-16	-14.9	-14.2	-13.9
4 OTHER DIRECT COSTS (3)	-16	-41.3	-40.1	-40	-40.6	-41.4
5 TOTAL	-55	-79.9	-73	-70.5	-69.8	-69.8
6 REVENUE: (4)	0	0	135.2	140.6	146.2	152.1
TAXES:						
7 OPERATING TAXES (5)	18.7	-18.8	-23	-25.7	-28	-30.1
8 DEPRECIATION TAX SHIELD (6)	4.9	8.3	6	4.3	3	3
9 TOTAL	23.6	-10.5	-17	-21.4	-25	-27.1
10 NET CASH FLOW: (7)	-131.4	-90.4	45.2	48.7	51.4	55.2
11 CUMULATIVE CASH FLOW:	-131.4	-221.8	-176.6	-127.9	-76.5	-21.3
12 NPV AT 18%	21.7					
13 IRR	0.201					

PART II (1997-2002) in millions of then-year dollars

	1997	1998	1999	2000	2001	2002
1 FACILITIES CAPITAL:	0	0	0	0	0	0
OPERATING COST:						
2 DIRECT LABOR (1)	-14.4	-14.3	-14.4	-14.4	-14.5	0
3 OVERHEAD (2)	-13.7	-13.7	-13.7	-13.6	-13.8	0
4 OTHER DIRECT COSTS (3)	-42.3	-43.3	-44.5	-45.8	-47.2	0
5 TOTAL	-70.4	-71.3	-72.5	-73.9	-75.5	0
6 REVENUE: (4)	158.2	164.5	171.1	177.9	185	192.4
TAXES:						
7 OPERATING TAXES (5)	-32	-33.9	-35.8	-37.8	-39.7	0
8 DEPRECIATION TAX SHIELD (6)	3	1.5	0	0	0	0
9 TOTAL	-29	-32.4	-35.8	-37.8	-39.7	0
10 NET CASH FLOW: (7)	58.8	60.8	62.8	66.2	69.8	192.4
11 CUMULATIVE CASH FLOW:	37.5	98.3	161.1	227.3	297.1	489.5
12 NPV AT 18%						
13 IRR						

See Notes for Tables on page 18.

Table 12-2B. - Projected Incremental Cash Flows for LCAMR: Reduced Subcontracting Case

PART I (1991-1996) in millions of then-year dollars

	1991	1992	1993	1994	1995	1996
1 FACILITIES CAPITAL:	-100	0	0	0	0	0
OPERATING COST:						
2 DIRECT LABOR (1)	-20	-26	-22.2	-20.6	-19.7	-19.2
3 OVERHEAD (2)	-19	-24.8	-21.1	-19.6	-18.7	-18.3
4 OTHER DIRECT COSTS (3)	-16	-28.5	-28.7	-29.2	-30.1	-31
5 TOTAL	-55	-79.2	-71.9	-69.4	-68.4	-68.5
6 REVENUE: (4)	0	0	135.2	140.6	146.2	152.1
TAXES:						
7 OPERATING TAXES (5)	18.7	-19	-23.4	-26.1	-28.5	-30.5
8 DEPRECIATION TAX SHIELD (6)	4.9	8.3	6	4.3	3	3
9 TOTAL	23.6	-10.7	-17.4	-21.8	-25.5	-27.5
10 NET CASH FLOW: (7)	-131.4	-89.9	45.9	49.4	52.3	56.1
11 CUMULATIVE CASH FLOW:	-131.4	-221.3	-175.4	-126	-73.7	-17.6
12 NPV AT 18%	25.3					
13 IRR	0.205					

PART II (1997-2002) in millions of then-year dollars

	1997	1998	1999	2000	2001	2002
1 FACILITIES CAPITAL:	0	0	0	0	0	0
OPERATING COST:						
2 DIRECT LABOR (1)	-19	-18.8	-18.9	-18.9	-19.1	0
3 OVERHEAD (2)	-18.1	-17.9	-17.9	-18	-18.2	0
4 OTHER DIRECT COSTS (3)	-32	-33	-34.2	-35.4	-36.7	0
5 TOTAL	-69.1	-69.7	-71	-72.3	-74	0
6 REVENUE: (4)	158.2	164.5	171.1	177.9	185	192.4
TAXES:						
7 OPERATING TAXES (5)	-32.4	-34.5	-36.3	-38.3	-40.3	0
8 DEPRECIATION TAX SHIELD (6)	3	1.5	0	0	0	0
9 TOTAL	-29.4	-33	-36.3	-38.3	-40.3	0
10 NET CASH FLOW: (7)	59.7	61.8	63.8	67.3	70.7	192.4
11 CUMULATIVE CASH FLOW:	42.1	103.9	167.7	235	305.7	498.1
12 NPV AT 18%						
13 IRR						

See Notes for Tables on page 18.

Table 12-2C. - Projected Incremental Cash Flows for LCAMR: Reduced Automation Case

PART I (1991-1996) in millions of then-year dollars

	1991	1992	1993	1994	1995	1996
1 FACILITIES CAPITAL:	-50	0	0	0	0	0
OPERATING COST:						
2 DIRECT LABOR (1)	-20	-27	-23	-21.4	-20.5	-20
3 OVERHEAD (2)	-19	-25.7	-21.9	-20.3	-19.4	-18.9
4 OTHER DIRECT COSTS (3)	-16	-41.3	-40.1	-40	-40.6	-41.4
5 TOTAL	-55	-94	-85	-81.8	-80.5	-80.3
6 REVENUE: (4)	0	0	135.2	140.6	146.2	152.1
TAXES:						
7 OPERATING TAXES (5)	18.7	-14	-18.9	-21.9	-24.3	-26.5
8 DEPRECIATION TAX SHIELD (6)	2.4	4.2	3	2.1	1.5	1.5
9 TOTAL	21.1	-9.8	-15.9	-19.8	-22.8	-25
10 NET CASH FLOW: (7)	-83.9	-103.8	34.3	39	42.9	46.8
11 CUMULATIVE CASH FLOW:	-83.9	-187.7	-153.4	-114.4	-71.5	-24.7
12 NPV AT 18%	26					
13 IRR	0.21					

PART II (1997-2002) in millions of then-year dollars

	1997	1998	1999	2000	2001	2002
1 FACILITIES CAPITAL:	0	0	0	0	0	0
OPERATING COST:						
2 DIRECT LABOR (1)	-19.7	-19.6	-19.6	-19.8	-19.8	0
3 OVERHEAD (2)	-18.8	-18.7	-18.6	-18.8	-18.8	0
4 OTHER DIRECT COSTS (3)	-42.3	-43.3	-44.5	-45.8	-47.2	0
5 TOTAL	-80.7	-81.6	-82.7	-84.4	-85.9	0
6 REVENUE: (4)	158.2	164.5	171.1	177.9	185	192.4
TAXES:						
7 OPERATING TAXES (5)	-28.5	-30.4	-32.4	-34.2	-36.2	0
8 DEPRECIATION TAX SHIELD (6)	1.5	0.8	0	0	0	0
9 TOTAL	-27	-29.6	-32.4	-34.2	-36.2	0
10 NET CASH FLOW: (7)	50.5	53.3	56	59.3	62.9	192.4
11 CUMULATIVE CASH FLOW:	25.8	79.1	135.1	194.4	257.3	449.7
12 NPV AT 18%						
13 IRR						

See Notes for Tables on page 18.

Table 12-2D. - Projected Incremental Cash Flows for LCAMR: Reduced Subcontracting/Automation Case

PART I (1991-1996) in millions of then-year dollars

	1991	1992	1993	1994	1995	1996
1 FACILITIES CAPITAL:	-50	0	0	0	0	0
OPERATING COST:						
2 DIRECT LABOR (1)	-20	-33.3	-28.3	-26.3	-25.2	-24.6
3 OVERHEAD (2)	-19	-31.6	-27	-25	-23.8	-23.3
4 OTHER DIRECT COSTS (3)	-16	-28.5	-28.7	-29.2	-30.1	-31
5 TOTAL	-55	-93.4	-83.9	-80.5	-79.1	-79
6 REVENUE: (4)	0	0	135.2	140.6	146.2	152.1
TAXES:						
7 OPERATING TAXES (5)	18.7	-14.2	-19.3	-22.3	-24.8	-26.9
8 DEPRECIATION TAX SHIELD (6)	2.4	4.2	3	2.1	1.5	1.5
9 TOTAL	21.1	-10	-16.3	-20.2	-23.3	-25.4
10 NET CASH FLOW: (7)	-83.9	-103.4	35	39.9	43.8	47.7
11 CUMULATIVE CASH FLOW:	-83.9	-187.3	-152.3	-112.4	-68.6	-20.9
12 NPV AT 18%	29.6					
13 IRR	0.214					

PART II (1997-2002) in millions of then-year dollars

	1997	1998	1999	2000	2001	2002
1 FACILITIES CAPITAL:	0	0	0	0	0	0
OPERATING COST:						
2 DIRECT LABOR (1)	-24.3	-24.1	-24.1	-24.3	-24.4	0
3 OVERHEAD (2)	-23	-22.9	-22.8	-23.1	-23.3	0
4 OTHER DIRECT COSTS (3)	-32	-33	-34.2	-35.4	-36.7	0
5 TOTAL	-79.3	-80	-81.2	-82.8	-84.4	0
6 REVENUE: (4)	158.2	164.5	171.1	177.9	185	192.4
TAXES:						
7 OPERATING TAXES (5)	-29	-31	-32.9	-34.7	-36.7	0
8 DEPRECIATION TAX SHIELD (6)	1.5	0.8	0	0	0	0
9 TOTAL	-27.5	-30.2	-32.9	-34.7	-36.7	0
10 NET CASH FLOW: (7)	51.4	54.3	57	60.4	63.9	192.4
11 CUMULATIVE CASH FLOW:	30.5	84.8	141.8	202.2	266.1	458.5
12 NPV AT 18%						
13 IRR						

See Notes for Tables on page 18.

Notes for Table 11-2A through Table 11-2D:

(1) The 1991 development cost simply equals the projected value. Estimated production costs in 1992 for each case are as follows in millions of 1992 dollars:

case	projected 1992 cost
base	$19
reduced subcontracting	$25
reduced automation	$26
reduced subcontracting/automation	$32

Real production costs for subsequent years are estimated using a learning rate of 82%. Nominal costs are calculated using a 4 percent inflation rate.

(2) Overhead is calculated on an incremental basis. It equals 95 percent of direct labor.

(3) The 1991 development cost simply equals the projected value. Estimated production costs for subcontracted items and raw materials in 1992 for each case are as follows in millions of 1992 dollars:

case	projected 1992 cost subcontracted items	projected 1992 cost raw materials
base	$26.4	$13.3
reduced subcontracting	$8.9	$18.5
reduced automation	$26.4	$13.3
reduced subcontracting/automation	$8.9	$18.5

Real production costs for subsequent years are estimated using a learning rate of 90 percent. Nominal costs are calculated using a 4 percent inflation rate.

(4) Real revenues equal $129.85 million annually (350 missiles at $371,000 per missile). Nominal revenues are calculated using an Inflation rate of 4 percent. Note that delivery (and thus receipt of revenues) lags one year behind production.

(5) Operating taxes equal 34 percent of revenue minus cost. Because Advanced Missiles Is required to use the percentage of completion method for purposes of tax calculations, taxes are due at the time costs are incurred rather than at the time of delivery or receipt of revenues. For example, missiles produced in 1992 would be delivered and paid for in 1993. However, taxes on the projected revenues would be due in 1992 when the production occurs.

(6) Depreciation of the test equipment for tax purposes is calculated using a seven year life and the 200 percent declining balance method. The tax shield equals 34 percent of the allowed depreciation.

(7) Net Cash Flow = Facilities Capital (line 1) + Operating Cost (line 5) + Revenue (line 6) + Taxes (line 9)

Table 12-3A. – PART I (1991-1996) Projected Costs by Program if LCAMR is Undertaken: Base Case (millions of then-year dollars)

	1991	1992	1993	1994	1995	1996
DIRECT LABOR:						
1 TSSCM	20	42	50.1	100	85.3	79
2 AMRAAM	120	102.3	94.8	90.8	88.5	87.4
3 THUNDERBOLT	18.9	18.7	18.6	18.6	18.7	18.9
4 COMMERCIAL	20.2	21	21.8	22.7	23.6	24.5
5 R&D	11.4	11.9	12.4	12.9	13.4	13.9
6 LCAMR	20	19.8	16.9	15.6	15	14.6
7 ALL PROGRAMS	210.5	215.7	214.6	260.6	244.5	238.3
OTHER DIRECT COSTS:						
8 TSSCM	0	300	300	220	217.4	219.4
9 AMRAAM	262	258.9	261.3	266	272.1	279.2
10 THUNDERBOLT	41.6	42.8	44	45.4	46.9	48.4
11 COMMERCIAL	63.2	65.7	68.3	71	73.8	76.8
12 R&D	2.8	2.9	3	3.1	3.2	3.3
13 LCAMR	30.3	65.8	57.6	52.5	49.5	50.3
14 ALL PROGRAMS	399.9	736.1	734.2	658	662.9	677.4
OVERHEAD BY TYPE:						
15 M&E	293.6	302.3	305.2	352.9	341.8	340.3
16 G&A	60	62.4	64.9	67.5	70.2	73
17 TOTAL	353.6	364.7	370.1	420.4	412	413.3
OVERHEAD BY PROGRAM:						
16 TSSCM	31.1	78.8	93.1	159.6	143	136.7
19 AMRAAM	203.8	168.5	160.2	148.4	150.9	153.4
20 THUNDERBOLT	32.1	30.6	31.1	29.9	31.3	32.5
21 COMMERCIAL	35.6	35.2	37.3	37.3	40.3	42.9
22 R&D	17.9	18.2	19.3	19.2	20.7	22
23 LCAMR	33.1	33.4	29.1	25.9	25.8	25.8
24 ALL PROGRAMS	353.6	364.7	370.1	420.4	412	413.3
TOTAL COST:						
25 TSSCM	51.1	420.8	443.2	479.6	445.7	435.1
26 AMRAAM	585.8	529.7	516.3	505.2	511.5	520
27 THUNDERBOLT	92.6	92.1	93.7	93.9	96.9	99.8
28 COMMERCIAL	119	121.9	127.4	131	137.7	144.2
29 R&D	32.1	33	34.7	35.2	37.3	39.2
30 LCAMR	83.4	119	103.6	94	90.3	90.7
31 ALL PROGRAMS	964	1316.5	1318.9	1339	1319.4	1329
OVERHEAD RATES:						
32 M&E RATE	1.39	1.4	1.42	1.35	1.4	1.43
33 G&A RATE	0.07	0.05	0.05	0.05	0.06	0.06
CAPITAL:						
34 NBV LAND	10.3	10.3	10.3	10.3	10.3	10.3
35 NBV BUILDINGS	53	71.3	83.6	78.3	73.9	69.5
36 NBV EQUIPMENT	86.9	143.9	206.9	197.1	187.2	177.5
37 NBV TOTAL	150.2	225.5	300.8	285.7	271.4	257.3
38 INVESTMENT	12	90.3	97.9	15	14.3	13
39 DEPRECIATION	16.2	15	22.6	30.1	28.6	27.1

Table 12-3A. – PART II (1997-2001) Projected Costs by Program if LCAMR is Undertaken: Base Case (millions of then-year dollars)

	1997	1996	1999	2000	2001	AVG
DIRECT LABOR:						
1 TSSCM	75.6	73.8	72.8	72.5	72.5	67.6
2 AMRAAM	87	87.1	87.5	88.3	89.4	93
3 THUNDERBOLT	19.1	19.4	0	0	0	13.7
4 COMMERCIAL	25.5	26.5	27.6	28.7	29.8	24.7
5 R&D	14.5	15.1	15.7	16.3	17	14
6 LCAMR	14.4	14.3	14.4	14.4	14.5	15.8
7 ALL PROGRAMS	236.1	236.2	218	220.2	223.2	228.9
OTHER DIRECT COSTS:						
8 TSSCM	223.3	228.5	234.4	241	248.2	221.1
9 AMRAAM	287.1	295.6	304.8	314.5	324.8	284.2
10 THUNDERBOLT	50	51.7	0	0	0	33.7
11 COMMERCIAL	79.9	83.1	86.4	89.9	93.5	77.4
12 R&D	3.4	3.5	3.6	3.7	3.8	3.3
13 LCAMR	51.2	47.8	44.5	45.8	47.2	49.3
14 ALL PROGRAMS	694.9	710.2	673.7	694.9	717.5	669.1
OVERHEAD BY TYPE:						
15 M&E	342.8	347.7	335.4	342.8	350.8	332.3
16 G&A	75.9	78.9	82.1	85.4	88.8	73.6
17 TOTAL	418.7	426.6	417.5	428	439.6	405.9
OVERHEAD BY PROGRAM:						
16 TSSCM	134.1	133.7	140.1	141.7	143.8	121.4
19 AMRAAM	156.1	159.4	169.9	174.1	178.6	165.8
20 THUNDERBOLT	33.5	34.6	0	0	0	23.2
21 COMMERCIAL	45.5	48.1	52.9	55.7	58.5	44.5
22 R&D	23.4	24.7	27.1	28.4	30	22.8
23 LCAMR	26.1	26.1	27.6	28	28.6	28.1
24 ALL PROGRAMS	418.7	426.6	417.5	428	439.8	405.9
TOTAL COST:						
25 TSSCM	433	436	447.3	455.2	464.5	410.1
26 AMRAAM	530.2	542.1	562.2	576.9	592.8	543
27 THUNDERBOLT	102.6	105.7	0	0	0	70.7
28 COMMERCIAL	150.9	157.7	166.9	174.3	181.8	146.6
29 R&D	41.3	43.3	46.4	48.4	50.8	40.2
30 LCAMR	91.7	88.2	86.5	88.2	90.3	93.3
31 ALL PROGRAMS	1349.7	1373	1309.2	1343.1	1380.3	1303.8
OVERHEAD RATES:						
32 M&E RATE	1.45	1.47	1.54	1.56	1.57	1.5
33 G&A RATE	0.06	0.06	0.07	0.07	0.07	0.1
CAPITAL:						
34 NBV LAND	10.3	10.3	10.3	10.3	10.3	10.3
35 NBV BUILDINGS	65.6	61.8	57.7	55	55.6	65.9
36 NBV EQUIPMENT	168.8	160.6	151.5	145.2	146.7	161.1
37 NBV TOTAL	244.7	232.7	219.5	210.5	212.6	237.4
38 INVESTMENT	13	12	10	14	23.1	28.6
39 DEPRECIATION	25.6	24	23.2	23	21	23.3

Table 12-3B. PART I (1991-1996) - Projected Costs by Program if LCAMR is Undertaken: Reduced Subcontracting Case (millions of then-year dollars)

	1991	1992	1993	1994	1995	1996
DIRECT LABOR:						
1 TSSCM	20	42	50.1	100	85.3	79
2 AMRAAM	120	102.3	94.8	90.8	88.5	87.4
3 THUNDERBOLT	18.9	18.7	18.6	18.6	18.7	18.9
4 COMMERCIAL	20.2	21	21.8	22.7	23.6	24.5
5 R&D	11.4	11.9	12.4	12.9	13.4	13.9
6 LCAMR	20	26	22.2	20.6	19.7	19.2
7 ALL PROGRAMS	210.5	221.9	219.9	265.6	249.2	242.9
OTHER DIRECT COSTS:						
8 TSSCM	0	300	300	220	217.4	219.4
9 AMRAAM	262	258.9	261.3	266	272.1	279.2
10 THUNDERBOLT	41.8	42.8	44	45.4	46.9	48.4
11 COMMERCIAL	63.2	65.7	68.3	71	73.8	76.8
12 R&D	2.8	2.9	3	3.1	3.2	3.3
13 LCAMR	30.3	53	46.2	41.7	39	39.9
14 ALL PROGRAMS	399.9	723.3	722.8	647.2	652.4	667
OVERHEAD BY TYPE:						
15 M&E	293.6	308.2	310.2	357.8	346.3	344.7
16 G&A	60	62.4	64.9	67.5	70.2	73
17 TOTAL	353.6	370.6	375.1	425.1	416.5	417.7
OVERHEAD BY PROGRAM:						
16 TSSCM	31.1	78.3	92.5	158.8	142.2	136
19 AMRAAM	203.8	167.1	159.1	147.7	150.2	152.6
20 THUNDERBOLT	32.1	30.3	30.8	29.8	31.1	32.3
21 COMMERCIAL	35.6	34.9	37	37.2	40.1	42.7
22 R&D	17.9	18.1	19.2	19.1	20.6	21.9
23 LCAMR	33.1	41.8	36.5	32.5	32.2	32.3
24 ALL PROGRAMS	353.6	370.6	375.1	425.1	416.5	417.7
TOTAL COST:						
25 TSSCM	51.1	420.3	442.6	478.8	444.9	434.4
26 AMRAAM	585.8	528.3	515.2	504.5	510.8	519.2
27 THUNDERBOLT	92.6	91.8	93.4	93.8	96.7	99.6
28 COMMERCIAL	119	121.6	127.1	130.9	137.5	144
29 R&D	32.1	32.9	34.6	35.1	37.2	39.1
30 LCAMR	83.4	120.8	104.9	94.8	90.9	91.4
31 ALL PROGRAMS	964	1315.8	1317.8	1337.9	1318.1	1327.6
OVERHEAD RATES:						
32 M&E RATE	1.39	1.39	1.41	1.35	1.39	1.42
33 G&A RATE	0.07	0.05	0.05	0.05	0.06	0.06
CAPITAL:						
34 NBV LAND	10.3	10.3	10.3	10.3	10.3	10.3
35 NBV BUILDINGS	53	71.3	83.6	78.3	73.9	69.5
36 NBV EQUIPMENT	86.9	143.9	206.9	197.1	187.2	177.5
37 NBV TOTAL	150.2	225.5	300.8	285.7	271.4	257.3
38 INVESTMENT	12	90.3	97.9	15	14.3	13
39 DEPRECIATION	16.2	15	22.6	30.1	28.6	27.1

Table 12-3B. PART II (1997-2001) - Projected Costs by Program if LCAMR is Undertaken: Reduced Subcontracting Case (millions of then-year dollars)

	1997	1998	1999	2000	2001	AVG
DIRECT LABOR:						
1 TSSCM	75.6	73.8	72.8	72.5	72.5	67.6
2 AMRAAM	87	87.1	87.5	88.3	89.4	93
3 THUNDERBOLT	19.1	19.4	0	0	0	13.7
4 COMMERCIAL	25.5	26.5	27.6	28.7	29.8	24.7
5 R&D	14.5	15.1	15.7	16.3	17	14
6 LCAMR	19	18.8	18.9	18.9	19.1	20.2
7 ALL PROGRAMS	240.7	240.7	222.5	224.7	227.8	233.3
OTHER DIRECT COSTS:						
8 TSSCM	223.3	228.5	234.4	241	248.2	221.1
9 AMRAAM	287.1	295.6	304.8	314.5	324.8	284.2
10 THUNDERBOLT	50	51.7	0	0	0	33.7
11 COMMERCIAL	79.9	83.1	88.4	89.9	93.5	77.4
12 R&D	3.4	3.5	3.6	3.7	3.8	3.3
13 LCAMR	40.9	37.5	34.2	35.4	36.7	39.5
14 ALL PROGRAMS	684.6	699.9	663.4	684.5	707	659.3
OVERHEAD BY TYPE:						
15 M&E	347.2	352	339.6	346.9	355.2	336.5
16 G&A	75.9	78.9	82.1	85.4	88.8	73.6
17 TOTAL	423.1	430.9	421.7	432.3	444	410.1
OVERHEAD BY PROGRAM:						
16 TSSCM	133.4	133	139.1	140.9	142.9	120.7
19 AMRAAM	155.3	158.5	168.8	173	177.5	164.9
20 THUNDERBOLT	33.3	34.4	0	0	0	23.1
21 COMMERCIAL	45.3	47.8	52.6	55.4	58.2	44.3
22 R&D	23.2	24.6	26.9	28.2	29.8	22.7
23 LCAMR	32.6	32.6	34.3	34.9	35.7	34.4
24 ALL PROGRAMS	423.1	430.9	421.7	432.3	444	410.1
TOTAL COST:						
25 TSSCM	432.3	435.3	446.3	454.4	463.6	409.5
26 AMRAAM	529.4	541.2	561.1	575.8	591.7	542.1
27 THUNDERBOLT	102.4	105.5	0	0	0	70.5
28 COMMERCIAL	150.7	157.4	166.6	174	181.5	146.4
29 R&D	41.1	43.2	46.2	48.2	50.6	40
30 LCAMR	92.5	88.9	87.4	89.2	91.5	94.2
31 ALL PROGRAMS	1348.4	1371.5	1307.6	1341.5	1378.8	1302.6
OVERHEAD RATES:						
32 M&E RATE	1.44	1.46	1.53	1.54	1.56	1.4
33 G&A RATE	0.06	0.06	0.07	0.07	0.07	0.1
CAPITAL:						
34 NBV LAND	10.3	10.3	10.3	10.3	10.3	10.3
35 NBV BUILDINGS	65.6	61.8	57.7	55	55.6	65.9
36 NBV EQUIPMENT	168.8	160.6	151.5	145.2	146.7	161.1
37 NBV TOTAL	244.7	232.7	219.5	210.5	212.6	237.4
38 INVESTMENT	13	12	10	14	23.1	28.6
39 DEPRECIATION	25.6	24	23.2	23	21	23.3

Table 12-3C. PART I (1991-1996) - Projected Costs by Program if LCAMR is Undertaken: Reduced Automation Case (millions of then-year dollars)

	1991	1992	1993	1994	1995	1996
DIRECT LABOR:						
1 TSSCM	20	42	50.1	100	85.3	79
2 AMRAAM	120	102.3	94.8	90.8	88.5	87.4
3 THUNDERBOLT	18.9	18.7	18.6	18.6	18.7	18.9
4 COMMERCIAL	20.2	21	21.8	22.7	23.6	24.5
5 R&D	11.4	11.9	12.4	12.9	13.4	13.9
6 LCAMR	20	27	23	21.4	20.5	20
7 ALL PROGRAMS	210.5	222.9	220.7	266.4	250	243.7
OTHER DIRECT COSTS:						
8 TSSCM	0	300	300	220	217.4	219.4
9 AMRAAM	262	258.9	261.3	266	272.1	279.2
10 THUNDERBOLT	41.6	42.8	44	45.4	46.9	48.4
11 COMMERCIAL	63.2	65.7	68.3	71	73.8	76.8
12 R&D	2.8	2.9	3	3.1	3.2	3.3
13 LCAMR	23.2	53.6	48.9	46.3	45.1	45.9
14 ALL PROGRAMS	392.8	723.9	725.5	651.8	658.5	673
OVERHEAD BY TYPE:						
15 M&E	293.6	309.1	311	358.4	347	345.5
16 G&A	60	62.4	64.9	67.5	70.2	73
17 TOTAL	353.6	371.5	375.9	425.9	417.2	418.5
OVERHEAD BY PROGRAM:						
16 TSSCM	31.1	78.1	92.3	158.6	141.9	135.7
19 AMRAAM	204.1	166.9	158.9	147.5	149.9	152.3
20 THUNDERBOLT	32.2	30.3	30.8	29.7	31.1	32.2
21 COMMERCIAL	35.6	34.9	37	37.1	40	42.6
22 R&D	17.9	18.1	19.2	19.1	20.6	21.8
23 LCAMR	32.7	43.3	37.8	33.9	33.7	33.8
24 ALL PROGRAMS	353.6	371.5	375.9	425.9	417.2	418.5
TOTAL COST:						
25 TSSCM	51.1	420.1	442.4	478.6	444.6	434.1
26 AMRAAM	586.1	528.1	515	504.3	510.5	518.9
27 THUNDERBOLT	92.7	91.8	93.4	93.7	96.7	99.5
28 COMMERCIAL	119	121.6	127.1	130.8	137.4	143.9
29 R&D	32.1	32.9	34.6	35.1	37.2	39
30 LCAMR	75.9	123.9	109.7	101.6	99.3	99.7
31 ALL PROGRAMS	956.9	1318.3	1322.1	1344.1	1325.7	1335.2
OVERHEAD RATES:						
32 M&E RATE	1.39	1.39	1.41	1.35	1.39	1.42
33 G&A RATE	0.07	0.05	0.05	0.05	0.06	0.06
CAPITAL:						
34 NBV LAND	10.3	10.3	10.3	10.3	10.3	10.3
35 NBV BUILDINGS	53	71.3	83.6	78.3	73.9	69.5
36 NBV EQUIPMENT	86.9	143.9	206.9	197.1	187.2	177.5
37 NBV TOTAL	150.2	225.5	300.8	285.7	271.4	257.3
38 INVESTMENT	12	90.3	97.9	15	14.3	13
39 DEPRECIATION	16.2	15	22.6	30.1	28.6	27.1

Table 12-3C. PART II (1997-2001) - Projected Costs by Program if LCAMR is Undertaken: Reduced Automation Case (millions of then-year dollars)

	1997	1998	1999	2000	2001	AVG
DIRECT LABOR:						
1 TSSCM	75.6	73.8	72.8	72.5	72.5	67.6
2 AMRAAM	87	87.1	87.5	88.3	89.4	93
3 THUNDERBOLT	19.1	19.4	0	0	0	13.7
4 COMMERCIAL	25.5	26.5	27.6	28.7	29.8	24.7
5 R&D	14.5	15.1	15.7	16.3	17	14
6 LCAMR	19.7	19.6	19.6	19.8	19.8	20.9
7 ALL PROGRAMS	241.4	241.5	223.2	225.6	228.5	234
OTHER DIRECT COSTS:						
8 TSSCM	223.3	228.5	234.4	241	248.2	221.1
9 AMRAAM	287.1	295.6	304.8	314.5	324.8	284.2
10 THUNDERBOLT	50	51.7	0	0	0	33.7
11 COMMERCIAL	79.9	83.1	86.4	89.9	93.5	77.4
12 R&D	3.4	3.5	3.6	3.7	3.8	3.3
13 LCAMR	46.8	45.6	44.5	45.8	47.2	44.8
14 ALL PROGRAMS	690.5	708	673.7	694.9	717.5	664.6
OVERHEAD BY TYPE:						
15 M&E	347.9	352.7	340.3	347.7	355.8	337.2
16 G&A	75.9	78.9	82.1	85.4	88.8	73.6
17 TOTAL	423.8	431.6	422.4	433.1	444.6	410.7
OVERHEAD BY PROGRAM:						
16 TSSCM	133.1	132.6	138.7	140.4	142.5	120.5
19 AMRAAM	155	158.1	168.3	172.4	177	164.6
20 THUNDERBOLT	33.3	34.4	0	0	0	23.1
21 COMMERCIAL	45.2	47.7	52.4	55.2	58	44.2
22 R&D	23.2	24.5	26.8	28.2	29.7	22.6
23 LCAMR	34	34.3	36.1	37	37.5	35.8
24 ALL PROGRAMS	423.8	431.6	422.4	433.1	444.6	410.7
TOTAL COST:						
25 TSSCM	432	434.9	445.9	453.9	463.2	409.2
26 AMRAAM	529.1	540.8	580.6	575.2	591.2	541.8
27 THUNDERBOLT	102.4	106.5	0	0	0	70.5
28 COMMERCIAL	150.6	157.3	166.4	173.8	181.3	146.3
29 R&D	41.1	43.1	46.1	48.2	50.5	40
30 LCAMR	100.5	99.5	100.2	102.6	104.5	101.8
31 ALL PROGRAMS	1355.7	1381.1	1319.3	1353.6	1390.6	1309.3
OVERHEAD RATES:						
32 M&E RATE	1.44	1.46	1.52	1.54	1.56	1.4
33 G&A RATE	0.06	0.06	0.07	0.07	0.07	0.1
CAPITAL:						
34 NBV LAND	10.3	10.3	10.3	10.3	10.3	10.3
35 NBV BUILDINGS	65.6	61.8	57.7	55	55.6	65.9
36 NBV EQUIPMENT	168.8	160.6	151.5	145.2	146.7	161.1
37 NBV TOTAL	244.7	232.7	219.5	210.5	212.6	237.4
38 INVESTMENT	13	12	10	14	23.1	28.6
39 DEPRECIATION	25.6	24	23.2	23	21	23.3

Table 12-3D. PART I (1991-1996) - Projected Costs by Program if LCAMR is Undertaken: Reduced Subcontracting/Automation Case (millions of then-year dollars)

	1991	1992	1993	1994	1995	1996
DIRECT LABOR:						
1 TSSCM	20	42	50.1	100	85.3	79
2 AMRAAM	120	102.3	94.8	90.8	88.5	87.4
3 THUNDERBOLT	18.9	18.7	18.6	18.6	18.7	18.9
4 COMMERCIAL	20.2	21	21.8	22.7	23.8	24.5
5 R&D	11.4	11.9	12.4	12.9	13.4	13.9
6 LCAMR	20	33.3	28.3	26.3	25.2	24.6
7 ALL PROGRAMS	210.5	229.2	226	271.3	254.7	248.3
OTHER DIRECT COSTS:						
8 TSSCM	0	300	300	220	217.4	219.4
9 AMRAAM	262	258.9	261.3	266	272.1	279.2
10 THUNDERBOLT	41.6	42.8	44	45.4	46.9	48.4
11 COMMERCIAL	63.2	65.7	68.3	71	73.8	76.8
12 R&D	2.8	2.9	3	3.1	3.2	3.3
13 LCAMR	23.2	40.8	37.5	35.5	34.6	35.5
14 ALL PROGRAMS	392.8	711.1	714.1	641	648	662.6
OVERHEAD BY TYPE:						
15 M&E	293.6	315.1	316	363	351.5	349.8
16 G&A	60	62.4	64.9	67.5	70.2	73
17 TOTAL	353.6	377.5	380.9	430.5	421.7	422.8
OVERHEAD BY PROGRAM:						
16 TSSCM	31.1	77.6	91.8	157.8	141.3	135
19 AMRAAM	204.1	165.6	157.8	146.8	149.2	151.5
20 THUNDERBOLT	32.2	30	30.6	29.6	30.9	32.1
21 COMMERCIAL	35.6	34.6	36.7	36.9	39.8	42.4
22 R&D	17.9	17.9	19	19	20.5	21.7
23 LCAMR	32.7	51.7	45	40.3	40.1	40.1
24 ALL PROGRAMS	353.6	377.5	380.9	430.5	421.7	422.8
TOTAL COST:						
25 TSSCM	51.1	419.6	441.9	477.8	444	433.4
26 AMRAAM	586.1	526.8	513.9	503.6	509.8	518.1
27 THUNDERBOLT	92.7	91.5	93.2	93.6	96.5	99.4
28 COMMERCIAL	119	121.3	126.8	130.6	137.2	143.7
29 R&D	32.1	32.7	34.4	35	37.1	38.9
30 LCAMR	75.9	125.8	110.8	102.1	99.9	100.2
31 ALL PROGRAMS	956.9	1317.8	1321	1342.8	1324.4	1333.7
OVERHEAD RATES:						
32 M&E RATE	1.39	1.37	1.4	1.34	1.38	1.41
33 G&A RATE	0.07	0.05	0.05	0.05	0.06	0.06
CAPITAL:						
34 NBV LAND	10.3	10.3	10.3	10.3	10.3	10.3
35 NBV BUILDINGS	53	71.3	83.6	78.3	73.9	69.5
36 NBV EQUIPMENT	86.9	143.9	206.9	197.1	187.2	177.5
37 NBV TOTAL	150.2	225.5	300.8	285.7	271.4	257.3
38 INVESTMENT	12	90.3	97.9	15	14.3	13
39 DEPRECIATION	16.2	15	22.6	30.1	28.6	27.1

Table 12-3D. PART II (1997-2001) - Projected Costs by Program if LCAMR is Undertaken: Reduced Subcontracting/Automation Case (millions of then-year dollars)

	1997	1998	1999	2000	2001	AVG
DIRECT LABOR:						
1 TSSCM	75.6	73.8	72.8	72.5	72.5	67.6
2 AMRAAM	87	87.1	87.5	88.3	89.4	93
3 THUNDERBOLT	19.1	19.4	0	0	0	13.7
4 COMMERCIAL	25.5	26.5	27.6	28.7	29.8	24.7
5 R&D	14.5	15.1	15.7	16.3	17	14
6 LCAMR	24.3	24.1	24.1	24.3	24.4	25.4
7 ALL PROGRAMS	246	246	227.7	230.1	233.1	238.4
OTHER DIRECT COSTS:						
8 TSSCM	223.3	228.5	234.4	241	248.2	221.1
9 AMRAAM	287.1	295.6	304.8	314.5	324.8	284.2
10 THUNDERBOLT	50	51.7	0	0	0	33.7
11 COMMERCIAL	79.9	83.1	86.4	89.9	93.5	77.4
12 R&D	3.4	3.5	3.6	3.7	3.8	3.3
13 LCAMR	36.5	35.3	34.2	35.4	36.7	35
14 ALL PROGRAMS	680.2	697.7	663.4	684.5	707	654.8
OVERHEAD BY TYPE:						
15 M&E	352.2	357	344.6	352	360.2	341.4
16 G&A	75.9	78.9	82.1	85.4	88.8	73.6
17 TOTAL	428.1	435.9	426.7	437.4	449	414.9
OVERHEAD BY PROGRAM:						
16 TSSCM	132.4	131.9	137.9	139.5	141.6	119.8
19 AMRAAM	154.2	157.3	167.3	171.3	175.9	163.7
20 THUNDERBOLT	33.1	34.2	0	0	0	23
21 COMMERCIAL	44.9	47.4	52.1	54.9	57.6	43.9
22 R&D	23.1	24.4	26.6	28	29.5	22.5
23 LCAMR	40.5	40.7	42.8	43.7	44.5	42
24 ALL PROGRAMS	428.1	435.9	426.7	437.4	449	414.9
TOTAL COST:						
25 TSSCM	431.3	434.2	445.1	453	462.3	408.5
26 AMRAAM	528.3	540	559.6	574.1	590.1	540.9
27 THUNDERBOLT	102.2	105.3	0	0	0	70.4
28 COMMERCIAL	150.3	157	166.1	173.5	180.9	146
29 R&D	41	43	45.9	48	50.3	39.9
30 LCAMR	101.3	100.1	101.1	103.4	105.6	102.4
31 ALL PROGRAMS	1354.3	1379.6	1317.8	1352	1389.1	1306.1
OVERHEAD RATES:						
32 M&E RATE	1.43	1.45	1.51	1.53	1.55	1.4
33 G&A RATE	0.06	0.06	0.07	0.07	0.07	0.1
CAPITAL:						
34 NBV LAND	10.3	10.3	10.3	10.3	10.3	10.3
35 NBV BUILDINGS	65.6	61.8	57.7	55	55.6	65.9
36 NBV EQUIPMENT	168.8	160.6	151.5	145.2	146.7	161.1
37 NBV TOTAL	244.7	232.7	219.5	210.5	212.6	237.4
38 INVESTMENT	13	12	10	14	23.1	28.6
39 DEPRECIATION	25.6	24	23.2	23	21	23.3

Table 12-4A. - Projected Fully Allocated Cash Flows for LCAMR: Base Case

PART I (1991-1996) in millions of then-year dollars

	1991	1992	1993	1994	1995	1996
1 FACILITIES CAPITAL:	-100	0	0	0	0	0
OPERATING COST:						
2 DIRECT LABOR (1)	-20	-19.8	-16.9	-15.6	-15	-14.6
3 OVERHEAD (2)	-33.1	-33.4	-29.1	-25.9	-25.8	-25.8
4 OTHER DIRECT COSTS (3)	-16	-41.3	-40.1	-40	-40.6	-41.4
5 TOTAL	-69.1	-94.5	-86.1	-81.5	-81.4	-81.8
6 REVENUE: (4)	0	0	135.2	140.6	146.2	152.1
TAXES:						
7 OPERATING TAXES (5)	23.5	-13.8	-18.5	-22	-24	-26
8 DEPRECIATION TAX SHIELD (6)	4.9	8.3	6	4.3	3	3
9 TOTAL	28.4	-5.5	-12.5	-17.7	-21	-23
10 NET CASH FLOW: (7)	-140.7	-100	36.6	41.4	43.8	47.3
11 CUMULATIVE CASH FLOW:	-140.7	-240.7	-204.1	-162.7	-118.9	-71.6
12 NPV AT 18%	-25.8					
13 IRR	0.156					

PART II (1997-2002) in millions of then-year dollars

	1997	1998	1999	2000	2001	2002
1 FACILITIES CAPITAL:	0	0	0	0	0	0
OPERATING COST:						
2 DIRECT LABOR (1)	-14.4	-14.3	-14.4	-14.4	-14.5	0
3 OVERHEAD (2)	-26.1	-26.1	-27.6	-28	-28.6	0
4 OTHER DIRECT COSTS (3)	-42.3	-43.3	-44.5	-45.8	-47.2	0
5 TOTAL	-82.8	-83.7	-86.5	-88.2	-90.3	0
6 REVENUE: (4)	158.2	164.5	171.1	177.9	185	192.4
TAXES:						
7 OPERATING TAXES (5)	-27.8	-29.7	-31.1	-32.9	-34.7	0
8 DEPRECIATION TAX SHIELD (6)	3	1.5	0	0	0	0
9 TOTAL	-24.8	-28.2	-31.1	-32.9	-34.7	0
10 NET CASH FLOW: (7)	50.6	52.6	53.5	56.8	60	192.4
11 CUMULATIVE CASH FLOW:	-21	31.6	85.1	141.9	201.9	394.3
12 NPV AT 18%	-25.8					
13 IRR	0.156					

See Notes for Tables on page 31.

Table 12-4B. - Projected Fully Allocated Cash Flows for LCAMR: Reduced Subcontracting Case

PART I (1991-1996) in millions of then-year dollars

	1991	1992	1993	1994	1995	1996
1 FACILITIES CAPITAL:	-100	0	0	0	0	0
OPERATING COST:						
2 DIRECT LABOR (1)	-20	-26	-22.2	-20.6	-19.7	-19.2
3 OVERHEAD (2)	-33.1	-41.8	-36.5	-32.5	-32.2	-32.3
4 OTHER DIRECT COSTS (3)	-16	-28.5	-28.7	-29.2	-30.1	-31
5 TOTAL	-69.1	-96.3	-87.4	-82.3	-82	-82.5
6 REVENUE: (4)	0	0	135.2	140.6	146.2	152.1
TAXES:						
7 OPERATING TAXES (5)	23.5	-13.2	-18.1	-21.7	-23.8	-25.7
8 DEPRECIATION TAX SHIELD (6)	4.9	8.3	6	4.3	3	3
9 TOTAL	28.4	-4.9	-12.1	-17.4	-20.8	-22.7
10 NET CASH FLOW: (7)	-140.7	-101.2	35.7	40.9	43.4	46.9
11 CUMULATIVE CASH FLOW:	-140.7	-241.9	-206.2	-165.3	-121.9	-75
12 NPV AT 18%	-28.9					
13 IRR	0.153					

PART II (1997-2002) in millions of then-year dollars

	1997	1998	1999	2000	2001	2002
1 FACILITIES CAPITAL:	0	0	0	0	0	0
OPERATING COST:						
2 DIRECT LABOR (1)	-19	-18.8	-18.9	-18.9	-19.1	0
3 OVERHEAD (2)	-32.6	-32.6	-34.3	-34.9	-35.7	0
4 OTHER DIRECT COSTS (3)	-32	-33	-34.2	-35.4	-36.7	0
5 TOTAL	-83.6	-84.4	-87.4	-89.2	-91.5	0
6 REVENUE: (4)	158.2	164.5	171.1	177.9	185	192.4
TAXES:						
7 OPERATING TAXES (5)	-27.5	-29.5	-30.8	-32.6	-34.3	0
8 DEPRECIATION TAX SHIELD (6)	3	1.5	0	0	0	0
9 TOTAL	-24.5	-28	-30.8	-32.6	-34.3	0
10 NET CASH FLOW: (7)	50.1	52.1	52.9	56.1	59.2	192.4
11 CUMULATIVE CASH FLOW:	-24.9	27.2	80.1	136.2	195.4	387.8
12 NPV AT 18%						
13 IRR						

See Notes for Tables on page 31.

Table 12-4C. - Projected Fully Allocated Cash Flows for LCAMR: Reduced Automation Case

PART I (1991-1996) in millions of then-year dollars

	1991	1992	1993	1994	1995	1996
1 FACILITIES CAPITAL:	-50	0	0	0	0	0
OPERATING COST:						
2 DIRECT LABOR (1)	-20	-27	-23	-21.4	-20.5	-20
3 OVERHEAD (2)	-32.7	-43.3	-37.8	-33.9	-33.7	-33.8
4 OTHER DIRECT COSTS (3)	-16	-41.3	-40.1	-40	-40.6	-41.4
5 TOTAL	-68.7	-111.6	-100.9	-95.3	-94.8	-95.2
6 REVENUE: (4)	0	0	135.2	140.6	146.2	152.1
TAXES:						
7 OPERATING TAXES (5)	23.4	-8	-13.5	-17.3	-19.5	-21.4
8 DEPRECIATION TAX SHIELD (6)	2.4	4.2	3	2.1	1.5	1.5
9 TOTAL	25.8	-3.8	-10.5	-15.2	-18	-19.9
10 NET CASH FLOW: (7)	-92.9	-115.4	23.8	30.1	33.4	37
11 CUMULATIVE CASH FLOW:	-92.9	-208.3	-184.5	-154.4	-121	-84
12 NPV AT 18%	-30.1					
13 IRR	0.148					

PART II (1997-2002) in millions of then-year dollars

	1997	1998	1999	2000	2001	2002
1 FACILITIES CAPITAL:	0	0	0	0	0	0
OPERATING COST:						
2 DIRECT LABOR (1)	-19.7	-19.6	-19.6	-19.8	-19.8	0
3 OVERHEAD (2)	-34	-34.3	-36.1	-37	-37.5	0
4 OTHER DIRECT COSTS (3)	-42.3	-43.3	-44.5	-45.8	-47.2	0
5 TOTAL	-96	-97.2	-100.2	-102.6	-104.5	0
6 REVENUE: (4)	158.2	164.5	171.1	177.9	185	192.4
TAXES:						
7 OPERATING TAXES (5)	-23.3	-25.1	-26.4	-28	-29.9	0
8 DEPRECIATION TAX SHIELD (6)	1.5	0.8	0	0	0	0
9 TOTAL	21.8	24.3	26.4	-28	-29.9	0
10 NET CASH FLOW: (7)	40.4	43	44.5	47.3	50.6	192.4
11 CUMULATIVE CASH FLOW:	-43.6	-0.6	43.9	91.2	141.8	334.2
12 NPV AT 18%						
13 IRR						

See Notes for Tables on page 31.

Table 12-4D. - Projected Fully Allocated Cash Flows for LCAMR: Subcontracting/Automation Case

PART I in millions of then-year dollars

	1991	1992	1993	1994	1995	1996
1 FACILITIES CAPITAL:	-50	0	0	0	0	0
OPERATING COST:						
2 DIRECT LABOR (1)	-20	-33.3	-28.3	-26.3	-25.2	-24.6
3 OVERHEAD (2)	-32.7	-51.7	-45	-40.3	-40.1	-40.1
4 OTHER DIRECT COSTS (3)	-16	-28.5	-28.7	-29.2	-30.1	-31
5 TOTAL	-68.7	-113.5	-102	-95.8	-95.4	-95.7
6 REVENUE: (4)	0	0	135.2	140.6	146.2	152.1
TAXES:						
7 OPERATING TAXES (5)	23.4	-7.4	-13.1	-17.1	-19.3	-21.3
8 DEPRECIATION TAX SHIELD (6)	2.4	4.2	3	2.1	1.5	1.5
9 TOTAL	25.8	-3.2	-10.1	-15	-17.8	-19.8
10 NET CASH FLOW: (7)	-92.9	-116.7	23.1	29.8	33	36.6
11 CUMULATIVE CASH FLOW:	-92.9	-209.6	-186.5	-156.7	-123.7	-87.1
12 NPV AT 18%	-33					
13 IRR	0.145					

PART II (1997-2002) in millions of then-year dollars

	1997	1996	1999	2000	2001	2002
1 FACILITIES CAPITAL:	0	0	0	0	0	0
OPERATING COST:						
2 DIRECT LABOR (1)	-24.3	-24.1	-24.1	-24.3	-24.4	0
3 OVERHEAD (2)	-40.5	-40.7	-42.8	-43.7	-44.5	0
4 OTHER DIRECT COSTS (3)	-32	-33	-34.2	-35.4	-36.7	0
5 TOTAL	-96.8	-97.8	-101.1	-103.4	-105.6	0
6 REVENUE: (4)	158.2	164.5	171.1	177.9	185	192.4
TAXES:						
7 OPERATING TAXES (5)	-23	-24.9	-26.1	-27.7	-29.5	0
8 DEPRECIATION TAX SHIELD (6)	1.5	0.8	0	0	0	0
9 TOTAL	-21.5	-24.1	-26.1	-27.7	-29.5	0
10 NET CASH FLOW: (7)	39.9	42.8	43.9	46.8	49.9	192.4
11 CUMULATIVE CASH FLOW:	-47.2	-4.6	39.3	86.1	136	328.4
12 NPV AT 18%						
13 IRR						

See Notes for Tables on page 31.

Notes for Table 11-4A through Table 11-4D:
(1) The 1991 development cost simply equals the projected value. Estimated production costs in 1992 for each case are as follows in millions of 1992 dollars:

case	projected 1992 cost
base	$19
reduced subcontracting	$25
reduced automation	$26
reduced subcontracting/automation	$32

Real production costs for subsequent years are estimated using a learning rate of 82%. Nominal costs are calculated using a 4 percent inflation rate.
(2) Overhead is calculated on a fully allocated basis. It is obtained from line 23 of table 3.
(3) The 1991 development cost simply equals the projected value. Estimated production costs for subcontracted items and raw materials in 1992 for each case are as follows in millions of 1992 dollars:

case	projected 1992 cost subcontracted items	projected 1992 cost raw materials
base	$26.4	$13.3
reduced subcontracting	$8.9	$18.5
reduced automation	$26.4	$13.3
reduced subcontracting/automation	$8.9	$18.5

Real production costs for subsequent years are estimated using a learning rate of 90 percent. Nominal costs are calculated using a 4 percent inflation rate.
(4) Real revenues equal $129.85 million annually (350 missiles at $371,000 per missile). Nominal revenues are calculated using an inflation rate of 4 percent. Note that delivery (and thus receipt of revenues) lags one year behind production.
(5) Operating taxes equal 34 percent of revenue minus cost. Because Advanced Missiles is required to use the percentage of completion method for purposes of tax calculations, taxes are due at the time costs are Incurred rather than at the time of delivery or receipt of revenues. For example, missiles produced in 1992 would be delivered and paid for in 1993. However, taxes on the projected revenues would be due in 1992 when the production occurs.
(6) Depreciation of the test equipment for tax purposes is calculated using a seven year life and the 200 percent declining balance method. The tax shield equals 34 percent of the allowed depreciation.
(7) Net Cash Flow = Facilities Capital (line 1) + Operating Cost (line 5) + Revenue (line 6) + Taxes (line 9)

PART IV

COMMENTARY AND PERSPECTIVES

Chapter 13

A NOTE ON THE INFORMATION PERSPECTIVE AND THE CONCEPTUAL FRAMEWORK

Gary L. Sundem
University of Washington Business School

Abstract: The FASB and IASB are reexamining and revising their existing conceptual frameworks. A conceptual framework consists of (1) objectives and (2) concepts that follow logically from those objectives. Most attention is being paid to the concepts, seemingly accepting the objective of wealth measurement. This paper suggests reconsideration of wealth measurement as the objective. Christensen and Demski (2003) suggest two views of accounting objectives: (1) the "value school" based on wealth measurement and (2) the "information content school" based on measuring and disclosing informative events. They make a case for the latter as the most logical objective of accounting. If one accepts the information-content approach to accounting, quite different concepts may arise. For example, the FASB and IASB are on record favoring the balance sheet approach over the revenue and expense approach. This is logical if wealth measurement is an appropriate objective. However, under the information content approach, the revenue/ expense approach, essentially focusing on the flows, which more directly reflect the events affecting an entity, may more logically follow. The revenue/expense approach seems to better align with the disclosure of information events and states.

Key words: conceptual framework, accounting objectives and concepts, information content school, balance sheet approach, revenue and expense approach

1. INTRODUCTION

Accounting standard setters worldwide agree that a conceptual framework is a great help in developing a coherent set of standards. The Financial Accounting Standards Board (FASB) in the United States developed its first framework in the 1970s. This was followed by similar frameworks developed in Canada, Australia, New Zealand, and the United Kingdom, as well as by the International Accounting Standards Committee, predecessor of the International Accounting Standards Board (IASB). The lack of a conceptual framework was seen as one of the main failings of the Accounting Principles Board (APB), as pointed out by Oscar Gellein (1992), a member of both the APB and FASB.

Although official conceptual frameworks have existed now for nearly three decades, they have not proved as useful as many expected. They have been incomplete and rife with internal inconsistencies. The goal of using the conceptual framework as a roadmap for the development of new standards has remained elusive. In addition, the accounting scandals in the early 2000s generated demands for "principles-based" standards. Although different parties had different definitions of what they meant by principles-based standards, the staff of the Securities and Exchange Commission (SEC) in the United States proposed the following reasonable definition (see Office of the Chief Accountant and Office of Economic Analysis, United States Securities and Exchange Commission (2003)): "[E]ach standard is drafted in accordance with objectives set by an overarching, coherent conceptual framework meant to unify the accounting system as a whole." Therefore, a conceptual framework is central to the development of principles-based standards. To address this issue, the FASB and IASB have instituted a joint project to reexamine and revise the existing conceptual frameworks of the two boards.

2.   OBJECTIVES AND CONCEPTS

According to L. Todd Johnson (2004), a conceptual framework consists of two parts, 1) objectives of financial reporting and 2) concepts that follow logically from those objectives. There seems to be little controversy over the objectives, and most attention is currently focused on the concepts that flow from the objectives. The purpose of this note is to suggest a reexamination of the objectives and how they lead to what Johnson calls the "fundamental building blocks" of financial statements – the elements of financial statements -- assets, liabilities, equities, revenues expenses, gains, losses, etc., which are defined in *Statement of Financial Accounting Concepts No. 6* (FASB, 1985).

The general objective accepted by most accountants is that financial reports facilitate economic decision making by investors and creditors. This is clearly an important objective if not the only objective. Following from this, it is reasonable to assume that the financial reports will focus on, as

Johnson (2004) points out, "an entity's economic resources, the claims to those resources, and changes in them (including measures of the entity's performance)." He continues, "The objectives, therefore, focus on matters of *wealth* [emphasis in original]. . . . It follows, then, that information about the wealth of those entities and the changes in it [are] relevant to investors and creditors." Johnson's use of "therefore" and "it follows" imply a logical progression from a focus on resources to a measure of wealth. Although I do not dispute the relevance of information on wealth, I think it is a large jump to assume that, just because information on wealth is relevant, the objective of accounting reports should be to provide information about wealth. There are many relevant pieces of information that accountants do not produce, so relevance of the information cannot be the only criterion for judging accounting information. Let's consider an alternative approach to accounting objectives.

3.   ACCOUNTING OBJECTIVES

Accounting systems provide the recorded history of an organization. To prepare a history, the historian has to decide what information to include and exclude in reports to the public (see Antle and Demski 1989 and Antle, Demski, and Ryan 1994). It is impossible to include all potentially relevant details, so choices are made to both exclude less-relevant data and summarize much of the more-relevant data. The role of accounting standard setters is to specify what details of history are important enough to include in accounting reports, how much detail to include in the reports, and in what format those details should be reported. One set of accounting standards should be judged against another based on the usefulness of its particular set of historical details. Further, usefulness depends on the objectives of accounting reports.

In a perfect and complete market, it might be a reasonable objective for accounting to measure wealth and changes in wealth. The values that comprise wealth would be well defined. But the world does not have complete and perfect markets. Thus, a focus on wealth measurement becomes problematic, as pointed out more than twenty-five years ago by Beaver and Demski (1979). This does not mean that an accounting system focused on wealth measurement is wrong. It is an empirical question as to whether such a system is better than alternatives. However, it is clear that a *prima facie* case for wealth measurement does not exist. It must be justified against other alternatives.

As mentioned earlier, most accountants (myself included) accept the view that accounting reports should facilitate economic decision making by investors and creditors. However, "facilitate" is a slippery term. There are various ways to facilitate decision making. We often slip into the easy interpretation that implies that accounting information must be in the set of information used directly by decision makers when making their decisions. However, there is another role for accounting information that may be more valuable – confirming information (see Sundem, Dukes, and Elliott 1996, 2005). This means that accounting information creates an agreed-upon structure for decision relevant information and ensures that more timely information from other sources will be validated by the later arrival of audited, validated, complete, and highly formatted accounting reports. For confirming information to be valuable, it must be related to the information used in decision making, but it need not be available at the time decisions are made. The more objective and verifiable the information is, the greater its power to confirm the more timely information used in decision making.

4.   VALUE VERSUS INFORMATION CONTENT PERSPECTIVES

Keeping in mind the confirming role of accounting information, I will next consider two alternative views of the objective of an accounting system presented by Christensen and Demski (2003). The first, the "value school," is based on wealth measurement. Such a system is judged by how well its measurements approximate the values that comprise wealth. In contrast, the "information content school" focuses on measuring and disclosing informative events. It would be judged by how well it communicates an underlying event structure.

Consider an accounting system as a financial history of an entity. The value school judges the history by how close its measures come to reflecting the "true" value of the entity. However, in the absence of perfect and complete markets, it is not clear what true value means. For some it may be the market value of the entity, for others it might be the aggregate of the market values of the entity's resources, for others the present value of the entity's future cash flows, and there may be many more definitions. What they have in common is that there is a value that exists and accounting systems attempt to measure that value.

In contrast, the information content perspective judges a system by what it reveals about states of the world and events affecting the entity. The concept is more vague and more difficult to apply because the underlying information to be disclosed by an accounting system is not a single measure of value but a multi-dimensional vector of events and states. Nevertheless, it gets to the heart of the purpose of accounting, revealing information that reduces uncertainty.

5.   THE LANGUAGE AND ALGEBRA OF VALUATION

The distinction between the value and information content schools is complicated by the common use of what Christensen and Demski (2003) call the "language and algebra of valuation."   A five-century tradition uses the terminology of economic valuation to convey accounting information. This terminology is natural for the value school; the information content school must simply accept it as a tradition that is not likely to change in the near future. It is logical to infer from the use of economic valuation terminology that the purpose of accounting reports is to mirror the economic valuation implied in the terminology. When most of an entity's value was derived from the value of its tangible resources, the linkage of economic value and accounting measures may have been useful. However, in today's complex world, where valuation reflects many dynamic stochastic variables, an accounting approximation to value may be far less valuable than the revelation of the events and states affecting an entity. While traditional accounting terminology, the "language and algebra of valuation," can reveal the events and states of interest (see Demski and Sappington 1990), the main question proponents of the information content school must ask is whether it can do so efficiently or whether non-accounting sources of information have a comparative advantage in revealing such information. Besides tradition, accounting has many advantages, especially the objectivity and verifiability of the reported information, which can aid greatly the confirming role of accounting information.

I will accept the constraint that accounting will continue to use the language and algebra of valuation. If this were not the case, we would abandon years of accounting tradition and face the task of creating a new language for the communication of events and states of concern. However, I will explore what this language and algebra is intended to communicate and how that might influence the concepts in a conceptual framework.

6.   MOVING FROM OBJECTIVES TO CONCEPTS

The traditional development of a set of concepts based on the objectives of accounting involves identifying information characteristics that best measure wealth and changes in wealth. However, this may not be a logical step when the objective is disclosing information about events and states. The logical link between information disclosure and wealth measurement is not obvious. That does not mean it does not exist, only that either a logical or empirical connection must be shown.

The full set of accounting concepts is beyond the scope of this note. Instead, I will focus on what Johnson (2004) calls the concepts with "conceptual primacy." These are the concepts that "are used to define other concepts . . . [and] provide unity and prevent the set of concepts from being internally inconsistent." According to Johnson, the FASB considered two alternatives as candidates for conceptual primacy, the "revenue and expense view" and the "asset and liability view."

The asset and liability view is essentially a stock approach – a focus on the measurement of the stock of assets and liabilities. The difference between assets and liabilities at two points in time is income, which can be divided into revenues (increases in assets or decreases in liabilities) and expenses (decreased in assets or increases in liabilities).

The revenue and expense view is essentially a flow approach – a focus on the direct measurement of revenues and expenses, that is, directly measuring the changes in assets and liabilities. This may appear to be nearly identical to the asset and liability view, since both approaches end up with measures for assets, liabilities, revenues, and expenses. However, the revenue and expense approach focuses on the events that cause changes in value, while the asset and liability approach focuses on the resulting values themselves. If the objective of accounting is measuring wealth, a focus on ending asset and liability values is sufficient. However, if the objective is revealing information about the events that cause changes in value, the revenue and expense view has definite advantages.

7.   A CASE FOR THE REVENUE AND EXPENSE VIEW

How should standard setters choose between information-content and valuation objectives and then, based on that choice, between the revenue/expense and assets/liabilities approaches to standard setting? This is not a question that can be answered by theory. It is an empirical question as to which objective and concepts lead to accounting information that has more net value. Nevertheless, I think some speculation may be useful.

Decision makers use information from a wide variety of sources. The subset called accounting information will have value (that is, benefit exceeding cost) in equilibrium only if no other information source can produce a similar uncertainty reduction at a lower price. This means that accountants must have a differential advantage at producing some type of information. Markets seem to have an advantage over accountants at producing information about values. Accountants might aggregate these values to produce valuable insights, but such a contribution would seem to have limited (though possibly positive) value.

In contrast, accountants have an advantage in recording, aggregating, and reporting the results of events affecting value. While accounting systems report on only a subset of events that affect value, traditionally accounting has staked claim on an important set of events – those meeting the definition of revenues and expenses. By bestowing conceptual primacy on revenues and expenses, accountants focus their attention on defining the types of events that will be reported. This focus on events seems more consistent with an information-content view of accounting than does a focus on assets and liabilities.

Nevertheless, the FASB, IASB, and others have chosen the asset/liability view as preferable. Why? By focusing on an objective of measuring wealth, these bodies concluded that the asset/liability view is more logically consistent. The revenue/expenses approach results in assets and liabilities that do not meet the criterion of wealth measures. In contrast, as reported by Storey and Storey (1998), under an asset/liability approach "[t]he only items that can meet the definitions of income and its components – revenues, expenses, gains, and losses – are those that increase or decrease the wealth of an enterprise." With wealth or value measurement the objective of accounting, the asset/liability approach is the logical conceptual primacy. The revenue/expense view results in asset and liability measures that are logically inconsistent with wealth measurement.

However, suppose information content, not wealth measurement, is the objective of accounting systems. The asset/liability approach would not necessarily be the logical conceptual primacy. Consistency with wealth measurement is not needed. What the accounting system should do is identify events and their effects which, if known by decision makers, will affect their decisions. Events, by their very nature, are akin to flows – something that happens rather than something that exists. An accounting system that focuses on flows may provide a better picture of the history of relevant events than one focused just on values. In addition, the history of events (or flows) may be more predictive of future events – those events that many decision makers want to predict – than is a simple history of wealth measures.

8.   RETURNS TO ACCOUNTING PROFESSIONALS

If the accounting profession wants to maximize the returns earned by those possessing accounting skills and knowledge, a conceptual framework must provide a structure within which those skills and knowledge can be put to their best use. It might be possible that we are entering a new era where traditional accounting skills and knowledge are not sufficient to produce a return warranting the cost of their development. In that case, a conceptual framework that highlights the need for the development of different skills and knowledge might be appropriate. Such a framework might focus on valuation, not a traditional strength on accountants. If the focus of accounting becomes valuation, the role of accountants changes. Either they identify, gather, summarize, and report values determined by others, or they develop skills and knowledge necessary for valuation. The former does not seem to be a highly rewarded skill, and the latter does not seem to build on the skills and knowledge accountants have traditionally used. Neither is good news for the future of the accounting profession.

I don't accept the demise of accounting skills and knowledge. I just think we tend to ignore the most important value created by these traditional skills and knowledge – confirming knowledge of relevant events. By focusing on confirming events we are likely to maximize the value and thereby the returns to accounting skills and knowledge.

9.   CONCLUSION

In this note I compare two objectives of accounting, valuation and information content, and two conceptual approaches that should be derived from the objectives, the revenue/expense view or the asset/liability view. Although both objectives can create information that has value, the information content approach is likely to better use the traditional skills and knowledge of accountants to create that value. If we accept information content as the objective of accounting, then the revenue/expense view better aligns with the disclosure of information events and states.

Therefore, I suggest a reexamination of the conceptual primacy that the FASB, IASB, and other have given to the asset/liability view. While it has advantages for the measurement of value, it may not provide as much uncertainty-reducing information as the revenue/expense view.

REFERENCES:

Antle, Rick, and Joel S. Demski, "Revenue Recognition," *Contemporary Accounting Research*, Vol. 5, No. 2 (Fall, 1989), pp. 423-451.

Antle, Rick, Joel S. Demski, and Stephen G. Ryan, "Multiple Sources of Information, Valuation and Accounting Earnings," *Journal of Accounting, Auditing & Finance*, Vol. 9, No. 4 (1994), pp. 675-696.

Beaver, William H., and Joel S. Demski, "The Nature of Income Measurement," *The Accounting Review*, Vol. 54, No. 1 (January, 1979), pp. 38-46.

Demski, Joel S., and David Sappington, "Fully Revealing Income Measurement," *The Accounting Review*, Vol. 65, No. 2 (April, 1990), pp. 363-383.

Christensen, John A., and Joel S. Demski, *Accounting Theory: An Information Content Perspective* (McGraw-Hill Irwin, 2003).

Demski, Joel S., and David Sappington, "Fully Revealing Income Measurement," *The Accounting Review*, Vol. 65, No. 2 (April, 1990), pp. 363-383.

Financial Accounting Standards Board, *Statement of Financial Accounting Concepts No. 6, Elements of Financial Statements* (FASB, 1985).

Gellein, Oscar S., "Financial Reporting: The State of Standard Setting," *Advances in Accounting*, Vol. 3 (JAI Press, 1986), p. 3-23.

Johnson, L. Todd, "Understanding the Conceptual Framework," *The FASB Report* (December 28, 2994).

Office of the Chief Accountant and Office of Economic Analysis, United States Securities and Exchange Commission, *Study Pursuant to Section 108(d) of the Sarbanes-Oxley Act of 2002 on the Adoption by the United States Financial Reporting System of a Principles-Based Accounting System, A Report* Submitted to Committee on Banking, Housing, and Urban Affairs of the United States Senate and Committee on Financial Services of the United States House of Representatives, available at **http://www.sec.gov/news/studies/principlesbasedstand.htm**, posted July 25, 2003.

Storey, Reed K. and Sylvia Storey. *The Framework of Financial Accounting Concepts and Standards* (FASB Special Report, 1998).

Sundem, Gary L., Roland E. Dukes, and John A. Elliott, *The Value of Information and Audits* (Coopers & Lybrand L.L.P., December 1996).

Sundem, Gary L., Roland E. Dukes, and John A. Elliott, *The Demand for Accounting Information and Audits,* Working Paper, 2005.

Chapter 14

ECONOMIZING PRINCIPLE IN ACCOUNTING RESEARCH

Shyam Sunder
Yale School of Managementy

Abstract: Joel S. Demski's work is characterized by the austere discipline of applying the economizing principle to accounting and management phenomena. In natural sciences optimization is used as a structural principle for understanding the organization of the physical universe. As social scientists applied it to our self-conscious selves, economizing acquired a behavioral interpretation, leading to unnecessary and avoidable confusion with the findings of cognitive sciences. Important aspects of aggregate level outcomes of social phenomena are structural. The use of the economizing principle for understanding social phenomena in general, and accounting in particular, has been highly productive, and it is not in conflict with cognitive limitations of human individuals. Demski's work defines the application of this powerful principle to problems of accounting.

Key words: economizing principle, self-selection, employee stock options, integrated financial-tax accounting, audit failures

Joel S. Demski's contributions to accounting are best characterized by use of the simple idea of economizing to build our understanding of accounting. Exploration of the reach and consequences of this idea for the discipline and practice of accounting is a good way to recognize his pioneering contributions.

All great ideas are simple, but not all simple ideas are great. The economizing principle is both simple as well as powerful. Borrowed from physics and biology where it is recognized as optimization principle, into management, economics, and social sciences, this principle serves as a domain of attraction, and the bedrock of our discipline.

1.   THE ECONOMIZING PRINCIPLE

When a marble rolls down the side of a bowl and comes to rest at the bottom, physicists know the marble minimizes its potential energy. When a photon leaves the sun and travels to the eye of a fish swimming under water on earth, the physicist knows that the photon bends just sufficiently at the surface of water so its total travel time from the sun to the eye of the fish is minimized. How does the marble decide where to go and where to stop? How does the photon know where to turn and by how much? Why do they, or anything else in the universe, care to minimize or maximize anything? These are not meaningful questions to a physicist. In physics optimization is used as a fundamental organizing principle of nature. Minima or maxima are guides to identify the domain of attraction of physical systems.

Similarly, in Biology:

At multiple hierarchical levels--brain, ganglion, and individual cell— physical placement of neural components appears consistent with a single, simple goal: minimize cost of connections among the components. The most dramatic instance of this "save wire" organizing principle is reported for adjacencies among ganglia in the nematode nervous system; among about 40,000,000 alternative layout orderings, the actual ganglion placement in fact requires the least total connection length. In addition, evidence supports a component placement optimization hypothesis for positioning of individual neurons in the nematode, and also for positioning of mammalian cortical areas.

A basic problem of network optimization theory is, for the connections among a set of components, to determine the spatial layout of the components that minimizes total connection costs. This simple goal seems to account for nervous system anatomy at several organizational levels. It explains "why the brain is in the head" of vertebrates and invertebrates—this placement in fact minimizes total nerve connection lengths to and from the brain. Proceeding to the internal structure of the brain, the working hypothesis of component placement optimization in cerebral cortex is consistent with known interconnections and spatial layout of cat visual and rat olfactory areas. In addition, the hypothesis exactly predicts contiguities among ganglia in the Caenorhabditis elegans nervous system. Finally, this "brain as ultimate VLSI chip" framework also applies to the lowest-level components, to predict grouping of individual neurons of the nematode into ganglion clusters, and even their positioning within ganglia. The observed harmony of component placement and connections in turn raises questions about whether in fact connections lead to optimal positioning of components, or vice versa. (Cherniak, 1994)

The objects of analysis in physics—marbles and photons—are inanimate. We do not ascribe intentionality to them. Physicists talk about the behavior of these elements only in the sense that they follow the immutable laws of nature the physicists seek to identify. Even in the passage quoted above from biology, two out of the three objects of analysis are ganglion and individual cells which are physical objects with no ascribable intentionality. Their behavior, too, is supposed to follow the immutable laws of nature the biologist seeks to identify. Physicists, biologists, chemists, and other natural scientists can talk about behavior of objects and use optimization as a structural principle to gain an understanding of the big-picture. Structural models are about the proverbial forests, not the trees; they concern the existence, type, and growth of the forest, not the location and height of individual trees. They shield us from getting lost in the detail.

Economics and management borrowed the optimization principle from physics, (and increasingly from biology, in recent decades). Demski has been instrumental in applying this principle to understand a variety of accounting problems (see Christensen and Demski, 2003). In economics, management and accounting, the application of this principle inevitably acquires a flavor of its own. Instead of inanimate marbles or photons to which the physicist applies this principle, we and the institutions in which we live and work, are the objects of economic and management analysis. When applied to our own self-conscious selves, "behavior" takes on the burden of intentionality not necessary, or present, in the natural sciences. It also gives rise to questions about the descriptive validity of optimization as a behavioral principle, about human rationality, and the related arguments.

Application of the optimization principle, combined with our concept of ourselves as sentient beings, led to the creation of the theory of choice.[55] We postulated for ourselves a definable and knowable preference ordering over all relevant objects of choice. The preference ordering, being directly unobservable to others, and possibly without the property of self-awareness, must be inferred from observable choices. In the absence of generalization to

---

[55] Whether, and in what sense, the choice theory allows us the opportunity to choose is replete with contradictions of its own, and perhaps I should not try to pursue that subject here. Briefly, on one hand, humans proudly claim to have unique attributes of free will, imagination, and creativity, placing how we act beyond the kind of laws physicists devise to describe the behavior of marbles and photons, and even other forms of life. Yet, social sciences try to identify general laws that may help us understand, explain and predict human actions as if we were some not-so-special kind of marbles.

contexts outside the choice data used to infer preferences, the theory of choice is essentially tautological—we choose what we prefer, and we must prefer what we do choose.

The power of the economizing principle derives from the discipline that its extreme simplicity imposes on our thinking. It does not allow us many degrees of freedom, nor lets us introduce new explanatory variables at will. We must force ourselves to think very hard about how and why our wants and behavior are linked to each other. If we assume that we choose what we want, and infer our wants from what we choose, we can identify one or more sets of mutually consistent wants and choice/behavior. Demski brought this mindset and tight discipline to accounting research, and used its remarkable power to identify internally consistent propositions in accounting and management contexts.

2.   BEHAVIORAL INTERPRETATION

In spite of the power and reach of the economizing principle, its results have come to be questioned due, I believe, to a deep misunderstanding of its roots. This has to do with the doubts about the rationality of individuals in making choices. It would be useful to make a short detour to touch on this subject here.

It was not surprising that in borrowing the concept of optimization from natural sciences, where it is used as a structural or organizing principle of the universe, economists and other social scientists were tempted to interpret it as a behavioral principle.[56] In economics, optimization came to be regarded as a matter of conscious and deliberate economizing—individuals choosing the best of the alternatives known and available to them. Cognitive psychology soon revealed, if it needed any revealing, that when acting by our intuition, we humans are not very good at optimization (Simon, 1957). While Simon was not a reductionist, and understood the distinction between structural and behavioral assumptions[57], not all those who claim his legacy do.

---

[56] Dixit (1991, p. 1): "Economics has been defined as the study of making the best use of scarce resources, that is, of maximization subject to constraints. The criteria being maximized, and the constraints being imposed on the choice, vary from one context to the next: households' consumption and labor supply, firms' production, and governments' policies. But all constrained maximization problems have a common mathematical structure, which in turn generates a common economic intuition for them."

[57] "This skyhook-skyscraper construction of science from the roof down to the yet unconstructed foundations was possible because the behavior of the system at each level

This literal interpretation of economizing as a behavioral principle has expanded to include some of those who use it in their own work. If people cannot intuitively choose what is best for them, they must be irrational[58], and therefore it follows that the results derived from the application of the economizing principle must be viewed with caution, even rejected.

There are three problems with this interpretation. First, failure to choose the best option does not necessarily arise from irrationality if the availability and the consequences of the option are not known. One cannot be expected to choose an unknown option, or one which is desirable without adequate information being available. In addition, if the unavailability of cognitive or computational tools of analysis leads to failure to choose the option which would have been best if such tools were available, irrationality would not seem to be the appropriate interpretation of the choice.

Second, a related problem of interpretation concerns generalization of evidence from contrived laboratory settings, with which subjects have had little living experience. Laboratory settings can yield valuable initial insights into a variety of real phenomena. However, their value for better understanding such phenomena depends on their generalizability outside the laboratory. We know that humans as well as animals adapt themselves by learning to solve complex problems over time through repetition, trial-and-error, and contemplation. We must be careful not to assume, either that human beings must already have adapted themselves to any task the experimenter can contrive for them in the lab, or that given the chance to learn through repetition, such learning cannot or would not occur.

Third, and most importantly, even if human ego supports the behavioral interpretation of the optimization principle, in the larger scheme of things, we cannot ignore its structural interpretation in aggregate or social level manifestations. In a largely serendipitous discovery, Gode and Sunder (1993a, b) found that under classic conditions, even markets populated by the so-called "zero-intelligence" traders[59] tend to converge, in price,

---

depended on only a very approximate, simplified, abstracted characterization of the system at the level next beneath. This is lucky, else the safety of bridges and airplanes might depend on the correctness of the 'Eightfold Way' of looking at elementary particles." Simon (1996, p. 16).

[58] Conlisk (1996), for example, gives four reasons for dropping the "infinite in faculties" assumption in favor of incorporating bounded rationality in economic models: empirical evidence on the importance of bounded rationality, proven track record of bounded rationality models (in explaining individual behavior), unconvincing logic of assuming unbounded rationality, and the cost of deliberating on an economic decision.

[59] A "zero-intelligence" buyer submits a randomly chosen number between zero and its value of the object as the price at which it is willing to buy the object. Similarly, a "zero-intelligence" seller submits a randomly chosen number between its cost and an arbitrary

allocations, and efficiency, to close proximity of the equilibrium predictions of economic theory. While the equilibrium predictions are derived using advanced mathematical techniques, and assuming optimization on part of the individual traders, the rules of a simple double auction (and many other forms of market organization) are sufficient to ensure that aggregate market outcomes are reached by individual traders whose behavior is far from optimizing. If our primary concerns are with aggregate social phenomena, we should not jump to the conclusion that the failure of individuals to optimize makes the predictions of economizing models inapplicable (Sunder, 2004).

3.   ECONOMIZING IN ACCOUNTING

The economizing principle has applications in, and implications for, many aspects of accounting. Most of these applications have been centered on managerial accounting, driven largely by the need for estimates of parameters in order to solve the problem on hand. This self-imposed limitation on the application of the economizing principle also appears to be driven by the behavioral and literal interpretation of the principle: In order to solve a problem we not only need to formulate it, but also need the knowledge of parameters to arrive at the actual solution in specific instances. I would like to argue that this interpretation is unnecessarily restrictive, confining accounting applications of the economizing principle to managerial contexts.

In accounting contexts where the aggregate or market level outcomes are of primary interest, the structural interpretation of economizing can be assumed to be more relevant. In such situations, we do not need to know the parameters of the problem in advance. If the market (or other aggregation) mechanism functions reasonably well, we do not need to know the parameters of the problem ex ante. Instead, if necessary, we can infer the parameters of the problem from observed outcomes of the aggregation mechanism. This, in essence, is the efficient markets argument.

---

upper limit as the price at which it is willing to sell the object. Such traders have no memory, learning, expectations, or attempt to optimize. They submit proposals to trade such that if a trade is completed, they would not incur a loss.

3.1   Employee Stock Options

With only a few exceptions (e.g., marketable securities), regulators of financial accounting in the United States (U.S.) have been reluctant to use economizing tendencies as reflected in even well-functioning, liquid markets to guide their actions. Feedback from such markets, when used in incentive compatible formats, can considerably simplify the regulatory burden by eliminating the need for objective estimation of parameters by individuals. For example, U.S. regulators have struggled mightily with the problem of measuring and recognizing the cost of employee stock options for well over 15 years, insisting throughout on model-based approaches. Proposals to construct scenarios so the economizing tendencies of markets (e.g., Sunder, 1994) can simplify the task of financial reporting received scant attention until quite recently when SEC's Office of Economic Analysis scrutinized such a proposal. The Chairman of the SEC said (SEC, 2005a):

> As the OEA memorandum makes clear, the use of an appropriate market instrument for estimating the fair value of employee stock options has some distinct advantages over a model-based approach. Most importantly, the instrument's price could establish the issuer's true cost of the option grant, by having it priced by the market.

> The Office of Economic Analysis (OEA) of the SEC concluded (SEC, 2005b):

- The market price obtained through a market-based approach value can efficiently reflect a consensus view among informed marketplace participants about an expense, asset or liability's utility, future cash flows, the uncertainties surrounding those cash flows, and the compensation that marketplace participants demand for bearing those uncertainties.
- The instrument's price could establish the true opportunity cost of the award to the issuer by having it priced by the market.
- Use of a market instrument may promote competition between different approaches to the estimation of the value of the market instrument, and thereby lead to innovations in models and techniques used to price employee stock options.
- There could be a positive externality for other firms that could use market prices to help improve their calibration of model-based estimates.

3.2   Integration of Financial and Tax Accounting

In the U.S. practice, financial and tax accounting have taken divergent paths over the years. I had always thought of this divergence as strength of the U.S. system in which corporations can solve two separate optimization problems independently, without worrying much about the other. On one hand, they decide what and how to report their financial results to the investors and general public, within the constraints of the applicable financial reporting rules, in order to optimize the interests of the shareholders and of their own. On the other hand, they decide how to report their results to the Internal Revenue Service (IRS), presumably to minimize the present value of taxes paid to the government. Within some limits, the former problem is often believed to induce a tendency to overstate the current performance of the firm while the latter problem induces corporations to report lower income. A corporation is free to paint a rosy picture for its shareholders and a dismal one for the tax collector.

Attempts to limit corporate discretion take the form of costly auditing. Independent financial auditors try to make sure that the financial reports are not excessively rosy. On the other hand, the IRS employs an army of auditors of its own to try to make sure that the tax returns do not present an excessively low income. Thus considerable amounts of real economic resources in the economy are devoted to these two kinds of audit services. In addition, the SEC on one hand, and the IRS on the other, devote resources to formulate their respective accounting rules to control the contents of the reports, not always successfully. Pressures to "clarify" the rules have led to an inevitable thickening of the two rulebooks.

An economizing approach to the problem might suggest that integration of the two accounting systems into one may help improve corporate financial reporting as well as taxation. If corporations were given wide reporting latitude with the provision that the same set of reports must be submitted to shareholders and the tax collector, the corporate tendency to overstate financial income and understate taxable income will have a disciplining influence on each other. If X were the "neutral," albeit unobservable, income of the firm, and if the firm were to try to report a higher amount $(X + Y)$, it would also have to pay taxes on the additional amount Y. The system will impose a real cost on the corporation for deviating from the neutral amount, and thus discourage it. If the firm were to report a lower amount as income to the tax collector $(X-Z)$ in order to pay lower taxes, it will also have to report the lower amount to the shareholders and the public, possibly lowering the performance evaluation and rewards to the managers who make such decisions. In other words, the corporate tendencies to overstate financial performance and avoid taxes will counterbalance each other. The self-serving behavior of managers, and a significant part of the corporate governance problem could be addressed by such a reform.

Such integration may have the additional advantage of substantially reducing the burden of dual auditing by independent and IRS auditors, as well as reduce the pressure on the SEC and the IRS to write evermore detail in their accounting rules.

While an application of the economizing principle to derive aggregate outcomes of interactions among individuals may yield equilibrium outcomes, the same principle also informs us that equilibria do not always exist. Even when they exist in open loop systems, designing a regulatory system in which markets and regulatory action are mutually dependent can create instability or indeterminacy (e.g., Brennan and Schwartz, 1982; Sunder 1989; and Marimon and Sunder, 1993 and 1995). Further, an inappropriate application of economizing principle, as well as ignoring it, can do more harm than good.

3.3   Failures of Accounting and Auditing[60]

The economizing principle, applied to the market for audit services, can help us better understand the large-scale and well-publicized audit failures during the recent years. While the antitrust laws, to promote competition in trade and industry, have been on the books in the U.S. since the late nineteenth century, these laws were not enforced on professionals such as doctors, lawyers and accountants. In their codes of ethics, the professional associations included provisions to proscribe advertising and solicitation of competitors' clients and employees as being unprofessional. The economic rationale for this informal exemption for the professions lay in the asymmetry of information. It is difficult for the clients of the professionals to see the quality of services rendered to them. Indeed, they often rely on the professionals to advise them on what services they should buy. Emphasizing competition in this setting, it was feared, would result in lowering not only the price but also the quality of the professional services, and thus result in a collapse of the market for such services. George Ackerlof, formalized this idea in his famously elegant model of economizing he called the "Market for 'Lemons'."

Economists also examined the robust of competition to information asymmetry, and the possibility of seller reputation about the quality of goods or services provided serving as an effective antidote for the problems caused

---

[60] This section is based on Sunder (2003).

by information asymmetries (Leland 1979, Smallwood and Conlisk 1979, Shapiro 1982, and Rogerson 1983). When sellers can develop reputations with the customers, we need not fear that the competition will lower the quality of goods or services provided.

The U.S. Supreme Court, which had heretofore sustained the ban on advertising in the market for professional services, ruled in 1977 that the Bar of the State of Arizona could not prevent its members from advertising their services. Though the case was decided on the grounds of (commercial) free speech guaranteed by the First Amendment to the U.S. Constitution, arguments about the opportunity to build reputations played an important role in this ruling.

Though not directed at them, it turned out to be a watershed ruling for the auditing profession in U.S. The Supreme Court ruling led the U.S. government to change its policy on professional competition, and the latter forced the professional associations to drop the anticompetitive provisions from their codes of ethics. The American Institute of CPAs changed its Code of Ethics effective 1979, resulting in major consequences.

Generalization of the reputation argument from the professions of medicine, dentistry, and law to auditing was fundamentally flawed because the results of the medical and legal services are observable, at least ex post, to the customers in a reasonably prompt manner. Such observations have a reasonable, albeit imperfect, correlation with the quality of services rendered; reputation has a fair chance of keeping markets from collapsing under competition.

This is not the case with the market for audit services. Corporate managers and directors hire the auditors. The real clients of the auditors— the investors— never see the auditors. Even if they could, they would not be able to tell by watching them if the auditors have done their job diligently. Managers who see the auditors hardly have any incentives to make sure that they properly check the representations made by the managers to the investors and others. Only on rare occasions, when a corporation runs into serious financial trouble, are questions raised about the fairness of its financial reports and the quality of the audit work used to certify the reports. More than 99 percent of the time, no questions are raised about the quality of the audit, and no one looks into what the auditors actually did.[61] In this environment, there is hardly any opportunity for the auditors to build their

---

[61] Attempts of the Public Oversight Board to scrutinize the quality of audit services proved to be ineffective. We would not know for a few more years whether the efforts of the newly created Public Company Accounting Oversight Board to do so will prove to be more effective after their novelty wears off.

reputation based on the quality of their work. Thus the reputation argument cannot be generalized from other professions to the auditing profession.

However it was generalized to the auditing profession, and under the pressure of competition, as Ackerlof's economizing model predicted, auditing turned into a "market for lemons." The prices dropped as the corporate controllers solicited new bids from audit firms, year after year, to get a better price from their auditors. At these ever-lower prices, the auditors could not continue to do what they had long done and still earn a decent living. Something had to change, and it did.

To survive in this new competitive environment forced upon them, auditors built themselves a new business model. It had three new elements— a new product mix, a new production function, and a new compensation policy. While I will not go into the details of what happened, this strategy did not work. Over the next 15 years, the audit firms tried various alternatives in business, political, and legal domains to recover their profitability. The widespread failures of auditing can, however, be traced to the misapplication of the economizing principle to promote competition in an industry whose product quality is virtually unobservable. In pushing competition on all professions in the late seventies, the government policy failed to consider the consequences of the economizing principle in this case and the special susceptibility of the market for audit services to become a "market for lemons." In pushing for competition, the government not only damaged auditor independence, but paradoxically, it damaged the competition too. After a quarter-century of efforts to promote competition, the number of large audit firms who audit most publicly held firms has been halved from eight to four.

4. RESEARCH AND PRETENSE

This is a special occasion for me to share with you a brief account of my second encounter with Demski. I first met him as a yet-to-be-minted PhD candidate visiting Stanford, hoping to get a job offer. Demski was my host for the visit. In one memorable instant, I knew that I was in the presence of a very special person—unconventional and independent. No pretense here— what you see is what you get. It took me five more months to find out, through another close encounter with him, the depth of thinking that accompanied that iconoclasm. It took me yet another ten years to discover that his thinking was the essence of the distinction between pretense and the real thing in research.

The second opportunity arose five month later. Nicholas Dopuch had asked me to present a paper (Sunder, 1973) from my PhD dissertation at the

1973 Journal of Accounting Research Conference, about a week before I was scheduled to defend it at Carnegie Mellon University. With the help of my mentors (Yuji Ijiri, Robert Kaplan, Richard Roll, Edward Prescott, and Marcus Bogue), data provided to me by Kaplan, and frequent conversations with Nicholas Gonedes who was visiting that year at Carnegie, I had moved from program entry to defense in about 24 months. This progress seemed to stall during the Spring Semester following the job market interviews.

At that time, the realization dawned upon me that my attempts to deal with the self-selection problem of my LIFO-FIFO sample were doomed to fail. Taking the argument one step up the ladder would not help any more than chasing my own shadow would help me catch up—the self-selection objections, too, simply move one step up the ladder. It reminds one of an oft-repeated story that has acquired the status of an urban legend under the label "turtles all the way down." [62] Various versions of the story share answers to the series of questions starting with: what does the earth rest on? A turtle. What does the turtle rest on? Another turtle, which rests on another, and another, and so on, all the way down. Whether in self-selection, or in cosmology, resorting to an infinite regress to shove inconvenient problems under the rug appears to be an old device.

When I had thought I only had to tie up a few loose ends in order to finish up my dissertation, this realization was becoming a growing psychological hurdle in my motivation. My advisors were kind enough to let me wrap up after pursuing the self-selection issues on inventory valuation one step above the conventional ladder. My tentativeness was reflected in the cautious title of the paper: Relationship between Accounting Changes and Stock Prices: Problems of Measurement and Some Empirical Evidence. I felt shaky defending it on logical grounds as I stood up at the JAR conference, unable to conceal how I felt through my halting, uncertain, and nervous delivery. I finished the talk with my results and caveats, and Dopuch called Demski to discuss the paper. Today is my chance to discuss Demski's comments.

An author's worst nightmare is that the discussant goes straight to the point. Without mincing many words, Demski did exactly that. After granting the justification for the study, he pointed out the gap between the theoretical demands of the question posed, and what could be learned from an empirical study of observed stock prices of samples of firms in the field. He went on, patiently, to list the internal and external validity problems of the study, and the gaps in the reliability of the claimed inference.

---

[62] See http://en.wikipedia.org/wiki/Turtles_all_the_way_down.

When Demski finished, Dopuch asked me to reply to his criticism. I said I agreed with him, and there was nothing for me to add. At the end of the session, while others thought I must have been crushed by the criticism, I felt amazingly good inside. Through his pointed critique Demski (1973) had freed me from having to defend what I knew could not be defended. He freed me from the pressure to pretend to do something that I knew could not be done.

For this early freedom, I am ever so grateful to him. I could move on to try to learn new things, without being tethered all my professional life to my very first research project. I returned, thirty years later to his criticism of my inability to establish a link between the individual behavior and aggregate market outcomes in the LIFO study, when Gode and I discovered (Gode and Sunder, 1993a, b), that the link between the two was tenuous, at best.

Each research method has limitations of its own. Demski had critiqued not just my paper, but the limitations of what could be learned from empirical method. To the best of my knowledge, it remains unsurpassed to this day. It is unfortunate to see that that branch of accounting literature has neither addressed, nor adjusted itself in light of this critique, and has moved along, as if pretending he never wrote or spoke those words.

Distinguishing pretense from the real thing has become increasingly difficult in many aspects of our lives, and this problem is, if anything, even worse in the field of research. When evidence suggests results that we don't like, we are often inclined to pretend even more. A few weeks ago, I learned of a study (Robinson and Adler, 2003) reporting that the periodical literature in accounting lags behind the literature of our sister management disciplines in publication and as well as citation statistics. Not only do we publish less often, each published paper is cited less often by others, both in and outside the accounting literature. This finding appears to have generated some discomfort and given rise to suggestions such as exhorting our colleagues to be more generous in acknowledging the work of others within accounting.[63] If I don't like my complexion in the mirror, will a rose-tinted mirror help? Can pretense substitute for the real thing?

Some twenty-two years ago, during our visit to the University of British Columbia, I walked into Vancouver's science museum with my three-and-a-half year old daughter. As we entered the lobby, a robot took a step forward and in its high-pitched, synthetic robotic voice asked: Where did you get your pretty blue dress? Richa could not be more pleased with the instant

---

[63] Occasionally, one hears allegations about the existence of citation rings or closed groups whose members supposedly agree to cite or download one another's work, and then promote the citations of the download statistics as evidence of accomplishment.

recognition, and gleefully responded: my aunt made it for me. The friendly robot, modeled after R2D2 of star wars, engaged in a few more sentences of banter with her before turning its attention to the next visitor. For Richa, that short conversation was the highlight of the visit.

Pretense is the essence of toys, dolls, learning, and imagination. If we cannot pretend, we cannot simplify; if we do not simplify, we cannot learn. Yet, if our learning is to amount to anything in the complex world we live in, the loop of imagination, simplification, pretension, learning and experience must be closed. To an engineer or scientist, it was clear that it would not have been possible for a robot, in the early 1980s, to do what it pretended to do. Pretending to do what tens of thousands of engineers and scientists have struggled mightily to do for decades was remarkably simple. On hearing the greeting, I had glanced around and had spotted a young woman sitting high up in the balcony with a microphone in her hand, greeting the visitors through speakers installed in the "robot" as they entered through the door.

Robots are designed to pretend to be people, and here was a "robot" designed to pretend to be a "real" robot. In the world we live in, we may often come across even more layers of pretense and modeling.[64] It may be worthwhile to look into these layers. That afternoon in the science museum, children were not the only ones who did not see through the layers of pretense. Some, unaware of the current limitations of robotic technology, and unaware of the young woman sitting in her high perch in the balcony, even objected to the suggestion that they were not looking at a "real" robot. What is a real robot, and what could it mean for accounting research?

The real driver of research, whether accounting or any other, is our curiosity to seek a better understanding of the world around us. Curiosity is a result of the interaction between our observation of the world, and contemplation that accompanies the integration of the observations with our internal model of the world. The internal model is a complex combination of memories, beliefs, expectations and their interrelationships about various phenomena. When new observations do not mesh with the existing internal model, a dissonance arises between the two. A scholar cannot afford to live with such dissonance, and must launch a search to find a way to eliminate it.

Such searches are curiosity-driven; they do not allow the mind to rest until a way has been found to reconcile the observation with the internal model. Reconciliation may involve either a parametric or structural revision of the model, or a correction of the observation. Given the frequency of

---

[64] For an example, see Blake Edwards' film Victor/Victoria (1982) in which Julie Andrews plays a woman who pretends to be a man, who in turn, goes on stage in drag to act like a woman.

observations and the range and complexity of models we carry in our heads, a scholar has a perpetual supply of inconsistencies that arouse curiosity, demand attention, and support the life of the mind. It is only a matter of deciding when to devote time to addressing which question. That choice is often made by the "excitement quotient" of the problem. One addresses the question that insists on being addressed first—the squeaky wheel principle. In any case, research is driven by internal, not external motivations, a palpable characteristic of Demski's work.

Demski's gift to accounting is the discipline of thinking deeply about problems within the strict constraints of the economizing principle. We think harder, and learn a great deal more, when we seek solutions for our problems within the confines of a few explanatory variables. The extraordinary power of economics among the social sciences arises from this discipline, and Demski's work is the best example of this approach to learning in accounting.

REFERENCES

Ackerlof, George A. 1970. "The Market for 'Lemons': Quality, Uncertainty and the Market Mechanism," Quarterly Journal of Economics, Vol. 84, No. 3, 488-500.

Brennan, M. J. and E.S. Schwartz, 1982. "Consistent Regulatory Policy under Uncertainty," The Bell Journal of Economics, Vol. 13, No. 2, 506-521.

Demski, Joel. 1973. "Discussion of 'Relationship between Accounting Changes and Stock Prices: Problems of Measurement and Some Empirical Evidence'," Journal of Accounting Research, Vol. 11, 46-54.

Cherniak, C. 1994. "Component Placement Optimization in the Brain," Journal of Neuroscience, Vol. 14(4), 2418-2427.

Christensen, John and Joel Demski. 2003. Accounting Theory. New York, NY: McGraw-Hill.

Conlisk, John. 1996. "Why Bounded Rationality?" Journal of Economic Literature, Vol. 34, No. 2: 669-700.

Dixit, Avinash. 1990. Optimization in Economic Theory. Oxford University Press.

Gode, Dhananjay K. and Shyam Sunder, 1993a. "Allocative Efficiency of Markets with Zero Intelligence Traders: Market as a Partial Substitute for Individual Rationality," Journal of Political Economy, Vol. 101, No. 1 (February), 119-137.

Gode, Dhananjay K. and Shyam Sunder, 1993b. "Lower Bounds for Efficiency of Surplus Extraction in Double Auctions," in D. Friedman and J. Rust, editors, The Double Auction Market: Institutions, Theories and Laboratory Evidence, Santa Fe Institute Studies in the Sciences of Complexity. New York, NY: Addison-Wesley, 199-219.

Leland, Hayne E. 1979. "Quacks, Lemons, and Licensing: A Theory of Minimum Quality Standards," Journal of Political Economy, Vol. 87, No. 6 (December), 1328-1346.

Marimon, Ramon and Shyam Sunder, 1993. "Indeterminacy of Equilibria in a Hyperinflationary World: Experimental Evidence," Econometrica, Vol. 61, No. 5, 1073-1107.

Marimon, Ramon and Shyam Sunder, 1995. "Does a Constant Money Growth Rule Help Stabilize Inflation?: Experimental Evidence," Carnegie-Rochester Conference Series on Public Policy, Vol. 43, 111-156.

Nicolaisen, Donald T. 2005. "Statement Regarding Use of Market Instruments in Valuing Employee Stock Options," Chief Accountant of U.S. Securities and Exchange Commission, September 9, 2005. http://www.sec.gov/news/speech/spch090905dtn.htm.

Robinson, Larry M. and Roy D. Adler, 2003. "Business Research in Eight Business Disciplines," Presented at the International Business and Economics Research Conference, Las Vegas, October 6, 2003. http://www.academicassessments.com/ArticlesFolder/pdfs/2-Las_Vegas_Paper.pdf.

Rogerson, William P. 1983. "Reputation and Product Quality," The Bell Journal of Economics Vol. 14, No. 2, 508-516.

Securities and Exchange Commission. 2005a. "Statement of Chairman Christopher Cox Regarding Use of Market Instruments in Valuing Employee Stock Options," Press Release 2005-129, September 9, 2005. http://www.sec.gov/news/press/2005-129.htm.

Securities and Exchange Commission, 2005b. "Economic Perspective on Employee Option Expensing: Valuation and Implementation of FAS 123(R)," Office of Economic Analysis Memo to Donald Nicolaisen, Chief Accountant, March 18, 2005. http://www.sec.gov/interps/account/secoeamemo032905.pdf.

Shapiro, Carl. 1982. "Consumer Information, Product Quality and Seller Reputation," Bell Journal of Economics, Vol. 13, No. 1, 20-35.

Simon, Herbert A. 1957. Models of Man, New York, NY: John Wiley & Sons.

Simon, Herbert A. 1996. The Sciences of the Artificial, 3rd edition. The MIT Press.

Smallwood, D. and J. Conlisk. 1979. "Product Quality in Markets Where Consumers are Imperfectly Informed," Quarterly Journal of Economics, Vol. 93, No. 1 (February), 1-23.

Sunder, Shyam. 1973. "Relationship between Accounting Changes and Stock Prices: Problems of Measurement and Some Empirical Evidence," Journal of Accounting Research, Vol. 11, 1-45.

Sunder, Shyam, 1989. "Proof That in an Efficient Market, Event Studies Can Provide No Systematic Guidance to Making of Accounting Standards and Disclosure Policy," Contemporary Accounting Research Vol. 5, No.2, 452-460.

Sunder, Shyam, 1994. "Economic Incentives as a substitute for Detailed Accounting Requirements: The Case of Compensation Value of Stock Options," Accounting Horizons, Vol. 8, No. 2 (June), 110.

Sunder, Shyam, 2003. "Rethinking the Structure of Accounting and Auditing," Indian Accounting Review, Vol. 7 No. 1 (June), 1-15.

Sunder, Shyam. 2004. "Markets as Artifacts: Aggregate Efficiency from Zero-Intelligence Traders," in M. E. Augier and J. G. March, editors, Models of a Man: Essays in Memory of Herbert A. Simon, Cambridge, MA: The MIT Press, 501-519.

Appendix: List of Published Writings of Joel S. Demski

Included in this Appendix are virtually all of Joel's major published writings as of March 2006. Given Joel's amazing scholarly productivity over the last four decades, we expect he will continue to produce more writings after the date of this list. So the list will grow for sure, to the benefit of readers.

We have tried our best to make the list complete, although it is close to impossible to make no error or omissions. We have excluded any translations into other languages of works originally published in English and we also excluded any reprints, in anthologies and other collections, of articles already listed here.

Books

Accounting Theory: An Information Content Perspective (McGraw/Hill-Irwin, 2002); with J. Christensen.

Managerial Uses of Accounting Information (Kluwer Academic Publishers, 1993).

Information Analysis (Addison-Wesley, 1972, 1st edition; 1980 2nd edition).

Cost Accounting: Accounting Data for Management's Decisions (Harcourt, 1974 2nd edition; 1982, 3rd edition); with N. Dopuch and J. Birnberg.

Cost Determination: A Conceptual Approach (Iowa State Press, 1976); with G. Feltham.

Essays in Honor of William A. Paton, Pioneer Accounting Theorist (University of Michigan, 1979); co-edited with S. Zeff and N. Dopuch.

Journal articles

"An Extension of Standard Cost Variance Analysis," *Accounting Review,* vol.42 (July, 1967; 526-536); with N. Dopuch and J. Birnberg.

"An Accounting System Structured on a Linear Programming Model," *Accounting Review,* vol.42 (October, 1967; 701-712).

"Analyzing the Effectiveness of the Traditional Standard Cost Variance Model," *Management Accounting,* vol.49 (October, 1967; 9-19).

"Some Considerations in Sensitizing an Optimization Model," *Journal of Industrial Engineering* (September, 1968).

"Research Proposal for Cost Measurement Criteria," *Journal of Accountancy* (February, 1969); with R. Jaedicke, G. Feltham, C. Horngren, and R. Sprouse.

"Predictive Ability of Alternative Performance Measurement Models," *Journal of Accounting Research,* vol.7 (Spring, 1969; 96-115).

"Decision-Performance Control," *Accounting Review,* vol.44 (October, 1969; 669-679).

"The Decision Implementation Interface: Effects of Alternative Performance Measurement Models," *Accounting Review,* vol.45 (January, 1970; 76-87).

"Optimizing the Search for Cost Deviation Sources," *Management Science,* vol.16 (April, 1970; B486-B494).

"The Use of Models in Information Evaluation," *Accounting Review,* vol.45 (October, 1970; 623-640); with G. Feltham.

"Some Decomposition Results for Information Evaluation," *Journal of Accounting Research,* vol.8 (Autumn, 1970; 178-198).

"Implementation Effects of Alternative Performance Measurement Models in a Multivariable Context," *Accounting Review,* vol.46 (April, 1971; 268-278).

"Forecast Evaluation," *Accounting Review,* vol.47 (July, 1972; 533-548); with G. Feltham.

"Information Improvement Bounds," *Journal of Accounting Research,* vol.10 (Spring, 1972; 58-76).

"Optimal Performance Measurement," *Journal of Accounting Research,* vol.10 (Autumn, 1972; 243-258).

"Simplification Activities in a Network Scheduling Context," *Management Science,* vol.19 (May, 1973; 1052-1062); with W. Abernathy.

"The General Impossibility of Normative Accounting Standards," *Accounting Review,* vol.48 (October, 1973; 718-723).

"Rational Choice of Accounting Method for a Class of Partnerships," *Journal of Accounting Research,* vol.11 (Autumn, 1973; 176-190).

"Choice Among Financial Reporting Alternatives," *Accounting Review,* vol.49 (April, 1974; 221-232).

"A Cooperative Formulation of the Audit Choice Problem," *Accounting Review,* vol.49 (July, 1974; 506-513); with R. Swieringa.

"The Nature of Financial Accounting Objectives: A Summary and Synthesis," *Journal of Accounting Research,* vol.12 (1974, Supplement; 170-187); with W. Beaver.

"Uncertainty and Evaluation Based on Controllable Performance," *Journal of Accounting Research,* vol.14 (Autumn, 1976; 230-243).

"Economic Incentives in Budgetary Control Systems," *Accounting Review,* vol.53 (April, 1978; 336-359); with G. Feltham.

"The Nature of Income Measurement," *Accounting Review,* vol.54 (January, 1979; 38-46); with W. Beaver.

"Variance Analysis Procedures as Motivational Devices," *Management Science,* vol.26 (August, 1980; 840-848); with S. Baiman.

"Economically Optimal Performance Evaluation and Control Systems," *Journal of Accounting Research,* vol.18 (1980, Supplement; 184-220); with S. Baiman.

"Strategic Behavior and Regulation Research in Accounting," *Journal of Accounting and Public Policy,* vol.1 (Summer, 1982; 19-32); with A. Amershi and M. Wolfson.

"Models in Managerial Accounting," *Journal of Accounting Research,* vol.20 (1982, Supplement; 117-148); with D. Kreps.

"Multi-Agent Control in Perfectly Correlated Environments," *Economic Letters* (1983); with D. Sappington.

"Decentralized Choice of Monitoring Systems," *Accounting Review,* vol.59 (January, 1984; 16-34); with J. Patell and M. Wolfson.

"Optimal Incentive Contracts with Multiple Agents, " *Journal of Economic Theory,* vol.33 (June, 1984; 152-171); with D. Sappington.

"Sequential Bayesian Analysis in Accounting Settings," *Contemporary Accounting Research,* vol.1 (Spring, 1985; 176-192); with A. Amershi and J. Fellingham.

"Accounting Research: 1985," *Contemporary Accounting Research* (Fall, 1985).

"Line Item Reporting, Factor Acquisition and Subcontracting," *Journal of Accounting Research,* vol.24 (Autumn, 1986; 250-269); with D. Sappington.

"On the Timing of Information Release," *Information Economics and Policy,* vol.2 (December, 1986; 307-316); with D. Sappington.

"Managing Supplier Switching," *Rand Journal of Economics,* vol.18 (Spring, 1987; 77-97); with D. Sappington and P. Spiller.

"Delegated Expertise," *Journal of Accounting Research,* vol.25 (Spring, 1987; 68-89); with D. Sappington.

"Hierarchical Regulatory Control," *Rand Journal of Economics,* vol.18 (Autumn, 1987; 369-383); with D. Sappington.

"Incentive Schemes with Multiple Agents and Bankruptcy Constraints," *Journal of Economic Theory,* vol.44 (February, 1988; 156-167); with D. Sappington and P. Spiller.

"Positive Accounting Theory: A Review," *Accounting, Organizations and Society,* vol.13 (1988; 623-629).

"The Controllability Principle in Responsibility Accounting," *Accounting Review,* vol.63 (October, 1988; 700-718); with R. Antle.

"Hierarchical Structure and Responsibility Accounting," *Journal of Accounting Research,* vol.27 (Spring, 1989; 40-58); with D. Sappington.

"Revenue Recognition," *Contemporary Accounting Research,* vol.5 (Spring, 1989; 423-451); with R. Antle.

"Fully Revealing Income Measurement," *Accounting Review,* vol.63 (April, 1990; 363-383); with D. Sappington.

"Resolving Double Moral Hazard Problems with Buyout Agreements," *Rand Journal of Economics,* vol.22 (Summer, 1991; 232-240); with D. Sappington.

"Contracting Frictions, Regulation, and the Structure of CPA Firms," *Journal of Accounting Research,* vol.29 (1991, Supplement; 1-24); with R. Antle.

"A Perspective on Accounting and Defense Contracting," *Accounting Review,* vol.67 (October, 1992; 742-753); with R. Magee.

"Sourcing with Unverifiable Performance Information," *Journal of Accounting Research,* vol.31 (Spring, 1993; 1-20); with D. Sappington.

"Market Response to Financial Reports," *Journal of Accounting & Economics,* vol.17 (January, 1994; 3-40); with G. Feltham.

"Multiple Sources of Information, Valuation, and Accounting Earnings," *Journal of Accounting, Auditing & Finance* vol.9 (Fall, 1994; 675-696); with R. Antle and S. Ryan.

"The Classical Foundations of "Modern" Costing," *Management Accounting Research,* vol.6 (1995; 13-32); with J. Christensen.

"The Changing Landscape of Academic Accounting," *Revision & Regnskabsvæsen* (June, 1995).

"Project Selection and Audited Accrual Measurement in a Multitask Setting," *European Accounting Review,* vol.4 (1995; 405-432); with J. Christensen.

"Product Costing in the Presence of Endogenous Subcost Functions," *Review of Accounting Studies,* vol.2 (November, 1997; 65-87); with J. Christensen.

"Profit Allocation Under Ancillary Trade," *Journal of Accounting Research,* vol.36 (Spring, 1998; 71-89); with J. Christensen.

"Performance Measure Manipulation," *Contemporary Accounting Research,* vol.15 (Fall, 1998; 261-286).

"Summarization with Errors: A Perspective on Empirical Investigation of Agency Relationships," *Management Accounting Research,* vol.10 (March, 1999); with D. Sappington.

"Risk, Return, and Moral Hazard," *Journal of Accounting Research,* vol.37 (Spring, 1999; 27-55); with R. Dye.

"Practices for Managing Information Flows Within Organizations," *Journal of Law, Economics & Organization,* vol.15 (1999; 107-131); with T. Lewis, D. Yao and H. Yildirim.

"Performance Measure Garbling Under Renegotiation in Multi-Period Agencies," *Journal of Accounting Research,* vol.37 (1999, Supplement; 187-214); with H. Frimor.

"Accounting Policies in Agencies with Moral Hazard and Renegotiation," *Journal of Accounting Research,* vol.40 (September, 2002; 1071-1090); with P. Christensen and H. Frimor.

"Corporate Conflicts of Interest," *Journal of Economic Perspectives,* vol.17 (Spring, 2003; 51-72).

"Factor Choice Distortion under Cost-Based Reimbursement," *Journal of Management Accounting Research,* vol.15 (2003; 145-160); with J. Christensen.

"Efficient Manipulation in a Repeated Setting," *Journal of Accounting Research,* vol.42 (March, 2004; 31-49); with H. Frimor and D. Sappington.

"Endogenous Expectations," *Accounting Review,* vol. 79 (April, 2004; 519-539), Presidential Lecture.

"Asymmetric Monitoring: Good versus Bad News Verification," *Schmalenbach Business Review,* vol.46 (July, 2004; 206-222); with J. Christensen.

"Audit Error," *Journal of Engineering and Technology Management* (forthcoming); with H. Frimor and D. Sappington.

"Quantum Information and Accounting Information: Their Salient Features and Conceptual Applications," *Journal of Accounting and Public Policy* (forthcoming); with S. FitzGerald, Y. Ijiri and H. Lin.

Other published papers

"Variance Analysis Using a Constrained Linear Model," in D. Solomons (ed.), *Studies in Cost Analysis* (Irwin, 1968).

"Cost Concepts and Implementation Criteria: An Interim Report," American Institute of Certified Public Accountants (December, 1969); with R. Jaedicke, G. Feltham, C. Horngren, and R. Sprouse.

"Performance Measure and Incentive Alternatives in a Multivariable Setting," in T. Burns (ed.). *Behavioral Experiments in Accounting* (Ohio State College of Adm. Science, 1972).

"Mathematical Models and Accounting," in S. Davidson and R. Weil (eds.), *Handbook of Modern Accounting;* 2nd edition (McGraw-Hill, 1977); with N. Dopuch.

"Evaluation of Social Effects," in H. Melton and D. Watson (eds.), *Interdisciplinary Dimensions of Accounting for Social Goals and Social Organizations* (Grid, 1977).

"Mathematical Concepts in Cost Accounting," in S. Davidson and R. Weil (eds.), *Handbook of Cost Accounting* (McGraw-Hill, 1978, 1st edition); in R. Weil and M. Maher (eds.) *Handbook of Cost Management,* (Wiley, 2005, 2nd edition).

"A Simple Case of Indeterminate Financial Reporting," in G. Lobo and M. Maher (eds.), *Information Economics and Accounting Research: A Workshop Conducted by Joel Demski* (University of Michigan, 1980).

"The Value of Financial Accounting," in G. Lobo and M. Maher (eds.), *Information Economics and Accounting Research: A Workshop Conducted by Joel Demski* (University of Michigan, 1980).

"Cost Allocation Games," in S. Moriarity (ed.), *Joint Cost Allocations* (University of Oklahoma Center for Economic and Management Research, 1981).

"Managerial Incentives," in A. Rappaport (ed.), *Information for Decision Making;* 3rd edition (Prentice-Hall, 1982).

"Demand for Accounting Procedures in A Managerial Setting," in K. Bindon, *Accounting Research Convocation: 1983* (University of Alabama School of Accountancy, 1983).

"Managerial Accounting," in G. Germane (ed.), *The Executive Course* (Addison-Wesley, 1986).

"(Theoretical) Research in (Managerial) Accounting," in B. Cushing (ed.), *Accounting and Culture* (AAA, 1987).

"Value of Information in Bimatrix Games," in G. Feltham, A. Amershi, and W. Ziemba (eds.) *Economic Analysis of Information and Contracts: Essays in Honor of John E. Butterworth.* (Kluwer Academic Publishers, 1988).

"Management Accounting," in H. Küpper and A. Wagenhofer, *Handwörterbuch Unternehmensrechnung und Controlling* (Schäffer-Poeschel, 2002).

"Analytic Modeling in Management Accounting Research," *Handbook of Management Accounting Research.* (forthcoming).

"Accounting and Economics," *The New Palgrave Dictionary of Economics* (forthcoming).

Comments

"Some Observations on Demski's Ex Post Accounting System: A Reply," *Accounting Review,* vol.43 (October, 1968; 672-674).

"Discussion of Testing a Prediction Method for Multivariate Budgets," *Journal of Accounting Research,* vol. 7 (1969, Supplement; 188-202).

"Discussion of The Relationship Between Accounting Changes and Stock Prices: Problems of Measurement and Some Empirical Evidence," *Journal of Accounting Research,* vol.11 (1973, Supplement; 55-59).

"Comments on Some Fruitful Directions for Research in Management Accounting," in N. Dopuch and L. Revsine (eds.), *Accounting Research 1960-1970: A Critical Evaluation* (Center for International Education and Research in Accounting, University of Illinois, 1973).

"An Economic Analysis of the Chambers' Normative Standard," *Accounting Review,* vol.51 (July, 1976; 653-656).

"Discussion of Behavioral Decision Theory: Processes of Judgment and Choice," *Journal of Accounting Research,* vol.19 (Spring, 1981; 32-41); with R. Swieringa.

"Accounting Standards Revisited: A Reply to Vickrey," *Quarterly Review of Economics and Business,* vol.22 (Spring, 1982; 140).

"Comments on Wilson and Jensen," *Accounting Review,* vol.58 (April, 1983; 347-349).

"Discussion of Legal Liabilities and the Market for Auditing Services," *Journal of Accounting, Auditing & Finance* (Summer, 1988).

"Further Thoughts on Fully Revealing Income Measurement," *Accounting Review,* vol.67 (July, 1992; 628-630).

"Discussion of Licensing and Technology Transfer," in J. Leitzel and J. Tirole (eds.), *Incentives in Procurement Contracting* (Westview Press, 1993).

"Additional Thoughts on Conditions for Fully Revealing Disclosure," *Journal of Business Finance & Accounting,* vol.23 (April, 1996; 481-490); with D. Sappington.

"On "Research vs. Teaching": A Long-Term Perspective," *Accounting Horizons,* vol.14 (September, 2000; 343-352); with J. Zimmerman.

"Some Thoughts on the Intellectual Foundations of Accounting," *Accounting Horizons,* vol.16 (June, 2002; 157-168); with J. Fellingham, Y. Ijiri, S. Sunder, J. Glover and P. Liang.

"Enron et al. -- A Comment," *Journal of Accounting and Public Policy,* vol.21 (Summer, 2002; 129-130).

Index